Linda Faye Williams

WITHDRAWN

the constraint of race

legacies of

white skin privilege

in america

The Pennsylvania State University Press University Park, Pennsylvania

Library of Congress Cataloging-in-Publication Data

Williams, Linda F.
  The constraint of race : legacies of white skin privilege /
  Linda Faye Williams.
      p.   cm.
  Includes bibliographical references and index.
  ISBN 0-271-02253-1 (cloth : alk. paper)
  1. United States—Race relations—Political aspects.
  2. United States—Social policy.
  3. Welfare state—United States—History.
  4. Whites—Race identity—United States.
  5. Whites—Civil rights—United States—History.
  6. Whites—United States—Social conditions.
  7. African Americans—Civil rights—History.
  8. African Americans—Social conditions.
  I. Title.

E185.61 .W7365   2003
323.1'73—dc21   2002154504

YBP $23.62 1-24-05 (J)

contents

preface

In 1992 William Jefferson Clinton promised to fundamentally reorient the relationship between markets and the state in order to produce a new generation of social policy. This book began as a short chapter evaluating the success of that attempt. But the more I sought to explain why Clinton's effort to transform his promise into policy was experiencing severe setbacks at best and complete failure at worst, the more heavily precedents from the past seemed to weigh on the potential for social policy making in the 1990s. Along with features of the American institutional structure (such as the Madisonian framework) and key policy legacies (such as the segmentation historically produced in the nation's social policy regime), the evolving politics of race emerged as a far more important historical precedent in constraining the development of American social policy than most other analyses have indicated. In fact, the central argument of this book is that to comprehend how America reached the current impasse in regard to social policy, one must understand not just the politics of race but in particular the politics of whiteness—that is, how the construction and use of race in American party politics has produced an American social policy regime that has advantaged whites, reproduces racial inequality much more often than it diminishes it, and at the same time constrains social citizenship for Americans of all races.

For starting me on this scholarly journey I am deeply grateful to the Russell Sage Foundation for including and financially supporting my research in a project (under the leadership of Margaret Weir) on the politics of social policy in the Clinton years. In addition to Weir, many others have influenced this work (although none may be totally comfortable with all of its conclusions). Among these mentors, assistants, and just plain encouragers are several of my most influential professors: Theodore Lowi, Kenneth Prewitt, William J. Wilson, Ira Katznelson, and Chandler Davidson. They are joined by my closest academic friends and colleagues who consistently have contributed to my thinking on race, inequality, politics, and policy: Ralph C. Gomes, Dianne Pinderhughes, Clarence Lusane, Philip Thompson, Sanford Schram, Robert Smith, Carol Page, Genna Rae McNeil, Adolph Reed, Clarence Stone, Jonathan Wilkenfeld, and Joe Oppenheimer. I am also grateful to several of my former graduate students who have mercilessly critiqued parts of earlier drafts of the book and often supplied new insights: Cedric Johnson, Avis and Guy DeWeever, Michael Gusmano, Tamelyn Tucker, Celeste Lay, Wendy Smooth, and Erika Gordon.

That brings me to the person who finally saw that this book (at points quite controversial) actually was published, Sanford Thatcher, Director of Penn State University Press. From submission of the first draft, Sandy encouraged me by his assurance that the ideas, argument, and research were important and needed to be published. With grace, patience, and perception he professionally guided the improvement of the manuscript. One especially important contribution Sandy made was to identify two exceptional reviewers for the manuscript: Charles V. Hamilton and Michael K. Brown. To be sure, I cannot say that my first reaction to their (then anonymous) criticisms was a happy one. Yet as soon as I got over wounded pride, I realized how sagacious, knowledgeable, and constructive their critiques were. I cannot overestimate the extent to which both Hamilton's and Brown's insights helped me to rethink and sharpen the book both substantively and organizationally. Barbara Salazar proved a tough and astute editor. I thank all of them for helping me complete a book that is significantly better than its first draft.

Finally, I owe a debt of gratitude to my family for putting up with me and pitching in and doing other kinds of work I would have been doing if I hadn't been working on this book. Thus I thank my husband, Ralph; my brother, Washington C. Williams Jr.; and my sisters, Susan Patterson and Zandra Williams. My father, Washington C. Williams Sr., remains my constant source of support in every arena imaginable.

Introduction

As the unmarked category against which difference is constructed,
whiteness never has to speak its name, never has to acknowledge its
role as an organizing principle in social and cultural relations.

—*George Lipsitz,* The Possessive Investment in Whiteness

Arguably, race has been the most endemic division in American politics and policy. Although class is the essential construct in understanding American economic life and in the workplace Americans often think of themselves as workers, managers, and owners, class remains the elusive little secret in American political life. Indeed few, if any, important political conjunctures in American history have crystallized around American workers acting as a class-conscious political force.

By contrast, a politics centered on race has characterized the United States of America since its birth as a republic. Thus the framers of the Constitution wrangled over how to count enslaved Africans for purposes of taxation and representation. A civil war was justified in the rhetoric of the hot-button issue of "freeing the slaves." The end of Reconstruction was sealed in the infamous Compromise of 1877, returning responsibility for civil rights to the states. The stability of the New Deal coalition rested in good part on refusal to enfranchise African Americans, to pass antilynching laws, and to include most blacks in social programs on an equal basis with whites. The Great Society—the biggest expansion of America's welfare state to date—ensued from the turmoil of the Civil Rights Movement of the 1960s, a fact that became almost instantaneously the battle cry for massive white resistance.

It was in the context of the dramatic changes wrought in the 1960s that African Americans, other people of color, and women of all races were finally included on a mass basis in the American welfare state. As African American, Latino, and Native American insurgency grew and urban strife became the order of the day, the meaning and object of American social policy was refocused. By the 1980s in most discussions, key parts of the social policy agenda, especially poverty, crime, and cities, were mapped to race.[1] In turn, a new and cryptic vernacular for racial politics developed. As Thomas and Mary Edsall put it in 1991, "when the official subject is presidential politics, taxes, welfare, crime, rights, or values . . . the real subject is RACE."[2] "Through these code words," writes Stephen Steinberg, "it is possible to play on racial stereotypes, appeal to racial fears, and heap blame on blacks," other people of color, and immigrants "without naming them."[3] In American politics, race, state, and party have been much more inextricably linked than class, state, and party.

This is a book about how, when, and why American social policy became fused with the politics of race, and with what effects for which racial groups over time. Rather than focus solely or primarily on the disadvantages suffered by blacks, as most analyses do, I widen the scope to make visible the other side of the coin: the advantages enjoyed by whites. What we find, in a nutshell, is that whites have been disproportionately the beneficiaries of the generous and more politically popular American social policies and that people of color (especially African Americans) have been disproportionately the beneficiaries of the more constrictive and politically challenged policies. The result has been a politics of social policy in which political parties and candidates use race as a weapon to constrain and at times turn back the American welfare state.

Thus we find an ironic situation: the American welfare state has denied people of color the social protections it has provided white Americans and then stigmatized them as welfare "dependents." This result is an outgrowth not simply of racially motivated *exclusion* but also of the particular and differential patterns, styles, and levels of racial *inclusion* and the way pejorative stereotypes are attached to some social policies and favorable ones to others. In effect, Ameri-

1. Michael B. Katz, *The Undeserving Poor: From the War on Poverty to the War on Welfare* (New York: Pantheon, 1989), 185.

2. Thomas Edsall and Mary Edsall, "When the Official Subject Is Presidential Politics, Taxes, Welfare, Crime, Rights, or Values . . . the Real Subject Is RACE," *Atlantic Monthly* 269 (May 1991): 52–86.

3. Stephen Steinberg, *Turning Back: The Retreat from Racial Justice in American Thought and Politics* (Boston: Beacon, 1995), 214.

can social policies have reproduced racial hierarchy and the American welfare state has been an instrument more often of social stratification than of social equality.[4]

Concomitantly, I argue that a full understanding of American social policy cannot be rendered without bringing race to the center of analysis. The American construction of race has powerfully influenced political and social policy strategies—privileging whites, wreaking havoc upon people of color, rendering organized labor less powerful, and generating the least comprehensive, most laggard and segmented welfare state among all the advanced industrialized democracies of the West.

To make the argument, I do not advance a grand theory of race. In fact, I hold that much of the inadequacy, incoherence, and contradictoriness of contemporary theorizing about race stems from, or is at least obscured by, a tendency to abstract too far from the concrete social processes within which people are shaped and shape themselves. Perhaps, then, the best way to try to make sense of the politics of race in the United States and its impact is by examining concrete instances of its complex operation.

Several theoretical accounts are, however, helpful in the examination: in particular the policy legacy approach and the rapidly developing literatures concerning whiteness and critical race theory. Both of these bodies of literature are grounded in an understanding of American political economy and what Rogers Smith has called the "multiple traditions" of the American ethos: liberal individualism, republicanism, and ascriptive inegalitarianism.[5] In short, the

4. Michael K. Brown, *Race, Money, and the American Welfare State* (Ithaca, N.Y.: Cornell University Press, 1999), 9.

5. Unlike either Louis Hartz or Gunnar Myrdal, who focus on how ascriptive traditions based on race, sex, and so forth conflict with the liberal ethos, in the following analysis I build on Rogers Smith's powerful critique of the notion that there is a single "American political tradition." As Smith points out, American liberalism has contended over time not only with republicanism but also with a variety of ascriptive traditions that have sought to define the "American ethos" in very different ways. Smith argues, "American political actors have always promoted civic ideologies that blend liberal, democratic republican, and inegalitarian ascriptive elements in various combinations designed to be politically popular." Each has been "centrally constitutive of American life" (Rogers M. Smith, *Civic Ideal: Conflicting Visions of Citizenship in U.S. History* [New Haven: Yale University Press, 1997], 30). For theses that focus on ways in which policies promoting ascriptive inequalities can be interpreted to be consistent with the liberal ethos or in conflict with it, see Louis Hartz, *The Liberal Tradition in America* (New York: Harcourt, Brace, 1955), and Gunnar Myrdal, *An American Dilemma: The Negro Problem and American Democracy* (New York: Harper & Row, 1962).

context of how the American racial order unfolded in economy, society, and polity, each reinforcing the other, each reflecting culture and recreating it, lies at the heart of the argument. My goal is not simply to include a cultural explanation based on critical race theory or simply an institutional one based on policy legacy, but to capture the complexities linking economy, constitutional structure, policy legacies, public opinion, coalitional and electoral political grievances, and culture—each an aspect of the American racial order—in the understanding of the relationship between race and social policy over time.[6] Let us examine the core theoretical elements of the argument.

The policy legacy approach grows out of the work of state-polity-centered theorists. This approach examines how the residue of past decisions and debates influences the views, interests, and actions of future political leaders—often creating a lock-in effect that acts as a brake on further change. Thus changing policy agendas, as Margaret Weir and her colleagues have explained, "emerge not only in response to new socioeconomic conditions but also on the basis of—or in reaction to—previous policy accomplishments."[7] The political identities of social groups and classes and the potential for political alliances, moreover, are reshaped by new policies.[8]

One policy legacy that is particularly important in understanding the American welfare state is segmentation. As most scholars of welfare have noted, unlike the Western European countries that have promoted broad, universal policies, the United States has a segmented welfare system. It has superior and inferior tracks: social insurance versus public assistance, hidden versus open,

6. For an analysis linking how U.S. political institutions, class politics, and racial divisions shaped a welfare state far less generous than other Western welfare states and how these structural, institutional, and organizational factors continue to limit the possibilities for change, see Charles Noble, *Welfare as We Knew It: A Political History of the American Welfare State* (New York: Oxford University Press, 1997).

7. Margaret Weir, Ann Shola Orloff, and Theda Skocpol, eds., *The Politics of Social Policy in the United States* (Princeton: Princeton University Press, 1988), 17.

8. For example, policy-centered theorists emphasize that the early enfranchisement of white men in the United States diminished their sense of themselves as a class-conscious political force. Although the concept of policy legacies is used in the following analysis, my main argument breaks with the policy-centered approach in some important ways, most spectacularly in regard to these theorists' view of states as "sites of autonomous actions" and the concomitant deemphasis on underlying social, cultural, and economic factors. In short, I avoid a narrow focus on political institutions per se. For an example of perhaps the best policy-centered approach, see Theda Skocpol, *Protecting Soldiers and Mothers: The Political Origins of Social Policy in the United States* (Cambridge: Belknap/Harvard University Press, 1992).

contributory versus noncontributory, federal versus state/local, rights-based versus needs-based, beneficiaries versus dependents, entitlements versus "welfare," and ultimately the deserving poor versus the undeserving poor.[9]

Yet despite all the attention devoted to describing and explaining the segmentation of the American welfare state, there is little agreement on the question of why the United States chose the path of segmentation versus the path of universalism in the first place. Virtually all that is assured is that segmentation was not created by social policy but grew out of preexisting features of American life.

Several of these features have been vigorously examined. For example, scholars have analyzed in great detail the roles played by the constitutional design of American government (obstacles imposed by Madisonian frameworks),[10] agenda-setting,[11] and other institutional-political processes[12] in shaping a segmented welfare state. Others have emphasized the role economic factors play.[13] These studies have produced important insights. Yet the role played by American political culture in this process remains relatively unexplored. Analyzing political culture is contextually and historically important, for neither the state nor the economy acts in a vacuum; rather, as Michael Omi and Howard Winant emphasize, they are embedded in a web of social relations, "the cultural and technical norms which characterize society overall." These norms "affect the organizational capacities of state agencies [and] their coordination," and react back upon the economy.[14] Yet most recent analyses have

9. For three particularly good books that make the segmentation argument, albeit focusing on different definitions of segmentation, see Linda Gordon, *Pitied but Not Entitled: Single Mothers and the History of Welfare* (New York: Free Press, 1994); Michael B. Katz, *In the Shadow of the Poorhouse: A Social History of Welfare in America,* 10th anniversary ed. (New York: Basic Books, 1997); and James T. Patterson, *America's Struggle against Poverty, 1990–1994* (Cambridge: Harvard University Press, 1995).

10. Richard E. Neustadt, *Presidential Power and the Modern Presidents: The Politics of Leadership from Roosevelt to Reagan* (New York: Maxwell Macmillan, 1990).

11. See discussion in Margaret Weir, "Political Parties and Social Policymaking," in Margaret Weir, ed., *The Social Divide: Political Parties and the Future of Activist Government* (Washington, D.C.: Brookings, 1998), 3.

12. See Weir et al., *Politics of Social Policy;* Theda Skocpol, *Social Policy in the United States: Future Possibilities in Historical Perspective* (Princeton: Princeton University Press, 1995); and Skocpol, *Protecting Soldiers and Mothers.*

13. For example, Michael Brown's excellent analysis in *Race, Money, and the American Welfare State* focused on the role of fiscal capacity in shaping segmentation.

14. Michael Omi and Howard Winant, *Racial Formation in the United States: From the 1960s to the 1990s* (London: Routledge, 1994), 84.

deemphasized culture as a defining force in shaping the American welfare state or ignored it altogether.

The nearly singular exception to this rule concerns the impact of the American ethos (usually defined as having a solitary strand: "liberal individualism") on shaping the welfare state. The well-known and widely subscribed emphasis on liberal individualism (also referred to as the "liberal values" approach) can be understood as a combination of laissez-faire values and Protestant morality. Openly embraced, essentially it is the belief in boundless economic opportunity for the industrious, and it measures persons and everything else by their success in earning income and their ability to secure wealth. According to liberal individualism, people who demonstrate individual responsibility and diligence in a free society will be able to take care of themselves and get ahead.[15] Thus all Americans can be independent; no one need be left out, unless he or she voluntarily chooses to be. In effect a standard of justice is set forth that holds each individual accountable, for it assumes that one's fate is in large measure under one's own control. Liberal individualism therefore leads inevitably to the moral condemnation of those who, for whatever reason, fail to prosper. Core components of liberal individualism are ideas such as a strong commitment to hard work and meritocracy.

As a civic ideology, liberal individualism gained a foothold as early as colonial days in large part because of the relative mobility the frontier setting afforded many white settlers. As the colonies grew in strength and numbers, so did the popularity of liberal individualism as both ethos and policy. Key aspects of the legal system and many of America's institutions embodied pervasive currents of liberal individualism. The framers of the United States Constitution, for instance, made strong efforts to keep public and private spheres separate and well defined. They adopted various provisions to protect private property and individual economic interests. The task of meeting the needs of the poor came to be regarded largely as a duty of religious institutions and private benevolence organizations, not of government.[16] According to Louis

15. John E. Schwarz and Thomas J. Volgy, *The Forgotten Americans: Thirty Million Working Poor in the Land of Opportunity* (New York: Norton, 1992), 3, 7–11.

16. For discussion, see Katz, *Undeserving Poor,* chap. 1; and Cedric Kweisi Johnson, " 'Forty Acres and a Mule' Revisited: The Freedmen's Bureau and the Coloring of American Social Policy," unpublished paper, December 1995.

Hartz, liberal individualism came to be felt so viscerally that it can be called "America's nationalism."[17]

A substantial number of social policy scholars have argued that liberal individualism played a prominent role in delaying the advent of the welfare state in America and shaped its segmentation.[18] That is, the extreme strength of the commitment to individualism, hard work, meritocracy, and self-help led not only to a tenacious resistance to social protection but also to castigation of the poor as responsible for their own plight. Thus American social policy, reflecting laissez-faire liberalism, rationalized contributory social insurance programs as "deserving" because they were "quasi-contractual" measures that enabled individuals to "earn the right to benefits" through their own contributions;[19] they stigmatized public assistance programs as "undeserving" because they depended on the arbitrary discretion of state and local authorities in a way that undermined individual dignity and delivered benefits on the basis of need, not as a matter of right. In effect liberal individualism undermined the development of altruistic policy outcomes in the United States.

But having come this far, scholars who point to the role of liberal individualism in shaping the American welfare state have gone no further. "At any given time," according to Weir and her colleagues, "some potential policy implications of liberal values are taken up, and others not; sometimes rhetorically well-crafted liberal arguments work and sometimes not."[20] In particular, the insights that illuminated the liberal values approach are overlooked in studies regarding race and social policy. From an intellectual perspective, it is a startling oversight; from a political perspective, it is all too easily explained by the overwhelming biases of the nation's tradition of liberal individualism itself.

In fact, as soon as race is considered, challenges to the usefulness and

17. Hartz, *Liberal Tradition in America*, 207.
18. See Robert Jackman, *Politics and Social Equality: A Comparative Analysis* (New York: Free Press, 1965); Harold Wilensky, *The Welfare State and Equality* (Berkeley and Los Angeles: University of California Press, 1975); Kirsten Gronbjerg, David Street, and Gerald D. Suttles, *Poverty and Social Change* (Chicago: University of Chicago Press, 1978); and Gaston Rimlinger, *Welfare Policy and Industrialization in Europe, America, and Russia* (New York: Wiley, 1971). Weir and her colleagues, however, dismiss even the role of liberal values in influencing the American welfare state. They conclude that "we must find more precise analytical tools than those offered by the national values approach": Weir et al., *Politics of Social Policy*, 13.
19. Rimlinger, *Welfare Policy and Industrialization*, 91.
20. Weir et al., *Politics of Social Policy*, 13.

veracity of liberal individualism emerge. One central problem resides in the ethos's social construction of freedom, independence, and citizenship. Historically to be independent in the United States, a household needed to own sufficient property or to have other means permitting it to produce an acceptable standard of living without having to become indebted or dependent on the will of anyone else. In an era when whites enslaved Africans and institutionalized forced labor of many types, liberal theorists pointed out, the concept "free" contained an economic dimension that was tied to the idea of independence. A "free man" or "free citizen," John Locke explained, was "one who is independent of others for life's sustenance," free to act "as he thinks fit without asking leave, or depending upon the Will of any other man."[21] A person who was not independent could not be said to be fully free or self-governing.[22] Nor could he or she be expected to be responsible. As James Madison pointed out in *Federalist* 63, "responsibility, in order to be reasonable, must be limited to objects within the power of the responsible party."[23] The premise that individuals can control and so be personally responsible for their own lives presumes that the opportunity to do so exists.

Such opportunity quite obviously did not exist for blacks throughout much of American history. Blacks were patently excluded from the enjoyment of liberal individualism and its link to citizenship; they were trapped behind another fundamental strand of the American ethos (albeit usually treated with silence or denial): ascriptive inequality or, more precisely, white skin privilege. Although scholars debate the precise point at which individual racist perceptions developed into a full-blown popular ideology, the system of economic, political, and social preferences for whites and subordination for blacks was in place well before the Constitution was framed.[24] By that time a plethora of local and state laws already defined the status of African Americans versus white Americans. This body of racial laws and statutes was uneven and varied from colony to colony; an equally diverse body of theoretical justifications for the disfranchisement and exploitation of blacks developed during this era.

21. John Locke, *An Essay Concerning Human Understanding and a Treatise on the Conflict of the Understanding* (Philadelphia: Hayes & Zell, 1854).

22. See discussion in John E. Schwarz, *Illusions of Opportunity: The American Dream in Question* (New York: Norton, 1997), chap. 2.

23. *The Federalist Papers* (New York: Modern Library, 1977), 408.

24. See Winthrop Jordan, *White over Black: American Attitudes toward the Negro, 1550–1812* (Baltimore: Penguin, 1969).

Hence even before the colonies became a nation, the relationship between thought and practice was established in respect to race. As Walter Trattner has pointed out, the first premises of white skin privilege were religious: most colonists viewed blacks as "Children of Satan" who were "not entitled to the same rights as whites and hence, excluded from the social welfare system."[25] Enlightenment "scientific" justifications for racial inequality followed. By the time the United States had become a new nation, political citizenship was explicitly racially inscribed by an act of Congress that declared that only "free white" immigrants could be naturalized.[26]

Notions of social citizenship implied by the multifaceted American ethos are even more problematic than definitions of political citizenship. The American ethos implies that work and the work ethic reside at the core of the American welfare state; but as it turns out, work, too, is a social construct, depending on who has the power to define it. The brutal, arduous work from "sunup to sundown" performed by enslaved Africans was not considered "work." Instead, as Judith Shklar argues, work—defined as earning a living—was historically identified in relation to its racial opposite, slavery.[27] A citizen was an independent worker. The very definition of work has depended on its relation to race and denoted the hierarchy of white over black.[28] In short, the American ethos mystifies the exploitative relations that not only allow the few to prosper at the expense of many others but also allow whites to prosper at the expense of people of color. While the liberal individualist strand of the American ethos posits, theoretically, a fundamental way in which all Americans, no matter the sources of their differences, can share a birthright—that is, that "all can belong no matter what their background or station, that everyone can succeed if they are conscientious and diligent"[29]—the reality of historic black subordination reveals just how untenable this myth is. Fixed, ascriptive hierarchies based on

25. Walter I. Trattner, *From Poor Law to Welfare State: A History of Social Welfare in America* (New York: Free Press, 1989). At the time, the colonies had meager government-supported welfare systems and most social welfare was provided privately. Blacks were excluded from both.

26. Matthew Frye Jacobson, *Whiteness of a Different Color: European Immigrants and the Alchemy of Race* (Cambridge: Harvard University Press, 1998), 13. See also Scott L. Malcomson, *One Drop of Blood: The American Misadventure of Race* (New York: Farrar Strauss Giroux, 2000).

27. Judith N. Shklar, *American Citizenship: The Quest for Inclusion* (Cambridge: Harvard University Press, 1991).

28. Brown, *Race, Money, and the American Welfare State*, 17.

29. Schwarz and Volgy, *Forgotten Americans*, 7.

such factors as race, ethnicity, and gender are as centrally constitutive of American life as liberal individualism and republicanism. America's illiberal and undemocratic traditions are as key to understanding the making of American social policy across time as its liberal and democratic ones.

Critical race theory, including theories of whiteness, helps develop a more complete understanding of both the various traditions of the American ethos and their impact on the making of American social policy. Developed over the last few decades of the twentieth century by historians, legal scholars, and sociologists of all races, critical race theory posits that race is neither a color nor solely or even primarily a biological construct. Both who is black and who is white are socially constructed, and the latter particularly has changed across time.[30] Thus race may have some biological meaning, but it is best understood as an element of the social, economic, and political terrain contested by "races" and classes in which whites display a sense of entitlement and make claims to social status and economic advantages, actively struggling to maintain both these privileges and their sense of themselves as superior.[31] To protect white privilege, boundaries are created that take the form not only of customs, norms, and traditions but also—and most important—of laws and public policies. The problem of race and racism, then, is not so much a problem of black people as a problem of whiteness. Therefore, to speak of whiteness is to assign everyone a place in the relations of racism.

And what is whiteness? It is first and foremost a result of hierarchy and collectivism. As Marguerite Ross Barnett wrote, hierarchy "specifically means the existence of a principle (racism) that ranks groups consistently and pervasively, *and is enforceable through social control.* Collectivism means that each individual member of a group is treated according to some principle that defines the whole."[32]

As a result of principles of hierarchy and collectivism, whiteness comes to have a property value. Monetary or property values associated with whiteness include but are not limited to intergenerational transfers of wealth, unequal

---

30. Jacobson, *Whiteness of a Different Color,* 4.

31. Brown, *Race, Money, and the American Welfare State,* 15.

32. Marguerite Ross Barnett and James A. Hepner, eds., *Public Policy for the Black Community: Strategies and Perspectives* (Port Washington, N.Y.: Alfred, 1976), quoted ibid. For a fuller discussion, see Barnett and Hepner's Introduction.

allocation of educational resources, substantial insider networks that funnel good jobs largely to whites, and social policies that deliver more generous benefits to whites. Critical race theorists also emphasize that the property values assigned to whites result not only from contemporary actions and policies but also from cumulative ones. Hence past discrimination cannot remain the elusive culprit, for it has legacies for the current historical conjuncture and the future. Critical race theorists therefore contextualize and historicize their study of whiteness, calling attention to the ways in which past discrimination helped whites in a cumulative manner, substantively altering their capacities to assess the abilities of people of color, and connecting the intentionality of white supremacist social relations to institutional discrimination.

Whites, however, usually do not have to confront their privilege. To whites, "race" generally has nothing to do with them; "racism" is a problem belonging to people of color, not to whites. Indeed, even the best and the brightest (and most progressive) scholars of American social policy rarely focus on whites.[33]

Yet, if one wants to fully comprehend why American social policy has developed as it has, whites, too, must directly enter the equation. Although a focus on black disadvantage logically implies a focus on white advantage, the tendency to ignore an explicit rendering of facts about the historical and current advantages of whites tends to minimize them, encouraging confusion about the relative statuses of racial groups,[34] hiding the element of force it takes to maintain white privilege, mystifying the kind of politics necessary to promote it, discouraging whites from understanding the privileges that accompany their own skin color, and encouraging them instead to perceive disadvantages. In short, without an explicit examination of both sides of the coin—groups advantaged and groups disadvantaged in the nation's social policy regime—whiteness becomes normalized and invisible, and relations of dominance are

33. For several particularly excellent analyses of race, gender, and welfare of recent vintage that focus on whites in such a limited way that "whites" does not even appear in their indexes, see Jill Quadagno, *The Color of Welfare: How Racism Undermined the War on Poverty* (New York: Oxford University Press, 1994); Gordon, *Pitied but Not Entitled;* Robert C. Lieberman, *Shifting the Color Line: Race and the American Welfare State* (Cambridge: Harvard University Press, 1998); and Brown, *Race, Money, and the American Welfare State.*

34. For data demonstrating the role of ignorance in shaping whites' views of blacks and select social policies, see Richard Morin, "Misperceptions Cloud Whites' View of Blacks," *Washington Post,* July 11, 2001, A1.

submerged.[35] As a result, whites develop such a powerful sense of entitlement that they do not question their ability to pass out the spoils of racial discrimination in banking practices, the criminal justice system, housing markets, media representations, educational arrangements, and social policies to succeeding generations. Instead they see themselves as the genuinely deserving progenitors and heirs of liberal individualism: people who have received their superior status the old-fashioned way, they "earned it"—a justification that has gone through religious, pseudo-scientific, and cultural renditions.

It should be clear, critical race theorists conclude, that little or none of white privilege is maintained by blatant racists; rather institutional and structural mechanisms and public policy maintain it, both materially and psychologically.[36] Moreover, white privilege is shared by all whites, affluent and poor, albeit to varying degrees. This sharing is especially salient in regard to the cultural and moral dimensions of white skin privilege.[37] Still, white skin privilege is usually less a matter of direct, referential, and snarling contempt than a system for protecting the privileges of whites by denying people of color opportunities for asset accumulation and upward mobility.

It also should be clear that opposing whiteness is *not* the same thing as opposing whites. White skin privilege is an equal opportunity employer; people of color can become active agents of white privilege as well as passive participants in its hierarchies and rewards. For some people of color, one means of becoming an insider is by participating in the exclusion of other outsiders. On the other hand, if every promoter of white skin privilege is not white, it follows that not all whites have to become complicit with white skin privilege, that there is an element of choice. Indeed, despite the material and sociopsychological interests white privilege confers, there are ample examples of whites actively struggling against whiteness. How else does one explain the Radical Republi-

35. Ruth Frankenberg, *White Women, Race Matters: The Social Construction of Whiteness* (Minneapolis: University of Minnesota Press, 1993). See also Richard Delgado and Jean Stefancic, eds., *Critical White Studies: Looking behind the Mirror* (Philadelphia: Temple University Press, 1997).

36. George Lipsitz, *The Possessive Investment in Whiteness: How White People Profit from Identity Politics* (Philadelphia: Temple University Press, 1998), xvii.

37. W. E. B. Du Bois made this point many years ago and critical race theorists have built upon it. See his *Dusk of Dawn: Autobiography of a Race Concept* (1940; New York: Schocken, 1968), 205. And see Howard Winant, "Behind Blue Eyes: Whiteness and Contemporary U.S. Racial Politics," in Michelle Fine, Lois Weis, Linda C. Powell, and L. Mun Wong, eds., *Off White: Readings on Race, Power, and Society* (New York: Routledge, 1997), 45–47.

cans of the Reconstruction era, or the white champions of civil rights in the 1960s and 1970s, or such presidents as Harry Truman and Lyndon Johnson, or for that matter the intellectuals who created the journal *Race Traitor* in 1992, whose manifesto is to abolish whiteness, defined as a barrier to justice and equality that cannot be overcome until the privileges of white skin are abolished? In short, critical race theorists emphasize that although people do not choose their assigned racial group, they do choose whether to be racist or not. This choice, however, is not made within a vacuum; it occurs within a social structure that gives value to whiteness and offers rewards for racism.

The following chapters apply insights from critical race theory and the policy-legacy approach to understanding the role of whiteness in structuring the American welfare state. Briefly, I argue that the welfare state was grafted onto preexisting conditions of race relations. Segmentation in American social policy had many roots, but since so many have previously underemphasized or ignored it, my focus is on how segmentation grew out of established boundaries that privileged whites and penalized blacks.[38] As the welfare state evolved, policy feedback, more often than not, further solidified the privileges of whiteness. This development was not simply an "inadvertent consequence" of a fiscally circumscribed welfare state.[39] Particularly up through the 1960s, the superior programs of the American welfare state were disproportionately white and male because they were designed to be so. Race and party politics interacted in ways that negatively shaped debates over social policies. Arguments during the legislative battles that shaped these programs often explicitly and openly discussed "the Negroes" and by corollary (though rarely directly) white racial interests. Since then, this battle has continued through code words in debates over the welfare state. For much of its history, the American welfare state officially, consciously, and intentionally advantaged whites as it disadvantaged blacks and other people of color. To focus attention only on black disadvantage is to allow citizens and policy makers alike to continue to ignore the privileges

38. Although race in the United States is clearly not a black/white dualism and more than ever before race relations are a complex phenomenon encompassing many groups (particularly Latinos, Asian Americans, and Native Americans), in order to make this study manageable I focus usually on blacks and whites. Arguably these two groups remain America's polar opposites in regard to race. Indeed, some groups, especially Latinos, remain socially constructed as an ethnic group that cuts across all races and many nationalities.

39. Brown, *Race, Money and the American Welfare State*, 8.

associated with whiteness and to allow these privileges to be considered simply normal.

The normalcy of white privilege in American social policy has both ideological and material sides. On the ideological side, the moral worthiness of those who benefit from social policies is racially cast, and the same stereotypes are used over and over until eventually the idea of dependency inscribed in social policy has a racial meaning.

On the material side, the American welfare state has been and remains steadfastly racially stratified or segmented. Whites benefit disproportionately from the good welfare programs, such as social insurance, employer-provided health and pension benefits, and hidden welfare of tax expenditures—programs so good that they are rarely even admitted to be "welfare." Meanwhile, people of color are relegated to the bad welfare programs, highly visible and readily stigmatized—that is, means-tested programs. The welfare state thus institutionalizes white privilege, a development that tends to serve as a constraint, particularly since the 1960s, on the development of social policy.[40]

It is this process of constraining the development of an appropriately formulated and sized welfare state in the United States that makes whiteness a problem for all those who would benefit from a guarantee of at least a modicum of economic security not dependent on the market or inheritance. Although people of color are most harmed by the holes and flaws in American social policy, ultimately the objective interests of the white working class and unemployed are also diminished. Through a battle that pretends to be about race and dependency, poor whites are encouraged to oppose the very policies they need. When poor whites are persuaded that "the blacks get more," they come to support the diminution of the welfare state in general and the cutting of specific policies that could improve their life chances in particular. Meanwhile, millions of poor whites, too, suffer from economic hardship, social stigma, and political disempowerment;[41] thus the significance of whiteness for the American welfare state and party politics. When liberal individualism and whiteness combine to reinforce derogatory meanings inscribed on beneficiaries of means-tested programs, poor people of color suffer most, but the poor of all races suffer.

40. I thank Michael Brown for assistance in clarifying this argument.
41. Matt Wray and Annalee Newitz, eds., *White Trash: Race and Class in America* (New York: Routledge, 1997).

In sum, developments in American social policy since the Civil War have persistently advanced the privileges that attach to whiteness through a variety of mechanisms, including the ongoing reinterpretation of the American tradition of liberal individualism in racialized ways, the slow accretion of policy legacies, the construction of whiteness itself as a political category, and the normal processes of coalition building and electoral politics. Through these connected processes, whiteness and the protection of white privilege have come to be fundamental to the operation of American democracy, and their centrality has been continually reinforced by American social policy, broadly considered.

Before we turn to the detailed development of this argument, one additional question needs to be addressed: how do class and gender enter the analysis of race and social policy?

First, despite linkages between whiteness and meager outcomes for the poor of all races, I will not argue that racial politics is a form of class politics. White skin privilege has been such a constant in America since colonial times that race has taken on a life of its own. Thus it bears repeating: a wide array of whites regardless to class demonstrate commitment to whiteness.

W. E. B. Du Bois explained this tendency many years ago. First, he pointed out that the decision of white workers to define themselves by their whiteness is understandable in view of its short-term advantages. At some times and in some places, such advantages show up in paychecks, where the wages of white workers are higher than those of people of color.[42]

But even when white workers receive a low wage, Du Bois added, they are compensated in part by a "public and psychological wage" that amounts to a tangible benefit acquired at the expense of people of color. They are given public deference because they are white; they are treated more leniently by the police because they are white; they are welcomed in any community where they can afford to buy a house because they are white; their children are more likely to be welcomed in the best schools because they are white; they can shop in any store without being treated as suspect because they are white; and so forth. By these means the status and privileges conferred by whiteness can be used to make up for alienating and exploitative class relationships. It is this psychologi-

---

42. W. E. B. Du Bois, *Black Reconstruction in the United States, 1860–1880* (1935; New York: Simon & Schuster, 1995), 727ff.

cal wage, more than anything else, that makes white workers forget their nearly identical objective economic interests with poor and working-class people of color and accept stunted lives both for themselves and for those more oppressed than themselves. In this way, white skin privilege undermines not only working-class unity but the very vision of many white workers.[43]

Thus, even when in practice poor whites have low economic and social status in comparison with other whites, their status concerns have the capacity to doom prospects for cross-racial collective action. In fact, social analysts and politicians alike have long remarked that racism plays an important role in maintaining the self-esteem of poor whites.[44] The very history of conservative politics, in many ways its essence, is based precisely on the exploitation of such apparently irrational behavior. Even among political elites, Sidney Verba and Gary Orren conclude,

> values do not merely rationalize action in accordance to self-interest. Often they arise quite independently of an individual's life experiences and in turn play an independent role in molding political behavior. Such behavior reflects people's group attachments and antipathies, and concern for larger purposes that transcend their own immediate situation. Thus, politics often resembles more closely the world of religion than the world of economics.[45]

It is in such a context that white skin privilege becomes the way in which white elites *and* white workers see the world. This problem has confounded class-based political organizing in the United States for more than two centuries. In fact, it is scarcely an exaggeration to conclude that white laborers in the United States are the least Marxian-acting working class in the world. In sum, in the United States, support for white skin privilege comes from both above and below. White workers do not just receive racist ideas but embrace, adopt, and at times murderously act upon those ideas. While false consciousness is certainly a problem, the more critical problem is that the white working class

43. Ibid., 30 and 700.
44. For examples of how whites scapegoat blacks for their own loss of social status, see Joe Feagin and Herman Vera, *White Racism* (London: Routledge, 1995), 24ff.
45. Sidney Verba and Gary Orren, *Equality in America: A View from the Top* (Cambridge: Harvard University Press, 1985), 248.

comes to think of itself and its interests as white.[46] In effect, white privilege and self-interest do not develop along separate tracks; rather white privilege helps construct individual whites' notion of self-interest across classes, in effect linking the presumed interests of the self to those of the collectivity.

Yet, despite the powerful role race plays in fracturing classes and genders, race, class, and gender remain inextricably linked. Thus my goal here is not to draw a precise line separating race and class but to draw a line around race and class to emphasize the interaction of race, class, and gender in political struggles and social policy outcomes. The focus is not only on the ways in which race has served as a barrier to the solidarity of the working class or women in the United States but also on the suppression of alternatives that could have permitted the poor and working classes of all races to join in demanding equal justice. In effect, class and gender issues are viewed through the prism of race, and race issues through the prisms of class and gender.

Quite arguably, this is the way race, class, and gender have always functioned in real life in the United States. That people of color are disproportionately part of the poor and working classes is an overt manifestation of the inseparable race/class link. That policies designed to maintain a cheap labor force end up disproportionately harming people of color is another overt demonstration of the race/class link. Moreover, in everyday life it has usually been impossible to separate race demands from class demands from gender demands. For example, the black women's club movement at the turn of the twentieth century—heavily engaged in the politics of providing services to blacks—viewed poverty work as race work as women's work, and race issues as poverty issues as gender issues. They could not and would not separate class, race, and gender as distinctive spheres. To work for welfare was to work against class inequality and against racial and gender discrimination. In their view, without some minimum level of economic well-being and dignity, people could not function as citizens. Social rights were civil rights were human rights.[47]

When civil rights activists of the late 1960s sloganized "What difference does it make to desegregate a lunch counter if you can't afford a hamburger?" they were clearly not just demanding the end of racial exclusion; at bottom they were also demanding class equality. When 250,000 people marched on

46. David Roediger, *The Wages of Whiteness: Race and the Making of the American Working Class,* rev. ed. (New York: Verso, 1999), 12.

47. See Gordon, *Pitied but Not Entitled,* chap. 5.

Washington for "jobs and freedom" on August 28, 1963, they were obviously cognizant of the interaction of race and class. Walter Reuther of the United Automobile Workers, speaking at the march, called for *full* and *fair* employment. A. Philip Randolph summed up the inextricable link between race and class by concluding: "But this civil rights revolution is not confined to the Negro nor is it confined to civil rights, for our white allies know that they cannot be free while we are not and we know that we have no future in a society in which six million black and white people are unemployed and millions more live in poverty."[48] When the Reverend Martin Luther King in his last crusade decided to dramatize the plight of the poor, the links between racial oppression and class exploitation in the United States had been brought to the center of the civil rights protest.

It is also evident that racial advancement has nearly always meant class and gender advancement. In the nineteenth century, white women, struggling for abolition of slavery, found voice for their own claims for political and equal rights; they did so again roughly a century later in the midst of the Civil Rights Movement. Similarly, providing education for "freedmen" after the Civil War boosted the provision of public schools for whites, too, throughout the South. Eliminating the poll tax midway through the twentieth century brought far more poor whites than blacks to the voting booths. Expanding welfare in the mid-1960s gave millions of poor white mothers and children access to improved government aid. Even a policy stigmatized as "race-specific," affirmative action, helped hundreds of thousands of white women enter colleges, secure employment, and gain promotions. There is a universal side of the demand for racial equality. Thus my goal here is to comprehend social policy in the United States by unpacking the package of whiteness as it has influenced the interaction of race, gender, and class.

A historical approach is appropriate for a study of race and American social policy for two principal reasons. First, this approach falls squarely within the tradition of studies of social policy. In fact, most of the important works on American social policy have been explicitly historical, concerned either with a decisive moment of creation (usually the New Deal) or with a period of development spanning several decades and seeking to answer a common set of ques-

---

48. Quoted in Dona Cooper Hamilton and Charles V. Hamilton, *The Dual Agenda: Race and Social Welfare Policies of Civil Rights Organizations* (New York: Columbia University Press, 1997), 127.

tions by using inductive reasoning and a wealth of empirical evidence: How are new programs created? What is responsible for their subsequent development?[49] Second, a historical approach is necessary because an inadequate confrontation with the past and examination of its effects on the current conjuncture has done a great deal to warp and distort perceptions of racial issues. These distorted perceptions have practical effects. Without an appreciation of the past, for instance, many whites are unable to appreciate the injustice and brutality that have been necessary to maintain them in their privileged position. This in turn makes them more unwilling to accept measures necessary to undo, to the extent possible, what has been done. Thus they continue to feel entitled to their privileged position and utterly fail to appreciate the accumulated injustices on which it rests. In sum, to begin in the current era and take a positivist approach would tend to hide the benefits of accumulated privileges; a historical approach enables one to see not only how such privileges originated and evolved but also what havoc they still play with any notion of a meritocracy in which whites (males especially) "deserve" to be at the top.

However, in the historical account that follows—covering nearly a century and a half—I quite obviously do not seek to provide a comprehensive description. Rather I seek to provide a compact and coherent reanalysis of key episodes in the development of American social policy, and thus to illuminate a deceptively simple and yet usually neglected theme of American political development: American social policy has consistently and cumulatively constructed and reinforced white privilege through the normal workings of American politics.

Chapter 1 begins the historical analysis by contrasting the politics that created the Freedmen's Bureau with the politics that created the Civil War veterans' pensions. The aid provided by the Freedmen's Bureau to black men and women and their children was from the start meager, time-limited, and stigmatizing. It rapidly disappeared from the American agenda. Veterans' pensions—going disproportionately to white men, women, and their children—however, were very generous by nineteenth-century standards, were open-ended, and rapidly increased in coverage and amounts of stipends. Contrary to the claims of some

49. Christopher Howard, *The Hidden Welfare State: Tax Expenditures and Social Policy in the United States* (Princeton: Princeton University Press, 1997), 12.

prominent social policy scholars,[50] Civil War pensions did not treat African Americans fairly and honorably. More important, political debates over the two federal programs foreshadowed what was to come. President Andrew Johnson and the Democrats in the mid–nineteenth century opposed the Freedmen's Bureau as likely to make blacks "dependent," as too expensive, as unfair to whites, and as very probably a threat to racial hierarchies. In the meantime, the generous aid to northern veterans of the Civil War and their widows and children was viewed as wholly justified, and in the end veterans' pensions became virtually an old-age insurance program. As we shall see, the ideological construction of difference surrounding the two programs foreshadowed debates on social policy for more than a century to come. Indeed, the origins of the link that joined race, moral worthiness, and social policy lie in the history of the Freedmen's Bureau, and in particular in Andrew Johnson's construction of it as a program that catered to special interests and promoted black dependency. As the American ethos and white skin privilege institutionalized moral worthiness or desert according to race during the mid– to late nineteenth century, so it would do in following periods of American social policy innovation.

Andrew Johnson's construction of social policy resurfaces in debates at the creation of the welfare state proper, the New Deal, and was used by its opponents. Chapter 2 explores how the New Deal, rather than upsetting the apple cart of whiteness, expanded it legally through exclusion of African Americans from its ultimately most successful innovation (social insurance) and allowing southern states to discriminate in distribution of "relief." The second leg in the development of the welfare state (hidden welfare benefits such as employer-provided health insurance, pensions, and so forth) also virtually excluded blacks and women. Differential treatment of black and white workers in labor markets is a central part of this development, and thus the policy process itself appears to be neutral in respect to race and gender. What really emerges, however, is an understanding of how seemingly neutral policies usually just reproduce the discriminatory systems they are grafted upon. In the creation of both social insurance and hidden welfare programs, white males were advantaged by virtue of the institutional racism that provided them most of the best jobs in the labor market. White worker organizations, especially

---

50. See, e.g., Skocpol, *Social Policy in the United States.*

craft unions, were complicit in this process. Finally, such programs as federal housing assistance and agricultural support also solidified white advantage. The bifurcation of the New Deal system solidified, not reversed, white skin privilege.

Chapter 3 shows how in a time of prosperity, with a president who could claim a mandate and a Congress heavily dominated by members of his party, an unprecedented assault on white privilege, the Civil Rights Movement, resulted in new, more inclusive social policies. From new civil rights legislation to the War on Poverty in particular and the Great Society in general, the formerly excluded found a measure of inclusion. For a brief moment the privileges of whiteness faced a substantial and, in some important ways, successful challenge. Still the legacies from the past were influential, if not determinant. Rather than benefiting from more universal programs, people of color (especially blacks) were walled off behind those programs that were most stigmatizing and least generous. To a large extent, whites rejected the Great Society programs because they saw African Americans and any program thought to be designed primarily to address their needs as unworthy. When the Civil Rights Movement subsided, the time was ripe for a counterattack on the newly segmented programs that isolated people of color. As a result of this mounting counterattack, it became clear that for all Johnson's attempts to understand "black power," for all blacks and their sympathetic white allies' attempts to challenge the entrenched benefits of whiteness, the assault on white privilege in the 1950s and 1960s would remain woefully incomplete. To be sure, after the civil rights revolution, the operation of white privilege would not and could not proceed as before. White racism in an era of legal racial equality would have to don new clothes. Modern racism, depending mainly on cultural arguments, was subtle and often unconsciously practiced. The principle of racial equality found widespread acceptance even as whites rejected policies to implement it and sought to maintain their social distance from people of color. Although most whites came to consider themselves free of racial bias, nevertheless they continued to prefer white skin and embrace its privileges. Indeed, by at least 1968, white Americans proved the power of their resistance to any further encroachment on white privilege and elected Republican Richard Nixon, who had campaigned on a promise to reinvigorate "states' rights"—a symbol well understood by southern whites in particular, who were highly vocal in their support of white power. In the face of a Democratic Congress, Nixon proved unable fully to overturn policies and programs that had cut modestly into the power of whiteness, but the process of retrenchment had begun.

Chapter 4 analyzes how Ronald Reagan and to a lesser extent George H. W. Bush sought to perfect what Nixon had begun. Devoted to fully restoring the normality of white skin privilege, Reagan through the use of racial symbolism and administrative efforts sought to undercut any social policy (and law) that challenged whiteness. Symbolically he railed against civil rights leaders and declared that racism was virtually a thing of the past. In fact, white men were now suffering from reverse discrimination, according to the most popular American president of the late twentieth century. When Reagan could not win in Congress, he appointed a man supportive of white privilege as secretary or under secretary of any department that oversaw any policy he deemed to cut into the property value of whiteness. He also, obviously with the complicity of Congress, cut spending for any agency whose job it was to enforce equal opportunity in particular and civil rights more generally. Reagan had the ability to convince a white population frantic about recent encroachments on its privileges that blacks had made not just some progress but tremendous progress. More than on any other single dimension, whites who believed that blacks had made "lots of progress" were the least likely to support policies now identified with blacks, such as welfare, affirmative action, full employment, and food stamps. Yet one demonstration of the changing ideology of white privilege is found in the necessity for a politics of racial code words, symbolism, and subterfuge in the Reagan-Bush years. Long gone were the days when unvarnished race appeals worked.

Chapters 5 and 6 examine the Clinton years. Social policy developments in three key areas (crime, welfare reform, and affirmative action) are at the center of the analysis. The focus is on how important historical and analytical contexts explain why Clinton, despite his rhetoric on race and his enormous popularity among African Americans, was largely a captive both of his own political surroundings and ambitions and of historical trends beyond his control. Chapter 5 presents the evidence in regard to crime and welfare reform; Chapter 6 examines affirmative action and other race initiatives. The roles racial politics and the legacy of white skin privilege played in constraining policy options and shaping policy outcomes in the 1990s are the main focus. These chapters pivot on an irony: Clinton was elected with the broad support of African Americans but presided over retrenchment in social policy and the enactment of policies that were detrimental to African Americans. And still his strongest support came from African Americans! The class implications of a "new black politics" in which black leaders and politicians vigorously mobilized to defend affirmative action but were nearly missing in action when it came to welfare reform are explained. In sum, these chapters explain why Clinton's progressive policy ambitions were so stunted in the first place and why in some notable instances policy moved farther to the right than many would have predicted. The results of welfare reform, the president's race initiative, crime policy, and other key social initiatives are revealed not only to have failed to challenge whiteness but to have supported it. It also is shown that arguments that emerged as far back as the mid–nineteenth century to rationalize the property value of whiteness remained the order of the day throughout Clinton's two terms. In many ways, it was déjà vu: Andrew Johnson could have been speaking for many Republicans once their party won control of Congress. In short, race has always figured in the calculations of policy makers, but its significance for the Clinton years was that a racial mythology of the welfare state had become so entrenched in party politics that it constrained the policy alternatives of a president who seemingly favored progressive change. The politics of race in reforming crime, welfare, and antidiscrimination policies during the Clinton years were, once again, shaped by underlying patterns of discrimination to the disadvantage of people of color.

Chapter 7 presents data to help draw conclusions about where, in a new millennium, white privilege stands. Socioeconomic data are adduced to show how dramatic racial inequality remains in practically any arena of desired values. Whites remain far ahead of blacks and Latinos and ahead of the much more highly educated Asian population in nearly every socioeconomic category imaginable. The extent to which social policy also continues to reflect white skin privilege is analyzed. It is shown that after more than sixty years of being a welfare state, the United States' particular brand of social policy elevates, not challenges, whiteness. Blacks and whites remain disproportionately served by different programs. Those in which whites are overrepresented are still the most generous; those in which blacks are overrepresented are still the least generous. Whites remain privileged in the nation's social policy regime.

Chapter 8 focuses mainly on what is to be done to produce a more just and equitable social policy regime. A short list for programmatic change is presented, but it is stressed that these programs are unlikely to materialize without a new politics. What is required is a frontal challenge to the power of whiteness and a demonstration to those at the bottom of the white hierarchy that their interest lies with their own class among racial minorities. Despite the difficulty of achieving such an outcome, there clearly is hope that the mainly dispiriting history chronicled in this book can be overcome. That the tide can turn is shown by suppressed historical alternatives, by the times in which whiteness was seriously challenged by many whites and people of color alike, and by the moments in which genuine progress was made. Twentieth-century America was hardly all stalemate in the politics of race and social policy. The fact that the years since 1980 can be seen as a period of turning back indicates that there were also moments in which the nation raced forward. With the development of a new politics, it could do so again. Thus, the book ends with an identification of some potential developments that might provide a window of opportunity to overcome the seemingly iron grip of white skin privilege.

The findings in this book strongly challenge the notion that the American social policy regime has disproportionately benefited people of color. Instead it is shown in copious detail that from its inception, the American welfare state has done a great deal more to solidify white privilege than to challenge it. From the mid–nineteenth century through the close of the twentieth century, white privilege in the American welfare state was the order of the day. The next chapter begins to flesh out the argument. It explains the prehistory of the welfare state: beginning with the post–Civil War period.

one

America's First Undeserving and Deserving Poor

Beneficiaries of the Freedmen's Bureau and Civil War Veterans' Pensions

This is a country for white men and by God, as long as I

am President, it shall be a government for white men.

—*President Andrew Johnson*

No sooner had the war to "free the slaves" ended than the nation's premier leaders make it clear to black and white alike that no fundamental shake-up in the nation's race relations was in store. Succeeding President Abraham Lincoln, "the Great Emancipator," after his assassination, President Andrew Johnson was blunt and direct in his defense of white skin privilege. A southerner by birth, a former slaveholder despite his poor white origins, and a staunch supporter of "states' rights" as an instrument for maintenance of white rule in the South, Johnson blatantly urged that the laws must distinguish between whites and blacks, or they would "place every spay-footed, bandy-shanked, hump-backed, thick-lipped, flatnosed, wooley-headed, ebon-colored negro in the country upon an equality with the poor white man."[1]

To be sure, there were, as there always have been, some white Americans opposed to "white rights"—for example, General Rufus Saxton, Senators Charles Sumner and Ben Wade, Congressman Thaddeus Stevens, and many other Radical Republicans. To be white did not (and does not) dictate that one also must be a white supremacist. Still, Andrew Johnson was no synthetic leader. In his determination to keep power in the hands of whites, Johnson was an authentic leader of his day, speaking for most whites, North and South. More significant, his views reflected more than a hundred years of the process of socially constructing whiteness on this soil.

1. *Congressional Globe,* 28th Cong., 1st sess., Apr. 4, 1844, 95–98.

As Arnold Rose put it, "racism grew up as an American ideology partly in response to the need to maintain a reliable and permanent work force in the difficult job of growing cotton."[2] Yet as Rose implies, economics alone cannot explain why government privileged whites in the first place. One needs to look further at the inextricable links and dialectical relations between structure (economic base) and superstructure (political and cultural bases) or more specifically at the complex cross-currents and confluence of capitalism in its drive for ever cheaper labor and higher profits and republicanism with its imperative of a "responsible" citizenry.[3]

Republicanism, capitalism, and racial formation are intertwined in American political development. Take the way republican notions of "independence" have had both racial and economic valences. The Native American's innate "dependency," the Mexican's "laziness," and the African American's "childlike nature" were assessments that had economic consequences in the form, typically, of dispossession of Native American land, appropriation of Mexican land and exploitation of Mexican labor, and total social control and exploitation of black labor. Another example is the way race was tied to American conceptions of property (who can own property and who can be property, for example). Property in turn was central to republican notions of self-possession and the "stake in society" necessary for participation in the democratic process.[4] Independence and property ownership, however, could not be freely chosen. Since colonial times, these conceptions had increasingly been preserved and reserved for whites only, not simply by custom but by law.

Colony charters of the early seventeenth century made it clear that those colonies were for whites. The very designation "white" appeared in laws governing who could marry whom, who could participate in the militia, who could vote or hold office, and in laws governing contracts, indenture, and enslavement. As already noted, the nation's first naturalization law in 1790 (limiting naturalized citizenship to "free white persons") demonstrated both the republican convergence of race and "fitness for self-government" and an unconflicted view of the presumed character and unambiguous boundaries of whiteness.

---

2. Quoted in Frances Piven and Richard Cloward, *Poor People's Movements: Why They Succeed, How They Fail* (New York: Pantheon, 1977), 185.

3. Matthew Frye Jacobson, *Whiteness of a Different Color: European Immigrants and the Alchemy of Race* (Cambridge: Harvard University Press, 1998), 19.

4. Ibid., 21.

Although "white" is not mentioned in the Constitution, it had appeared in the Articles of Confederation.[5]

The importance of the developing whiteness project was hardly limited to the South. African American political standing in the free states of the North underscored the extent to which citizenship and whiteness were conjoined throughout the nation. At a constitutional convention in Pennsylvania in 1837, in a rousing speech urging extension of the suffrage "to every American citizen," a delegate added, "I use the word citizens as not embracing the colored population." There were no objections. Similarly in the free state of Michigan, a state senator comfortably asserted that "our government is formed by, for the benefit of, and to be controlled by the descendants of European nations. Negro suffrage would thus be inexpedient and impolitic."[6] Then in 1857 Chief Justice Roger Taney handed down the *Dred Scott* decision, in which he asserted that blacks possessed no rights "which the white man is bound to respect."[7]

Meanwhile, through a set of specific religious, partisan, and power struggles, a line was being drawn around Europe to establish just who was white. This was by no means a harmonious undertaking or instant achievement, and at times it was by no means certain that the Irish, Jews, and other groups would be part of the growing conception of whiteness. Abraham Lincoln—himself personally against the granting of citizenship to blacks, but in the midst of a campaign against the Know-Nothings, a nativist party—put it this way: "Our progress in degeneracy appears to me to be pretty rapid. As a nation, we began by declaring that 'all men are created equal.' We now practically read it 'all men are created equal except negroes.' When the Know-Nothings get control it will read 'all men are created equal, except negroes and foreigners and Catholics.' "[8] It took the need of the Democratic Party for voters in the North, the persistent efforts of the Catholic Church, and both violent and nonviolent efforts of white ethnics to disassociate themselves from blacks to avoid this calculus. By these processes the Irish, Jews, Germans, and a variety of Eastern and Southern Europeans—once conceived ethnically or even as

5. Gordon S. Wood, *The Creation of the American Republic, 1776–1787* (New York: Norton, 1969), 30–31, 47–50.

6. Quoted in Jacobson, *Whiteness of a Different Color,* 29.

7. *Dred Scott v. Sanford,* 19 How. 393 (1957).

8. Quoted in Richard Hofstadter, *The American Political Tradition* (New York: Knopf, 1973), 131.

"a race apart"—became white in large part on the backs of people of color.[9] Blacks remained enslaved; American Indians were constructed as neither "citizens" nor "nations" but as "domestic dependent nations"; Asian immigrants were "ineligible for citizenship"; and Mexican Americans became strangers in their own land during the period when many European ethnics were winning inclusion in whiteness.

Making white men the only group fit for self-government and excluding all others on the basis of race and gender did not represent mere lacunae in an otherwise liberal philosophy and democratic creed. These inclusions and exclusions were inseparably woven in the same ideological tapestry of republicanism. Perhaps there is no place this is better seen than in the views of that paragon celebrator of the egalitarian tendencies of republicanism, Thomas Jefferson. Jefferson, known best for penning the Declaration of Independence, with its famous salute to the equality of "all men," was elsewhere quite clear that he did not include black men in that equation. In *Notes on the State of Virginia* Jefferson explained: "It will probably be asked [if slavery is ended], why not retain and incorporate the negroes into the state." This would not be a prudent course of action, Jefferson maintained: "Deep rooted prejudices entertained by the whites; ten thousand recollections, by the blacks, of the injuries they have sustained; new provocations; the real distinctions which nature has made; and many other circumstances, will divide us into parties, and produce convolutions which will probably never end but in the extermination of the one or the other race." The republican emphasis on a homogeneous polity did figure in Jefferson's thinking. But he went on to detail "the real distinctions which nature has made" between the two races. He wrote fondly of the greater beauty of whites; he noted with unelaborated portent "the preference of the Orangutan for the black woman" over those of his own species; and he asserted that "in reason [blacks] are much inferior" and "in imagination they are dull, tasteless, and anomalous."[10] Such a group was not capable of self-government or of being equal citizens in any way.

---

9. See David Roediger, *The Wages of Whiteness: Race and the Making of the American Working Class,* rev. ed. (New York: Verso, 1999), and Jacobson, *Whiteness of a Different Color* for two excellent analyses of how ethnic whites became simply whites. Many of the stereotypes first used to derogate and oppress the Irish were actually later transferred to blacks, not vice versa.

10. Thomas Jefferson, *Notes on the State of Virginia,* new ed. (Richmond, Va.: J. W. Randolph, 1853), 147.

That Jefferson would couch the Declaration, a politically legitimating document for the coming war against Britain, in universalist language and the *Notes on Virginia* in openly exclusionary and racist tones shows that the disjunction between the celebrated American abstract ideal of individualism and actual understandings and expectations was apparent from the beginning of the nation. As Richard Hofstadter concludes, the idea that "all men are created equal" meant "only that British colonials had as much natural right to self-government as Britons at home; that the average American was the legal peer of the average Briton."[11] The freedom to hold and accumulate property was a much more important concern for the Founding Fathers. Most, preferring, as Jefferson did, the rule of a "natural aristocracy," feared the leveling tendencies of the masses, saw themselves as tremendously different from the masses, and defined women, blacks, Native Americans, and other people of color as groups disqualified for full citizenship by their dependency or lack of the great Enlightenment equalizer, reason.

When it came to practically structuring the polity, these actual understandings took priority. For example, the list of qualifications for office was long: white, male, propertied, and Protestant.[12] Thus from the very start of the nation, racism appears not anomalous to the working of American democracy but fundamental to it.

In short, by the time of the Civil War, after more than a hundred years of development in America, race was not only a social construction but also a perception. Whites were conceived and perceived as "fit" for self-government; the darker races were "unfit." Thus long before Andrew Johnson promoted white rights in the aftermath of the Civil War, race was the prevailing idiom for discussing both citizenship and the relative merits of a given people.[13] It was also the most fundamental labor organizing principle in the South.

It is in the context of the mid- to late nineteenth-century construction of race that the nation's first excursions in federal social policy emerge. As Ann Shola Orloff contends, "histories of American social provision often presume that the federal government had no role in providing welfare benefits until the

11. Hofstadter, *American Political Tradition*, 15.

12. J. R. Pole, *The Pursuit of Equality in American History* (Berkeley and Los Angeles: University of California Press, 1978), 91.

13. John P. Kaminski, *A Necessary Evil? Slavery and the Debate over the Constitution* (Madison, Wis.: Madison House, 1995), 214–19.

1930s when President Franklin Delano Roosevelt (FDR) introduced social security programs as part of the New Deal. Until then, the story goes, the needs of those Americans unable to care for themselves through participation in the labor market were addressed only, if at all, by the state—and especially—local levels of government." Orloff adds that this account is "superficially accurate but potentially quite misleading." She then points to the Civil War pension system as one "rather spectacular exception to local predominance in the welfare field in the late nineteenth and early twentieth centuries."[14]

Yet Orloff, too, overlooks still another exception, one critical to understanding the legacy of racial politics in the making of American social policy: the relief efforts of the short-lived Freedmen's Bureau.[15] Not only Orloff but most scholars of American social policy tend to ignore the historical significance of the Bureau.[16] It is much more common to set the origins of American social policy in the Civil War pensions, as Orloff does, or in the state and local-level programs for widowed mothers during Reconstruction. Indeed, most scholars consider the pension program to be the first social security system in the United States. With respect to social security per se, this claim has some truth; yet the story Orloff, Theda Skocpol, and most others writing on the prehistory of the American welfare state tell is incomplete, neglecting other significant welfare activities during the Reconstruction period. In fact, had they also included the Bureau, they would have seen bifurcation and segmentation in American social policy much earlier than the New Deal.

Officially known as the Bureau of Freedmen, Refugees, and Abandoned Lands, the Bureau was established before the soldiers' pension program, and in many respects these two programs mirror the segmented system that was to become the New Deal. Compared to the Bureau's efforts, the soldiers' pension program was generous, was politically legitimated, and considered to serve the

14. Ann Shola Orloff, "The Political Origins of America's Belated Welfare State," in Margaret Weir, Ann Shola Orloff, and Theda Skocpol, eds., *The Politics of Social Policy in the United States* (Princeton: Princeton University Press, 1988), 38.

15. I thank Cedric Johnson for first calling to my attention the social policy nature of the Freedmen's Bureau's work. See Cedric Kweisi Johnson, " 'Forty Acres and a Mule' Revisited: The Freedmen's Bureau and the Coloring of American Social Policy," unpublished paper, December 1995.

16. For another prominent work on early federal social provision that ignores the Freedmen's Bureau, see Theda Skocpol, *Protecting Soldiers and Mothers: The Political Origins of Social Policy in the United States* (Cambridge: Belknap/Harvard University Press, 1992).

"deserving poor" in much the same way as modern social insurance programs.[17] The Freedmen's Bureau occupied the lower rung of the Reconstruction welfare system. The Bureau, like Aid to Families with Dependent Children from at least the 1960s onward, was politically unpopular and vulnerable and considered to serve the "undeserving poor."

At the same time, as Walter Trattner notes, the Bureau demonstrated that the federal government could provide for the welfare of people on a broad scale when poverty and hardship could (or would) not be addressed locally.[18] Thus there is much to be learned from the Bureau's experience and demise; in fact, many of the debates over the Bureau foreshadowed debates over the American welfare state ever since. Contrasting the Bureau's efforts with those of the veterans' pension system is instructive for what it reveals about the way the privileges of whiteness were first modestly challenged, then fully restored. This was perhaps the first missed opportunity to produce a genuine multiracial democracy in the United States since the nation's founding fathers betrayed the noble principles enshrined in the Declaration of Independence by sanctioning the slave trade.

Race, Class, Gender, and the Freedmen's Bureau

During the short-lived Reconstruction period, the task of challenging whiteness and replacing it with a new multiracial democracy in the South fell largely to the Freedmen's Bureau. In fact, the Bureau was an experiment in social policy that perhaps, as Eric Foner concludes, "did not belong to the America of its day."[19] Its official responsibility was to address two problems: the mushrooming economic crisis after the Civil War and the so-called Negro question. What should happen to free blacks? Should they be treated as full and equal citizens or as demicitizens, or should they be recolonized in Africa, the Caribbean, Canada, or perhaps some unsettled area of the United States?

By far the most popular of these alternatives was colonization. Even the

---

17. Black Civil War veterans were not entirely excluded from the veterans' pensions, no more than all blacks were excluded from Social Security in the 1930s. In both instances, however, the black recipients represented only a meager proportion of recipients of these more generous programs.

18. Walter I. Trattner, *From Poor Law to Welfare State: A History of Social Welfare in America* (New York: Free Press, 1989). Trattner, like a few others who have mentioned the Bureau as an early component of the history of American social policy, did not develop the argument.

19. Eric Foner, *A Short History of Reconstruction* (New York: Harper & Row, 1990), 64.

most radical blueprints for the abolition of slavery involved, in one way or another, the disappearance of the formerly enslaved. Either a colonization scheme would remove them to some distant land or, by the magic of eighteenth-century ethnological principles, "in the process of time the very color would be extinct and there would be none but whites."[20] That blacks should somehow just vanish was such a popular theme that it not only became part of political debates but appeared regularly in popular culture. One of the best-selling children's books of the day was *The Ten Little Niggers,* a story in which ten little black children disappear one by one "until there was none."[21]

Many blacks opposed colonization, arguing that they were born in the United States, they had fought for their country, and they hoped to remain here in the full enjoyment of "enfranchised manhood and its dignities."[22] There is some evidence, however, that at least some blacks favored colonization—they desired a chance to leave what for them had been primarily a land of misery or at least to be sent to an unsettled region of the West where they would live apart from whites.[23] The most successful colonization scheme was that sponsored by the American Colonization Society, which received government aid to send more than 3,000 blacks to Liberia. The costs were high. To send just 618 adults and 145 children to Liberia in 1868 cost $6,290, or the combined average monthly wages and earnings of more than 350 workers.[24] So the question became: who would pay for colonization on a mass scale and which country was willing to take the wholesale resettlement of the ex-slaves. These were sticking points that ultimately doomed colonization schemes.

Meanwhile, the destruction of crops, farmlands, and infrastructure throughout the South displaced thousands of workers of all races. The war had

20. Winthrop Jordan, *White over Black: American Attitudes toward the Negro, 1550–1812* (Baltimore: Penguin, 1969), 542–69.

21. This book was so popular that numerous publishing houses produced or reproduced it throughout the 1800s. In addition, a tune with a merry beat was written to accompany it so that children could actually sing the story. For elaborately illustrated examples, see *The Ten Little Niggers* (New York: McLoughlin Bro's, 1847, 1894); and *Mother Goose's Ten Little Niggers Book* (New York: Mother Goose, 1877).

22. "Resolution of Convention of Negroes in Virginia," in National Archives, RG 105, Microform 732, Roll 23, p. 574.

23. Charles F. Oubre, *Forty Acres and a Mule: The Freedmen's Bureau and Black Land Ownership* (Baton Rouge: Louisiana State University Press, 1978), 7.

24. Ibid., 6, and U.S. Bureau of the Census, *Historical Statistics of the United States, 1789–1945* (Washington, D.C., 1949), 67.

removed primary wage earners from many homes, increasing the ranks of the poor. Literally tens of thousands of people—both black and white—found themselves landless, jobless, and homeless.[25] Whites and blacks alike experienced nearly a complete breakdown of everyday life. What should happen to the families of men who had lost their lives in the Civil War? What could be done for those disabled during the war? Who would assume responsibility for those too old, too ill, too infirm to work? What would happen to all those—black and white—now cast out of the routine of work and the regulatory framework it had imposed?

In the face of mounting need, it became increasingly clear that local resources would not be even close to sufficient. The sources of relief for African Americans in particular were limited. The nineteenth-century feminist-led Mothers' Aid movement in the North focused on poor European immigrants, not black women in the North or South.[26] Most private aid societies in the South either had little interest in providing assistance to black persons or simply were unable to do so because resources were so scarce. As the size and intensity of the relief crisis grew, however, a number of new private aid societies in the North sprang up with the express objective of demanding that the federal government create a more formal support system for the former slaves and refugees.[27] In short, it was forces in civil society, not government, that first sought to push the creation of programs of relief.

As Du Bois explains it, "it was a Pierce of Boston . . . who became in a sense the founder of the Freedmen's Bureau . . . [and] started the Freedmen's Aid Societies. Among the Aid Societies were the American Missionary Association, the various church organizations, the National Freedmen's Relief Association, the American Freedmen's Union, the Western Freedmen's Aid Commission—in all fifty or more active organizations, which sent clothes, money, school books, and teachers southward."[28]

These groups, however, soon concluded that their meager resources were

25. Jacqueline Jones, *The Dispossessed: America's Underclass from the Civil War to the Present* (New York: Basic Books, 1992), chaps. 1–2.

26. Linda Gordon, *Pitied but Not Entitled: Single Mothers and the History of Welfare* (New York: Free Press, 1994).

27. Paul Pierce, *The Freedmen's Bureau* (Iowa City: University of Iowa, 1904); W. E. B. Du Bois, "The Freedmen's Bureau," *Atlantic Monthly,* March 1901, 345–65; and George Bentley, *A History of the Freedmen's Bureau* (Philadelphia: University of Pennsylvania Press, 1955).

28. Du Bois, "Freedmen's Bureau."

no match for the enormity of the problem. As the members of the Thirty-eighth Congress were gathering for their first session, freedmen's aid societies in Boston, Cincinnati, New York, and Philadelphia pooled their efforts and wrote a letter to President Lincoln, imploring him to "interpose" with Congress and urge "the immediate creation of a bureau of emancipation." They sought a "regularly constituted government bureau, with all the machinery and civil powers of the government behind it." Emancipation alone was not enough if liberty was to be anything more than a curse, the letter argued, and only the national government had the resources to provide necessary compensatory assistance; the voluntary agencies, faithful as they had been, would have been inadequate to the situation "were their resources ten times what they are, and ten times what they can be made."[29]

Politics, it has been said, makes strange bedfellows, and so it was with the proposal to create the Freedmen's Bureau. Support came from two distinct corners with different, albeit not wholly conflicting, ambitions. On the one hand, support came from textile manufacturers who believed that the Bureau had much to offer not only blacks but New England businessmen as well. Businessmen such as Edward Atkinson, John Murray Forbes, and George O. Hovey had concluded long before the Civil War that the landowning aristocracy of the South was holding up the price of raw cotton, and they wanted the system of slave labor broken so that cotton production might become more competitive. If they could break the southern plantocracy's semimonopoly, they expected free labor to produce more and cheaper cotton, as the Port Royal Sound experiment in the South Carolina and Georgia Sea Islands showed it would. There the widely reported successes in planting cost-efficient crops and raising the first regiment of black troops did much to persuade the northern public that blacks would work without compulsion and would defend their own freedom. They also fed the idea that in time blacks would have their own land. Here, northern industrialists intoned, was the model for a new South. In sum, from the vantage point of northern cotton manufacturers, one important job of the Freedmen's Bureau would be to establish a free-labor society in the South and help the northern investor "guide and protect the Negro in the ways of free labor, *but it must not go too far in regulating the relations of the new planters and their potential field hands.*"[30] In sum, the northern business support for the Bureau

29. Quoted in Bentley, *History of the Freedmen's Bureau,* 30.
30. Ibid., 31–34; emphasis added.

was anything but entirely altruistic. It owed far more to the politics of class and class factions than to the politics of race.

The second source of support was Radical Republicans in Congress. The Radicals were the leftmost faction of the Republican party, bitterly opposed to slavery and stern in their judgments of the South. It was the Radicals who pushed and pulled Abe Lincoln, not only president but leader of the conservative wing of the party, to win support for freedmen. As the war progressed toward a restoration of the Union, the Radicals' ambition grew toward controlling Reconstruction—an ambition that could be realized only if blacks had the vote. To the Radicals, a Freedmen's Bureau could be a useful tool. It could provide patronage, authority to direct the labor of the South, and a strategic position for influencing the new black vote. All of these developments would help to "Republicanize" the South. Thus the Radicals were eager to do their share in creating the bureau that the cotton manufacturers and freedmen's aid societies had asked Lincoln to promote.

On December 14, 1863, two weeks after the freedmen's aid societies had written their letter to Lincoln, a moderate Republican, Thomas D. Eliot, introduced in Congress a bill to create a bureau of emancipation. It called for an agency in the War Department with a commissioner and assistant commissioners to have general supervision over freed blacks, to permit them to cultivate abandoned and confiscated lands, and to help secure them fair wages. The hotly debated bill was opposed by all the usual suspects—in particular southern Democrats, who argued that the bill was unconstitutional and full of loopholes that would be abused by northern speculators and investors.[31] As debates mushroomed, the Eliot bill stalled.

Yet, despite the furor of the constitutional debate and matters such as under which department (Treasury, Interior, or War) the bureau should be placed, a bill to create the Freedmen's Bureau passed, without division, on March 3, 1865. On the same day Lincoln signed it into law.[32] The Freedmen's Bureau bill would prove to be one of the last bills he signed in the six weeks left before his assassination. Lincoln named Major General Oliver Otis Howard as the Bureau's commissioner, but before the appointment could be made, Lincoln was dead. It fell to his successor, Andrew Johnson, to actually appoint Howard.

31. For discussion of the arguments advanced by Democrats, see ibid., 36–39.
32. Ibid., xv.

When Howard took over the Bureau, a new era of federal social services provision began, but what would it mean? Whose bureau was it going to be and for whose purposes was it to be chiefly used—the freedmen's, the Radical politicians, or northern industrialists? What impact would it have on white privilege?

The Policies and Programs of the Freedmen's Bureau

Perhaps the most noteworthy characteristic of the Freedmen's Bureau bill was negative: it provided the Bureau a very tenuous status, vulnerable from its inception to opposing forces. For instance, the Bureau was established as a temporary division of the War Department and slated to operate for only one year after the end of the war.[33] The Bureau's financial status, too, was anything but encouraging. In fact, Congress appropriated no funds to support the Bureau's work.[34] For its first year of operation, the Bureau depended on donations from benevolent societies and rents collected from tenants working abandoned lands. The rents declined significantly once President Andrew Johnson, ever a white supremacist, pardoned many planters and restored lands to them.[35] Although the Bureau never won consideration as a permanent agency, after a bitter struggle between Johnson and Congress, its life was extended for six years and it won some direct federal funding. Indeed, annual congressional appropriations were essential for the Bureau's survival. Congress appropriated roughly $17 million for the Bureau over its lifetime.[36] Still, as its housing in the War, not Treasury, Department indicated, the Bureau was always viewed as a wartime or temporary agency.

Despite these limitations, the Bureau undertook the monumental task of providing welfare services to freed persons and white refugees. Its day-to-day responsibilities were daunting. It provided food, clothing, and fuel to the destitute, aged, ill, and insane among both white refugees and freedmen; established schools for freedmen; supplied medical services; implemented a workable system of free labor in the South through the supervision of contracts between

33. Ira Colby, "The Freedmen's Bureau: From Social Welfare to Segregation," *Phylon* 46, no. 3 (August 1985): 220–23.

34. Ibid., 221.

35. Bentley, *History of the Freedmen's Bureau,* 74.

36. W. E. B. Du Bois, *Black Reconstruction in the United States, 1860–1880* (1935; New York: Simon & Schuster, 1995).

the freedmen and their employers; managed confiscated or abandoned lands, leasing and selling some of them to freedmen; and attempted to secure for blacks equal justice before the law. Each local Bureau agent was expected not only to accomplish these formidable tasks in the post–Civil War environment but also to win the confidence of blacks and whites alike in an atmosphere poisoned by centuries of mutual distrust and conflicting interests.[37] As Lerone Bennett concluded, "the Bureau combined the governmental functions of the WPA, the Office of Economic Opportunity and Medicare with the defense functions of the NAACP and Urban League."[38]

How successful the Bureau was in accomplishing these monumental tasks—whether in land and labor policy, education, or relief—hinged on the ability of individual agents to make their case before blacks and whites and to inculcate respect for law. Since the Bureau lacked the institutional and financial resources to fully effect relief, recovery, and reform, and since local differences in culture and conditions meant constantly having to adapt broad Bureau philosophy and interests to very particular conditions, results across the South were far from uniform. What was uniform was that Bureau agents were overworked in the field, for there were never enough agents. According to Eric Foner, a total of only 2,441 men served as agents over the life of the Bureau and just 900 were spread across the South at the height of Bureau staffing. The job of a Bureau agent was not a happy one. Many agents lived and operated alone, with diminishing military support and unrelenting local white opposition. Their caseloads were staggering. Blacks presented the agents with a constant stream of concerns, including family and personal matters, and even as whites decried the Bureau's interference, they regularly pressed the agents to make the freed people work and abide by their contracts.[39]

Nevertheless, historians generally agree that the Freedmen's Bureau's experiment in social policy relieved much suffering among blacks and whites. During its brief life span the Bureau provided between $13 and $17 million in goods, services, and cash disbursements. John Hope Franklin and Albert Moss Jr. point out that "between 1865 and 1869 . . . the Bureau issued 21 million

37. Foner, *Short History of Reconstruction*, 64–65.
38. Lerone Bennett, *Black Power U.S.A.: The Human Side of Reconstruction, 1867–1877* (Chicago: Johnson, 1967), 26.
39. Foner, *Short History of Reconstruction*, xxviii–xxix.

rations, approximately 5 million going to whites and 15 million to blacks."[40] Ira Colby discusses the contents of these rations as outlined in General Order No.120 of the War Department. One ration included pork/bacon (16 ounces), fresh beef (16 ounces), flour/soft bread (16 ounces), hard bread (12 ounces), corn meal (16 ounces), peas, bacon or hominy (10 pounds), sugar (8 pounds), vinegar (2 quarts), candles (8 ounces), soap (2 pounds), salt (2 ounces), and pepper (2 ounces). Colby notes that women and children received tea (15 ounces) and roasted rye coffee (10 pounds); children under the age of fourteen received one-half the specified amounts.[41] As a result of the types of rations issued, most freed persons' diets consisted of hominy, corn bread, fat bacon, coffee, molasses, rice, pork, and starchy vegetables such as beans and peas. Thus the rations the refugees and freed persons received reflected both an unhealthy diet and their poverty.[42]

Nonetheless, the practice of providing food, clothing, and other necessities to the destitute served as a key point of contention among Bureau officials and supporters and critics alike. Some feared the "pauperizing" effects of these handouts. Word soon spread throughout the South that many blacks were taking "undue advantage" of the government's benevolence.[43] As a result, many officials encouraged the withholding of rations to force the able-bodied to work. As resentment grew, the quantity of disbursements tapered off significantly.

The size of the Bureau-sponsored hospital system is also noteworthy. By 1867 forty-six hospitals staffed by physicians, surgeons, and nurses were operating under Bureau supervision. The medical department spent over $2 million to improve the health of freedmen and treated more than 450,000 cases of illness.[44] Ira Colby points out that during a typical month 45,898 freed persons received care in Bureau-supervised hospitals.[45] Judging from available data on the Bureau's medical care programs, such activities apparently had a positive impact on the health and welfare of freed persons and refugees. The quality and

40. John Hope Franklin and Alfred Moss Jr., *From Slavery to Freedom: A History of African Americans,* 7th ed. (New York: Knopf, 1994), 229.

41. Colby, "Freedmen's Bureau," 226.

42. Randy Finley, *From Slavery to Uncertain Freedom: The Freedmen's Bureau in Arkansas, 1865–1869* (Fayetteville: University of Arkansas Press, 1996), 97.

43. Bentley, *History of the Freedmen's Bureau,* 76–79.

44. Franklin and Moss, *From Slavery to Freedom,* 229.

45. Colby, "Freedmen's Bureau," 227.

effectiveness of Bureau hospitals is reflected in the downward-sloping trends in mortality rates among patients under their care. In 1865, 13 percent of freed persons and 9 percent of white refugees died in Bureau-supervised hospitals. By 1869 those rates had been reduced to 2 percent for freed persons and 1 percent for white refugees. Predictably, the quality of such health care services for blacks deteriorated rapidly once the Bureau's powers were dissolved by Congress in 1869. From that point on, mortality rates among black patients in public hospitals ballooned upward to 17 percent by June 30, 1872.[46]

The Bureau achieved its greatest success in education. It set up or supervised all kinds of schools: day, night, Sunday, and industrial as well as colleges. Many of the nation's best-known black colleges were founded with aid from the Bureau: Howard University, Hampton Institute, St. Augustine's College, Atlanta University, Fisk University, and Biddle Memorial Institute (now Johnson C. Smith University). When the education work of the Bureau stopped in 1879, there were 247,222 students in 4,329 schools.[47]

To be sure, these statistics in some ways overestimate the Bureau's success in education. First, most of the schools were located in or near towns while the majority of blacks were still rural. As a result, most black school-age children did not attend school at all, and even those who went to school did so for only a few months out of the year and often just for a few years overall. Second, virtually every school was segregated by race, for whites refused to attend freedmen's schools and the Bureau did not push for racial integration. Third, the Bureau could not take credit for all of those schools, many of which were staffed by blacks and in some cases southern whites and had no relation to the Bureau. Clearly black education in the postemancipation South was a joint venture combining the common efforts and philosophy of the Bureau, benevolent associations, and blacks themselves. Fourth, it is important to understand just how tentative and limited the Bureau's efforts were. Even in 1879, only a minority of white children of school age was actually enrolled in the South and half or more of those enrolled were likely to be absent on any given day. "Education for blacks lagged far behind even this minimal achievement. . . . As late as the end of the century, the great majority of Southern [blacks] were still imprisoned in illiteracy."[48]

46. Pierce, *Freedmen's Bureau*, 87–94.
47. Franklin and Moss, *From Slavery to Freedom*, 230.
48. Dan Lacy, *The White Use of Blacks in America: 350 Years of Law and Violence, Attitudes and Etiquette, Politics and Change* (New York: McGraw-Hill, 1973), 86–87.

Yet to discount the Bureau's educational achievement is to miss the dynamic of the Bureau's role in Reconstruction. Without the Bureau's resources and resolve, the freedmen's education would have been even more sporadic and limited than it was. The Bureau laid a foundation, but its overtaxed agents could not remake the southern educational system; nor did it seek to do so. The Bureau's goal in education was to set a course for others to follow rather than carry the load by itself, and its efforts should be judged on that basis. On balance, across the board the Freedmen's Bureau did much good.

The Limits of the Freedmen Bureau's Success

By law the Bureau was to set apart "for their use abandoned lands within the Confederate states, or such land to which the United States had acquired title, to be assigned to loyal refugees and freedmen in plots of not more than 40 acres at the annual rent of six percent of its value for three years, at the end of which the occupants might buy them."[49] It was the Bureau's most revolutionary promise: the authorization to produce a permanent transformation of the condition of the emancipated slaves by providing them a means to economic security by becoming independent farmers in a free-labor South. While hardly a definitive commitment to land redistribution, the law establishing the Bureau indicated, at the very least, that the Freedmen's Bureau was to be a settlement agency, leasing abandoned properties to black and refugee cultivators. This, however, is where the Bureau failed most tragically.

Control and ownership of land were critical to black needs. Coming out of slavery, African Americans had considerable agricultural skills. Along with the protection of their rights, what they needed most was land on which they could use those skills and funds and teachers to begin the task of agricultural educational and vocational training.

Landownership was also what many, if not most, blacks saw as the ultimate meaning of freedom. As Garrison Frazier, a Baptist minister who had known bondage for sixty years before purchasing his liberty in 1857, put it on January 12, 1865, to General William T. Sherman, freedom meant "placing us where we could reap the fruit of our own labor." The best way to achieve this goal, he added, was "to have land, and . . . till it by our own labor."[50] The

---

49. Quoted ibid., 30.
50. Quoted in Foner, *Short History of Reconstruction,* 32.

freedmen's view of economic security came down not to an unearned dole but rather to ownership of land they could work to provide for their own needs and for profit.

The problem was that meeting the needs of freed blacks for land required an alternative vision of the South in which white privilege no longer ran rampant. For this vision to be realized, unearned white advantages, white racial preferences, and conferred white dominance would have to be openly addressed and challenged, if not destroyed—for the conflict over land was in a very immediate sense a conflict over whiteness as a real and imagined property value.

Thus the "land question" was essentially a question about both class and white skin privilege. After all, the land to be given to freed blacks could have come only from the confiscation and redistribution of plantation holdings. The Confiscation Act of 1861 had laid the legal basis for such action, but this statute never commanded the support of the administration of either Abraham Lincoln or Andrew Johnson and was never seriously enforced. Nonetheless, by 1865 the Bureau controlled over 850,000 acres of abandoned land. Although hardly enough to accommodate all the former enslaved, it was sufficient to make a start toward creating a black yeomanry.

That a black yeomanry could have been productive had been demonstrated. During the Civil War and immediately after it, there were various experiments in which freedmen had the opportunity to operate for their own profit lands abandoned by Confederate owners, and they had done so successfully. Perhaps the best known of these experiments was the settlement of freedmen on so-called Sherman land. This experiment began four days after Garrison Frazier's plea to Sherman in January 1865, when Sherman issued Special Field Order No. 15, setting aside the Sea Islands and a portion of the lowcountry rice coast south of Charleston, South Carolina, extending thirty miles inland, for the exclusive settlement of blacks. Sherman authorized each family to receive forty acres of land and a mule, lent to them by the army. Here, perhaps, lies the origin of the phrase "forty acres and a mule," which ultimately echoed throughout the South. As a result, some 40,000 freedmen had been settled on 400,000 acres of Sherman land by June 1865. Similarly, the Bureau leased over 60,000 acres in Louisiana to blacks.

Then on July 28, 1865, the Bureau made its boldest move: Howard issued Circular 13, which directed the assistant commissioners to set aside lands under their control and begin dividing them among the freedmen. Although President Johnson had already issued his proclamation granting amnesty and pardon to all but leading former Confederates on May 29, the July circular specified that the amnesty proclamation did not affect the lands in question. In effect, Circular 13 instructed Bureau agents to "set aside" forty-acre tracts for the freedmen as rapidly as possible.[51]

The set-asides posed no challenge to the American ethos; rather they were an outgrowth of it. Howard believed that the freedmen should have land and that the South could be reconstructed only if it became a land of small farms rather than a land dominated by aristocrats, but he also firmly believed that freedmen should earn land and not receive it as a gift. Not only did he encourage freedmen to work and save money in order to purchase land, but he instructed his assistants to rent the land to the freedmen and use the rents thus generated to pay for the rations, clothing, medical care, schools, and shelter provided by the Bureau. Thus, during the entire first year of the Bureau's work, the freedmen, through their own labor, paid for the care of many who were unable to work and the Bureau was self-supporting.

But even the Protestant work ethic imposed by Circular 13 was too much for white southerners and their man in the White House. White southerners who lacked the money to plant all their land nevertheless refused to sell to the freedmen. To get around this logjam, Howard recommended that northerners, including Bureau agents, purchase or lease farms to provide work for the freedmen.

These actions infuriated President Johnson. Although he had become popular in the North as the only senator from a seceding state who remained loyal to the Union, he fully shared the Confederacy's racist views. That he did not oppose the black codes passed by the states that he sought to reconstruct gave ample proof of Johnson's determination to keep power in the hands of southern whites. His preferred means of doing so was states' rights. These preferences explain why Johnson always hated the Bureau. To him the Bureau seemed not only to interfere with states' rights but also to create "special" support for freedmen. His veto of the bill to create it had to be overridden. Then in July 1865 Andrew Johnson ordered the withdrawal of Circular 13.[52]

51. Ibid., 71–74.
52. Hans L. Trefousse, "Andrew Johnson and the Freedmen's Bureau," in Trefousse, *Impeachment of a President: Andrew Johnson, the Blacks, and Reconstruction* (Knoxville: University of Tennessee Press, 1975), 31–33, 42.

Consequently, on September 12, 1865, Howard replaced Circular 13 with Circular 15. Drafted in the White House, Circular 15 ordered that no land was to be considered confiscated until it had been legally condemned. Property not so condemned was to be restored to the original owners, and those pardoned by the president were eligible to recover their property. In effect Circular 15 not only cut off prospects for black landownership but also returned to the planters the land of the few freedmen who had cobbled together the means to plant crops on their leased lands in 1865. In effect, once those black farmers had harvested their crops, virtually all the land under the Bureau's control reverted to its former owners, and freedmen who refused to work for the planters were evicted. Johnson had already rescinded a previous order turning over to the Bureau all tax funds collected for the benefit of refugees and freedmen or accruing from abandoned lands or property set aside for their use.[53] Revolutions, as the historian Willie Lee Rose has noted, "do go backward."[54]

As blacks' dreams of landownership as a route to self-reliance began to fade, the former Confederate claimants of land temporarily farmed by the freedmen "were treated with a tenderness quite lacking in the confiscation of Loyalist estates" during the American Revolution.[55] This outcome was predictable on two grounds. First, the elites were vigorous in seeking to restore southern white dominance and impede blacks' attempts at autonomy through landownership. What the former masters wanted and attempted to recreate in the immediate post–Civil War South was a disciplined labor force, and they, like the freedmen, understood that questions of land and labor were directly linked. Planters clearly saw that their control of black labor required them to retain access to the productive land of the plantation belt. Even if relatively few freedmen established themselves as independent farmers, plantation discipline would dissolve, since, as William H. Trescot explained, "it will be utterly impossible for the owner to find laborers that will work contentedly for wages alongside of these free colonies."[56] Hence planters resolved, at public meetings and in their private correspondence, never to rent or sell land to freedmen.

Second, providing confiscated or abandoned land to blacks had little or

53. Ibid., 33.
54. Willie Lee Rose, *Rehearsal for Reconstruction: The Port Royal Experiment* (Indianapolis: Bobbs-Merrill, 1964), 378.
55. Lacy, *White Use of Blacks,* 84ff.
56. Quoted in Foner, *Short History of Reconstruction,* 74.

no support in official Washington. To be sure, a few Radical Republicans, especially Thaddeus Stevens, continued to agitate for expropriation measures to distribute land to blacks, but Stevens's argument was overwhelmingly rejected on the grounds that such a policy was a "violation of the property rights" of southern landowners and a clear departure from the principle of competition.[57] The Congress dallied with the idea that blacks might be given preferential access to free lands in the public domain through the Southern Homestead Act, but this idea, too, came to almost nothing.[58] Thus, while the freed people continued to be, in biblical terms, "prisoners of hope," nurturing rumors of forty acres and a mule during the Christmas seasons of 1865 and 1866, at least from the Johnson-inspired Circular 15 onward (if not before), the fundamental view of the Bureau was that most freed people must return to plantation labor under their former masters.

Howard set about informing the freed people of the Bureau's latest policy shift, contending that they must "lay aside their bitter feelings, and become reconciled to their old masters." Even as some black freedmen equated Circular 15 with a practical return to slavery, the idea of the Bureau as an active promoter of black landownership came to an abrupt end. Agents who continued to be sympathetic to black ownership, such as General Rufus Saxton, a prewar abolitionist who headed the Bureau in Georgia, Florida, and South Carolina, and Thomas W. Conway, a Radical Republican of Louisiana, Johnson ordered removed.[59]

Unlike Saxton and Conway, the vast majority of Bureau agents, black and white, made every effort to induce freed people to sign contracts with their former masters, and federal troops forcibly evicted those who refused. The restoration of land ultimately required the displacement of tens of thousands of freed people throughout the South, leaving in its wake only about 2,000 freedmen in South Carolina and Georgia who actually received the land they had been promised in 1865. As Merrimon Howard, a freedman of Mississippi, put it, blacks had been left with "no *land,* no *house,* not so much as a place to lay our head. . . . Despised by the world, hated by the country that gives us birth, denied all our writs as a people, we were friends on the march . . . brothers on the battlefield, but in peaceful pursuits of life it seems that we are strangers."[60]

57. Ibid., 182.
58. Lacy, *White Use of Blacks,* 85.
59. Trefousse, "Andrew Johnson and the Freedmen's Bureau," 33.
60. Quoted in Foner, *Short History of Reconstruction,* 77.

Once it was clear that blacks had been relegated to the status of outsiders and hirelings, not equals and competitive landowners, southern elites moved unwaveringly to find ways to keep blacks steadily and dependably employed as plantation labor without the necessity of compensation significantly above the bare subsistence level of slavery. One result was that most blacks ended up working as sharecroppers or tenant farmers, systems that amounted to a form of debt servitude that restricted their freedoms and kept them tied to the white planters' land.[61]

The new debt servitude of blacks moderated though it did not transform the evils of exploitation suffered unambiguously in slavery. Indeed, the planters attempted through written contracts to reestablish their authority over every aspect of their laborers' lives. "Let everything proceed as formerly," one advised, "the contractual relation being substituted for that of master and slave." Many contracts not only prescribed labor from "sunup to sundown," as in antebellum days, but required complete subservience to the planter's will, "the same as in slavery time," as one South Carolina planter put it. The presumption of white over black was so robust that when one white North Carolinian hired a freedman in the spring of 1865, he promised only to give him "whatever was right" after the crop had been gathered. Behavior entirely normal in the free-labor North, such as leaving the employ of a farmer because the freedman "thought he could do better," provoked cries of outrage and charges of ingratitude in Georgia. Most contracts prohibited blacks not only from leaving plantations but from entertaining guests or holding meetings without the employer's permission. And it was not just southern white elites who insisted on the restoration of white skin privilege. "If the freedmen were to become productive free laborers," wrote the *New York Times* with unintended irony, "it must be done by giving them new masters."[62]

Blacks persisted in wanting to be their own masters. They used whatever weapons they could find, refusing to do work they found odious, and conflict between blacks and whites was endemic on plantations in the chaotic economic conditions of the postwar South.[63] Still, it was easy to see that not just white elites but white workers were restored to privilege.

61. Stephen Steinberg, *Turning Back: The Retreat from Racial Justice in American Thought and Politics* (Boston: Beacon, 1995), 206.

62. Quoted in Foner, *Short History of Reconstruction*, 84.

63. Ibid., 61–62.

In the last years of the Freedmen's Bureau's existence, with Johnson-approved commissioners virtually running the operation at the state and local levels, the Bureau joined the army in rounding up unemployed black laborers in both cities and countryside for shipment to plantations. Bureau courts dispatched impoverished blacks convicted of crimes to labor for whites who would pay their fines. To be sure, propertyless white people—South and North—also were compelled to labor for wages; but their compulsion was supplied by economic necessity, not public officials, law and contracts that prevented them from leaving work whenever they chose. No idle white person was required to sign a labor contract or ordered to leave a city for the countryside, certainly not by a government bureau whose professed goal was equal treatment.

How, then, does one assess the Bureau's land and labor policies? If one judges its land policy by its effectiveness in laying a foundation on which a minority of blacks might construct stable lives, some data suggest that it was not a complete failure. Although it is impossible to determine precisely the amount of land purchased by freed people and the value of that land during the latter part of the nineteenth century, census figures for 1900 suggest that blacks made progress in at least owning land. As Table 1.1 shows, 25.2 percent of blacks in the South owned their own farms by 1900. When one considers

Table 1.1.   Farm tenure in the South, 1900, by race and tenure of operators

	White		Black		Black/White
	Number	Percent[a]	Number	Percent	Ratio
Total population	16,521,970	67.4	7,922,969	32.3	0.48
Total farm	1,879,721	100.0	740,670	100.0	1.00
Owners	1,183,806	63.0	186,676	25.2	0.40
Full	1,078,635	57.4	158,479	21.4	0.37
Part	105,171	5.6	28,197	3.8	0.67
Managers	17,172	0.9	1,593	0.2	0.22
Tenants and croppers	678,743	36.1	552,401	74.6	2.07

NOTE: A farm operator, according to the census definition, is a person who operates a farm, either performing the labor himself or directly supervising it. The number of farm operators, for all practical purposes, is identical to the number of farms. While the population statistics are for whites and blacks, the farm operator statistics are for whites and nonwhites. The racial/color classification of farm operators includes Mexicans with whites. The nonwhite group includes blacks, Indians, Chinese, Japanese, and others constructed as "nonwhite" in 1900. Blacks composed 96.2% of the nonwhite population in 1900.

[a] Except in the case of population, "percent" refers to the percentage of each racial group. Percentage may not add up to 100 because other races are excluded.

SOURCE: U. S. Bureau of the Census, *Historical Statistics of the United States, 1789–1945* (Washington, D.C., 1949), 96.

that there were relatively few black landowners in the South in 1865, this represents a sizable increase in thirty-five years of freedom.

Still the overwhelming pattern one sees in Table 1.1 is white advantage. Blacks were substantially less than half as likely as whites to own or manage farms, and they were twice as likely as whites to be tenants and sharecroppers. While only slightly more than one out of three whites were farm workers, three out of every four blacks were. Indeed, although whites composed only 67 percent of the southern population in 1900, they accounted for more than 85 percent of southern farm owners and managers. By contrast, blacks composed nearly a third of the population but less than 15 percent of farm owners and managers.

In the end, the Bureau did not represent a significant or sustained challenge to whiteness as a real or imagined property value. Freed people were denied means of economic independence even as they remained uncompensated for more than 250 years of unpaid labor. Culturally, the racial mores of the nation barely inched forward. Although there were no public opinion polls in the late nineteenth century to confirm the finding, it appeared that the vast majority of whites of all classes and regions were committed to whiteness. As long as the government, too, was committed to advancing the privileges of the dominant race and held in contempt and even hatred the subordinate one, there was small hope for equality of opportunity.

Perhaps, however, the most important conclusion to draw is that whatever the Bureau's shortcomings, it surely accomplished more for the freed people than they would have gotten if there had been no Bureau. If the result fell far short of success, the alternative might well have been total failure. At a time when there was no tradition of federal responsibility for a huge poor population and the states had only the most limited capacity to administer welfare, employment, and land reform programs, and in a setting where as a temporary agency it had to overcome the determined opposition of both the president and most southern whites, the Freedmen's Bureau was forced to grope in the dark. Its architects having had no previous experience and no role models, the Bureau created the precedents for others to follow.

The Social Policy Legacies of the Freedmen's Bureau

The experience of the Freedmen's Bureau established precedents, patterns, and themes that would influence debates over federal social policy in the United

States for a long time to come. First, it demonstrated severe limitations in the willingness of the federal government to pursue a course of social rights for blacks or any other poor population. Given the strength of the American ethos, the poor in general were viewed as responsible for their own plight and undeserving of assistance from government. The interaction of the ethos with the ideology of whiteness made blacks, in the eyes of most white people, "the truly undeserving." Hoary stereotypes of blacks as lazy, shiftless, dependent, and naturally inferior had rendered them unworthy of assistance even in the minds of the feminist-led Mother's Aid movement. Only a crisis of gigantic proportions could alter these stakes and temporarily reveal the utter defenselessness of many poor Americans. The Civil War was such a crisis. In the face of the extreme shocks and mass suffering generated by the war, the federal government for the first time stepped into the job of delivering relief. Just how averse to relief the government remained and how strong a hold the ethos of liberal individualism had, however, was demonstrated by the Bureau's authorization as only a "temporary" expedient, Congress's refusal to appropriate funds for its first year of operations, and persistent underfunding and understaffing throughout the Bureau's short life. Some states that led in resistance to the Bureau had very few agents indeed. Only a dozen served in Mississippi, and the largest contingent in Alabama at any time numbered twenty. That this was a recipe for failure was acknowledged at the time: "It is not . . . in your power to fulfill one tenth of the expectations of those who framed the Bureau," General Sherman advised General Howard, the Bureau's chief. "I fear you have a Herculean task."[64] Despite Sherman's warning, it would hardly be the last time the view would prevail that American social policy could be effectively conducted on the cheap. In sum, one precedent established by the Bureau was the view that the cost of social provision must be low.

Second—and obviously relatedly—the Bureau established the precedent that the real job of welfare agencies is to put themselves out of business as rapidly as possible. In fact, there was the outrageous optimism that the Bureau could in an exceptionally modest amount of time overturn a social and economic order that it had taken over 250 years to consolidate. As a result, the number of services provided and the numbers and kinds of people served steadily dropped. During the early months of the Bureau's existence it provided

64. Quoted ibid., 165.

relief to destitute southerners both black and white, going so far as to supply white planters and farmers with rations to aid them "in the subsistence of their employees." By July 1865, however, the Bureau's headquarter in Washington began to place limitations on the agency's relief policies by establishing stricter eligibility requirements for federal assistance. By the end of the summer of 1865, the Bureau had ended government relief for white employers and destitute whites who were not refugees. "Only such white persons as have been forced to leave their homes, because of their loyalty," Howard directed agents, were to be "fed by the government." As a result, the Bureau became yet more closely identified with blacks and blacks alone. Agents were further directed in September 1965 to "carefully investigate the matter of issues of rations to refugees and freedmen, and order their discontinuance, whenever in their judgment such issues can be dispensed with." Consequently, by October 1866, restrictions had essentially limited government aid to blacks who were orphans, elderly, disabled, ill, or members of Union soldiers' families. In fact, the Bureau increasingly attempted to restrict the rations issued to freedwomen with young children, although agents generally regarded them as "unproductives" who could not find work, whether they wanted it or not. By January 1867, the Bureau officially had further limited assistance to black orphaned children and freed people in "regularly organized hospitals." The message was clear: federal relief was to be given only to the nineteenth's century's version of the "truly disadvantaged" to prevent extreme suffering.[65]

Quite clearly, the Bureau hoped to end the need for assistance by encouraging employment and returning the responsibility for destitution among blacks to private charities and state and local governments as soon as possible. It did not matter that the southern states resisted assuming responsibility for penniless, starving, and homeless blacks. For example, when William Armstrong, president of the overseers of the poor in Virginia's Stafford County, was asked whether his county would feed the poor freed people residing there should the Bureau cease issuing rations, Armstrong answered: "Not a *damn* bite will I give them; I would choose hell first."[66] Nevertheless, by the fall of 1866, federal relief had been discontinued except for those in hospitals and orphan asylums.

65. Ibid., 166.
66. Mary J. Farmer, "'Because They Are Women': Gender and the Virginia Freedmen's Bureau's 'War on Dependency,'" in Paul Cimbala and Randall M. Miller, eds., *The Freedmen's Bureau and Reconstruction: Reconsiderations* (New York: Fordham University Press, 1999), 168.

Some Radical Republicans had sought from the outset to avoid this situation. Senator Charles Sumner (R-Mass.), for example, had proposed establishing the Bureau as a permanent agency with a secretary of Cabinet rank, but he was rebuffed by both Congress and President Johnson. Thus a second precedent established by the experience of the Bureau was the withdrawal of social policy gains as soon as the immediate crisis began to subside.

The third and probably most important precedent established by the Bureau's experience was the honing of themes and ugly rhetorical flourishes that built opposition to altruistic social policy in the United States and ratcheted up the power of whiteness. Andrew Johnson's message vetoing the Bureau's creation touched on most of these themes. Johnson derided the Bureau as an "immense patronage" unwarranted by the Constitution and unaffordable, since "the condition of our fiscal affairs" required "severe retrenchment." Congress, he pointed out, had never provided economic relief, established schools, or purchased land for "our own people—the thousands, not to say millions of the white race, who are honestly toiling from day to day for their subsistence." Such aid, moreover, threatened the "character" and "prospects" of the freedmen by implying that they did not have to work for a living.[67] In effect, Johnson argued that the Bureau should be opposed on the grounds of "big government," too much spending, budgetary concerns, catering to special interests, and promotion of dependency. Nor did Johnson miss the opportunity once again to construct whites as the people who actually worked hard for a living and blacks as the people who sought unearned handouts. In sum, in appealing to fiscal conservatism, raising the specter of an immense federal bureaucracy overriding citizens' rights, and insisting that self-help, not outside assistance, offered the surest route to economic advancement, Andrew Johnson voiced themes that to this day have sustained opposition to federal assistance for blacks in particular and the poor in general.

It was Johnson's emphasis on relief as ruinous to blacks that has had the longest and most consequential life. As Johnson put it: "Any legislation that should imply that they [freed people] are not expected to attain a self-sustaining condition must have a tendency injurious alike to their character and their

---

67. Andrew Johnson, "Veto of the Freedmen's Bureau Bill," Feb. 19, 1866, in *Essential Documents in American History, 1492–Present* (electronic database), 3596.

prospects."[68] Here the venerable racist who had rarely if ever indicated that blacks—any blacks—had character and had never shown care for their life chances now used a supposed concern for blacks to justify opposing legislation designed to provide freed people a bootstrap by which they might lift themselves up. Quite simply, the Andrew Johnson so concerned about black character in his veto message stood in stark contrast to the Andrew Johnson who told his secretary in February 1866, immediately after meeting Frederick Douglass and a black delegation lobbying for suffrage, "I know that damned Douglass; he's just like any nigger, and would sooner cut a white man's throat than not."[69]

Johnson's views were widely held. In fact, white northerners and southerners alike discouraged the disbursement of rations for fear of undermining the work ethic and fostering pauperism and dependency. Most whites were convinced that now that slavery had been abolished, some other force had to be applied to compel blacks to work. Even General Howard considered public assistance to the poor "abnormal to our system of government," and the Bureau's "war on dependency" led it to close with unseemly haste camps for fugitive and homeless blacks that had been established during the war to provide direct assistance to children, the aged, and those unable to work. Blacks, declared Orlando Brown, head of the Virginia bureau, must "feel the spur of necessity, if it be needed to make them self-reliant, industrious, and provident." Although this position reflected a belief about the dangers of encouraging dependency among the lower classes in general, its application by Bureau officials to blacks in particular made it certain that they, more than other groups, were stigmatized as undeserving and victimized by badly conceived and administered relief programs.

The Bureau's relief policies were closely tied to its labor policies, with the concomitant emphasis on getting freed people to work, irrespective of gender and often of age, and without regard to whether employment was actually available. Commissioner Howard instructed his state assistant commissioners and local agents "not [to] issue rations to any person able to work." If a freed person lived in an area where potential laborers were abundant but jobs were

---

68. Ibid.
69. From *The Papers of Andrew Johnson* as quoted in Trefousse, "Andrew Johnson and the Freedmen's Bureau," 42.

scarce, she was instructed to move; if she did not, relief was denied. If she remained unemployed, she would be arrested, hired out, and forced to work without compensation.[70]

In short, Bureau agents perceived blacks as being "unschooled in the work ethic, people who needed to be taught that a day's honest work would yield its reward."[71] Apparently few saw the irony in ascribing laziness to the people who for centuries had performed the vast majority of work for a white leisure class. It was as if slavery had been a 250-year holiday from work.

Logic aside, the Bureau's assumption that blacks *wished* to be dependent on the government persisted in the face of evidence that wherever possible the black community itself (particularly black women's clubs, church groups, and mutual benefit societies) shouldered the task of caring for orphans, the aged, and the destitute. Also ignored was the fact that in many localities more whites than blacks received Bureau aid. The *New York Times* reporter Whitelaw Reid observed in 1867 that so many whites in Mobile, Alabama, survived only by depending on the food rations and medical services provided by the Bureau that "a stranger might have concluded that it was the white race that was going to prove unable to take care of itself, instead of the emancipated slaves."[72]

The Freedmen's Bureau institutionalized one final precedent that would influence American social policy for generations: its social construction of gender. Fears that federal assistance could easily result in an unhealthy dependency on government stemmed from antebellum concerns about men's as well as blacks' responsibilities and independence. Despite its name, the Freedmen's Bureau obviously established programs also for freedwomen and children. While on their face the Bureau's policies were gender neutral, freedwomen and freedmen did not always have the same experiences with the Bureau. For instance, the Bureau was insistent that a man who could work had no right to government support, and black men were compelled to find employment or face prosecution as vagrants. Often, however, similarly situated freedwomen did not suffer the same fate. Bureau officials were much more likely to regard able-bodied freedwomen who could not find work as acceptable "dependents on the government," rather than vagrants, and provide them with relief.

70. Quotes from Farmer, "'Because They Are Women,'" 167–68.
71. Jones, *Dispossessed,* 15.
72. Quoted in Foner, *Short History of Reconstruction,* 69.

Assumptions about manhood clearly informed the practices of the Bureau's agents. Men, they believed, should be independent, show initiative, provide for the well-being of their families, and have a public life. Women belonged in the sphere of domesticity. Concomitantly, Bureau policy encouraged black men to get married and take responsibility for themselves and their families. Bureau officials were directed to remind black men of these duties regularly. "Husbands must provide for their families," one agent told a group of freed people. "Your wives will not love you if you do not provide bread and clothes for them. They cannot be happy and greet you with a kiss when you come home, if they are hungry, ragged, and cold. By industry and economy you can soon provide a real good home, and plenty of food and clothing for your family; and you should not rest until this is done."[73] To a recently freed slave whose wife and children were also slaves, and not necessarily of the same master, the idea of "coming home" to the domesticated housewife must have been laughable. Yet in the eyes of Bureau agents, assistance to able-bodied black men would undermine the very sense of manly independence and responsibility that the Bureau thought it needed to inculcate. It would encourage not only dependency on others but also independence from the responsibilities of family.

Black women were another matter. Bureau officials viewed them as naturally dependent—preferably on black men, not on the federal government. Thus when freedwomen were married or separated, the Bureau sought to help them hold black men accountable. Officials were directed wherever possible to send home all able-bodied freedmen who had deserted their families without "good" cause.

The freedwomen who were most troubling to the Bureau were mothers who were dependent on the federal government because they had no husbands. The Bureau's goal was to end such "inappropriate" dependency. One tactic tried was what today would be called "family caps," that is, to refuse to issue additional rations to an unwed mother who had another child; she would have to be responsible for that child herself. Another approach was to urge unwed freedwomen with many children to have all or some of them apprenticed to white employers who could provide "good homes." Freedwomen no longer "encumbered" with children would then—like freedmen—be forced to work. Bureau agents were shocked that most freedwomen refused to send their chil-

73. Farmer, "'Because They Are Women,'" 163.

dren to work for their old masters or new white employers, even when doing so deprived them of government assistance altogether. At times the Bureau moved in directly and took custody of children and apprenticed them despite their mothers' wishes.

Another approach was simply to encourage black women receiving government aid to return to the workplace. The obligation to work had not ended with emancipation. If black women receiving assistance could not find jobs, several southern states gathered them in one central location and forced them to do "community service," such as washing the clothing of any whites who wanted it done without payment.

Still another approach was to transport unemployed single freedwomen, including those with children, to places where jobs were more plentiful. Agents usually advocated a return to their former masters' homes or to northern cities where the demand for domestics, laundresses, and cooks was higher. Some freedwomen returned to their former homes; some took the opportunity to go north; many more just refused to go. Some were fearful of their former masters and realized that most of their family and friends might no longer be in the area; others were suspicious of efforts to find them homes and employment elsewhere and preferred to rent or purchase small plots of land to cultivate and enjoy the fruits of their own labor.[74] They understood that when they found employment, they risked abuse and were paid less than subsistence wages, not enough to provide for their children.

Thus many black women defied the Bureau's policies and chose personal autonomy and their children over the dictates of the Bureau and the market. The grudging willingness of the Bureau to refrain from enforcing its policies to the letter afforded black women a modicum of protection black men did not have. Assumptions about women's natural dependency; the fact that women were almost always the caretakers of children, the elderly, ill, and disabled; and realities of the labor market encouraged the Bureau to provide assistance to black women far longer than to black men. As one Bureau agent put it, the Bureau provided aid to destitute freedwomen "because they are women, helpless with infants either in their arms or unborn, with no place to go . . . totally destitute . . . [and] who would be beggars anywhere [else]."[75] In short, by the

74. Ibid., 175–79.
75. Quoted ibid., 181.

time of the Bureau's demise, it had established the precedent that efforts to eliminate dependency were aimed primarily at blacks but that independence was not to be expected of women of any color.

The Death of the Freedmen's Bureau

From its inception the Bureau's days were literally numbered; it was underfunded and understaffed, its powers were continually undercut, and its own proposals were reversed by the president and Congress. Radical Republicans and other sympathizers fought to extend the Bureau's life on several occasions, but it was dissolved on January 1, 1869, and ceased all operations by 1872. Thus a dramatic chapter in the early history of American social services ended.

President Johnson had contributed mightily to this result. When he could not win in Congress, he turned to his executive powers to undermine the Bureau. By pardoning former Confederates wholesale and restoring their lands, Johnson undercut the Bureau's capacity to raise money and to settle blacks on land they could control. By removing military officers and Bureau commissioners he found too sympathetic to the freed people and replacing them with men of his own choosing, he undermined the Bureau's authority and morale. By refusing to enforce Republican Reconstruction, he emboldened white southerners to oppose it as well. For these and other acts of obstruction the House Republicans impeached Johnson in 1868. A chastened Johnson relaxed his interference in the work of the Bureau, but by then its days were nearly at an end. Andrew Johnson did not defeat the Freedmen's Bureau, but his actions weakened it sufficiently to frustrate its efforts, discourage its supporters, and limit its authority.

Yet Johnson's actions could not have been so influential were it not for wider forces at work. Despite the moderating impact that the ideologies of the American ethos and white skin privilege had on its policies, the Freedmen's Bureau challenged some of the prevailing assumptions about racial inequality, the role of government, and the manner in which poverty should be addressed. For this reason the Bureau was perceived as radical by a substantial portion of the populace of its day. This perception had major political implications.

In the eyes of many whites, the Bureau's policies posed a formidable threat to established social mores and existing power relations throughout the South. Many whites felt that the Bureau gave blacks unfair advantage. Southern whites charged that the Republicans sought to "Africanize the South" and institute "Negro rule and domination."

Of course, some were more vocal about their views than others. The intensity of resentment toward activist government and the fear of racial equality were openly expressed by the Ku Klux Klan (KKK). In the words of Ryland Randolph, a leader of the KKK in Tuscaloosa, Alabama: "They came from the galling despotism that breeds like a nightmare over these southern states" and arose in response to "a persistent prostitution of all government, all resources, all powers to degrade the white man by the establishment of Negro Supremacy."[76] In Randolph's interpretation of Reconstruction, whites were the victims of "reverse discrimination." Whites were the losers in a zero-sum contest for scarce political and economic resources.

The Klan was not alone in holding these views. In 1866 the *Galveston Daily News* argued that the Texas Freedman's Bureau had been "guided by a manifest hostility to the white man and an inordinate and preposterous partiality for the Negro."[77] These perceptions of victimization and loss were shared by many whites and gave rise to a conservative social movement that virtually ended all efforts to establish racial equality.

Indeed, the Klan was arguably just the handmaiden of the Democratic Party. The Democrats played a far more crucial role in securing the full restoration of white skin privilege. To further their aim they defined any person of European ancestry as white in order to gain a toehold among white ethnics, such as the Irish in the North; worked for the removal of all federal troops from the southern states; dismantled racial egalitarian policies; resurrected indigenous southern rule; and returned to states' rights and local governmental autonomy in the South. Allen Trelease refers to the Reconstruction-era Democratic Party as the "party of White Supremacy."[78] The harassment, beating, and murder of southern black and white Bureau officials and supporters at the hands of local vigilante groups complemented the efforts of Capitol Hill Democrats who filibustered and voted down proposed Bureau legislation. As a result, the lives of the Bureau and of not a few of its workers met an untimely end.

---

76. Quoted in David M. Chalmers, *Hooded Americanism: The First Century of the Ku Klux Klan, 1865–1965* (Garden City, N.Y.: Doubleday, 1965), 16.

77. Quoted in Bentley, *History of the Freedmen's Bureau,* 104.

78. Allen W. Trelease, *White Terror: The Ku Klux Klan Conspiracy and Southern Reconstruction* (Baton Rouge: Louisiana State University Press, 1971), 14.

To be sure, the Freedmen's Bureau fell victim to institutional-political processes, but these processes were conditioned by both the American ethos and
white skin privilege, and its demise foreshadowed the debate over American
social policy for more than a century to come.

A Post–Civil War Program for the "Deserving" Many

One federal social policy initiative that began in the mid–nineteenth century
fared far better than the Freedmen's Bureau. That initiative was the Civil War
veterans' pensions program. Its federal appropriations, unlike the Bureau's,
were assured from the start and grew dramatically over the course of the late
nineteenth century. Unlike the Bureau, it increased both the numbers and
kinds of its beneficiaries. Unlike the Bureau, it provided cash assistance, not
mainly goods and services. Unlike the Bureau, it had a disproportionately white
clientele. Unlike the Bureau, it viewed the carrot rather than the stick as the
way to discourage dependency, and it saw its beneficiaries as deserving of the
aid it offered. As the 1888 Republican platform put it, generous pensions for
veterans were necessary "to provide against the possibility [that] any man who
honorably wore the Federal uniform shall become the inmate of an almshouse
or dependent upon private charity."[79] In short, honorable and generous public
assistance to Union veterans was openly defined in opposition to the demeaning
assistance offered the freedmen and refugees of the South as well as the poor
white immigrants of the North. The very point of the pensions was to keep
those deserving men and their families from the degrading fate of private charity or public relief.

The Creation of the Civil War Veterans' Pension System

The history of the Civil War veterans' pension system has received so much
attention from scholars of American social policy that only its main outlines
need to be sketched here.[80] Historically, there has always been a strong belief
in the United States that the government is under a moral obligation to provide
for the aid and relief of those who have been disabled in its military service and

79. Quoted in Skocpol, *Protecting Soldiers and Mothers*, 150.
80. For an update of the typical argument, see Theda Skocpol, *Social Policy in the United
States: Future Possibilities in Historical Perspective* (Princeton: Princeton University Press, 1995).

for the support of widows and dependent relatives of the slain.[81] Whenever they have needed assistance, veterans, their widows, and their children have been constructed as the deserving poor. As it had been since the days of the American Revolution, so it was in the nation's worst military conflagration, the Civil War.

During 1861, preexisting regular army benefits were granted to the first volunteers in the Civil War. This, however, was understood to be only a stop-gap approach. In February 1862, a bill specifically addressing the needs of Union soldiers and sailors and their dependents was enthusiastically passed by the Republican-dominated Congress. On July 14, 1862, President Lincoln signed the bill into law. The 1862 act provided for monthly payments to men totally disabled and to the widows, orphans, and other dependents of those who died for causes traceable to their Union military service. Pensions were graded according to rank. A lieutenant colonel or above totally disabled for manual labor received $30 per month; a private equally disabled got $8; pensions for partial disability were proportionate.

From 1864 onward, veterans' pensions were made more generous and systematic by a steady stream of legislative tinkering, each phase relaxing eligibility requirements. Under the 1862 law, the award of pension benefits was directly linked to disabilities "incurred as a direct consequence of military duty" or, after the end of the war, "from causes which can be directly traced to injuries received or disease contracted while in military service." Many claims were rejected because claimants had difficulty proving that the serviceman's disability or death was due to military service. Political pressure mounted in the late 1880s to eliminate this requirement by providing Civil War pensions to all who had served in the Union forces, regardless of disability status.

On June 27, 1890, the Dependent Pension Act was passed, authorizing a pension for any disabled veteran who was honorably discharged. Unlike the 1862 act, the 1890 act did not require the disability to be attributable to Civil War service. Assistance was provided to thousands of Union veterans as they became incapacitated by illnesses associated with aging and the number of Civil War pension beneficiaries soared, rising from 126,722, or only 2 percent of Union veterans, in 1866 to a high of 999,446, or 83 percent, in 1902. In effect, by the turn of the twentieth century, the federal government had developed a

---

81. Skocpol, *Protecting Soldiers and Mothers*, 1.

very extensive, expensive, and open-ended system of disability, old-age, and survivors' benefits for anyone who could claim even the most minimal service for the Union during the Civil War. By 1915, 93.5 percent of Union veterans were on the pension rolls. Thus decades before the advent of Social Security, nearly all veterans received a form of old-age assistance from the federal government, and when widows and dependents of deceased Union soldiers and sailors are considered, a large proportion of Americans in general benefited from federal aid. Theda Skocpol points out that the rates for veterans and their dependents were generous by both historical standards in the United States and standards of that time in Europe.[82]

While it is difficult to estimate exactly how important veterans' pensions were for nineteenth-century Americans, some general conclusions have been drawn. The average recipient received $122 annually in 1866 and $139 annually in 1900, when the average annual income of employees was $375. The average Civil War pensioner, then, received nearly 40 percent of an earner's wage—a substantial sum by nineteenth-century standards. Moreover, since the 1890 act did not make veterans' payments conditional on destitution, these funds must have been supplementary income for some beneficiaries.

A large proportion of the pension recipients were widows and children. In 1883, widows accounted for one in six on the pension rolls, and more than half had children under sixteen years of age. To receive a pension, a widow had to prove that her husband had died from a service-related wound or disease. When she had done so, she received the same pension as a totally disabled veteran. And there were no family caps: a widow received an additional allotment for each child under the age of sixteen. Since women's wages were only about 60 percent of the wages of a man, her pension payments represented a larger proportion of the wages that she could otherwise earn.[83] Moreover, the 1890 act made women eligible who had married Union veterans up to twenty-five years after the war ended.

Some Union veterans, of course, were black. Blacks—free and enslaved—had two main reasons for joining the Union forces: they wanted to help win their own and their people's freedom and they hoped to show that they were

---

82. Ibid., 212–14, 23, 106–7.
83. Amy E. Holmes, "'Such Is the Price We Pay': American Widows and the Civil War Pension System," in Maris Vinovskis, *Toward a Social History of the American Civil War: Exploratory Essays* (New York: Cambridge University Press, 1990), 172.

equal to whites in courage and effectiveness on the battlefield. Black soldiers, however, experienced a sharply different war than white soldiers. Despite promises of equal treatment, black soldiers encountered substantial discrimination in the Union army. The Union sought to pay them less than whites, refused to commission them as officers, and often assigned them to work details or garrison duty rather than combat. Black troops usually were forced to live in conditions so unsanitary that many sickened and died. Some 188,571 blacks served in the Union armies, including 7,122 who served as lower-level officers in black units. All told, blacks made up about 9 percent of Union forces. (See Table 1.2.)

Attempting to Become Part of the Deserving Poor

Much has been made of the fact that the Pension Bureau, unlike most American institutions of its day, was not formally racist. The Pension Bureau in the Civil War period was a Union institution. It was only after Reconstruction that Confederate soldiers and sailors received even minimal federal or state aid. The Pension Bureau was in effect a regional and partisan operation. At a time when northerners and Republicans were fighting a war against southerners and Democrats over the issue of slavery, it would have been unseemly to fashion a pension system that excluded black veterans de jure. As a result, it has been argued, "African Americans who fought in the Civil War were included fairly and honorably in the system of Civil War pensions that flourished in the late

Table 1.2.   Survival rates of black and white Union and Confederate veterans, 1890

	White Union veterans	Confederate veterans	Black Union veterans
Civil War enlistments (Army and Navy)	1,911,429	882,000	188,571
Died in service	322,474	260,000	38,823
War survivors	1,588,955	622,000	149,748
Percent war survivors	83.1%	70.5%	79.4%
Alive in 1890	980,274	432,000	53,799
Percent alive in 1890	51.3%	49.0%	28.5%

SOURCE: Joseph P. Reidy and Leslie S. Rowland, eds., *Freedom: A Documentary History of Emancipation, 1861–1867; Series II: The Black Military Experience* (Cambridge: Cambridge University Press, 1982), 12; Frederick H. Dyer, *A Compendium of the War of the Rebellion*, vol. 1 (New York: Thomas Yoseloff, 1908), 12; Donald R. Shaffer, "Marching On: African-American Civil War Veterans in Postbellum America, 1865–1951" (Ph.D. diss., University of Maryland, 1996); and U.S. Bureau of the Census, *Report on Population of the United States at the Eleventh Census: 1890, Part II* (Washington, D.C., 1897), 803.

nineteenth century," although systematic evidence of precisely how black and white Union veterans fared in the pension application process is lacking.[84]

There is little argument that simply serving in the Union forces left a beneficial legacy overall for those black men who survived the Civil War. Many black soldiers learned to read and write in the army, gained positions of responsibility as noncommissioned officers, and garnered the respect of others through performance of military duties. In a sense, the Union army was an academy of freedom, transforming the enslaved into free men. In the wake of emancipation, African American servicemen, now experienced in military command structures, often became leaders in articulating the needs and demands of their people—an ability that often made them the targets of organized white mob violence in the postwar South.[85]

Service in the Union army also had financial rewards for black men, as Donald Robert Shaffer has pointed out: "Fed, clothed, and housed by the army, thrifty soldiers could accumulate significant savings." Since the army infrequently paid its troops, it inadvertently encouraged accumulation. Moreover, when many black regiments refused to accept lesser pay than white soldiers and the government ultimately equalized pay scales, many black soldiers received sizable sums in back pay. Lump-sum rewards or bounties were also paid to some black soldiers for joining the army. Consequently what little capital existed in black communities after the war often belonged to veterans. For instance, black Union servicemen made 60 percent ($3,000) of the initial deposits ($5,000) at the Freedman's Savings Bank branch in Baltimore. According to one white officer in a black Maryland regiment, his men had saved $90,000 by the time they left the army.[86] In sum, military service gave black soldiers a head start over other emancipated people in the transition to freedom and played an important role in reproducing and advancing embryonic class divisions among blacks.

When black Civil War veterans received pensions, their financial well-being was further enhanced. Perhaps nothing set former soldiers apart from the rest of black Americans in the immediate postwar era than access to money from military claims and pensions. The average black family income of less

84. Skocpol, *Protecting Soldiers and Mothers*, 138.

85. Donald Robert Shaffer, "Marching On: African-American Civil War Veterans in Postbellum America, 1865–1951" (Ph.D. diss., University of Maryland at College Park, 1996), 33.

86. Ibid., 69, 81.

than $200 per year was increased by over 50 percent by a veteran's pension under the 1890 law.[87]

We cannot assume, however, that all black veterans received pensions, for fragmentary published statistics and contemporaneous accounts call into question the conclusion that blacks were included "fairly and honorably" in the Civil War veterans' pension system. At best, hints from the historical record suggest that blacks who were free before the war and who had records of stable residency in the North probably did as well as their white counterparts in being awarded veterans' pensions. Even if they did, however, northern black veterans represent only a small minority of black Union soldiers, about one out of four. Of the 53,799 black Civil War veterans who survived in 1890, when the pension system relaxed eligibility requirements and became far more generous, only 14,427 lived in the North (Table 1.2).

The vast majority of black Civil War veterans came from and returned to the former slaveholding states. For these roughly 75 percent of black veterans, seemingly neutral policies ironically made their paths to pensions difficult. Indeed, nearly all of this large contingent were freed slaves who were disadvantaged by procedures required to qualify for a pension. Just as the cumulative advantages of whites during slavery helped whites, the cumulative disadvantages of blacks hurt them in the pension application process. Poor black tenant farmers, sharecroppers, and day laborers rarely had the money to track down witnesses, execute legal documents such as affidavits, and pay for other expenses associated with their applications. One needed a lawyer to work claims through the Pension Bureau bureaucracy, but few blacks could afford to hire one. Illiteracy increased the costs, since African Americans who could not read and write had to pay others exorbitant amounts to write letters for them and file even simple court forms. The claims of black applicants without sufficient funds to pay expenses inevitably lapsed despite their validity.

Just proving one's identity could be an obstacle in the application process. While fighting for the Union, they had usually been designated by their master's last name. After emancipation, black men eager to shed the names of former masters often adopted their own father's surname. Name changes made it difficult for many black veterans to prove to the Pension Bureau they served in the army.

87. Kenneth Ng and Nancy Virts, "The Value of Freedom," *Journal of Economic History* 49 (December 1989): 960–61.

This problem paled in comparison with the one faced by the widows of black veterans in establishing proof of marriage. Family law was the province of the states; there was no national standard for judging the legality of slave marriages. A marriage could be recognized as valid in one southern state and not in another. In addition, the Pension Bureau could deny the legality of a slave marriage if the husband and wife had not complied with any requirement of their state, such as postwar registration of the marriage union, even if the couple had cohabitated for many decades.

The inability to prove birth dates also hampered many blacks in the pension application process. Some slave masters deliberately kept knowledge of birth dates from the enslaved, and freedmen were often unable to provide specific dates. Birth dates became especially important after the passage of the 1907 pension law, which based a veteran's qualification on his age: the older a former soldier was, the higher the monthly pension he received. Birth dates and birth certificates also were important in the claims of children, since they not only had to demonstrate that they were the "legitimate" offspring of a Civil War soldier but lost their pensions when they turned sixteen. In general, the lack of written records documenting their lives made black applicants for pensions vulnerable to the grudges of uncooperative witnesses and unscrupulous claim agents and lawyers.[88] Consider the case of Harriet Berry, who applied for a widow's pension on the basis of the service of her husband, Joseph Berry. Martha Burgess, the widow's former owner, claimed to a federal investigator she did not even know of Joseph Berry's existence, let alone that he was married to her former slave. Refusing to sign Harriet Berry's deposition, Burgess told the investigator, "I don't know why I should sign anything for her to get money from the government; she ran away from me and I never got anything for her."[89] Only when black community activists rallied to her defense and testified that she was indeed a war widow was Berry's claim approved. By then it had been delayed for years.

In sum, the cumulative disadvantages inherited from slavery explain why far fewer eligible black veterans and their families applied for Civil War pensions than eligible whites. By 1890 pension claims were based on the service of

88. Shaffer, "Marching On," 216–20.
89. Deposition of Martha Burgess, Apr. 3, 1884, in pension file of Joseph Berry, 37th USCI, RG 15, National Archives, quoted ibid., 220–21.

just over 51 percent of black soldiers and their families; the comparable rate for white soldiers and their families was 80 percent.[90]

Other cumulative racial inequalities shaped inequalities in Civil War pensions. Because black soldiers had been barred from serving as superior officers, black veterans and their widows and children were also ineligible for the more lucrative pensions received by white former officers and their dependents. The most numbing statistic of all is seen in survival rates. A substantially smaller percentage of black veterans than former white troops survived the quarter-century after the end of the Civil War. As Table 1.2 shows, black Union soldiers were not substantially less likely than white Union soldiers to have survived the war and were a good deal more likely to have survived than Confederate soldiers. By 1890, however, less than 30 percent of African American veterans were still alive compared to half of the white men who joined the Union and Confederate forces. These data suggest that the difficulties encountered by black men in civilian life killed more of them than the war called the bloodiest in the nation's history. Hard physical work, poverty, and related unsanitary living conditions apparently took a high toll on the health and life expectancy of black veterans.[91] Since for all racial groups, establishing a pension claim was easier for the veteran than for his family, the lower survival rates of black veterans also suggest a racial discrepancy in receipt of pensions.

In sum, while African Americans formally enjoyed equal access to Civil War veterans' pensions, in practice they continued to experience greater difficulty getting pensions than white Union veterans and their survivors. Scholars' claims of the biracial character of Civil War pensions are seriously overblown. Informal presumptions and the rampant racial inequality that was now institutionalized privileged white male northerners in what was supposed to be a universal program for Union veterans of all races. For many black veterans of the Civil War, the road to being considered "deserving" was actually an obstacle course too difficult to travel. True equality of opportunity would have required compensatory measures that took the cumulative advantages of whites and cumulative disadvantages of blacks into consideration.

Conclusion

In the midst of an economic, political, and military crisis, the federal government took its first steps toward provision of social services: the creation of the

90. U.S. Bureau of the Census, *Report on Population: 1890,* 804.
91. Shaffer, "Marching On," 114–16.

Freedmen's Bureau and pensions for Civil War veterans. Neither program was racially exclusive. Thousands of white refugees received relief from the Freedmen's Bureau; thousands of black veterans received pensions. The issue was one of proportion: the beneficiaries of the Freedmen's Bureau were largely black; those of the Civil War veterans' program were largely white.

Class and gender concerns also shaped both programs. The Freedmen's Bureau served not only the interests of freed people and southern white refugees but also the needs of northern industrialists for cheaper cotton production and of Radical Republicans for leadership in reconstructing the South. At the same time, the pension system permitted middle- and working-class northern whites, generally without property, to enjoy a higher standard of living. The Freedmen's Bureau strictly enforced work requirements for black men but encouraged black women to retreat to the domestic sphere—provided they were married. White widows and their children were considered so worthy of state aid that they received more in benefits than they could have earned in the gender-stratified labor market.

Neither the Freedmen's Bureau nor the Civil War veterans' pensions were fully consonant with the individualism at the heart of the American ethos. Both provided benefits to large categories of people without regard to actual or potential earnings or other sources of income. The Freedmen's Bureau provided its relatively meager relief to all people who could meet eligibility requirements (which were rapidly tightened); the Veterans' Bureau provided its relatively generous benefits to all former members of the Union armed services (and rapidly loosened eligibility requirements). At first the Freedmen's Bureau provided relief to the black and white destitute, going so far as to help white planters provide subsistence for their workers, but in a very short time its benefits were cut off for virtually all except blacks in orphanages and Union-certified hospitals. At first veterans' pensions were provided only to those who could prove disability attributable directly to their service in the Union forces, but over time all Union veterans became eligible, whether or not they had actually fought or were disabled, and to their widows and children.

Why the two programs moved in such opposite directions has much to do with the social construction of moral desert and the role whiteness played in that process. The veterans' pensions came to be seen as a program for the deserving core of a special generation—a generation that had contributed to victory at a moment when the nation's very life was at risk. That many Union veterans did not need material assistance and that many more people who were not Union veterans—North and South—needed help desperately was unimportant in shaping the aid lavished on this selected subset of the American working and middle classes. What counted most was the social construction of moral worthiness.

Generally, aid to Civil War veterans was justified on moral and instrumental grounds. It was argued that veterans deserved special rewards because fighting for one's country was a special sacrifice. Veterans were seen as especially deserving of benefits because they had *earned* them by service to the nation. Besides, it was argued, many veterans not only had given up careers to serve their country but had come out of the Civil War with disabilities that made civilian life hard for them. They deserved a cushion to assist their reentry in civilian life and to ensure them opportunities to survive respectably and perhaps to prosper. Further, benefits provided to veterans would promote love of country and willingness to fight for it in future wars.

It is at least theoretically possible that an alternative argument could have developed that would have undercut the generous pension program that developed. It could have been argued, for example, that the status and character of these men would be debased by treating them as inferiors incapable of making their own way in a land of free competition. It could have been contended that the veterans' program was too inclusive and open-ended, since it had no expiration date. It could have been concluded that the pension system represented an "immense patronage" at a time when the nation needed to be fiscally prudent. It could have been pointed out that pensions were going to men who had simply fulfilled a citizen's obligation. It could have been emphasized that veterans' pensions were going only to a "special interest" and so were unfair to women and the vast majority of the previously enslaved, and to men who had been sick or disabled at the time of the war. The payment of benefits to stay-at-home widows could have been questioned on the grounds that these women had demonstrated no particular loyalty to the nation. In short, to be fully consonant with classical liberal theory, the pension system would have had to be open to all if the nation were committed to equality of opportunity.

Indeed, many of these arguments actually were made to undercut the Freedmen's Bureau. The argument that members of the armed forces deserved help by virtue of the great sacrifices they had endured might surely just as well have been advanced about African Americans recently freed after 250 years of involuntary servitude. Given the profits northern-based manufacturers made from cotton, it could certainly have been argued that the enslaved were forced to sacrifice their very freedom for the economic well-being of the nation.[92] It surely could have been argued that the problems of the freedmen were particularly acute and merited prolonged, generous, and special consideration. In short, the discourse of compensation for sacrifice makes at least as much sense in support of aid for freedmen as for aid to veterans. Indeed, a logic of compensation would actually have supported a claim for monetary reparations.[93]

What best explains the emergence of arguments in favor of veterans' pensions and in opposition to the Freedmen's Bureau is the meaning of race that kept the two in seemingly separate universes. Help through the Freedmen's Bureau was objected to and delimited primarily because its main beneficiaries were not white. Capitalism, republicanism, and racial formation combined to construct the Civil War veterans' program in a way that solidified whiteness and the Freedmen's Bureau in a way that delegitimized blacks and their claims to justice. What difference did it make to most blacks that veterans' pensions grew to be so generous that they became an old-age insurance program when most blacks, living in the South and not emancipated until near the end of the Civil War, had not been able to participate in the war, and many of the minority who did were beset by costly obstacles when they sought to navigate the bureaucracy established by the pension system?

Meanwhile, as whites prospered disproportionately through the Civil War veterans' pensions, blacks were forced back into an economic position in many ways like slavery in the aftermath of the Bureau's demise. It was a situation that would last for decades. Until nearly midway through the twentieth century, when the mechanical cotton picker arrived in the South, the majority of African Americans, officially free but landless and desperate for work, remained yoked to the southern plantocracy through the sharecropper system. As sharecroppers, African Americans were leased farmland and provided housing, seed, horses and mules, and farm tools. In return, a proportion (usually 40 to 50 percent) of each year's harvest had to be given to the landowner. Although in theory the African American sharecropper was able to keep the remainder of his crop, it seldom worked out that way. To survive during the months before harvest, sharecroppers were almost invariably forced either to borrow directly from the planter or to buy on credit from the plantation general store. Exorbi-

92. John David Skrentny, *The Ironies of Affirmative Action: Politics, Culture, and Justice in America* (Chicago: University of Chicago Press, 1996), 59.

93. Boris I. Bittker, *The Case for Black Reparations* (New York: Random House, 1973), 69.

tant markups and interest rates and manipulated records guaranteed that sharecroppers inevitably owed the landowner more money than their share of the harvest was worth, perpetuating the stranglehold of the planters on the necks of blacks.[94] Thus, by the end of Reconstruction and throughout the long period of Jim Crow, southern white elites had nearly completely restored their power over the vast majority of blacks. As Du Bois concluded, the enslaved "went free; stood a brief moment in the sun; then moved back again toward slavery."[95] The privileges of whiteness had been secured by a comprehensive system of both legal and extralegal controls.

It did not have to work out that way. Had the promises of genuine Reconstruction been kept, including a massive redistribution of land (as envisioned by a few Radical Republicans); had a social policy regime emerged that provided enough bootstrap services to enable blacks to help themselves; had black farmers been provided greater opportunity to establish themselves as independent owners; had the freedmen been considered among the deserving poor, the paths of the American welfare state, self-sufficiency, and multiracial democracy could have been different.[96]

But instead, of the two incipient federal social policy initiatives of the late nineteenth century, only the Civil War pension system, which benefited mainly whites, was successful. Ultimately it fell prey to charges of corruption, but by that time more than a million whites had been provided a means out of suffering and into the middle class.

Only another crisis could have shaken up the American political economy so fundamentally that the ideology and actuality of whiteness might be challenged, and people of color, too, might prosper. The Great Depression of the 1930s was such a crisis.

94. Jeremy Rifkin, *The End of Work: The Decline of the Global Labor Force and the Dawn of the Post-Market Era* (New York: Putnam, 1995), 69–71.

95. W. E. B. Du Bois, *Black Reconstruction in the United States, 1860–1880* (1935; New York: Simon & Schuster, 1995), 30.

96. Steinberg, *Turning Back,* 205–6; and Gunnar Myrdal, *An American Dilemma: The Negro Problem and American Democracy* (New York: Harper & Row, 1962), 237.

two
White Security
The Birth of the American Welfare State

We have had no work since last season. A great many have been on federal relief.

When they tell us to register for civil work hundreds done so. Then they give all the

work to the whites except three days before thanksgiven when about sixty Negroes

was put in the Flamingo Swamp to work in the mud. After Thanksgiven no other

Negroes have had a single hour's job. Hundreds of whites work every day.

—Anonymous black man, 1933

The modern story of partisan politics, race, and social policy begins with the abolition of the Freedmen's Bureau and the overturn of Radical Reconstruction. The fate of social policy was sealed by the economic relations, dominant ideologies, and party alignments then constructed.

The Democratic Party, as the party of the Old South, came out of Reconstruction bent on restoring white skin privilege in every domain. To do so, the Democrats played a key role in reinventing just who was white and what it meant to be white. A new racial alchemy developed in which a wide range of Europeans, an earlier era's Celts, Slavs, Hebrews, and Iberians among them, were now granted the "scientific" stamp of authenticity as members of a unitary Caucasian race.[1] The Democratic president James Buchanan, for instance, called Mexicans a "mongrel" race unfit for freedom but characterized "Americans" as a "mixed" population of English, Welsh, French, Scotch-Irish, and German ancestry. Senator Thomas Hart Benton (D-Mo.) harped on a "Celtic-Anglo-Saxon race," superior to, in descending order, the yellow, brown, red,

---

1. Matthew Frye Jacobson, *Whiteness of a Different Color: European Immigrants and the Alchemy of Race* (Cambridge: Harvard University Press, 1998), 8.

and black races.[2] The latter groups came to be lumped together as the inverse of whites: "nonwhites." In short, the Democrats in the post-Reconstruction era constructed a line around whiteness, turning diverse Europeans who were once identified according to national origin into one big white identity group, based largely on opposition to a "nonwhite" or "colored" other.

This new social construction of race had material consequences. By the early decades of the twentieth century, most nonwhites had experienced dramatic setbacks. Almost all Native Americans had been forced onto reservations controlled by the federal government. Not surprisingly, reservation land was usually of so little value that nobody wanted it.[3] By 1930, 55 percent of all Native Americans had a per capita annual income of less than $200 and only 2 percent had incomes of more than $500 per year. By 1933, Indians had lost about 60 percent of the 138-million-acre land base they had controlled at the time of the Dawes Allotment Act in 1887.[4]

Meanwhile, through conquest Mexicans had become the cheap labor force of the Southwest and West. Mexican farm workers became destitute as their average wage dropped from 35 cents an hour in the 1920s to 15 cents in the 1930s, and the average time worked was drastically reduced.

During the same period a vocal and often violent anti-Chinese movement coalesced in the West, especially in California, where white workers decried the labor competition of "Mongolians" and demanded a "white man's republic." Racial antagonism in the mines, factories, and fields of the West forced thousands of Chinese into self-employment—small stores, restaurants, and particularly laundries.[5]

"Different strokes for different folks" may have applied to America's treatment of its diverse people of color, but all the strokes had oppression based on color in common. In Democratic propaganda of the day, this was how things should be. Drawing a line around all of Europe was the way for this southern-based party to encourage groups like the Irish, who had once been treated as

2. David Roediger, *The Wages of Whiteness: Race and the Making of the American Working Class*, rev. ed. (New York: Verso, 1999), 141–42.

3. For discussion, see Peter Nabokov, ed., *Native American Testimony: A Chronicle of Native-White Relations from Prophecy to the Present, 1492–1992* (New York: Viking, 1991).

4. Ronald Takaki, *A Different Mirror: A History of Multicultural America* (Boston: Little, Brown, 1993), 238.

5. Ibid., 201.

"a race apart," to join the Democrats, thereby giving the party an important electoral toehold in the North.

But constructing whiteness was not just a Democratic project; the Republicans, too, were contributing to the construction. Rutherford B. Hayes, Republican governor of Ohio, not only agreed to the Compromise of 1877 when he was brought to the presidency but made it clear where he stood on race. The "present Chinese invasion," he argued in 1879, was "pernicious and should be discouraged. Our experience in dealing with the weaker races—the Negroes and Indians.—is not encouraging. . . . I would consider with favor any suitable measure to discourage the Chinese from coming to our shores."[6] Three years later Congress prohibited Chinese immigration; six years after that the prohibition was broadened to include "all persons of the Chinese race." Renewed in 1892, the Chinese Exclusion Act was extended indefinitely in 1902.[7] Indeed, as the twentieth century began, the race question surfaced in every region of the nation and most of the world. Henry Stanley's reports from Africa aroused tremendous popular enthusiasm for the adventure of taming "the dark continent."[8]

In the midst of these national and international developments, hypocritical and conflicting racial discourses indicated the political character of race in America. At the same time that Hayes was denigrating the Chinese, blacks, and Native Americans, the Republican Party, as the party that had "freed the slaves," ritually called every four years in its platforms for congressional action to end lynching and disfranchisement and to provide "equal justice for all men, without regard to race or color." In fact, however, the Republicans' appeal to people of color, especially African Americans, was illusory; as Ira Katznelson has so pithily expressed it, the party's "most attractive quality was a memory."[9] For all the magic of the name of Lincoln, no late nineteenth- or early twentieth-century Republican had sought to emulate Lincoln's image as an even halfway responsible leader for blacks. With both parties staunchly supporting white skin privilege in practice and neither party ready to make the fundamental

6. Stuart C. Miller, *The Unwelcome Immigrant: The American Image of the Chinese, 1752–1882* (Berkeley and Los Angeles: University of California Press, 1969), 190.

7. Takaki, *Different Mirror*, 206–7.

8. Jacobson, *Whiteness of a Different Color*, 140–41.

9. Ira Katznelson, *Black Men, White Cities: Race Politics and Migration in the United States, 1900–1930, and Britain, 1948–1968* (Chicago: University of Chicago Press, 1976), 46.

commitments that might have elicited African Americans' support, those few blacks who could vote (almost all of them in northern cities) remained passively with the Republicans. The hard fact of life was that Republican pledges were not redeemed because African Americans had nowhere else to turn. It would take a crisis of major proportions to move them into the Democratic Party and take even a tiny step toward promoting policy change. The Great Depression and the Hoover administration gave African Americans ample reason to turn their backs on the GOP.

This deep and staggering economic crisis was brought about in part by the introduction of new labor-saving technologies (the internal combustion engine, the automobile, electric power) and new management practices (the Ford assembly line, the General Motors organizational revolution). These developments combined to increase productivity and concomitantly to displace workers, especially between 1919 and 1929, with a resultant sharp drop in sales.[10] In response, labor unrest, particularly in the East and Midwest, racked the nation and raised questions about the white working class itself.

It was people of color, however, that were disproportionately afflicted. Last hired, first fired, African Americans in particular figured prominently among workers uprooted from jobs when factories closed, farmers and share-croppers forced off the land, families evicted from their homes, and hundreds of thousands forced to roam the land begging for food and seeking a job—any job.

President Herbert Hoover not only was slow to respond to the failure of the economy; he rigidified racial segregation in federal employment, ignored black Republican leaders in the southern states, made other mistakes on racial questions, and virtually littered his speeches with racial slurs.[11] For the first time African Americans began to look seriously at the Democratic Party as a potential ally.

Yet in 1932 Franklin Delano Roosevelt (FDR) was not much for blacks

10. Jeremy Rifkin, *The End of Work: The Decline of the Global Labor Force and the Dawn of the Post-Market Era* (New York: Putnam, 1995), 60.

11. Nancy J. Weiss, *Farewell to the Party of Lincoln: Black Politics in the Age of FDR* (Princeton: Princeton University Press, 1983), 5; and Dan Lacy, *The White Use of Blacks in America: 350 Years of Law and Violence, Attitudes and Etiquette, Politics and Change* (New York: McGraw-Hill, 1973), 163.

to get excited about. He had few contacts with African Americans. He used the word "nigger" casually in private conversation and correspondence.[12] And although he promised everything to nearly everybody in his presidential campaign, he did not respond when Walter White, head of the National Association for the Advancement of Colored People (NAACP), sent him a questionnaire asking where he stood on eleven issues ranging from segregation to Haitian independence.[13] As Walter Trattner concludes, "Roosevelt's actual commitment to the Negro was slim."[14]

Despite some symbolic civil rights gestures by Eleanor Roosevelt, the New Deal paid only the most limited attention to African Americans during Roosevelt's first two terms. President Roosevelt in particular did as little as possible on the race question; his constant answer to African Americans and their white allies was that he needed the southerners' support in Congress—especially in the Senate—so he could not afford to alienate them by actively backing antilynching laws or black enfranchisement in the South. Instead he offered an early "universalist" approach, arguing that African Americans could best progress by being loyal to the New Deal, thus benefiting from the array of social and economic legislation it sponsored. In effect (as "New Democrats" would advise half a century later), the civil rights issue was submerged in order to maintain party unity. Between 1937 and 1946 more than 150 civil rights bills—focused principally on lynching, poll taxes, and fair employment practices—were introduced in Congress and not a single one prevailed.[15] One main reason for their defeat was FDR's refusal to provide public support. What Roosevelt did do was to not wholly exclude African Americans from the economic benefits of the New Deal. Nonetheless, there is ample evidence to support the view that the New Deal, in some critical instances, did little or nothing to shake up the system of white privilege and in some others bolstered it.

An impressive body of knowledge focuses on how the New Deal's most

12. Kenneth O'Reilly, *Nixon's Piano: Presidents and Racial Politics from Washington to Clinton* (New York: Free Press, 1995), 110.

13. Walter White, *A Man Called White* (New York: Arno Press/New York Times, 1969), 139.

14. Walter I. Trattner, *From Poor Law to Welfare State: A History of Social Welfare in America* (New York: Free Press, 1989), 281.

15. Edward G. Carmines and James A. Stimson, *Issue Evolution: Race and the Transformation of American Politics* (Princeton: Princeton University Press, 1989), 31.

important legacies—social insurance and relief—disproportionately benefited whites, not blacks.[16] Less attention has been paid to other policies (agricultural, housing, labor) that advantaged whites.

The First Phase of the American Welfare State

The creation of the New Deal and particularly the Social Security Act of 1935 cannot be understood without consideration of civic action. According to most scholars of the period, relief was not a high priority with Roosevelt. In his first days in office he ordered a bank holiday, began federal budget cutbacks, started the process of repealing Prohibition, and abandoned the gold standard. Initially his was an orthodox fiscal policy: he favored retrenchment, not spending.[17] Even at the passage of the Social Security Act of 1935, Roosevelt seemingly was as gravely cynical about relief as Andrew Johnson had been. He called welfare "a narcotic" and "a subtle destroyer of the human spirit" and proclaimed that "continued dependence upon relief induces a spiritual and moral disintegration fundamentally destructive to the national fiber."[18] Thus it is quite probable that the New Deal would never have happened were it not for demands blistering up from a suffering populace. Civic activists lobbied, organized disruptive demonstrations, influenced a rapid shift in public opinion regarding government responsibility, and thereby stimulated welfare proposals. Organized labor was a key player and had a substantial impact on social policy expectations (and, as we shall see, not always to the betterment of people of color). Other members of the working class—largely ignored by the unions because they were jobless or unorganized—created a militant social movement of the unemployed. Often organized by Socialists and Communists, this movement was the most cross-racial and cross-gendered in adherents. The women's movement was largely silent, with the predictable consequences for women. African American organizations, from the NAACP to the Urban League, the Brotherhood of Sleeping Car Porters, and the National Council of Negro

16. For two excellent analyses, see Robert C. Lieberman, *Shifting the Color Line: Race and the American Welfare State* (Cambridge: Harvard University Press, 1998); and Michael K. Brown, *Race, Money, and the American Welfare State* (Ithaca, N.Y.: Cornell University Press, 1999).

17. Linda Gordon, *Pitied but Not Entitled: Single Mothers and the History of Welfare* (New York: Free Press, 1994), 188.

18. Franklin D. Roosevelt, "Annual Message to Congress, January 4, 1935," in *The Public Papers and Addresses of Franklin D. Roosevelt* (New York: Random House, 1938), 4:19.

Women, sought influence but were virtually ignored. Their lack of influence on the New Deal was quickly revealed in policies that reinforced racial segregation and discrimination.

Work relief under the Federal Emergency Relief Act (FERA)—the first New Deal federal aid program—vividly demonstrates this result. FERA left the design of work projects and the allocation of funds to local officials, who more often than not discriminated against African Americans, especially but not exclusively in the South. Although some studies conclude that overall relief rates were higher among blacks than among whites, the same studies show that black workers and families were forced to rely on general relief, "the dole," rather than work relief.[19] While the Works Progress Administration (WPA) and the Civilian Conservation Corps (CCC) created jobs for millions of out-of-work Americans at a cost of over $90 million (adjusted for inflation),[20] most blacks were either placed in dirty jobs or, as the unemployed worker laments in the epigraph to this chapter, excluded from employment altogether.[21] In fact, officially blacks faced a quota in the CCC. Although blacks were proportionately represented among the extremely impoverished, the CCC restricted the enrollment of blacks to 10 percent of the total—a quota not met in most places.[22]

There was similar discrimination against other people of color. In California and Texas impoverished Mexican Americans were heavily represented on the relief rolls at the beginning of the Depression—an unsurprising finding, given the destitution of farm workers in the 1930s. Instead of finding their way into the new government jobs, however, persons of Mexican descent became victims of a massive campaign to "repatriate" them to Mexico, even though many were U.S. citizens. Ultimately approximately 160,000, or roughly 40 percent of their population, were intimidated into returning to Mexico by 1936. New York's Puerto Ricans, too, suffered from the same coercion, although all of them were citizens.[23]

19. Brown, *Race, Money, and the American Welfare State*, 76–81.

20. Senator David Boren (D-Okla.), "A Modern WPA: A Proposal to Empower and Rebuild Our Country," *Yale Law Journal* 102, no. 6 (April 1993): 24.

21. See, for discussion, Herbert Hill, *Black Labor and the American Legal System: Race, Work, and the Law* (Cambridge: Harvard University Press, 1977).

22. Trattner, *From Poor Law to Welfare State*, 282.

23. Carlos Cortes, "Mexicans," in Stephen Thernstrom, ed., *Harvard Encyclopedia of Ethnic Groups* (Cambridge: Harvard University Press, 1980), 711.

Native Americans also received short shrift. Many of them lived in isolated areas where no WPA projects were set up, but they were reminded that the federal government was already subsidizing them by providing reservations for them. Some Western states actually argued that Native Americans were not entitled to any of the benefits of the Social Security Act.[24]

Women of all races were excluded or segregated into stereotyped, low-wage jobs. Indeed, the way women were treated by the WPA and CCC reveals how inextricably race, class, and gender are linked. In 1936, 56 percent of all women enrolled in WPA projects worked in sewing rooms. The percentage was greater in states with large populations of racial minorities; in New Mexico it was 84 percent. The CCC, originally only for men, eventually added a complement of 85,000 women to the 2.5 million men enrolled. The program was then disbanded in 1937.[25]

In these instances it is impossible to separate out gender from race and class as the basis for discrimination. Relief workers in New Mexico rationalized discrimination against Latinas by arguing that their culture required them to stay home to care for their families. The fact that most black women wage earners' work experience was in domestic service (82 percent in 1930) was used to lock them into the unskilled category. In sum, women of color were triply discriminated against. Their need was greater because race-based poverty placed them at the bottom of the class hierarchy; because disproportionately more of them were the heads of their households, at least among African Americans; and because of direct racial discrimination. Not surprisingly, more African American than white women wrote letters to the Roosevelt administration complaining about discrimination.[26]

The Women's Bureau strongly protested gender discrimination, as civil rights organizations protested racial discrimination. The black press was full of articles denouncing racism and exclusion in New Deal work programs.[27] Instead of redressing their grievances, the National Recovery Administration (NRA), in its approval and enforcement of industry codes for the self-regulation of the economy, gave official sanction to local patterns of discrimination in employment, including lower wage rates for black and Hispanic men and all

24. Trattner, *From Poor Law to Welfare State,* 284.
25. Gordon, *Pitied but Not Entitled,* 195.
26. Ibid., 198.
27. See discussion in Lieberman, *Shifting the Color Line,* 39 and 262.

women. Although no formal racial or gender differentials were included in wage rates on federal work relief projects, there were sharp differentials in type of work done, size of community, and region. This situation, writes Dan Lacy, "had, and was intended to have, the result of fixing the level of relief payments to southern agricultural workers at levels below the minimum payments for marginal farm labor. The local authorities who administered the WPA were less concerned that black field hands have enough to eat than that the planters' opportunity to exploit the distress of the times by getting their farm work done at a minimum cost should not be interfered with."[28]

There was marked discrimination in favor of whites even at the point of enrollment in federal work programs. Only after all or most whites seeking government employment had been hired were destitute blacks likely to be enrolled. On the one hand, clerical and other white-collar jobs and those requiring manual skills were especially likely to be reserved for whites. On the other hand, black men were likely to be assigned to arduous tasks such as ditch digging and road building, and black women to cleaning and other menial jobs.[29] With the federal government failing to require or enforce equal access to government jobs for all races, the ultimate effect of the New Deal employment programs was to widen the gap between the economic conditions of minority and white workers. In short, the New Deal's labor policies contributed to, not narrowed, the racial and gender divides. The NRA fell into such disrepute that it became known among blacks as "Negro Run-Around" or "Negroes Ruined Again."[30]

The New Deal's agricultural policies also had negative implications for racial minorities. In fact, nowhere was white skin privilege more firmly bolstered than in this facet of the New Deal. In the face of mountains of unmarketable cotton, wheat, and other basic crops, the administration's first emergency agricultural action was to plow under a third of crops in the field in 1933. It then launched a program to take acreage out of staple crop production and provide price supports for the crops grown on the remaining land. The problem was that to withdraw land from use was to withdraw workers from use. While a small independent landowner could cut his cotton acreage and

28. Lacy, *White Use of Blacks*, 164–65.
29. Ibid.
30. Robert Dallek, *Lone Star Rising: Lyndon Johnson and His Times, 1908–1960* (New York: Oxford University Press, 1991), 136.

use the land and time he freed up to grow uncontrolled crops, a planter whose extensive acreage was farmed by sharecroppers could get rid of them altogether when he removed from cultivation the land they worked. Sharecropping and tenant farming were not practical for the production of other than staple commercial crops that are not perishable or consumable and that commanded a steady and known commercial value, such as cotton and tobacco. Thus, while agricultural diversification and conservation practices that removed land from intensive cultivation were undoubtedly sound in respect to general regional development, they cut significantly into the need for agricultural field labor and cut off tens of thousands of black croppers and tenants and Mexican farm workers from the little income they had.[31]

It did not help that the Agricultural Adjustment Act of 1933, passed to help farmers experiencing mounting crop surpluses and depressed prices for farm products, gave considerable autonomy to local landowners in the administration of the program. The result was great variation in the treatment of tenant farmers and sharecroppers. Many African American sharecroppers and tenant farmers and Mexican laborers were excluded altogether and others were underpaid, as an investigation by the NAACP substantiated. One historian concluded that the AAA's cotton program in particular "achieved about as much for the mass of the nearly three million black farm tenants as a plague of boll weevils."[32]

Thus, taken together, the labor and agricultural policies of the New Deal reproduced and even expanded while skin privilege. In fact, Arthur Ross, a former commissioner of the Bureau of Labor Statistics, noted that significant disparities between black and white unemployment rates did not begin until the Depression of the 1930s. After the New Deal, the disparities increased.[33]

But it was not only labor and agricultural policies that granted new advantages to whites while denying them to people of color. When the federal government began to finance the construction of low-cost housing and to guarantee mortgages on private dwellings, it gave formal recognition to residential segregation, a practice that had hitherto been informal and unofficial. Under

31. Ibid., 165–66.
32. Dona Cooper Hamilton and Charles V. Hamilton, *Dual Agenda: Race and Social Welfare Policies of Civil Rights Organizations* (New York: Columbia University Press, 1997), 13–14.
33. Arthur Ross, "The Negro in the American Economy," in Arthur Ross and Herbert Hill, eds., *Employment, Race, and Poverty* (New York: Harcourt, Brace & World, 1967), 141ff.

the New Deal, however, from the passage of the Housing Act of 1937 public policy mandated the selection of tenants by race and located new projects in racially segregated neighborhoods, ensuring that public housing developments were all white or all black. In addition, as has been well documented elsewhere,[34] the FHA instituted "redlining," a practice in which a red line was literally drawn on a map around areas considered too risky for loans for economic or racial reasons. This practice had long-term damaging consequences for African Americans, since most redlined neighborhoods were theirs. At the same time, appraisers who determined the size of the mortgage the government would guarantee on a private house or apartment building were officially instructed to consider the racial homogeneity and stability of the neighborhood in which it was located. Until 1949, restrictive covenants to enforce such stability and homogeneity (by banning African Americans in certain neighborhoods and refusing to insure mortgages in integrated ones) were considered to make the property insurable at a higher value and were often insisted on.[35] As a result, less than 2 percent of all houses financed by the FHA before 1960 were purchased by African Americans. Especially from the mid-1940s onward, federal housing programs helped those who could help themselves, and most of the billions of dollars in tax expenditures and public services for housing were available only to people who could afford to buy a house, and typically this meant whites only. Between 1945 and 1960, 21 million new private housing units were completed and just 536,000 public housing units; and the federal investment of roughly $800 million in low-cost housing assistance was only a small fraction of the assistance given to middle-class home buyers.[36] In this way the FHA played a crucial role not only in cementing racial segregation but simultaneously in guaranteeing that middle-class whites would be dramatically privileged in homeownership, always the most successful generator of wealth for average Americans.

34. See, e.g., Herman H. Long and Charles S. Johnson, *People vs. Property: Race Restrictive Covenants in Housing* (Nashville: Fisk University Press, 1947); Karl Taeuber and Alma Taeuber, *Negroes in Cities: Residential Segregation and Neighborhood Change* (Chicago: Aldine, 1965); Gary A. Tobin, ed., *Divided Neighborhoods: Changing Patterns of Racial Segregation* (Newbury Park, Calif.: Sage, 1987); Gregory D. Squires, ed., *From Redlining to Reinvestment: Community Responses to Urban Disinvestment* (Philadelphia: Temple University Press, 1992); and Robert D. Bullard et al., eds., *Residential Apartheid: The American Legacy* (Los Angeles: CAAS, 1994).

35. Lacy, *White Use of Blacks*, 164.

36. Ibid.

What made these developments even more problematic was the fact that housing segregation was tied to other forms of discrimination and segregation. In deciding where to locate military installations, for instance, the Department of Defense ignored local housing policies in its off-base housing programs. Doing so meant that African Americans could not work at many installations because they could not find housing nearby. Similarly the General Services Administration awarded the government's enormous rental and leasing business to real estate agents whose housing operations were racially restricted, and the Atomic Energy Commission located the world's largest atom smasher, a huge jobs-generating facility, in an area notorious for housing discrimination. In each instance the New Deal's housing policy ended up depriving people of color not only of housing but also of jobs.[37] Nor did the New Deal's two most important legacies, social insurance and relief, make a dent in racial inequality.

Race, Politics, and the Social Security Act of 1935

African Americans and whites did not benefit equally from the social welfare programs spawned by the Social Security Act of 1935, the foundation on which modern American social policy rests. First, as the price for southern members of Congress's acquiescence in the creation of old age insurance (OAI), the exclusion of the self-employed, farm laborers, domestic servants, schoolteachers, clerics, and so forth meant that blacks were twice as likely as whites to be excluded from social insurance. In 1940—the first year a decennial census was taken after the act was passed—seven of every ten whites (71.1 percent) were covered while nearly six of every ten blacks (58.8 percent) were excluded from coverage by OAI and similarly from minimum wage laws and unemployment insurance on the basis of occupation alone.[38] The high representation of African Americans in just two occupations, farm laborers and domestics, virtually guaranteed this result.

Thus although the Social Security Act of 1935 made no explicit distinction on the basis of race and millions of black workers were eligible for coverage, the exclusion of occupational categories cut out the majority. Black women were particularly affected. In 1940 nearly a million black women (60 percent

37. Jill Quadagno, *The Color of Welfare: How Racism Undermined the War on Poverty* (New York: Oxford University Press, 1994), 91–92.
38. Calculated on the basis of data in U.S. Bureau of the Census, *Sixteenth Census of the United States: 1940, Population—Labor Characteristics,* Table 62, pp. 88–90.

of the entire black female labor force) worked as domestics in private homes. Many of the excluded farm laborers and teachers were also black women. All told, approximately eight of every ten black women were excluded from social insurance coverage (Table 2.1), leaving them worse off than not only white men and women but black men. Moreover, while statistics were not kept in the 1940s on the numbers of black women who were employed but failed to accumulate the continuous employment record required for coverage, it seems likely that many were excluded from workmen's compensation, unemployment insurance, and OAI precisely because the kinds of jobs that women and racial minorities were (and are) most likely to have were in small enterprises, for low wages, and seasonal and "casual" employment.

Table 2.1. Total employed persons and workers excluded from old-age insurance coverage by race and sex, 1940

Category	White males	Black males	White females	Black females
Total employed persons[1]				
Number	30,931,506	2,936,795	9,563,583	1,542,273
Excluded				
Farmers, farm managers, farm laborers and foremen	6,490,206	1,202,242	219,492	244,765
Percent of employed persons	21.0%	40.9%	2.3%	15.9%
Domestic service workers	50,687	85,566	1,045,726	917,942
Percent of employed persons	0.2%	2.9%	10.9%	59.5%
Self-employed[2]	689,603	13,927	146,814	63
Percent of employed persons	2.2%	0.5%	1.5%	0.0%
Railroad managers and workers	520,374	54,991	0	0
Percent of employed persons	1.7%	1.9%	0.0%	0.0%
Teachers, nurses, clergy, and college professors	431,985	31,240	1,070,312	58,699
Percent of employed persons	1.4%	1.1%	11.2%	3.8%
Other government and nonprofit	994,849	23,252	47,234	1,855
Percent of employed persons	3.2%	0.8%	0.5%	0.1%
TOTAL EXCLUDED	9,177,699	1,411,218	2,529,578	1,223,324
PERCENT OF EMPLOYED PERSONS	29.7%	48.1%	26.5%	79.3%

[1]Persons on Public Emergency Work are excluded.
[2]Self-employed includes occupations such as fishermen, lumber-owners, architects, artists, authors, dentists, insurance agents, lawyers, musicians, physicians, veterinarians, cleaners and laundry owners, retail dealers, seamen, etc.

SOURCE: U.S. Bureau of the Census, *Sixteenth Census of the United States: 1940, Population—Labor Characteristics,* Table 62, pp. 93–94, 96.

In short, when the Social Security Act provided protection against poverty in old age and minimum wage laws established a floor under income, it offered little of value to a substantial majority of blacks.[39] Thus, when the Social Security Act of 1935 advanced a new definition of social citizenship based on work but socially constructed "work" in ways that deprived many workers of the right to earn benefits, it not only perpetuated both race and gender inequality but showed that the very definitions of "worker" and a right to earn benefits were politically negotiable. The political manipulation of the category "wage worker" led to the exclusion of a majority of blacks engaged in paid employment and a substantial proportion of southerners of all races and genders.[40] In effect, these groups were left trapped in an inferior form of social citizenship.[41]

African American interest groups decried these flaws in the Social Security Act. When Charles Houston, NAACP board member and law professor, testified against the decision to exclude agricultural workers, laborers, and domestics, he pointed out that the NAACP had been inclined to favor the creation of the contributory system that became known as Social Security, but the more it studied the proposal, the more it began to look "like a sieve with holes just big enough for the majority of Negroes to fall through."[42] Both the National Urban League (NUL) and the NAACP favored legislation introduced by Representative Ernest Lundeen (Farmer-Labor, Minn.). Lundeen called for a "workers' bill" based on the belief that unemployment "was a disease of the capitalist system" and proposed that the beneficiaries of capitalism should compensate its victims.[43]

Under the Lundeen proposal, a federal system of insurance would have been created for all categories of workers who suffered involuntary unemploy-

39. Jill Quadagno, "From Old-Age Assistance to Supplemental Security Income: The Political Economy of Relief in the South, 1935–1972," in Margaret Weir, Ann Shola Orloff, and Theda Skocpol, eds., *The Politics of Social Policy in the United States* (Princeton: Princeton University Press, 1988), 238.

40. In 1940, for instance, 57% of southern white men worked in excluded occupations. See U.S. Bureau of the Census, *Sixteenth Census of the United States: 1940, Population—Labor Characteristics,* Table 62, pp. 93–94, 96.

41. It would be 1960 before most of the labor force was covered by Social Security, after a series of bills in 1954 and 1956 extended coverage to farm and domestic workers and to nearly all professional groups. See Quadagno, *Color of Welfare,* 157–58.

42. Hamilton and Hamilton, *Dual Agenda,* 30–31.

43. Gordon, *Pitied but Not Entitled,* 298.

ment due to sickness, accident, maternity, or old age. In this system, to be administered by elected committees of workers, benefits would have equaled the prevailing local wage and been indexed to the cost of living and funded by individual and corporate income taxes and inheritance and gift taxes. All workers, including professionals, the self-employed, domestics, agricultural workers, laborers, and people who worked part-time because they were unable to find full-time jobs, would have been covered under a completely federal plan. There would be no exclusion of blacks or women from the plan.

The Lundeen bill, however, was heavily denounced by the Roosevelt administration. Virtually all of the old arguments raised against the Freedmen's Bureau resurfaced: The bill was too expensive; it was fiscally unsound; it would require a huge bureaucracy; it would make people dependent, and so on and so on. Practically the only new criticism that emerged was that the Lundeen bill was a "Communist plot."

What was really at stake, however, was whether the country actually needed a radical redistribution of wealth, more consumption, and less capitalization. But in the heated rhetoric aimed at defeating the bill, this debate never surfaced. Although the bill was reported out of committee, it was killed by the Rules Committee. It would be 1952 before the Social Security Act was finally amended to extend coverage to vast numbers of women and people of color.

While social insurance schemes excluded a majority of African Americans before the 1950s, Title IV of the 1935 Social Security Act did provide for welfare relief, old age assistance (OAA), and its handmaiden, Aid to Dependent Children, or ADC, albeit on a very different basis from social insurance schemes. Both OAA and ADC required that clients be "needy," but ADC was unique among welfare programs in its subjection of applicants to a morals test. Sexual behavior became the most frequent measurement of a "suitable home" for a child. What made a home unsuitable was the presence of a man in the house or the birth of an "illegitimate" child. Protecting the line drawn around whiteness, a home could also be declared unsuitable if the child was the offspring of an interracial couple. The search for these "moral" infractions led to heavy supervision and violations of privacy.[44]

The most troubling aspect of relief programs was that they were often

44. U.S. Bureau of the Census, *Sixteenth Census of the United States: 1940, Population—Special Report: The Nonwhite Population,* Table 1, p. 5.

administered on a discriminatory basis. Racial discrimination was a direct result of labor segmentation and local administration, since in theory, relief was not constructed as having any connection to race. OAA officially served all the needy aged; ADC officially served all single mothers; there was no explicit mention of race in the law. In practice, however, state regulations could be arbitrary and discriminatory. States, allocated varying amounts of ADC benefits, excluded "employable mothers," demanded "suitable homes," policed sexual behavior, and made similar decisions regarding which aged persons actually deserved help through OAA. African American women and the African American aged bore the brunt of these practices in the South. Indeed, as Jill Quadagno concludes regarding OAA, African Americans unilaterally received lower benefits than whites in the South during the 1930s, generally less than the subsistence furnished by planters. Not only were rates of relief lower for African Americans, but proportionately only half as many received benefits, although rates of poverty were substantially higher among blacks in the South. Table 2.2A shows that blacks were significantly more likely than whites to be poor in every region of the country, but in the South (where 77.5 percent of all blacks lived in 1940)[45] nearly the entire black population was poor. Of course, part of the problem was that the South itself was a poor region; whites, too, were more likely to be poor in the South than in other regions. Still the gap between black and white poverty rates tended to be higher in the South; more important, as Table 2.2B shows, while other regions apparently made higher relief grants to blacks on the basis of their deeper poverty, the South did not. Whites received more a month throughout the South, from $1.43 more in the West South-Central region to $2.52 more in the South Atlantic region. A difference of $2.52 a month may not sound like much today, but it amounted to nearly 20 percent more than elderly blacks were getting—a big advantage in the late 1930s.

Furthermore, at planters' requests, relief offices in many rural counties were closed for two months at the height of the cotton-picking season. In one county in Alabama no OAA grants at all were paid to older black persons because local authorities feared they might subsidize whole African American families. Similarly, in 1937 the governor of Louisiana arbitrarily ordered that payments to African Americans—but not to whites—be cut in half during

45. Quadagno, "From Old-Age Assistance," 237ff.

Table 2.2.   Percentage of wage earners earning less than $1,000 in 1939, and average monthly old-age assistance grant by race and region in fiscal year, 1938–39

	White	Black	Difference
A. Percent earning less than $!,000[1]			
New England[2]	54.6%	78.3%	− 23.7%
Mid-Atlantic[3]	50.7	78.6	− 27.9
East North Central[4]	50.0	75.1	− 25.1
West North Central[5]	61.5	85.0	− 23.5
South Atlantic[6]	59.8	92.5	− 32.7
East South Central[7]	66.8	94.5	− 27.7
West South Central[8]	64.1	95.4	− 31.3
Mountain[9]	56.8	81.7	− 24.9
Pacific[10]	48.3	80.7	− 32.4
B. Average grant per month per recipient			
New England	$26.50	$27.37	+ $0.87
Mid-Atlantic	20.47	21.47	+ 1.00
East North Central	18.21	19.55	+ 1.34
West North Central	18.08	18.53	+ 0.45
South Atlantic	13.45	10.93	− 2.52
East South Central	10.70	9.11	− 1.59
West South-Central	12.96	11.53	− 1.43
Mountain	NA	NA	NA
Pacific	30.54	30.24	− 0.30

NOTE: A negative sign (−) indicates the amount/percent of black disadvantage relative to whites; a positive sign (+) indicates the amount/percent of black advantage relative to whites.

[1]According to a Works Program Administration study in 1935, this figure is less than the average minimal income required to maintain a family of four ($1,261).

[2]New England states in the table are: Maine, New Hampshire, Vermont, Massachusetts, Rhode Island, and Connecticut.

[3]Mid-Atlantic states in the table are: New York, New Jersey, and Pennsylvania.

[4]East North Central states in the table are: Ohio, Indiana, Illinois, Michigan, and Wisconsin.

[5]West North Central states in the table are: Minnesota, Iowa, Missouri, North Dakota, South Dakota, Nebraska, and Kansas.

[6]South Atlantic states in the table are: Delaware, Maryland, District of Columbia, Virginia, West Virginia, North Carolina, South Carolina, Georgia, and Florida.

[7]East South Central states in the table are: Kentucky, Tennessee, Alabama, and Mississippi.

[8]West South Central states in the table are: Arkansas, Louisiana, Oklahoma, and Texas.

[9]Mountain states in the table are: Montana, Idaho, Wyoming, Colorado, New Mexico, Arizona, Utah, and Nevada.

[10]Pacific states in the table are: Washington, Oregon, and California.

SOURCE: U.S. Bureau of the Census, *Sixteenth Census of the United States, 1940, Population, Wage or Salary Income in 1939* (Washington, D.C., 1943), 75–86; and Social Security Board, Bureau of Research and Statistics, Division of Public Assistance Research, National Archives, RG 47.

June and July.[46] Southern white planters had few or no objections to "keeping their peons alive during the slack season on pork and meal," but they wanted all relief suspended during the work season "so these niggers will be good and hungry," as one official of the Tennessee Valley Authority (VA) put it in the early years of the New Deal.[47]

In sum, the Social Security Act of 1935 created a two-tier system. The superior social insurance programs applied mainly to whites and men, as they were designed to do. The inferior relief programs—or "welfare," as they came to be known—applied mainly to people of color and women, as they were designed to do. And even in the latter case, relief was distributed on a discriminatory basis in favor of whites.

The first major amendments to the Social Security Act deepened the racial divide. The 1939 amendments, which restructured OAI to provide benefits for survivors, separated the widowed mothers (disproportionately white) from the never-married or divorced mothers (disproportionately black). The widowed mother was cast as "deserving" (because she had *depended* on her deceased husband, who had qualified for social insurance) in the developing morality play, while the never-married or divorced mother was cast as "undeserving" (because she did not have a man to mediate her relations with the state even from the grave). Thus the 1939 amendments provided widows and their children survivors' insurance (old age survivors insurance, or OASI) while poor single mothers received ADC (changed to Aid to Families with Dependent Children, or AFDC, in 1962). Unlike the federally set survivors' insurance, as previously noted, ADC consisted of federal funds matched by the states, which ran their own programs with minimal federal supervision. Initially ADC funds covered only children, not caregivers; a grant for caregivers was authorized in 1949 in the belief that "it was necessary for the mother or another adult to be in the home full time to provide proper care and supervision."[48] In effect, the 1939 and 1949 amendments meant that white women at least benefited from their husbands', fathers', and brothers' coverage under the superior federal programs, but to be a survivor or dependent of a black man was also often to be

46. Quoted in Harvard Sitkoff, "The New Deal and Race Relations," in Harvard Sitkoff, ed., *Fifty Years Later: The New Deal Evaluated* (New York: Random House, 1985), 94–95.

47. Eileen Boris, "When Work Is Slavery," in Gwendolyn Mink, ed., *Whose Welfare?* (Ithaca: Cornell University Press, 1999), 38.

48. Gordon, *Pitied but Not Entitled,* 293–94.

left out of the primary beneficiary stream. The treatment of both survivors and dependents varied according to the status of their men. By 1967, the average benefit to a child of a deceased worker under OASI was $62; under AFDC the average benefit was $37. The premier losers were not women and children in general but those of subordinated races and classes.[49]

In effect, both symbolically and practically two tiers of social citizenship had been created in two arenas: federal on the one hand, state and local on the other. White men were usually covered by federal programs, women and racial minority men by state-controlled programs. The federal programs had higher standards, more generous stipends, a bigger tax base to support them—and dignity. The state programs were far more vulnerable to political attacks, declining tax bases, interstate competition—and stigma. The exclusions of people of color from Social Security programs and the defeat of federal standards for welfare programs in 1935 were directed, implicitly if not explicitly, at minority and low-wage labor of both genders.[50] To be sure, protecting white skin privilege was not the only factor that led to the splitting of social insurance from relief programs,[51] but it was not a negligible one.

Why White, but Not Black, Interests Were Secured in 1935

The bifurcated welfare state with its differential impact on whites versus people of color and men versus women was not accidental or incidental. This outcome was due in part to the ideology of the men who shaped the legislation; southern Democrats' inclusion in the New Deal coalition practically ordained it. And it was due in part to the general restorative rather than structurally reformist (much less revolutionary) goals of the New Deal. A brief look at these three factors demonstrates why the result in 1935 was increased security for whites, especially white males, and continued peril for people of color of both genders.

First, neither people of color nor white women were key players in shaping the legislation. To be sure, white women were at first intricately involved in developing the new social policies. Aid to Dependent Children was grafted

49. Ibid., 294.

50. For several excellent analyses of factors beyond racial matters that led to a segmented welfare state and alternative explanations of the policy decisions involved, see Weir et al., *Politics of Social Policy;* Brown, *Race, Money, and the American Welfare State;* and Michael B. Katz, *The Price of Citizenship: Redefining the American Welfare State* (New York: Henry Holt, 2001).

51. Gordon, *Pitied but Not Entitled,* 287.

onto the Roosevelt administration's economic security proposal by the female leadership of the Children's Bureau as a way of expanding and regularizing state mothers' pensions. In congressional deliberations, however, the Children's Bureau lost operational control of ADC, which was given over to the Social Security Board to run alongside the social insurance programs to which its leadership was more committed. Thus, ultimately, the Social Security Act was written by two kinds of people, sometimes by the same people in two roles—white male social planners and politicians.[52] Whereas in earlier years welfare had been almost totally a state and local function and white women had predominated in shaping it, both the social planners and the politicians who constituted Roosevelt's Brains Trust were white men who had little interest in relief but discovered a profound interest in the social insurance schemes developed in Europe. The crux of events in 1935, from a gendered and racialized perspective, was that as federal social policy grew in size and importance, white men took it over. Behind this development were factors ranging from the increasing professionalization of social work which made men more interested in these and related occupations to the weakness of women's voting habits and the fact that most blacks remained deprived of the vote. If politicians in the 1930s had had to be concerned about securing the women's vote, the black vote, the Latino vote, and so forth, they might have been more willing to listen to the concerns of these groups. Without the constraining influence of these groups, the white men shaping the Social Security Act of 1935 viewed social citizenship from the standpoint of white male workers. This tendency need not have been conspiratorial or bereft of good intentions; more likely it was simply the prevailing conception of the day in the 1930s. Masculinist and racialized visions of what constituted useful work shaped law.

Equally important were coalitional politics. Before FDR was elected president, the Democratic Party was dominated by southerners, who despite their minority position in Congress maintained a controlling influence on national legislation through the organizational and procedural structure of that body. FDR's landslide victory in 1932 brought many states outside the South under the Democratic umbrella for the first time. The result was an uneasy coalition. Northern Democrats, representing not only northern capital and midwestern

52. See Lee J. Alston and Joseph P. Ferrie, "Paternalism in Agricultural Labor Contracts in the U.S. South: Implications for the Growth of the Welfare State," *American Economic Review* 83 (September 1993): 852–76; and Quadagno, "From Old Age Assistance," 244–47.

farmers but also organized labor, favored permanent national programs operated by the federal government; southern Democrats opposed any possibility of federal intrusion in the South's cheap labor system. The compromise was to strengthen the committee system and thereby the southern hand in legislative outcomes.[53] In 1933, southern whites chaired twelve of the seventeen major House committees and nine of the fourteen major Senate committees. In control of these key veto points, southern legislators were able to hold the Democratic Party hostage to their demands for regional autonomy on questions of race, gender, and class.[54]

The Social Security Act of 1935 grew out of this kind of compromise. It balanced the desires of organized labor for a permanent, bureaucratically controlled old-age pension program with the demands of southerners to keep relief for the aged and female poor decentralized. Thus the legislation created two different programs to provide economic assistance to the aged. The nationally administered OAI program (Social Security) was financed entirely by payroll taxes collected from employers and employees in industries and was from the start federally controlled. OAA (welfare relief) was from the first (as the southerners wished) locally control. Eliminated from initial proposals was a "decency and health" provision, leaving the states free to pay pensions of any amount and still recover 50 percent of the costs from the federal government. States were also granted the right to impose additional provisions that would make criteria for eligibility more stringent than those stipulated in the bill, such as the ability to exclude people on the basis of age, residence, or citizenship. So while federal authority became the path of social insurance, it was narrowly circumscribed when it came to relief.

Given the power to control assistance, the South did what it wanted, and what it wanted was to manipulate federal funds in a way to maintain its cheap labor force. Cash grants to African Americans were monitored so as not to undermine prevailing wage rates and to intrude as little as possible into the sharecropper system. Thus the political economy of the southern cotton plantation areas dictated the structure of public assistance and guaranteed that relief would not undermine the control of African American labor by the dominant

53. V. O. Key, *Southern Politics in State and Nation* (Knoxville: University of Tennessee Press, 1977), 667–68.
54. Quadagno, "From Old-Age Assistance," 244–47.

white planter class.[55] Few of the nation's leaders saw this as a problem; it was simply taken for granted that African Americans earned substantially less than whites. Indeed, until well past the half-century mark, some African Americans never even knew the meaning of wages. Dr. Martin Luther King Jr. told of his astonishment when he visited a plantation in Alabama in 1965 and met sharecroppers who had never before seen United States currency.[56]

In sum, the political economy of the South, southern dominance of the committee system in Congress, the political needs of FDR and the Democratic Party, and the concomitant politics of race dictated the structure of the American welfare state at its official birth. The result was segmented policies that would not undermine the control of African American labor by the dominant planter class. In consequence, the private practices that isolated blacks in the plantation South and in low-paid unskilled employment in declining areas of the economy and in ghetto areas of the North received tacit official sanction and reinforcement from the federal government.[57]

The general thrust of the New Deal was not to transform the American system but to restore the existing economy to effective operation and to protect every individual's established stake in it. Dan Lacy sums up the situation: "The landowning farmer was assured an income. The depositor's bank account was guaranteed. The investor was assured an honest securities market. Credit was made more easily available to land-owning farmers, the real-estate developer, and the homeowner or purchaser. The industrial worker was protected in his right to join a union, and the union in turn in its right to represent employees, to strike, and to negotiate union, or closed-shop agreements."[58]

These measures, however, benefited only those who already had a stake in the economy as property owners or industrial and commercial labor, and by and large, that meant white men and their families. Federal mortgages meant nothing to the black worker who could not dream of buying a house, or federal deposit insurance to one with no money in the bank. The protection of the National Labor Relations Act and the creation of Social Security were worthless to domestic servants, agricultural workers, and unskilled laborers whose occupations were not organized or covered—jobs held by the vast majority of black

55. Rifkin, End of Work, 74.
56. Lacy, White Use of Blacks, 168.
57. Ibid., 166–67.
58. Ibid., 167–68.

workers. The minimum-wage and pro-union legislation, while clearly important bulwarks for white male workers, denied or reduced the competitive position of the many blacks who were not welcomed by the unions. Similarly, the housing legislation and administrative practices of the New Deal strengthened the barriers that protected the exclusivity of white neighborhoods and suburbs. Even welfare relief flowed disproportionately to the nonblack.

Thus—and to be certain—the New Deal restored and strengthened the American society and economy and bolstered the economic position of many citizens, but it was a racist society and economy that were strengthened and whites whose economic lives were secured. The jobs, the homes, the farms, the savings, the statuses and futures of many Americans were protected by federal action, but one of the things these values were protected against was the intrusion of blacks into "white jobs" and "white neighborhoods." The New Deal did little to end segregation, to improve black education, or to open jobs to blacks; and it did nothing to restore the vote to blacks or even to end lynching.[59] Throughout the New Deal, black peril and its flip side, white skin privilege, continued. In effect, the New Deal granted a modicum of economic security to whites while denying to people of color the full perquisites of democracy.

Thus the official birth of the American welfare state in the 1930s reproduced, not transformed, the subordination, domination, and oppression of African Americans and other people of color. Although African Americans were not excluded outright from New Deal programs and many benefited from them, the institutional arrangements by which blacks were incorporated in or eliminated from programs meant that the new American welfare state had little or no effect on the subordination of blacks. The relative advantage of whites continued in every regard throughout the New Deal.

Exclusion of African Americans in Phase 2 of the Welfare State

Still, economic recovery for many whites hardly occurred overnight. With many workers still suffering as the 1940s began, organized labor stepped up its pressure on Congress for further protections. When Republicans took control of Congress in the 1946 off-year elections and coalesced with southern Boll Wee-

59. Ibid., 121. See also Beth Stevens, "Labor Unions, Employee Benefits, and the Privatization of the American Welfare State," *Journal of Policy History* 2, no. 3 (1990): 233–60.

vil Democrats, unions' hopes for protective legislation vanished. At a time when many European nations were expanding their welfare states, the United States failed to enact programs such as full employment and national health insurance, and expanded existing programs such as Social Security slowly. The chief barriers to expanding social protections were business interests and congressional conservatives.

Realizing that new social spending initiatives were politically infeasible, unions expanded collective bargaining negotiations to include such fringe benefits as health care, disability insurance, life insurance, and pensions. Labor's strategy received support from the executive branch and the Supreme Court.[60] The Truman administration helped to broker a deal in 1946 between striking mine workers and owners that included welfare and retirement benefits. In 1948 the National Labor Relations Board (NLRB) ruled in *Inland Steel Company v. United Steel Workers of America* that private pensions were equivalent to wages and thus could not be excluded from collective bargaining agreements. The board even suggested that since Social Security benefits were not large enough to provide a comfortable retirement, employers had a social obligation to provide pensions for their workers. The Supreme Court upheld the NLRB ruling in 1949. Then in 1954 Congress passed legislation to exclude from employees' income all employer contributions to health and retirement programs, so that they were not subject to income tax.[61]

These decisions were motivated primarily by the desire to secure labor peace during and after World War II. Employers had good reason to agree to labor's demands: their contributions to pension plans were exempt from taxation; they were legally required to bargain over pensions; union strength was substantial even after the Taft-Hartley Act of 1947 gave the NLRB new powers to enjoin or curtail any strike it deemed to imperil national health or safety; employers in such capital-intensive industries as steel and autos, usually among the first to offer pensions, could ill afford work stoppages; and most companies were largely unfettered by international competition and could thus afford to provide benefits. As a result, the number of workers with fringe benefits soared.

60. For a discussion of court rulings and legislation undergirding hidden welfare benefits, see Richard J. Butler, *The Economics of Social Insurance and Employee Benefits* (Boston: Kluwer Academic, 1999), chap. 2.

61. Michael K. Brown, *Remaking the Welfare State* (Philadelphia: Temple University Press, 1988), 194–95.

The number of workers covered by private pension plans more than doubled between 1940 and 1950, from 4.1 to 9.8 million, and almost doubled again to 18.7 million by 1960. This increase was not solely a function of an expanding labor force. Pension coverage increased from 15 percent of all private wage and salary workers in 1940 to 41 percent in 1960.

These benefits, developed in lieu of openly provided public ones, were rooted in favorable tax treatment, and most economists agree that federal subsidies (tax expenditures) for fringe benefits are analytically equivalent to budgetary outlays. The only difference is that the federal government, rather than write checks to a particular group, simply indicates to the favored parties that they can write smaller checks to the government. In effect, most fringe benefits are "hidden welfare."

These hidden welfare benefits flow disproportionately to people who work in manufacturing and large firms, those in unionized or professional occupations, full-time and high-wage workers, and those with long tenure on the job. Since white men, at least partially as a result of past and current discriminatory practices by both employers and unions, predominate in these categories, they gained the most from the establishment of hidden welfare in the 1940s and 1950s. In fact, when fringe benefits are added to wages or salaries, the development of hidden welfare actually broadens racial and gender gaps in total compensation.[62] By settling for winning new fringe benefits in the 1940s and 1950s only for the best-off sector of workers, organized labor ignored and scuttled the interests not only of most people of color and women but of poor, marginalized agriculturalists as well.

In sum, both the first and second phases of the New Deal system hardly tinkered with the system of unequal racial opportunities or outcomes "normal" in the United States. This was in large part a result of discrimination in the labor market, which laid the groundwork for even race-neutral policies to be reproductive of inequality. To the extent that the welfare state is designed to decommodify labor, differential treatment of black and white workers and female and male workers was a central mechanism generating this result. Segregated jobs and industries were the order of the day in the 1940s. Facing unemployment at worst or working disproportionately in agriculture or the

62. Brown, *Race, Money, and the American Welfare State*, 14, 68. See also Hamilton and Hamilton, *Dual Agenda*, and Michael Reich, *Racial Inequality: A Political-Economic Analysis* (Princeton: Princeton University Press, 1981).

secondary labor market of small, nonunionized businesses in jobs with little security at best, most blacks suffered not only lower wages and more temporary employment than whites who worked in the developing unionized corporate world, but also lack of access to the new hidden welfare benefits. Even the benefits of those blacks in occupations covered by Social Security at its initiation lagged behind those of white workers because of lifetime wage differences and work histories. As Michael Brown explains, "wage-related contributory social insurance forges a right link between work and eligibility. . . . Job discrimination undermined the eligibility of black (and female) workers for unemployment benefits as well." Moreover, the Wagner Act, which legitimated the closed shop, tended to reify the perverse relationship between race and labor market processes. By refusing to add an antidiscrimination provision, as black political leaders had sought, the Act in an era in which many unions excluded blacks "left black men and women with little protection from white workers who believed that their racial privileges were more important than class solidarity."[63] In effect, it is impossible to separate the effects of labor market discrimination from the effects of social policy. Social policy need not mandate overt discrimination to advantage whites; whites' access to greater social benefits is generated by more favorable treatment in labor and housing markets, segregated education systems, and so forth. A policy universally applied in a system that already advantages some and disadvantages others tends to reproduce, not eradicate, inequality.

Thus it is not surprising that a system that stratified workers by race and gender was reproduced in a welfare system that recognized two arenas of social citizenship: one federal, one local. White men were usually covered by federal programs and hidden welfare, women and men of color by locally controlled programs. Both the federal programs and hidden welfare had higher standards, more generous benefits, and a bigger tax base to support them. State programs, from the start, were more vulnerable to political attacks, declining tax bases, and interstate competition.

These differences among welfare programs exacerbated group resentments. As we shall see, the resulting politics of resentment ultimately weakened both the welfare state and the Democratic Party. As taxes increased, recipients of the more stingy targeted programs became scapegoats. Mean-

---

63. Gordon, *Pitied but Not Entitled,* 301.

while, the rise of hidden welfare lessened the support of organized labor and professionals for a shared social citizenship and further distanced them from those who could not obtain or could not afford private health insurance and pensions. Many beneficiaries of hidden welfare did not recognize their dependence on the welfare state. Nonetheless, the gains "welfare" offered to the poor—disproportionately racial minorities—were undercut by the reverse redistributory effects of the programs not labeled as "welfare." Benefits to white middle- and upper-working-class men and their dependents were greater absolutely and proportionately than contributions to the female and minority poor.[64]

Even in the 1930s and 1940s, African American interest groups understood the flaws in the emerging American welfare state and predicted dire consequences for their constituency. As each bill that constructed the welfare state in this period was debated (especially the Social Security Act, the National Labor Relations Act of 1935, and the Fair Labor Standards Act of 1938), African American interest groups sought, unsuccessfully, to address its faults. Time after time they testified in favor of fair and full employment as the key welfare program needed. Again and again they lobbied in favor of comprehensive programs with universal coverage and federal administration. Over and over these groups, realizing that without adequate safeguards African Americans would not benefit equally from New Deal policies, sought to secure antidiscrimination amendments to legislation. But consistently their hopes were dashed. Lacking the political capacity to achieve their goals, African American organizations reluctantly supported social welfare policies that reproduced racial segregation, discrimination, and white skin privilege in exchange for sharply delimited economic benefits for their constituents.[65]

Indeed, more than just the leaders and activists of the NAACP, the NUL, the National Council of Negro Women, and the Brotherhood of Sleeping Car Porters—the key African American interest groups of the era—recognized that the social policies of the first two phases of the American welfare state were seriously flawed. The testimony of contemporaries clearly demonstrates that most African Americans were not so seduced by rhetoric, style, and symbolism that they were unable to perceive the inequities in the way they were being

64. Hamilton and Hamilton, *Dual Agenda*, 8–42.
65. Weiss, *Farewell to the Party of Lincoln*, 14, 244.

treated. However, there was nothing most African Americans could do about their unequal treatment under New Deal–era social policy; the basic problem was the relative insignificance of the black vote. The great majority of African Americans still resided in the South, and the vast majority of the southern black population remained disfranchised throughout the New Deal era. Of the 6 million African Americans of voting age in the states of the Old Confederacy in 1940, only about 275,000 were registered to vote.[66] Change, however, was in the making.

National Electoral Instability and Embryonic Signs of Policy Change

The one section of the nation where many blacks could vote in the 1930s and 1940s was the North. The pattern of that vote shifted dramatically in the New Deal period. In 1932, when many other Republican constituencies supported FDR, the northern black vote stayed with the GOP. Then in 1936, despite racial inequalities in New Deal program distribution and critical flaws in legislative intent, strong African American support shifted to Roosevelt's Democrats. In the crucible of economic despair, a strong majority of African Americans bade farewell to the party of Lincoln.[67]

The reasons were straightforward: blacks endured such excessive suffering in the Great Depression that they appreciated any efforts to ameliorate it. In the crucible of despair, objective not relative gains were key. Thus, as Nancy Weiss concludes, African Americans became Democrats in response to their small share of economic benefits from the New Deal, and they voted for Franklin Roosevelt in spite of the New Deal's lack of a substantive record on race. It was notions that Democrats favored the "little man" and FDR's ability to provide at least some jobs and cash assistance, not his embrace of civil rights and equal opportunity, that made him a hero to African Americans.[68]

Perceptive observers recognized the irony in the outpouring of northern black support for the New Deal in the election of 1936. One need not have been a diehard Republican to wonder at the marriage between a black electorate and the party of the Old South, which purposefully evaded any important issue related to race. How could a president who sidestepped antilynching leg-

66. Weiss's *Farewell to the Party of Lincoln* provides an excellent description of African Americans' transformation from Republicans to Democrats in this period.
67. Ibid., 168.
68. Ibid., 241–77.

islation, seemed undisturbed by disfranchisement and segregation, and presided over relief programs teeming with discrimination win an overwhelming majority of African American votes?

First, the masses of African Americans did not hope for much on race in those days. There was no reason for them to hope for an attack on white skin privilege. The federal government had not done anything significant for the particular benefit of African Americans for as long as most could remember. Racial expectations and racial consciousness were considerably more limited than they became after World War II. The struggle to survive took precedence over the struggle for racial equality, and in the struggle to survive, even the crumbs of many New Deal programs made the crucial difference. Moreover, as blacks moved out of the South, more, especially more black women, became eligible for relief. Thus meager economic assistance paid large dividends to the Democratic Party. The transcendence of economic over racial concerns during the Depression—indeed, the close congruence of race and class for African Americans—made it possible for the Democratic Party to win African American voters by the simple expedient of not totally excluding them from the economic benefits that it brought to suffering Americans generally.

To be sure, the New Deal's excursions into racial symbolism, especially the rhetoric of Eleanor Roosevelt, helped appreciably to cement the bond between African Americans and the Democrats, but the essential political tie was forged in the cauldron of economic despair. Roosevelt was singled out as a personal hero in plain defiance of the facts. It may be tragic that it took so little to win African Americans' support for the New Deal, but the hard facts are that the black embrace of the Democratic Party was a realistic response to the economic and political circumstances of the time.[69]

The shift to the Democratic Party was, however, part of a larger process of politicization that was changing the political habits of African Americans. The New Deal not only changed blacks' partisan presidential preference; it also increased their interest in political participation. Further stimulating African American political activism was migration from the rural South. Migration and the continued urbanization of African Americans was the upside of the downside of the New Deal agricultural policies, which stimulated the mechanization,

<hr />

69. Frances Piven and Richard Cloward, *Poor People's Movements: Why They Succeed, How They Fail* (New York: Pantheon, 1977), chap. 4.

consolidation, and internationalization of American agriculture and in turn drove out millions of African American sharecroppers. The massing of African Americans with similar economic and civil rights needs in limited geographical areas outside the South (the African American populations of northern cities roughly doubled between 1920 and 1940) made possible the articulation of common political interests.[70] It fostered the development of specialized interest groups with particular political objectives. It created an environment conducive to the emergence of African American political leadership. It brought African Americans under the sway of local Democratic political machines, and it made the black vote a sufficient force in northern cities to warrant attention from the national parties.

One of the first results of growing African American electoral influence in the North and political consciousness nationally was Roosevelt's Executive Order 8802, issued in 1941, to make discrimination in government employment illegal and to establish a Committee on Fair Employment Practices (FEPC) to enforce a nondiscrimination policy in all defense areas. Issued largely in response to the threat that African Americans, led by A. Philip Randolph's Brotherhood of Sleeping Car Porters, would mount a march on Washington, Executive Order 8802 was soon followed by Executive Order 9346, which extended the scope of the FEPC to include all federal contract areas. Both executive orders concerned only federal employment; provisions often were not enforced; and the FEPC was abolished at the end of World War II. In short, both orders had only a very limited effect on employment discrimination.[71] Nonetheless, Executive Order 8802 proved to be an important development, principally as a precedent. For the first time the equal treatment of blacks in employment had been defined as a national policy and a matter of appropriate governmental concern. Before 1940 few whites, whatever their feelings about the injustice of employment policies that closed opportunities to blacks, would have thought it legal or proper for the federal government to tell a private employer, even one with a federal contract, whom he might or might not hire. Nor did most whites see anything unusual or improper about the closing of whole categories of jobs to blacks. The categorization of some jobs as "white" and others as "black" had been taken for granted. For the first time, such segre-

70. Carmines and Stimson, *Issue Evolution*, 32.
71. Lacy, *White Use of Blacks*, 179.

gation and discrimination in private employment—even if only in private employment in the fulfillment of government contracts—was defined as a wrong, and as a wrong remediable by government action.[72]

A second result of growing black political participation—both conventional (voting and filing lawsuits) and unconventional (protest)—was a Roosevelt-oriented Supreme Court that declared the white primary unconstitutional in the early 1940s. Even such minor concessions in Roosevelt's final years marked the beginning of a new posture by national Democratic leaders toward the black cause. These acts also, however, engendered intense antagonism among white southern leaders, thus creating a deep strain between the northern and southern wings of the Democratic Party.

Increasingly it appeared that a coalition of southern whites, northern blacks, and white liberals could endure only so long as the issue of race was ignored. As late as 1944, Edward Carmines and James Stimson conclude, the Democratic Party managed to submerge the race debate so well that it remained clearly the conservative party on issues of race. While the 1944 Republican platform provided a clear, specific, and detailed call for a congressional inquiry into the mistreatment, segregation, and discrimination of African Americans in the military, federal legislation to deal with abuse found, the establishment of a permanent FEPC, a constitutional amendment abolishing poll taxes, and legislation to make lynching a federal crime, the Democratic platform contained only the simple assertion: "We believe that racial and religious minorities have the right to live, develop, and vote equally with all citizens and share the rights that are guaranteed by our Constitution."[73]

But the politics of the Democratic Party was perched on the precipice of change, largely as a result of its need to maintain a biracial coalition in the North if it were to continue to be the majority party. Maintaining this coalition proved to be an increasingly daunting challenge after FDR's death in 1945. On the one hand, the spiraling racial consciousness of African Americans as a consequence of World War II, further urbanization, and the diminution of the economic emergency brought racial issues to the fore in the 1940s in ways that had not occurred in the previous decade. African Americans themselves, in the words of Ralph Bunche, the first black to head a division of the State Depart-

72. Carmines and Stimson, *Issue Evolution,* 31.
73. Quoted in Weiss, *Farewell to the Party of Lincoln,* 234, 238.

ment and winner of the Nobel Peace Prize in 1950, developed from the experience of the 1930s and 1940s "a much keener sense than formerly of the uses to which the ballot [could] be put." They now knew that the ballot was "negotiable" and that it could "be exchanged for definite social improvements for themselves."[74] Thanks to the politicization stimulated by the New Deal, blacks moved increasingly to use the ballot as a lever to encourage attention to their concerns. Civil rights groups adopted a new strategy: to overcome the persistent exclusion of enforceable antidiscrimination clauses in social welfare legislation, henceforth they would refuse to support legislation that did not explicitly prohibit discrimination and segregation. Never again would social welfare trump civil rights. By 1948 African American leaders served notice to Democrats and Republicans alike that they would encourage the expanding ranks of black voters to support the party that took the strongest stand in favor of civil rights. Both parties responded by courting black votes as never before. The Republicans adopted a platform supporting antilynching legislation and opposing discrimination in strong language. Democrats, who for the first time had African American delegates at their nominating convention, worked closely with civil rights activists to get out the black vote and generally reminded blacks of the economic assistance provided by the Roosevelt-Truman administration.

Northern white Democrats interested in civil rights but especially in the electoral fortunes of their party represented another pressure point for change. Growing impatient with their party's silence on race even after millions of African Americans had become "Roosevelt Democrats," many white northerners encouraged the party to act. A central goal was to make the party competitive well outside of its natural base of support in the South; in fact, the party's success in maintaining a majority coalition depended critically on its electoral fortunes beyond Dixie. And winning the electoral votes of northern states depended on winning the cities in that region by large margins. In turn, winning the cities depended on winning increasing numbers of northern African American voters. The electoral logic of the New Deal coalition, in short, was forcing Democrats to begin to confront racial issues to an extent they had never had to do before.[75] As a result, Harry S. Truman looked to civil rights as a

74. Ibid., 32–33.
75. Barton Bernstein, "The Ambiguous Legacy: The Truman Administration and Civil Rights." in Barton Bernstein, ed., *Politics and Policies of the Truman Administration* (Chicago: Quadrangle, 1970), 171, 174, 177.

means to transform black Roosevelt supporters into black Democrats. A virtual sea change was occurring in the party of the Old Confederacy. Whiteness as an ideology faced a new, even if modest, challenge within the very party that had so long openly championed it.

This new challenge produced a counterattack. By 1948 the influence of African Americans and white liberals in the Democratic Party had begun to rankle its staunchest white supremacists, disproportionately in the South. When in February of that year President Truman called for legislation to abolish the poll tax, make lynching a federal crime, curtail discrimination in employment, and prohibit segregation in interstate commerce, southern Democrats were outraged. As they had denounced the Freedmen's Bureau as the work of those out to "Africanize" the South, vocal southern white leaders now denounced Truman's call as the work of liberals out to "harlemize" the nation. They threatened to bolt the party, and buttressed their threats by convincing southern contributors to cancel several hundred thousand dollars in pledges to the Democratic National Committee. Despite these efforts, a coalition of liberals, civil rights leaders, and labor leaders succeeded in incorporating Truman's proposal in the party platform. The delegates to the Democratic convention erupted in applause when Hubert Humphrey, then mayor of Minneapolis, declared: "The time has arrived for the Democratic Party to get out of the shadow of state's rights and walk into the bright sunshine of human rights."[76] Mississippi's delegation and part of Alabama's decided it was time for them to get out of the Democratic Party. Bolting the convention, they eventually formed a third party, the States' Rights Democrats—a.k.a. the Dixiecrats—to run a presidential candidate more to their liking: Strom Thurmond, then governor of South Carolina.

Southern discontent with the Democrats deepened during the campaign when Truman issued Executive Orders 9980, creating a Fair Employment Practices Board within the Civil Service Commission, and 9981, desegregating the military. In effect, Truman was courting the black vote as no Democratic presidential candidate had ever done before. His electoral arithmetic was clear: the fleeting southern white vote could be made up for by a strong black vote in sixteen northern states, with a total of 278 electoral votes—151 more than

76. Jack M. Bloom, *Class, Race, and the Civil Rights Movement* (Bloomington: Indiana University Press, 1987), 76.

the 127 electoral votes controlled by the South. The war for the racial soul of the party had clearly begun. What was then a serious fissure between the Democratic Party and a growing number of southern whites would ultimately become a gaping fault line.

The defiant splinter candidacy of Strom Thurmond notwithstanding, the civil rights platform, both executive orders, and a last-minute appeal to black voters in the North helped to secure victory for Truman in 1948. In what was an exceptionally close election, Truman won despite the loss of four Deep South states—Louisiana, South Carolina, Alabama, and Mississippi—to the States' Rights Party. He was amply rewarded for his efforts on behalf of civil rights: a strong majority of African Americans not only cast their votes for the Democratic nominee but abandoned the party of Lincoln and joined the party of Roosevelt and Truman. They did so in such substantial numbers that politicians could never again dismiss their votes as of little consequence in national elections.[77]

In sum, the election of 1948 placed civil rights high on the national agenda and helped force national leaders to begin to address the ethos of white skin privilege and the position of African Americans in society. As Roy Wilkins, executive director of the NAACP, saw it, "the message was plain: white power in the South could be balanced by black power at the northern polls. Civil Rights was squarely at the heart of national politics—if we could keep them there."[78]

This was no small task. In 1952 the Democrats took a giant step backward toward the ethos of white skin privilege. In an attempt to regain the South, the party asserted in its platform that "the Party of Jefferson and Jackson pledges itself to continued support of those sound principles of local government which will best serve the welfare of our people and the safety of our Democratic rights."[79] This statement sent a coded message to segregationists that the party planned to steer a more conciliatory course on civil rights after its near disaster in 1948. The choice of Adlai Stevenson to be the party's presi-

77. Henry Lee Moon, *Balance of Power: The Negro Vote* (Garden City, N.Y.: Doubleday, 1948), 217.
78. Quoted in William Berman, *The Politics of Civil Rights in the Truman Administration* (Columbus: Ohio State University Press, 1970), 325.
79. Quoted in Carmines and Stimson, *Issue Evolution,* 35.

dential nominee in 1952 was part of this approach. Stevenson, never deeply committed to civil rights, was much more concerned about the potential of the "race issue" to divide the party. He made strenuous efforts to court the South, even praising the Constitution of the Confederacy. Stevenson's southern strategy apparently worked: the four Dixiecrat states that had deserted the party in 1948 all returned to the Democratic column in 1952. Nevertheless, it was not a winning strategy. When Dwight D. Eisenhower won in 1952, the Democrats were forced to rethink their electoral arithmetic.

For the remainder of the 1950s, both major parties took relatively moderate stands on civil rights, although Republicans reclaimed their traditional position of being more supportive. Thus it was Eisenhower who was president when the first civil rights acts since Reconstruction were passed and signed into law. The Civil Rights Act of 1957 created a temporary Commission on Civil Rights, gave the Justice Department an assistant attorney general for civil rights, and specified those circumstances requiring jury trials in contempt cases. The 1960 act provided for court-appointed referees to ensure that eligible African Americans were allowed to register and vote. Neither act, however, included strong enforcement powers. Yet the very fact that they passed during a Republican administration reinforced the party's image as being the more progressive on race. When Eisenhower sent federal troops to Little Rock to enforce a school desegregation order, his action was further evidence that the Republican Party was not yet a viable alternative for segregationists and other staunch protectors of white privilege.[80]

As a result of the relative uniformity on race issues, polls taken before 1964 showed that American public opinion was bifurcated on the question of which party was "good for civil rights." As late as 1960 a substantial minority of African Americans continued to vote for the Republican presidential nominee. In the contest that year between Richard M. Nixon and John F. Kennedy, 32 percent of black voters cast their ballots for the Republican nominee, Nixon.[81] It would take the Civil Rights Movement and the social policy legislation of the 1960s to change all that.

80. Ibid., 37.
81. Stanley Greenberg, *Middle-Class Dreams: The Politics and Power of the New Majority* (New Haven: Yale University Press, 1996), 14.

Conclusion

In an address at Howard University near the start of the New Deal, Franklin Delano Roosevelt announced that his social policy would proceed upon the conviction that "among American citizens there should be no forgotten men and no forgotten races."[82] The irony of this statement is apparent, for African Americans were indeed forgotten at best and singled out for exclusion and unequal treatment in the welfare state at worst. Whites were the prime beneficiaries of most New Deal legislation, from its agricultural policies and its Housing Authority's pro-segregation mortgage loans to its social insurance and relief schemes.

In part because black-white relations took on new salience with the New Deal and the migration of blacks out of the South, many other peoples were in a sense forgotten, too. That was the time when Europeans who previously had been consigned to alien identities with suitably funny names—Wops, Polacks, Hunkies, Eyteys, Frogs—became ever more likely to be recognized as simply whites. As Matthew Frye Jacobson concluded, by the 1950s, what was "'forgotten' was that these groups had ever been distinct races in the first place."[83] Race politics had ceased to concern the white "races" of Europe and come to refer exclusively to black-white relations and the struggle over civil rights as both political and social conceptions for African Americans.

Arguably, the New Deal was the crowning American legislative achievement of the twentieth century. It provided at least a modicum of income security not dependent on the market for the elderly, the unemployed, and poor children. Its guarantees of home mortgages, subsidized "private" pensions, Social Security, and health insurance generated important benefits for the American middle class. And for the first time, workers were guaranteed strong rights to organize into unions and to earn a minimum wage. In each instance the New Deal posed a challenge to the American ethos. With no end of the Great Depression in sight, for the first time a major political party tentatively embraced the idea that responsible, hardworking people are sometimes unable to make their way and that the federal government had the responsibility to promote individual economic security.

82. Quoted in Harvard Sitkoff, *A New Deal for Blacks: The Emergence of Civil Rights as a National Issue—the Depression Decade* (New York: Oxford University Press, 1978), 62.
83. Jacobson, *Whiteness of a Different Color,* 246.

To be sure, the New Deal did not embrace sweeping notions of social rights. Roosevelt and his advisers constantly expressed concern about fiscally irresponsible and politically motivated "unearned handouts."[84] Nonetheless, the New Deal advanced important new ideas about both the causes of individual need and the role of the federal government in addressing that need. Yet most of the new benefits established by the New Deal were provided in a discriminatory pattern, guaranteeing white but not black security. Before Truman's presidency the Democratic administration made few attempts indeed to challenge America's racial status quo.

This is not to say that the New Deal represented a total failure from the standpoint of racial concerns. The inadequacy of its efforts should not lead us to minimize the achievement of 1935. People of color and white women would have been even worse off without federal assistance. Although assistance was provided on a discriminatory basis and was never enough and never sustained, federal relief was nevertheless a major accomplishment. It helped people of all races and both genders to subsist; it provided hope; and most important, it firmly established that the federal government could manage a huge distribution system. It also raised expectations, awakened consciousness of civil rights, and prompted demands for equal treatment. Both the good and the bad of the New Deal made people want more. Thus the New Deal not only heightened citizens' sense of entitlement but also increased their desire to participate.

Perhaps, more than anything else, it was these new participatory norms that would produce change. Black politics in northern cities moved the "American dilemma" from the periphery to the center of national politics. Racial injustice was no longer understood as just a southern problem, for the nation as a whole was forced to confront this issue. By the mid-1950s, a civil rights movement swept across the nation, demanding that the United States finally and immediately grant to *all* its citizens the basic prerequisites of a democratic society—the right to vote, the right to a job, the right to live wherever one could afford to buy a home[85]—all demands that challenged the belief system and reality of white skin privilege.

84. Margaret Weir, "Political Parties and Social Policymaking," in Margaret Weir, ed., *The Social Divide: Political Parties and the Future of Activist Government* (Washington, D.C.: Brookings, 1998), 17.
85. Jill Quadagno, "Race and American Social Policy," *National Forum,* Summer 1996, 35–36.

three

An Assault on White Privilege

Civil Rights and the Great Society

I'll tell you what's at the bottom of it. If you can convince the lowest white man

that he's better than the best colored man, he won't notice you picking his pocket.

Hell, give him somebody to look down on, and he'll empty his pockets for you.

—*Lyndon Baines Johnson*

Lyndon Baines Johnson (LBJ), the thirty-sixth president of the United States, understood the power of whiteness as both property value and social and psychological wage. He often spoke of the naked suffering experienced by blacks and Latinos in his native state, Texas, as well as how playing the "race card" was an important means of manipulating the white poor and working classes into supporting racially discriminatory social policies even when those policies hurt their own material interests. He contended that he wanted to be president precisely to address and alter these situations. As Johnson put it: "Some men want power simply to strut around the world and to hear the tune of 'Hail to the Chief.' Others want it simply to build prestige, to collect antiques, and to buy pretty things. Well, I wanted power to give things to people—all sorts of things to all sorts of people, especially the poor and the blacks."[1]

An ample historical record exists to support his claim. Both before and after becoming president, Johnson wanted to be remembered as a person who saw that most blacks and Latinos really did not have a chance for good health, decent housing, and jobs, that they were always skating right on the edge, struggling to keep body and soul together; and he wanted to rectify these conditions. At the same time, Johnson thought action on altering the racial mores

1. Quoted in Doris Kearns, *Lyndon Johnson and the American Dream* (New York: Harper & Row, 1976), 53–54.

of the country was important for the economic development of his region, the South. Improved conditions for blacks would ultimately serve all southerners. Thus the challenge in the 1960s, from Johnson's viewpoint, was to overcome the southern obsession with race—its continued insistence on conjuring up the ghost of Reconstruction and get on with the business of tackling its economic and educational problems.[2] The very well-being of the South, as Johnson saw it, depended on convincing southern white leaders to accept the inevitability of some progress on civil rights and to enact federal civil rights legislation that reduced racial strife.

In many ways, however, Johnson was an unlikely warrior in this struggle. Throughout the 1940s, whenever he confronted civil rights measures to prevent lynchings of black southerners, eliminate poll taxes, and deny federal funds for lunch programs to segregated schools, Johnson consistently voted with his southern colleagues. Like his hero, FDR, he gave utilitarian political excuses. He could go "only so far" as an official elected from Texas; if he went further, he might lose his congressional seat, and "there's nothing more useless than a dead liberal." At other times, Johnson justified his votes against civil rights by saying he was not against blacks but rather for states' rights, adding that these bills would not have passed anyway, and he did well to vote with southerners on civil rights as a way to command their help on other "important" issues. Moreover, Johnson shared many conventional southern attitudes toward blacks and often privately and publicly used the word "nigger," especially when he was putting on a show for such rabid racists as Senator Theodore G. Bilbo of Mississippi. Viewing Johnson's statements, votes, and other actions against civil rights in the 1940s, Walter White, executive secretary of the NAACP, denounced him in the fall of 1951.[3] When Johnson became president after the assassination of John Fitzgerald Kennedy, most blacks—leaders and masses alike—were seriously concerned at best and distraught at worst. As the black nationalist leader Malcolm X saw it, Johnson was nothing but "a southern cracker, that's all he is."[4] Yet it was during Johnson's years in the White House that the most serious challenge to whiteness and to liberal individualism as central organizing principles of American social policy faced their biggest challenge up to that time.

2. Ibid., 149.

3. Robert Dallek, *Lone Star Rising: Lyndon Johnson and His Times, 1908–1960* (New York: Oxford University Press, 1991), 168–69, 276–77, 405.

4. Quoted in Richard Kluger, *Simple Justice* (New York: Knopf, 1975), 957.

Economic, Demographic, and Political Harbingers of the Challenge to Whiteness

By the time Johnson assumed the presidency, technological developments had altered the American economy and inspired demographic and social change. The years of war and intense development of weaponry for World War II and the Korean War produced technological advances that were transferred to civilian production. The result was an outpouring of physical production that rapidly raised most Americans to a new level of affluence.

Although the dramatic increases in productivity resulting from science-based technological innovations are usually associated with manufacturing, in fact the most startling technological advances of all were made in agriculture. Because southern agriculture had lagged so far behind before World War II, it experienced these changes with special force.[5] Technological change altered both the cotton culture and the demand for black labor in the South. As late as 1949, only 6 percent of the South's cotton was harvested mechanically; African American sharecroppers harvested most of the rest. By 1964, however, machines harvested 78 percent of the cotton; and by 1972 nearly 100 percent was picked by machines.[6] For the first time blacks were no longer needed in the cotton fields. The southern sharecropper system had been made obsolete by technology.

As a result, African American men and women poured out of the rural South and into the nation's northern urban centers—New York, Chicago, Detroit, Philadelphia, and numerous smaller cities. The population shift was dramatic: in 1940, 77 percent of African Americans lived in the South; by 1970 only 53 percent still did.[7] The tractor and chemical defoliants did more to liberate African Americans from the rural South than both the Emancipation Proclamation and the recruitment of black labor by northern manufacturers during World Wars I and II.

For many African Americans, however, the migration northward proved to offer only temporary improvement. To be sure, at first they found limited access to unskilled jobs in the durable goods manufacturing sector, especially in

5. Dan Lacy, *The White Use of Blacks in America: 350 Years of Law and Violence, Attitudes and Etiquette, Politics and Change* (New York: McGraw-Hill, 1973), 207–11.

6. Jeremy Rifkin, *The End of Work: The Decline of the Global Labor Force and the Dawn of the Post-Market Era* (New York: Putnam, 1995), 73.

7. Claudette Bennett, *The Black Population in the United States* (Washington, D.C.: U.S. Government Printing Office, 1995), 2.

steel, rubber, chemical, and auto production, and they received more equitable treatment in social programs in northern cities. More black women were able to obtain welfare in the North. The economic well-being of blacks in the North improved steadily until the mid-1950s.

But the cities blacks migrated to in the 1950s were also being radically transformed in ways that would stall, if not end, black progress. Five interlocking factors were at the root of change: postwar housing programs, the automobile, the interstate highway system, educational trends, and deindustrialization of inner cities—each influenced by public policy.

Quality housing for the new migrants was scarce. After a decade and a half of minimal construction, the return of millions of veterans from World War II and the concomitant burst of marriages and children that followed brought a housing shortage of major proportions. By the 1950s, it was certain that the New Deal's promise to construct low-cost housing was broken. Of the millions of low-cost housing units authorized by various acts of Congress, only about 190,000 were actually constructed by 1950.[8] Not surprisingly, it was the poor—especially the black poor—that suffered most from this inaction. Not only were they desperately overcrowded, many were packed into houses not fit for human habitation. "In 1950," writes Dan Lacy, "about one-fifth of all Americans lived in houses without running water or indoor toilets or otherwise dilapidated or deteriorating. More than half of all blacks were compelled to live so."[9]

Yet despite the alarming plight of these new urbanites, it was the millions of middle-class white families, newly married or new parents or at last having the means to buy homes, that got the attention of federal, state, and local governments when they turned again to the housing problem. State governments in the 1950s joined the federal government in providing tax expenditures, making capital available to savings and loan associations, providing subsidies for other private lenders, and allowing the deduction of home mortgages and real estate taxes from taxable income. Local governments eagerly cooperated in opening new areas for residential development, changing zoning, paving streets, widening highways, installing sewer systems, and building schools. The

8. Lacy, *White Use of Blacks,* 207.
9. Ibid.

dramatic growth in production of new automobiles and trucks (97 million in the years from 1945 to 1960) simultaneously killed off hopes of early development of mass transit and opened up the potential for suburban development.[10]

The new suburbia that exploded into being around every major city was totally white or very nearly so. Even after the Supreme Court held racial covenants to be unenforceable[11] and the federal government withdrew its instructions to discourage the guarantee of mortgages on homes in racially integrated areas, the combined policies of real estate agents, developers, banks, and savings and loan associations kept the suburbs white. Even had blacks been welcomed to the suburbs, however, few could have afforded to accept the invitation.

In the 1950s, scholars and public officials alike claimed the mushrooming number of poor families in inner cities, driven to seek refuge from mines and farms by unemployment and rural poverty, was not a pressing problem. In their housing trickle-down theory, the families of the poor would move into the housing vacated by families who moved to the suburbs from the inner cities and to newer suburbs from older ones. In actuality, the vacated housing of good quality was occupied by expanding white families of moderate means. "The worst, already physically deteriorated and rat and insect infested was left available for blacks," Lacy points out. "But there was never enough of it, and hideous overcrowding compounded the squalor of dingy neighborhoods and decaying buildings."[12] Moreover, such housing was located in declining, often abandoned neighborhoods with the oldest school buildings, the most decrepit hospitals, and the most potholed streets. Perhaps the devastating physical quality of the schools was the worst omen of all. It suggested to the children what their adult conditions were expected to be, and it turned away competent staff who did not want (or no longer wanted) to work in an environment of deterioration and social disorganization.

Developments in education policy in the twenty years after World War II further hardened the obstacles faced by the new black migrants. The first source of change was the GI Bill of Rights—officially the Servicemen's Readjustment Act of 1944—which offered veterans the opportunity to earn a col-

10. Ibid., 209.
11. *Shelley v. Kraemer,* 334 U.S. 1 (1948).
12. Lacy, *White Use of Blacks,* 214.

lege or technical education at public expense.[13] Adopted as a democratizing measure, the GI Bill succeeded in blurring the educational boundaries between the middle and upper classes. In the 1930s about one American in eight entered college and about one in eighteen graduated. By the 1960s almost half entered and about one in four graduated.[14]

As for racial inequality, the nature, role, and impact of the GI Bill is complex. While the conventional wisdom is that the GI Bill benefited black veterans enormously, in actuality their experience after World War II is in many ways reminiscent of their experience after the Civil War. The GI Bill, like the legislation establishing the veterans' pensions, had no discriminatory provisions. Indeed, some of its provisions were directly helpful to blacks. First, veterans could select their own schools and pursue any course they wanted, and the federal government was authorized explicitly to "protect the rights of smaller schools, including some Negro institutions."[15] Thus historically black colleges and universities (HBCUs) were protected against almost certain discrimination by southern states, since schools otherwise would have had to be certified by their state boards of education before being deemed eligible to receive federal funds. Second, a subsidy of $20 a week was granted for 52 weeks for veterans who were unemployed. This provision, often called "the 52/20," went to veterans regardless to race. Third, coinciding with the GI Bill was the parallel Lanham Act of 1946, which funded the improvement and expansion of educational facilities required to make room for the vast increase in enrollment as veterans entered. Because HBCUs were in greater disrepair than predominantly white institutions, proportionately more of them received these funds. Finally, the GI Bill financed not only higher education but vocational training programs, even in neighborhood storefront trade schools that taught television repair, auto repairs, and so forth. These relatively inexpensive and quick skills training programs undoubtedly helped some black veterans who either did not qualify for admission to colleges and universities or did not have the luxury of waiting four years before they could begin to earn a living. In view of these salutary aspects

13. To help World War II veterans, the law also subsidized mortgages, which disproportionately helped whites move to the new suburbs. It also provided $20 a week for a maximum of 52 weeks in jobless benefits.

14. Lacy, *White Use of Blacks*, 214.

15. Michael J. Bennett, *When Dreams Came True: The GI Bill and the Making of Modern America* (Washington, D.C.: Brassey's, 1996).

of the GI Bill, many people have concluded that blacks received its benefits at rates equal to whites in every region of the country, and were slightly more likely to be the beneficiaries of education and readjustment benefits.[16] Certainly, black enrollment in colleges went up. In 1940, enrollment at HBCUs was 1.08 percent of the total United States college enrollment; in 1950, it was 3.6 percent.[17] Many black men who received college educations as a result of the GI Bill consider it nearly heresy to find any flaws in it.

Yet, as with the Civil War veterans' pensions, the real social and historical legacy of the GI Bill lies in its demonstration of how little difference presumably race-neutral and "universal" policies make when they are instituted within the context of widespread racial inequality and white advantage. To give just one example: although African Americans were not overtly excluded from the GI Bill's benefits, blacks as a group were clearly underrepresented because proportionately more of them had been disqualified from military service in World War II. In 1950, the first census year after World War II ended, of 15,386,000 veterans eligible for GI benefits, 920,000, or 6 percent, were African Americans, although they accounted for 10 percent of the adult male population. Disqualification in most instances was a direct consequence of segregated, inferior schools and poor health in a society where discrimination was rampant. "Nor did black veterans receive the same occupational and educational lift as did white veterans," reports Michael K. Brown. "At all income thresholds, black World War II and Korean War veterans did not earn as much by 1970 as white veterans, nor did they advance as far educationally."[18] Aside from a few anecdotal accounts, there are no data revealing how many of the eligible

16. Ronald Roach, "From Combat to Campus," *Black Issues in Higher Education* 14, no. 13 (Aug. 21, 1997): 26. This is also Michael Bennett's conclusion in *When Dreams Came True*, 27, 179, 260–76. For a more complex understanding of the GI Bill that sees it as a form of relatively generous "truncated universalism" for a narrow group of men, who were treated "very differently" from poor women trapped in means-tested programs, see Michael K. Brown, *Race, Money, and the American Welfare State* (Ithaca, N.Y.: Cornell University Press, 1999), 117–19, 169–70, 189–91. Indeed, Brown shows how segregation and discrimination in labor markets, housing markets, educational institutions, and other elements of American society undermined the potential benefit of the GI Bill and other veterans' programs for black men. In short, his analysis shows the limits of universalist social policies in a society heavily structured by racial and class inequalities.

17. Based on data from Biennial Survey of Education, 1948–50, in Bennett, *When Dreams Came True*, 243–68.

18. Brown, *Race, Money, and the American Welfare State*, 189, 191, with table of supporting data on 190.

black men actually took advantage of the benefits. All that is certain is that despite the increase in male enrollment in colleges and universities, 70 percent of veterans of all races were employed in the year after World War II ended, 14 percent were in colleges and universities, and 3 percent were in vocational training programs.[19]

Black veterans received a visibly different homecoming than white veterans. They found pervasive discrimination in the labor market and were shut out of local American Legion posts in many places, particularly in the South. Because they had greater difficulty than whites finding jobs, they remained recipients of the inferior "52/20" unemployment benefits for a much longer time. When white employers refused to accept black applicants, their files were put in the inactive pile, and ultimately many black veterans gave up on using the U.S. Employment Office. To be sure, black veterans were advantaged over black nonveterans, but less so than white veterans and nonveterans of the same age.[20]

In short, while it is difficult to draw any final conclusions about the GI Bill's impact on whiteness, several results seem clear. First, the GI bill, to its credit, diminished the distance between the middle and upper classes, but it sharply increased the distance between the middle and working classes, men and women, and blacks and whites. As generous as was the education assistance it offered, it was irrelevant to the hundreds of thousands of young men, disproportionately black and poor, whose poor health and level of literacy were so low as to bar their entrance to the armed services and who hence never benefited from any of the GI Bill's provisions. Like previous demonstrations of government largesse—the Civil War pensions, Social Security, union protection, unemployment insurance, agricultural programs, federal deposit insurance—the GI Bill ignored those who most desperately needed help.

In fact, the radical change in college attendance actually worked to the disadvantage of the undereducated. On the one hand, it enabled the more rapid transformation of the economy through the general use of a technology in which the undereducated had a dwindling role to play. On the other hand, it

19. Calculated from data reported in Bennett, *When Dreams Came True,* 25. The remaining 13% were drawing checks to supplement farm work or help establish businesses or professional practices, drawing unemployment benefits, on vacation, or hospitalized.

20. See Brown, *Race, Money, and the American Welfare State,* Table 11, p. 190, and discussion on 191.

permitted educational criteria to become a barrier to entry. Even when educational criteria had little or no relevance to job performance, they became an essential part of hiring standards as a way to narrow the applicant pool—that is, a kind of barrier to entry. As a result, the job and promotional opportunities for those who lacked a college degree or a high school diploma became fewer and fewer. In the days of Andrew Carnegie, John D. Rockefeller I, Henry Ford, and the Wright brothers, even a high school education was needed only if one planned to attend college, and a college degree was needed only if one planned to enter a learned profession. But by the 1960s, at least, a high school diploma and preferably a college degree were becoming indispensable to almost any but low-paid and futureless employment.[21]

Of all the factors that negatively altered the prospects of black migrants to American cities in the 1950s, deindustrialization (a product of automation and out-migration of industries) was key. As revolutions in communications and transportation technologies occurred, employers became free to locate throughout suburban areas in pursuit of cheap land and lower taxes. Suburban locations were especially attractive to electronics and service industries, which ranked among the industries growing most rapidly and providing the most attractive job opportunities.[22] Federal public policy facilitated these moves by funding the interstate highway system and the ring of metropolitan expressways around cities and by heavily subsidizing the construction of housing for the white middle-class suburbanites who would fill the new jobs. Stuck in central cities and unable to afford or maintain automobiles, many people of color were hopelessly excluded from these new arenas of employment opportunity.

Making matters worse was the rapid disappearance of unskilled and semi-skilled jobs in manufacturing as a result of automation. Between 1944 and 1962, 1.6 million blue-collar jobs disappeared in the manufacturing sector and almost all the increase in well-paid employment was in jobs requiring high levels of education or advanced skills. This was a situation considerably different from the one faced by the millions of peasants who arrived from Ireland, Italy, and Central and Eastern Europe in the decades from 1880 to 1924. These European immigrants, as Lacy reminds us, "came to cities with roads to be graded, streets to be paved, ditches to be dug, freight to be loaded and

21. Lacy, *White Use of Blacks,* 219–20.
22. Ibid., 214.

unloaded, burdens to be moved, and all by hand. They came to factories in which simple labor served primitive machines and to mines not yet mechanized." When blacks migrated north after World War II, they came from mechanized farms to automated cities, "where the laborer's muscle was almost as useless as the ancient skill with mules and hoes or the fingers trained to snap cotton from the boll."[23] As Tom Kahn quipped, "it is as if racism, having put the Negro in his economic place, stepped aside to watch technology destroy that place."[24]

In sum, in the postwar decades blacks were pushed by the relentless closing of opportunities in the South but not pulled by northern demand for their labor. Several million blacks, whose labor major sectors of the economy in both North and South had once depended on, now were excluded from a needed and productive economic role. Whereas the unemployment rate of blacks had never exceeded 8.5 percent between 1947 and 1953 and the rate of white unemployment had never gone beyond 4.6 percent, by 1964 blacks were experiencing an unemployment rate of 12.4 percent while white unemployment was only 5.9 percent.[25]

It did not help matters that public sector jobs (for example, in sanitation, police, welfare, and school systems) operating in black neighborhoods were almost entirely supervised and largely manned by whites, many of whom were from lower-middle-class neighborhoods that felt threatened by the expanding black population. These white workers' own insecure social position sometimes led to hostile racial altercations, especially in regard to police/black community relations. With the conditions of everyday life breaking down for not only southern but northern blacks, the times were ripe for the Civil Rights Movement, begun in the North in the 1940s, to spread throughout the nation.

The Civil Rights Movement and the Challenge to Whiteness

Although it has been argued that it was the actions of the federal judiciary that actually inspired the Civil Rights Movement,[26] a more realistic reading

23. Ibid.
24. Tom Kahn, "Problems of the Negro Movement," *Dissent,* Winter 1964, 115.
25. Rifkin, *End of Work,* 76.
26. Some of the best textbooks on American government advance this argument; e.g., Benjamin Ginsberg, Theodore J. Lowi, and Margaret Weir, *We the People: An Introduction to American Politics* (New York: Norton, 1997), 685ff.

demonstrates a dialectical relationship between the movement and judicial action, albeit with black organizations and activists and their white allies taking the lead role. It was, after all, movement activists, particularly those in the NAACP, who brought the cases to federal courts, and indeed a full understanding of the evolving role of the courts in the area of civil rights in the first half of the twentieth century can be understood only in the context of the campaign for black equality waged by these early activists. Activist lawyers of the NAACP, for instance, won a string of cases from at least 1917 onward that presaged the coming changes, though none more than *Brown v. Board of Education* in 1954, which tore down the legal edifice of "separate but equal."[27]

A Court ruling, however, does not in itself change social reality, and the most prevalent response to *Brown* was what came to be called "massive white resistance." Most southern states refused to cooperate until they were sued and employed a host of ingenious schemes to avoid compliance ; the favorite ploy was to pay the tuition for white students to attend newly created "private" segregated academies. Even when school boards began to stop enforcement of school segregation, racially segregated housing guaranteed de facto school segregation in both North and South.

Brown made it obvious to all that adjudication alone would not succeed in the face of massive white resistance in the South and generally negative national public opinion toward racial integration nationwide. Increasingly it became certain that a successful challenge to white skin privilege would not be made through the courts, Congress, or federal agencies unless it was accompanied by intense, well-organized mass action. The process of direct action began locally; but over time grassroots efforts culminated in the organization of new regional and ultimately national groups, most prominently the Congress of Racial Equality (CORE), the Southern Christian Leadership Conference (SCLC), and the Student Nonviolent Coordinating Committee (SNCC).

Mexican Americans were also spurred to action. Most of the four million persons of Mexican ancestry, still gathered in barrios throughout the Southwest and West in the 1960s, were also held back by discrimination and inadequate schooling and job training, as well as language issues. They, too, had been ignored by policy makers. Similarly, some 450,000 Native Americans, perhaps

---

27. *Brown v. Board of Education of Topeka, Kansas,* 347 U.S. 483 (1954). See Kluger, *Simple Justice,* for a discussion of the central cases and the issues involved.

the nation's poorest and most deprived group, also took on a new militancy. Native American organizations such as the National Congress of American Indians (NCAI), the National Indian Youth Council (NIYC), and the American Indian Movement (AIM); and Latino organizations such as the National Farm Workers' Association, the Political Association of Spanish-Speaking Organizations (PASO), the Mexican-American Political Association (MAPA), the Alianza de Mercedes, and many other groups inspired by Chicanismo mobilized.

As the decade matured, welfare mothers also organized. In the 1930s welfare mothers had been too few, too scattered, and too lacking in a sense of entitlement to engage in collective action; now they organized the National Welfare Rights Organization (NWRO). By the late 1960s the NWRO was staging sit-ins and engaging in confrontations at welfare offices to demand increased benefits, jobs, an established right to a fair hearing to obtain or maintain benefits, and the removal of a host of odious regulations that prevented women from receiving benefits. The fact that the NWRO was part of the Civil Rights Movement meant that welfare rights organizing took on a black face, even though the majority of women on welfare remained white.

More generally, the women's movement was reborn. Many new women's organizations were formed, with the National Organization for Women, formed in 1966, playing a leading role. The women's movement was disproportionately of, by, and for middle-class white women, and as it grew more radical, it ignored such issues as child care, welfare, and the concerns of women who were not in the workforce because some women viewed these issues as associated with the subordination of women. All the same, it played a key role in promoting the demand for a more inclusionary, equal, and just social order.

Finally, perhaps the most radical of all these mushrooming activists were the students. Predominantly white groups such as Students for a Democratic Society (SDS) not only fought against the Vietnam War but linked their demands for a just foreign policy to a just domestic policy and interacted with all the various groups working on human rights. Similarly, predominantly black student groups such as SNCC increasingly linked their demand for justice at home to justice in Vietnam. Taken together, these racial/ethnic, women's, and students' organizations built a movement that stretched across the nation. It was the largest, most unprecedented, and most fundamental challenge to white male privilege the nation had ever seen. (Perhaps here lies the biggest part of the reason the 1960s are held in such disdain in the current era.)

There was never a time, however, when movement politics was the only strategy. At the same historical moment that mass action politics flourished, legal action expanded enormously. Both types of action, each bolstering the other, engendered hostile responses from many whites. Grassroots activists were, not surprisingly, on the front line receiving these responses. In defense of white skin privilege, it was common for white hecklers in the South to push lit cigarettes against the backs of young women trying to integrate lunch counters; to throw hot French fries and saliva-soaked gum at demonstrators; to spit and blow cigar smoke in the faces of civil rights activists; to beat and kick white "nigger lovers"; to set dogs upon protesters, flog them with chains, throw acid in their faces. The violence escalated to murder. Horror stories were televised as in city after city the savage core of racism ended all notions of southern hospitality.[28]

"Massive white resistance" was not confined to hoodlums. Southern uniformed officials often made up the front line of the defense of white privilege. When on May 2, 1963, over a thousand black children, some only six years old, marched out of the Sixteenth Street Baptist Church in Birmingham, Alabama, to demonstrate, they were met by police with snarling dogs and by firemen whose high-pressure hoses, sounding like gunfire, sent streams of water to blast the children against buildings and sweep many down slippery streets. The hundreds of pounds of pressure ripped the bark off trees; tore the clothes off children's backs, cut through their skins, and jerked their small limbs as though they were weightless. In two days of demonstrating, white police arrested nearly 1,300 children.[29]

Massive white resistance had, of course, a material basis. Attitudes and interests were in sync. The flip side of black exclusion from social policies that served middle- and stable working-class whites was white inclusion. Thus massive white resistance was not just the actions of an irrational group of bigots; rather it was the product of markets protecting whiteness. What massive white resistance most demonstrated was an almost overwhelming sense of the intensity of commitment to unearned privilege for whites. To be sure, affluent whites may have had the greatest stake in white privilege. As Michael Reich has demonstrated, racism works far more to the economic advantage of affluent whites

28. Harvard Sitkoff, *The Struggle for Black Equality, 1954–1992* (New York: Hill & Wang, 1993), 69.
29. Ibid., 127–29.

and often to the economic disadvantage of working-class whites.[30] But massive white resistance grew out of the stakes that all whites had in racism. Beyond economic interests were the compensatory factors of racism that provided, at least in the short run, significant gains for all whites—that is, the social, cultural, political, and psychological dimensions of racism that whites have accrued and continue to accrue as the results of the system of racism. Like economic forces, these noneconomic forces, as LBJ indicated, ensure white solidarity.

The response to massive white resistance and its flagrant lawlessness was intensified struggle and flagrant lawlessness on the side of the challengers. Indeed, a genuine leftist politics came to characterize the Civil Rights Movement by the mid-1960s. SNCC, the Black Panther Party, the Student Organization for Black Unity (SOBU), and other youthful groups joined the mostly white SDS and had a tremendous influence on the New Left.

Yet although it may have been the radical left that most directly sought to link race and class in the politics it promoted, mainstream black organizations, as the 1963 March for Jobs and Freedom and the Urban League's Marshall plan amply demonstrate, also merged concerns for racial justice with class justice. Concomitantly, as insurgency, violent confrontations with students, and urban strife became the order of the day, American party politics and American social policy were transformed.

Civil Rights and the Transformation of American Party Politics

The first clear sign that Congress and presidential hopefuls were beginning to see the inevitability of progress on civil rights emerged in the struggle over the Civil Rights Act of 1957. Movement activism increased pressure for legislation to implement the *Brown* decision on school desegregation and enforce black voting rights in the South. With the House likely to pass a civil rights bill, as

---

30. Michael Reich demonstrates in "The Economics of Racism," in David Gordon, ed., *Problems in Political Economy: An Urban Perspective* (New York: D. C. Heath, 1971), 107–13; and *Racial Inequality: A Political-Economic Analysis* (Princeton: Princeton University Press, 1981), that racism generates greater inequality among whites by two main mechanisms: (1) the total wages of white labor are reduced by racial antagonisms in part because union growth and labor militancy are inhibited, since racism deflects attention from workers' grievances, permitting employers to cut costs; and (2) the supply of public services available to low- and middle-income whites is reduced when racial antagonism reduces the ability to join in a unified political movement for more and better services.

in 1956, the Senate was the focus of congressional action. There Lyndon Johnson was majority leader. By then Johnson's presidential ambitions were well known and well documented.[31] He reasoned that if he could lead a major civil rights bill through the Senate, it would help transform him from a southern leader into a national one. At the same time, Republican presidential aspirants were also grasping the newly attained importance of civil rights. Richard M. Nixon, who had an unimpressive voting record on civil rights, suddenly became a champion of legislative advance.

A noticeable shift of northern black votes from Democrats to Republicans in 1956 gave the issue an electoral urgency the Democrats had not felt since 1936. It was also increasingly apparent that the split between the southern and northern wings of the Democratic Party on the question of civil rights was having injurious effects on the party's electoral fortunes. Finding a compromise and muting civil rights as a divisive force in party affairs took on added significance. Arthur Schlesinger Jr. gave Johnson another reason to support a civil rights bill. Such a law, he counseled, would remind voters that Democrats had not abandoned their determination to use activist government as a tool for serving the people and enlarging rights and opportunities. Johnson, weighing carefully each of these concerns and their relation to his personal ambitions, decided to back civil rights legislation in 1957.

Most of his southern Democratic colleagues remained dead set against civil rights legislation. When a bill authorizing "the reimposition of post–Civil War Reconstruction" was introduced, many were livid. Only after deletion of strong enforcement provisions and a record twenty-four-hour filibuster by Strom Thurmond could enough votes be found to pass the bill, in August 1957. The bill created a permanent United States Commission on Civil Rights, made the Justice Department's Civil Rights Section a division headed by an assistant attorney general, and enhanced the powers of the Justice Department to protect voting rights. On September 9 President Eisenhower signed the bill.[32] And thus, for the first time in eighty-two years, the Congress of the United States passed civil rights legislation.

Not surprisingly, given the compromises required for this legislative advance, the 1957 bill had no teeth and was soundly criticized by both liberal

31. Discussed in Kearns, *Lyndon Johnson,* and Dallek, *Lone Star Rising.*
32. Philip A. Klinkner and Rogers M. Smith, *The Unsteady March: The Rise and Decline of Racial Equality in America* (Chicago: University of Chicago Press, 1999), 248.

whites and African Americans. Ralph Bunche and A. Philip Randolph declared it would have been better to have no bill at all. To Joseph Rauh of the liberal Americans for Democratic Action, "Johnson's triumph was so tarnished that it proved his unfitness for national leadership." Johnson's critics had a point, of course. The 1957 law did little to increase black voting rights and nothing to protect other civil rights. Two years after the bill became law, there were only 205 black voters on the rolls in four Alabama counties with huge black populations. What the bill principally delivered were two key results. First, it improved Johnson's standing with the northern wing of his party. So venerable a friend to civil rights as Hubert Humphrey came to see Johnson as a "pragmatic moderate." Immediately after the Senate passed the 1957 bill, Humphrey handed Johnson a note: "I was never more proud of you! Your speech was a masterpiece—more important, it came from the heart and soul. It's a genuine privilege to be included amongst your friends."[33] In effect, Johnson had succeeded in becoming the first southern Democratic leader since the Civil War to be considered a serious candidate for presidential nomination. Second, the 1957 act proved to be a watershed in congressional consideration of civil rights. It meant, first and foremost, that legislation enacting civil rights was no longer out of reach.

The coming transformation in American party politics became yet more visible during the presidential campaign of 1960, when both major parties and their respective nominees took comparable positions on civil rights. The Democrats adopted a strong civil rights plank despite southern opposition, and the Republicans would not be outdone. Nixon threatened to wage a floor fight if strong pro–civil rights language was not adopted in the party platform; and the final plank included an extensive array of civil rights commitments, including support for equal voting rights, establishment of a Commission on Equal Job Opportunities, and a prohibition against discrimination in federal housing and in the operation of federal facilities. With both party platforms addressing civil rights and both candidates demonstrating roughly equal commitment, about all that gave the Democratic nominee, John Fitzgerald Kennedy (JFK), an advantage among blacks was his well-publicized telephone call to Coretta Scott King inquiring about the status of her recently arrested husband, the

33. Quotes and discussion are in Dallek, *Lone Star Rising*, 524–27, 688.

SCLC leader Martin Luther King Jr. Kennedy won the election narrowly, with the help of roughly two-thirds of the black vote.[34]

In office, however, JFK was cautious on civil rights. As Kenneth O'Reilly concludes, despite the mythology surrounding the slain president, there is little hard evidence to suggest that the cause of civil rights was of deep moral concern to Kennedy. Like FDR, he had no plans to sacrifice his domestic and economic programs on the altar of civil rights.[35] Thus, at first, Kennedy decided not to send a civil rights bill to Congress; what he could do he would attempt to do through his executive powers. It was a decision that could not last, for neither the movement nor the massive white resistance to it was about to let the issue die.

Another pressure point forcing action on civil rights stemmed from Washington's efforts in the 1960s to expand American influence in the Third World, where the British and French empires had recently disintegrated. As America's image became tarnished worldwide by its version of racial apartheid and the scenes of struggles in Birmingham, Selma, Montgomery, and elsewhere in the South, JFK was virtually forced to use persuasion, dispense federal troops, and send a comprehensive civil rights bill to Congress in June 1963. Arguably, the decision to move on civil rights had grown out of a choice between legal action and mounting violence.

Within a month of the 1963 March on Washington, however, John Kennedy was assassinated and Vice President Johnson became president. Having publicly committed himself to the pending civil rights bill, the new president was now determined to see it enacted into law. Using the full powers of the presidency and his legendary political skills, he pressed Congress to action. As Johnson put it, "there is but one way to deal with the Congress, and that is continuously, incessantly and without interruption."[36] Hammering away and working closely with his Capitol Hill allies—particularly Humphrey, now majority whip—LBJ played a key role in securing the passage of the Civil Rights Act of 1964 by a wide margin in the House and Senate.

34. Edward G. Carmines and James A. Stimson, *Issue Evolution : Race and the Transformation of American Politics* (Princeton: Princeton University Press, 1989), 39.

35. Kenneth O'Reilly, *Nixon's Piano: Presidents and Racial Politics from Washington to Clinton* (New York: Free Press, 1995), 241.

36. Quoted in "Fulfilling the Great Society," *Congressional Quarterly Weekly Report,* June 10, 1995, 1615.

The Civil Rights Act only spurred the determination of many southern whites to protect white skin privilege by any means possible. Within days of Johnson's signing of the bill, three Mississippi civil rights workers were reported missing. Three months later, the bodies of James Chaney, Andrew Goodman, and Michael Schwerner were found buried beneath a dam near Philadelphia, Mississippi.

It was not only southern whites that opposed change. A poll conducted in 1963 found 64 percent of whites believed that blacks were moving "too fast" in their quest for equality; and in 1964 only 30 percent of whites wanted blacks to have more influence in government. Perhaps the most visceral symbol of how far some northern whites were willing to go in their defense of white privilege was in the outpouring of support for the proudly racist governor of Alabama, George Wallace, in several presidential primaries in 1964. Wallace won 34 percent of the vote in the Wisconsin primary, 30 percent in Indiana, and 45 percent in Maryland, Yet, as Lyndon Johnson's landslide victory would demonstrate, white resistance was not yet strong enough to forestall advances in civil rights and other social polices.[37]

Constraining de Jure Privileges of Whiteness and an Emerging New Politics

By the end of the 1960s, the legal basis of white privilege had been seriously eroded by three civil rights laws. The 1964 law made it a federal crime to apply a literacy or other voting test in a racially discriminatory way, even if the test itself made no mention of race or color. Literacy tests were required to be in writing and to be preserved so that discrimination in their use could be discovered and proved. The law mandated that voting rights cases could have prompt hearings in a special federal court to prevent the delays that had made earlier actions fruitless.

But the 1964 act attended to far more than voting: its mandates attacked three other major areas of discrimination directly: segregation in public facilities, discrimination in jobs, and discrimination in schools. Thus, for the first time since 1875, Congress made unlawful any private discrimination against blacks in hotels, restaurants, theaters, sports arenas, gasoline stations, and all other public accommodations affecting or affected by interstate commerce. No longer would civil rights protections be left to the chance successes of scattered

37. Klinkner and Smith, *Unsteady March*, 275–77.

individual suits brought by poor and vulnerable plaintiffs and the financially strapped organizations that represented them. For the first time, the United States government was given the power to intervene directly to ensure recognition of the constitutional rights of all its citizens in every state.

Most important, the 1964 act set up mechanisms to ensure compliance, including the withdrawal of federal funding. Since local schools and hospitals, especially in the South, tended to be desperate for financial assistance, this one provision could be more effective than any other in forcing at least an ostensible end of discriminatory practices.

The provision outlawing both racial and sexual discrimination in employment in businesses engaged in interstate commerce initially applied only to those businesses with a labor force of more than 100 persons; it was to be extended gradually to employers of 25 or more. Labor unions as well as employers were subject to the provisions, but the enforcement mechanisms were mild, relying heavily on citations, negotiations, and the use of state legislation and agencies.

Finally, the act gave the attorney general authority to initiate or intervene in suits to enforce school desegregation as well as to protect other civil rights. The commissioner of education was instructed to make a study of racial segregation at each educational level throughout the United States and to give technical assistance to schools in the process of desegregation. Funds were authorized to give training to educators in methods to accomplish desegregation smoothly.[38]

Supporters of the hard-fought bill claimed not only that it was the most important piece of legislation concerning equal opportunity ever passed by Congress, but also that it would be the backbone of efforts to eliminate discrimination throughout American society and actually guarantee people of color equal opportunity. By allowing private litigation, it was thought, the bill would make every victim a monitor and put enforcement potential in the hands of those with intimate knowledge of workplaces, educational institutions, and public accommodations. As polls showed, civil rights moved to the top of the nation's list of important issues;[39] and as the vote for the 1964 act revealed, civil rights had strong bipartisan support in Congress. Consequently, many

38. Lacy, *White Use of Blacks*, 198–99.
39. For poll results, see Edmund S. Ions, *The Politics of John F. Kennedy* (New York: Barnes & Noble, 1967), 174.

looked in the mid-1960s to a new and nearly universal consensus on the nation's historically most contentious issue: race.

Yet in reality the votes on the Civil Rights Act of 1964 in both bodies of Congress revealed a sharp regional split: northern Democrats overwhelmingly in support, southern Democrats overwhelmingly opposed. Only one wing of the party had altered its historical position on civil rights. As the bitter fight at the 1964 Democratic Convention over seating the Mississippi Freedom Democratic Party would later make viscerally clear, the segregationist wing of the party was up for grabs by another force.

The 1964 Republican presidential nominee, Barry Goldwater, proved to be the first of a slew of Republican nominees who sought to be just such a force. Perhaps, as Edward Carmines and James Stimson conclude, Goldwater, with his preference for a minimalist government in domestic affairs, had much more in common with classical liberals of the nineteenth century than with twentieth-century white supremacists, with their preference for a strong state to guarantee the separate and unequal treatment for America's two most obviously unequal races. But what mattered most to many white southerners who supported Goldwater was that a limited role for the federal government would allow those "governments closest to the people," southern states and localities, to continue the policies and practices that bolstered white skin privilege.[40]

Thus when Goldwater's campaign highlighted his opposition to the landmark 1964 act—he was one of only eight senators outside the South to vote against it—he became a magnet for white southerners. Strengthening his appeal to segregationists was the racial conservatism embodied in the Republican platform. Goldwater's 1964 strategy meant the Republican Party was going where the ducks were, and for them the ducks were southern segregationists at a time when Johnson's strong backing for civil rights converted a healthy black majority for the Democrats into a nearly unanimous bloc for decades to come. Indeed, in just four years, 1960–64, blacks' identification with the Democrats went from 58 percent to 82 percent. It had been only 44 percent in 1936 and 56 percent in 1948.[41]

40. Carmines and Stimson, *Issue Evolution,* 47.
41. The 1936–56 data are from Everett Carll Ladd Jr. and Charles D. Hadley, *Transformations of the American Party System: Political Coalitions from the New Deal to the 1970s* (New York: Norton, 1975), 60 and 112; the 1960–64 data are from Paul R. Abramson, John H. Aldrich, and David W. Rohde, *Change and Continuity in the 1984 Elections* (Washington, D.C.: Congressional Quarterly Press, 1986), 213.

The 1964 election was a landslide for LBJ. Goldwater won the electoral votes of only six states (five in the Deep South—Mississippi, Alabama, South Carolina, Louisiana, and Georgia) by large margins, the first time Republicans had won these states since Reconstruction, when Confederates could not vote. But if Goldwater represented the future of what would become known in Nixon's 1968 campaign as the "southern strategy," he also completely severed the African Americans' tie to the Republican Party. Forty percent of African Americans had voted for Dwight Eisenhower in 1956, nearly a third for Nixon in 1960, less than 10 percent for Goldwater. Thus 1964 marked a decisive turning point in the political evolution of racial issues: Republicans turned their backs on 100 years of racial leadership; the historical party of slavery became the home for nearly all blacks. As Carmines and Stimson conclude, the 1964 presidential election transformed American politics for decades to come. Public opinion shifted dramatically. As late as 1962, polls showed the public found little difference between the two parties on issues of race, but by 1964, 60 percent said Democrats were more likely to favor "fair treatment in jobs for blacks"; only 7 percent cited the Republicans.[42] In 1964, race, party, and state became much more intimately linked than class, party, and state, a development with major consequences for the coalition-building potential of the two major parties in a fundamentally racist state.

After the 1964 election, partisan differences on civil rights widened. Spurred by the march from Selma to Montgomery for voting rights and by Governor Wallace's bullying response, and also by the Democratic Party's need to compensate for defections of southern whites, Johnson pressed ahead on civil rights. Voting had not been fully dealt with in the 1964 act, and it became the next arena of action. On August 6, 1965, Johnson signed the Voting Rights Act, which recognized unlawful restrictions wherever literacy tests or similar devices had been employed in 1994 and fewer than half of persons of voting age had cast ballots. In the jurisdictions so identified (Alabama, Georgia, Louisiana, Mississippi, South Carolina, Virginia, and twenty-six counties in eastern North Carolina), all literacy tests and similar devices were forbidden, and federal registrars could be appointed to register all those who sought to vote. No new electoral tests or devices could be adopted unless submitted to and approved by the attorney general. Even in areas not so identified, the Justice

42. Carmines and Stimson, *Issue Evolution,* 45–47.

Department was given full authority to intervene or to initiate actions to ensure the voting rights of African Americans. Puerto Ricans were also aided by a provision that anyone who had completed the sixth grade of a school under U.S. jurisdiction should be presumed to be literate, whatever the language of instruction. For the first time, any person of color who wanted to register and vote had a realistic opportunity to do so. Because voting was totally under public control and because the system of federal registrars was under centralized national direction, it was possible to enforce the antidiscrimination provisions of this act far more completely than those of the 1964 Civil Rights Act relating to housing, employment, public accommodations, and education. The Department of Justice began to make good Johnson's promise of implementation of voting rights from the start.[43] Concomitantly, as the historian Stephen Lawson reported, "on the first anniversary of the passage of the Voting Rights Act, an average of 46 percent of adult blacks in the five Deep South states to which examiners had been assigned could vote, thereby doubling the percentage from the year before."[44]

Then in 1966 Johnson went further. Responding to the open-housing campaign begun by the SCLC in Chicago in early 1965 and white Chicagoans' violent demonstrations against it, Johnson asked Congress for legislation to ban discrimination in housing. Eliminating housing discrimination was viewed as key to progress in other areas. Residential segregation defeated efforts to integrate schools and impeded equal employment opportunity programs, especially in the rapidly growing suburban plants and in service and white-collar jobs. The action to produce fair housing policy did far more than the Civil Rights Act of 1964 or the Voting Rights Act of 1965 to bring the movement home to the North.

Indeed in the North, housing segregation was at the heart of racial inequality in the 1960s and it produced heated conflict. More than half the new industrial buildings, stores, hospitals, and schools were built outside inner cities between 1954 and 1965. In 1966 twenty states had fair housing laws and legislation was pending in ten more, but a white backlash against fair housing was gaining ground in big cities across the North. In California, voters passed Proposition 14 in 1966, repealing that state's fair housing laws, and the

43. Lacy, *White Use of Blacks*, 201, 255.
44. Stephen F. Lawson, *Black Ballots: Voting Rights in the South, 1944–1969* (New York: Columbia University Press, 1976), 330.

debate brought down Governor Pat Brown, whose Republican opponent, Ronald Reagan, campaigned against fair housing legislation as "an infringement of one of our basic individual rights." Following the California victory, thirteen other states introduced similar legislation. For many whites, property rights superseded civil rights.[45] In fact, for all the equal rights laws on the books of northern states, whites and blacks lived with far less contact with one another in northern cities than in the rural areas and small towns of the South. It was the segregation in northern ghettos more than anything else that led the President's Commission to Investigate the Cause of Social Disorders (better known as the Kerner Commission) to conclude in 1968 that the United States was becoming two nations, one black and one white.

At first northern Republicans in Congress refused to support the fair housing measure and it failed in 1966. But LBJ reintroduced fair housing legislation in 1967, and this time it won. On April 11, 1968, after the assassination of Reverend King and a week of riots across the nation, LBJ signed the bill into law. Title VIII of the Civil Rights Act, the last of the series of major civil rights acts passed during the fifteen years following *Brown,* banned discrimination against anyone because of race, color, or national origin in the sale, rental, or financing of most housing units and brought millions of single-family homes owned by private individuals under federal fair housing law. The only exceptions were in connection with the sale or rental of individually owned single-family houses without the use of a real estate agent and the rental of a room or apartment in what was essentially a private home. The housing bill was plagued, however, by weak enforcement mechanisms and depended on state and local agencies and voluntary cooperation. It should also be noted that while the principal thrust of the act aimed at lessening discrimination and segregation in housing, it also increased the powers of the federal government to deal with riots and disorder.[46]

Taken as a group, the three major civil rights acts of the 1960s challenged white skin privilege and advanced the potential for full inclusion of people of color. In fact, there is no denying that the series of judicial decisions and federal statutes, many of them paralleled by state legislation, constituted a major legal revolution. Until 1954, in the states in which most African Americans lived,

45. Jill Quadagno, *The Color of Welfare: How Racism Undermined the War on Poverty* (New York: Oxford University Press, 1994), 98.
46. Lacy, *White Use of Blacks,* 202–3.

white skin privilege was not only de facto but de jure. Whatever the pretenses of complying with the "separate but equal" provision of *Plessy v. Ferguson*,[47] the separate arrangements made for whites a vastly superior existence. Front of the bus symbolized white skin privilege; back of the bus, black subordination. Southern states, with the acquiescence of the federal government, required white racial preference in all aspects of life. Both employers and labor unions practiced affirmative action for whites by barring African Americans from all but the meanest jobs; white owners and brokers of real estate saved the best for whites; white custom preserved key social circles for whites. All of these actions protecting white skin privilege expressed the sense of southern communities in particular and had the police to enforce them.

Thus civil rights policy, in its formal expression, had diametrically reversed itself in fifteen years. By 1968, white skin privilege had been challenged in law in a way it had not been since the demise of the Freedmen's Bureau and the end of Reconstruction. The next job would be to lessen the additional burdens of economic inequality. This was the role of the Great Society.

The Great Society's Attempt to Be Inclusive

As the transformation of civil rights proved to be a predicate for reconstruction of the Democratic and Republican parties, the transformation of the American party system became a predicate for alterations in the New Deal system more generally. To a substantial extent, these conversions were facilitated by electoral arrangements and economic conditions in the 1960s.

On the electoral side, there was a president who could claim a mandate for change. LBJ's 61 percent of the popular vote exceeded even FDR's 1936 triumph over Alfred Landon; indeed, it was the greatest landslide since the popular vote was first counted nationally in 1832. Moreover, on Johnson's coattails came huge Democratic congressional majorities: 68 of the 100 Senate seats, 295 of the 435 House seats.[48] These large political majorities go a long way toward explaining why Johnson leaped into the high-stakes game in transforming the nation's social policy.

---

47. 163 U.S. 537 (1896).
48. "Fulfilling the Great Society," *Congressional Quarterly Weekly Report*, June 10, 1995, 1616.

On the economic side, the strength of the American economy was a key source of the amazing optimism that characterized the period and facilitated change. In the 1960s, the United States was the most powerful nation in the world by virtually every conceivable measure. Not only the key military superpower, the nation enjoyed steady growth in the gross national product (GNP) and comparatively low rates of unemployment and inflation. It was a time that fitted Aristide Zolberg's definition of "moments of madness," when not just a few thought "all was possible."[49] The United States could actually abolish poverty, if it tried.

After November 1963, now president in his own right, Johnson was clearly caught up in that wave of optimism. Thus, not surprisingly for a president who hailed in his first State of the Union address "the excitement of great expectations" and who described the "Great Society" he wanted to build as "a place where the city of man serves not only the needs of the body and the demands of commerce but the desire for beauty and the hunger for community," not "the changeless, and sterile battalion of the ants," LBJ promised to wage an "unconditional war on poverty." The very sweep of the programs, however, show that in Johnson's view no one, no group, no class would be left out of progress. In fact, however, much of the Great Society initiative was intended for the advantage of the white middle class. The members of the white middle class concerned about automobile safety would get government regulations on seat belts; those who could afford to visit a national park would have parks protected; those who longed for more in-depth news would be able to switch on *All Things Considered;* more important, those covered by social insurance would see their benefits rise; those getting fringe benefits would be treated more favorably by tax laws—all products of the talents of government put to solving social problems and to establishing what Johnson called "a creative federalism between the National Capitol and the leaders of local communities."[50] In short, the programs he sought to create reflected a postscarcity sensibility and a psychology of abundance—the idea that within the vast riches of America lay the possibility that each citizen could have an equitable share.

The sweep of Johnson's ambition was the most far-reaching since the

---

49. Aristide Zolberg, "Moments of Madness," in Ira Katznelson and Aristide Zolberg, eds., *Working-Class Formation: Nineteenth-Century Patterns in Western Europe and the United States* (Princeton: Princeton University Press, 1986).

50. Quoted in "Fulfilling the Great Society," 1615.

dawn of the New Deal. He demanded the first national health insurance for the aged, the first massive federal assistance for education, the first stiff controls on polluters, the first federal patronage of the arts and broadcasting. He called for aid to cities, to the poor, to the police, to small farmers, to Appalachia. And, decrying racial injustice, he pledged "equal rights for Negroes" if the United States were truly to be a great society and Americans a great people. If America did not meet the challenge of equal rights for blacks, it would "have failed as a people and as a nation," even if it defeated every enemy, doubled its wealth, and conquered the stars.[51]

To fulfill his promises, Johnson knew he had to move quickly. He might have won by 16 million votes, he said, but the total was inflated by Goldwater's extremism, and his popular support was sure to subside. "So I want you guys to get off your asses and do everything possible to get everything in my program passed as soon as possible," he told his congressional lobbying team.[52]

Johnson also understood that building his governing coalition required a structural project involving efforts to alter the government's capacities in ways that locked in the coalition's agenda and facilitated further transfers in the future. Political rules and institutions would have to be changed in ways that advanced his policy action.

One immediate task was to find institutional ways to deal with his biggest obstacle: southern Democrats. Although the House Rules Committee had lost its iron grip in 1961, Chairman Howard W. Smith of Virginia was still a powerful enemy not only of civil rights bills but also of federal aid to education (inspiring the in-house slogan "no rules for schools"). On the Ways and Means Committee, the folksy, Harvard-trained Wilbur Mills of Arkansas was at the peak of his power. His committee was known as the graveyard for Medicare and other welfare reforms. Understandably, an immediate objective of the administration was to neutralize southern committee chairs. Thus in the first days of the new Congress, liberal House Democrats—watched by 1,400 senior citizens bused in from across the country—set out to tether the committee barons. They gave the Speaker new power to circumvent the Rules Committee if it stalled legislation for more than twenty-one days. Ways and Means, which traditionally had allotted fifteen of its twenty-five seats to the majority, saw its

51. Ibid., 1616.
52. Ibid.

ratio altered to 18 to 7, with all the new Democratic seats going to pro–Great Society members. To warn southerners in general, the majority stripped of their seniority two Democrats who had openly supported Goldwater in 1964.

Johnson's legislative strategy was remarkably successful. All told, 181 of 200 bills requested by his administration were enacted. His only significant defeats came on his push for home rule for the District of Columbia and for the repeal of the section of the Taft-Hartley labor law that protected state right-to-work laws.[53]

Among the 181 bills passed after the civil rights revolution, those that were at the heart of the War on Poverty had the greatest impact on politics and policy during the Johnson years. The Economic Opportunity Act of 1964, passed even before Johnson was elected in his own right, initiated the War on Poverty and poured resources for community development, job training, and housing into local communities. While the New Deal and the privatized welfare benefits won by organized labor in the 1940s and 1950s failed to address the status of African Americans in any fundamental way, the War on Poverty targeted African Americans for inclusion.

The core antipoverty program was community action, which was under the jurisdiction of the new Office of Economic Opportunity (OEO). The OEO, in turn, delegated responsibility to Community Action Agencies (CAAs). CAAs established neighborhood health centers, emergency food and medical services, job and literacy training, counseling for alcoholics, drug rehabilitation, and other assistance efforts. They also fed resources into local civil rights organizations, which used these resources to pursue the struggle for political equality.[54] The central idea of the CAAs was that each city and rural area would devise its own "community action program," to be planned and carried out by agencies in which the poor themselves played an active role. The belief—"maximum feasible participation," it was called—was that the citizens of each locality, especially those who were themselves suffering poverty, would best know what particular ways of using federal funds would most effectively meet local problems. Perhaps even more important, it was thought that the responsible participation of the poor would in itself help to restore hope and dignity and commitment. As Johnson explained it, "I propose a program which relies on

53. Ibid., 1617.
54. Jill Quadagno, "Race and American Social Policy," *National Forum*, Summer 1996, 35.

the traditional time-tested American methods of organized local community action to help individuals, families, and communities to help themselves."[55]

This attempt to empower the poor and expand local citizenship was by far the most innovative and the most controversial element in the economic opportunity programs since it most directly challenged white elite privilege. The very participation of the black poor in planning and managing community action programs was feared and resisted by local politicians and most city officials, who saw it as undercutting their own authority and diminishing the power they hoped to gain by granting or withholding at their own discretion the boons of the poverty program. This concern was heightened by programs that provided legal advice and services to the poor, the more so since many of their complaints were against local governments and welfare agencies for discriminatory treatment. In addition, wherever CAAs began militantly to organize the poor as a meaningful political force, able to affect the outcomes of elections and the distribution of power within the community, the opposition of local officials and the caution of national grant-making officers grew.[56]

A second focus of the War on Poverty, education and job training, ultimately led to affirmative action. The principal efforts of the slew of education and training programs were based on the conviction that inadequate basic education and related vocational skills were the principal causes of poverty, white as well as black. The goal was to equip the no longer needed unskilled labor force to play a more productive role in the booming high-tech economy. Three groups became the targets: preschool children who might enter first grade already disadvantaged by the meagerness of their experience with language and the behavior patterns expected in school; talented youth of poor families who could benefit from a college education but would not attain it without counseling and financial aid; and unemployed adolescents and young adults who lacked the experience and skills to enter the workforce.

Operation Head Start became the key programmatic thrust of the view that preschool experiences could give poor children skills to compete on an equal footing in elementary school. A special effort was made to give vocabulary and speech training that would ready the children for reading. At the other end of the schooling spectrum, an Upward Bound program was created to

---

55. Quoted in James L. Sundquist, "Origins of the War on Poverty," in James L. Sundquist, ed., *On Fighting Poverty: Perspectives from Experience* (New York: Basic Books, 1969), 23.
56. Lacy, *White Use of Blacks*, 238–39.

encourage high school students from poor families to apply for college admission and to prepare them for a successful college experience. For other adolescents and young adults, two programs were planned: the Neighborhood Youth Corps, funded under the Economic Opportunity Act but administered by the Labor Department, and the Jobs Corps. The former attempted to give teenagers training and job experience while they lived at home; the latter removed older youths from their homes for several months of training in a residential center to focus on remedial education in reading and mathematics and development of specific job skills. The Jobs Corps concentrated on the most difficult cases, not youths with good school records who needed only specific vocational training or young adults who were the victims of technological unemployment who had been good workers and needed only new skills, but rather school dropouts who not only had no employable skills but had never known the discipline of continuous work in the regular job market. The program was considered to be expensive; Congress came to view it with disfavor; and some communities resisted Jobs Corps centers in their neighborhoods. As a result the Jobs Corps enrolled relatively few trainees a year and was never able to reach a large proportion of youth desperately in need of training.

What was most significant for the new education and job training programs created in the 1960s was that they targeted African American children and youths and refocused federal attention not just on skills improvement and employers but also on unions, especially craft unions. The focus on unions was an outgrowth of the difficulties in placing the newly trained African American youths in jobs. By 1968 African Americans, although 11 percent of the population, constituted 47 percent of the Neighborhood Youth Corps, 81 percent of the Concentrated Employment Programs, and 59 percent of the Job Corps. Yet, as poor African American men in particular moved out of federal job-training programs and into the labor market, their inability to obtain employment made visible the protections for white men erected by the unions.[57]

At first the Johnson administration merely encouraged the unions to comply with Title VII of the Civil Rights Act of 1964, which banned discrimination in employment on the basis of race and prohibited discrimination in union membership. When the unions continued to discriminate, Johnson issued Executive Order 11246 in 1965, requiring each nonexempt contractor

57. Quadagno, "Race and American Social Policy," 35–36.

or subcontractor to take "affirmative action" and created the Office of Federal Contract Compliance (OFCC; since 1975 Office of Federal Contract Compliance Programs, or OFCCP) to administer the order. In 1967 he issued Executive Order 11375 to include sex as a protected category under affirmative action.

In a very real sense affirmative action was not a novel approach. Indeed, it had been prefigured for over a hundred years by at least one relatively popular program: veterans' preference. Veterans' preference had been customary as far back as the patronage-ridden civil service under President Andrew Jackson. It was coded into law under Abraham Lincoln as part of the generous provisions accorded to Civil War veterans.[58] Over time, veterans' preferences had been enshrined not only in federal law but in forty-seven state laws. They had become relatively uncontroversial and protected by the courts. In most states and in the federal government, veterans and wives of veterans who took civil service examinations simply, openly, and directly had 10 points added to their scores if they were disabled and 5 points otherwise. It did not matter whether a veteran had ever seen action on the battlefront or had served his entire duty at a desk or in a kitchen. Clearly the wives' preferences were not based on any unusual personal service to the nation. All one needed to be to get the preference was a veteran or spouse of a veteran. Moreover, after the bonus points were added, veterans were preferred over nonveterans with equal scores in several states. In addition, since the Veterans Preference Act of 1944, veterans were exempted from minimum educational requirements, antinepotism regulations, layoffs, and so forth. As we have seen, under the GI Bill veterans also had their own home loan program through the Veterans Administration (VA). Since 1944, the VA operated like the FHA, insuring low-interest, long-term loans for the purchase of single-family homes, usually in segregated neighborhoods.[59] As John David Skrentny concludes, outright preferences for veterans have been naked, not hidden by nebulous terms such as "affirmative action," and yet there has been little resistance to them.[60]

Despite centuries of racial exclusion and oppression of people of color, nothing so dramatic was planned for affirmative action. There was no plan to

---

58. Theda Skocpol, *Protecting Soldiers and Mothers: The Political Origins of Social Policy in the United States* (Cambridge: Belknap/Harvard University Press, 1992).

59. Quadagno, *Color of Welfare*, 90.

60. John David Skrentny, *The Ironies of Affirmative Action: Politics, Culture, and Justice in America* (Chicago: University of Chicago Press, 1996), 38–60.

automatically award blacks, any other racial minorities, or women 5 or 10 extra points or to exempt them from educational requirements because of their past sacrifices or because of the discrimination openly practiced against them at least until the mid-1960s. Neither the unrecompensed work of the enslaved, their sacrifice of freedom, and the role they played in building the American economy nor more than half a century more of Jim Crow would entitle African Americans to the kind of special consideration and compensation for past sacrifice that went to veterans.

Still, the nebulous proposal for affirmative action was clearly within the legacy of veterans' preferences. The federal government was using a tool within its experience. Thus, from its inception, affirmative action presented no sharp break with the American past of rewarding or making up for past sacrifice. What was novel was that the policy presented a modest challenge to the system of white preference in regard to desired values and positions of affluence and influence in American society. What was significant and controversial in Executive Orders 11246 and 11375 was not their hint of awarding preferences but awarding them to people of color and women.

As administered by the OFCC, Executive Orders 11246 and 11375 required that all employers with federal contracts must file written affirmative action plans with the government. Moreover, the OFCCP, which regulated about one-third of private employment, could intervene pro-actively to reduce barriers to minority and women's employment. Plans could be either mandatory or voluntary, however, since many institutions might adopt voluntary plans to gain or retain federal contracts or to enhance their social and political status. These measures were needed, Johnson argued in a speech at Howard University in 1965, if the nation was ever to fully transcend the exclusion "because of race or color—a feeling whose dark intensity is matched by no other prejudice in our society."[61]

When the emphasis on desegregating unions was added in 1968, taking affirmative action meant proving that minorities would be represented in all trades on the job and in all phases of the work. Under the new regulations, the Equal Employment Opportunity Commission (EEOC) could require all unions to report on whether they were complying with affirmative action and then

---

61. Lyndon Johnson, "To Fulfill These Rights," in Lee Rainwater and William Yancey, eds., *The Moynihan Report and the Politics of Controversy* (Cambridge: MIT Press, 1967), 127.

decide whether the union was discriminating. If the union was, the EEOC could turn the case over to the attorney general to bring a civil suit against the offenders.

The requirement for both employers and unions to take affirmative action meant that for the first time in the history of the African experience in the United States, the federal government committed itself not just to enacting new rules that promoted fairness and justice from that point into the future, but mandated actions to correct the injustices of the past. In effect, it was seeking to overturn historical forces that had worked over time to benefit whites. It was precisely the gains accrued as a result of racism and the system of white preference that put whites in a unique position and made white workers both oppressors and exploited. Affirmative action, however, threatened to end the "gentleman's agreement" between employers and unions that bolstered the accumulated privileges of white workers.

A third focus of the War on Poverty was increasing housing for the poor and improving the quality of life in inner cities. Toward this end, the department of Housing and Urban Development (HUD) and its Model Cities program, enacted in 1968, were created to provide more and better housing for the poor and put local housing authorities under HUD's jurisdiction. The newly developed HUD was authorized to handle specific cases of housing discrimination and a broad range of affirmative action activities. Both Model Cities and HUD signaled the nation that urban aid would have a special place at the federal level. In practice, however, HUD was more often than not unwilling to take on local recalcitrants, and in general working through city governments made undoing the New Deal's segregationist legacy in housing difficult or impossible.

Other key reform targets were in the areas of health care and education. In 1965 the Medicaid and Medicare programs were created to improve health care for the poor and elderly, and the Elementary and Secondary Education Act brought the federal government into the business of directly aiding local school districts for the first time and helped financially strapped districts especially. To be sure, these were relatively costly programs, but the Johnson administration, like Kennedy's before it, assumed that services could be used to train, educate, and in other ways assist poor people in finding full-time employment; in turn these full-time employees would pay taxes. Thus federal outlays for education, employment training, social services, and health services (exclusive of Medicaid) directed to the poor increased from $883 million in fiscal year 1964 to almost $7 billion in fiscal 1969. Outlays for cash and in-kind transfers increased from $3.2 billion to $7.4 billion during the same period.[62]

Among the public aid outlays was significant new spending on food stamps and AFDC. Although the Department of Agriculture had been distributing commodities for decades (mainly as a way to help farmers eliminate surpluses), the Food Stamp Act was signed into law in 1964 both to enable poor families to purchase more healthy foods and to boost demand for agricultural products. The average number of monthly participants in the food stamp program grew rapidly, from 366,800 in 1964 to 2,878,800 in 1969.[63]

Beneficiaries of AFDC followed a similar pattern. From 588,000 in 1960, the numbers grew by more than half to 903,000 in 1966; and they would rise still faster so that millions were obtaining aid by the turn of the decade.[64] As with food stamps, blacks were overrepresented among AFDC recipients in substantial part because of higher rates of extreme poverty.

Despite all the later complaints that the Great Society expanded black "dependency" on AFDC, this is one arena in which new and more generous policies may not have had substantial influence, either negative or positive. In fact, despite the rise in AFDC rolls, the main AFDC policies enacted during the Great Society were aimed at compelling recipients to enter the labor market; eligibility requirements were made more difficult in the hope of reducing the number of recipients. AFDC-UP was created to include unemployed fathers, who became obligated "to accept job referrals in order to remain eligible since in those families the mother would be able to remain home to care for her child." In 1962, Community Work and Training programs were developed primarily for unemployed fathers.[65] WIN sought to encourage welfare recipients to work for wages by disregarding their income. In late 1967 Congress enacted a series of amendments to the Social Security Act directly intended to slow the rise in

---

62. Lacy, *White Use of Blacks,* 240.

63. Kenneth Finegold, "Agriculture and the Politics of U.S. Social Provision: Social Insurance and Food Stamps," in Margaret Weir, Ann Shola Orloff, and Theda Skocpol, eds., *The Politics of Social Policy in the United States* (Princeton: Princeton University Press, 1988), 223. In succeeding years, food stamps rose even faster.

64. Frances Piven and Richard Cloward, *Poor People's Movements: Why They Succeed, How They Fail* (New York: Pantheon, 1977), 274–75.

65. Eileen Boris, "When Work Is Slavery," in Gwendolyn Mink, ed., *Whose Welfare?* (Ithaca, N.Y.: Cornell University Press, 1999), 38–40.

AFDC rolls. States were required to establish job training and referral programs for recipients identified as "employable." To receive assistance, these recipients were to be compelled to enter the training and referral programs. To ensure that states would attempt to cut the rolls, in 1967 Congress enacted a freeze on AFDC reimbursements: each state's reimbursement would depend on the number of AFDC children as a proportion of all children in the state as of January 1967. This meant that a state with a rising ratio of children in impoverished female-headed families, regardless of the cause, would be obliged either to raise more of its own revenues to pay the cost of the increased caseload or to spread the federal money among a larger number of cases by lowering grant levels.

These measures went largely unenforced, however, as those on the local front line feared the political repercussions in poor neighborhoods (as well as the loss of the fruits of patronage) if large-scale efforts were made to force mothers and children off the rolls. Indeed, state and local officials vigorously protested the freeze. In response, the Johnson administration (and later Nixon's) postponed the effective date so long that the policy was forgotten.[66] Thus the huge increases in AFDC rolls had more to do with the activism of welfare rights advocates and the price that had to be paid to maintain or restore social acquiescence in the nation's inner cities than it did with new federal policy.

Moreover, as Figure 3.1 makes clear, black representation on AFDC rolls was rising sharply through Democratic and Republican administrations well before the Great Society was launched. In 1936, despite the much steeper levels of poverty among blacks, they composed only about 14 percent of those on ADC. The percentage had risen to 20 percent by 1942 and to 40 percent by 1960. Clearly black representation among AFDC beneficiaries continued to increase during the Great Society, rising to 45 percent by 1969 before it tapered off. It is not the Great Society that lies behind this pattern but demographic and state and local political factors. Higher levels of black migration out of the South in the 1940s and years later made it possible for more black women and their children to benefit from AFDC. As we have seen, the Social Security Act of 1935 structured public aid in such a way as to permit southern states to limit the number of black beneficiaries. Southern states had increasingly used the tactic of discretionary application of "suitable home" policies, giving caseworkers wide latitude to deny benefits to families with children born

66. Piven and Cloward, *Poor People's Movements,* 275.

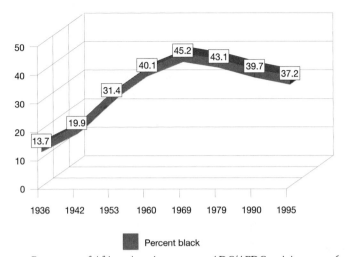

Figure 3.1. Percentage of African Americans among ADC/AFDC recipients, 1936–1995

SOURCE: Data for 1936–53 are from Bobbie Green Turner, *Federal/State Aid to Dependent Children in America, 1935–1985* (New York: Garland, 1953); for 1960, from Frances Fox Piven and Richard Cloward, *Regulating the Poor: The Functions of Public Welfare* (New York: Vintage, 1971); and for 1969–1995, from U. S. House of Representatives, *Background Material and Data on Programs within the Jurisdiction of the Committee on Ways and Means, 1999* (the "Green Book") (Washington, D.C., 1999).

out of wedlock or to mothers even just believed to be engaged in illicit relationships. Such policies excluded African Americans disproportionately from ADC in the late 1930s. Migration out of the South eroded this denial of access to resources. The 1939 amendments, which disproportionately provided benefits to white widows, removed many of them from ADC rolls, thereby increasing the percentage of black women among those remaining.[67] Moreover, an increase in the federal matching-grant contribution to the ADC program from one-third to one-half of total state expenditures encouraged some southern states either to expand their coverage or to begin participating in the ADC program for the first time. In effect, during the Great Society, patterns of racial discrimination in the distribution in AFDC were reversed.[68] If the extension of AFDC to African American women and their children produced dependency, then white women who had been covered by and advantaged in the program for decades should have been the most dependent of all.

67. Martin Gilens, *Why Americans Hate Welfare* (Chicago: University of Chicago Press, 1999), 106.
68. Discussed in Brown, *Race, Money, and the American Welfare State,* 334.

To the extent that Great Society policies played a role in increasing black representation on AFDC rolls, it was due not to new policies but to a more equitable enforcement of old ones, especially in regard to eligibility requirements. Before the early 1960s, the number of AFDC cases did not reflect the size of the population eligible for assistance. Indeed, only a relatively small percentage of eligible families actually received AFDC because many eligible women did not apply or because officials arbitrarily denied them relief. By the mid-1960s, however, as advocates of welfare rights campaigned to extend public assistance and loosen eligibility requirements, the number and proportion of AFDC cases began to increase phenomenally. In essence, the "welfare explosion" of the 1960s developed from changing rates of use and eligibility standards, not new policy. As more eligible families applied for AFDC, increasing numbers of the "newly eligible" were women of color and their children—a development encouraged by the rights-conscious efforts of the civil rights movement, the War on Poverty, and the welfare rights movement.[69] Civil rights and legal services lawyers overturned "man in the house" rules and established a right to a fair hearing to prove eligibility for benefits.[70] Still, as Figure 3.1 demonstrates, although African Americans by 1969 made up a very substantial minority of AFDC beneficiaries, the proportion of blacks in the program had been growing steadily for decades and was almost as high in 1960 as it was in 1969. This evidence suggests that it was not the Great Society that produced higher numbers and proportions of blacks on the welfare rolls but a more just enforcement of eligibility requirements.

One major source of improvement for poor and low-income people of all races was a steadily rising minimum wage. The magnitude of the increase is easily demonstrated when one considers its value in constant dollars compared to the value of the minimum wage in earlier and later years. In 1996 dollars, the minimum wage in 1960 was $5.30 an hour; in 1968 it had risen to $7.21 (or a 36 percent increase) but by 1996 it had fallen to only $4.75.[71]

In sum, the Great Society, spurred by actions in the streets and courts of

69. Michael B. Katz, *The Undeserving Poor: From the War on Poverty to the War on Welfare* (New York: Pantheon, 1989), 48, 68.

70. Piven and Cloward, *Poor People's Movements*, 274–75.

71. U.S. Employment Standards Administration, <http://www.dol.gov/esa/minwage/main.htm>. Effective Sept. 1, 1997, the federal minimum wage rose to $5.15 ($5.03 in 1996 dollars.)

America, produced not only a new politics but a transformation of American social policy and the ideology of whiteness. The Great Society broke with Andrew Johnson's policies aimed at securing a "white man's country" and with the New Deal's insistent suppression of the "race issue." No longer were blacks counseled to be patient as they waited for universal programs to help them somewhere down the road; they were targeted for inclusion in the Great Society. Emphasis was no longer on the "dependency" of blacks but on the barriers erected against equal opportunity. No longer did the privileges of whiteness go unchallenged. In 1968 for the first time an American president gave a major address that spoke forthrightly of "the crippling legacy of bigotry and injustice," and concluded, arms raised and speaking slowly, with the words of the anthem sung by civil rights marchers: "And . . . we . . . shall . . . overcome."[72] It was the Great Society that made an attempt to delegitimize white supremacy and thereby became a "new deal" for America's people of color. At the very least, the Great Society was a period in which some American political leaders turned their backs on brazen racism and support for an obdurate racial tyranny.

Achievements of the Great Society

Despite this signal achievement, by the 1980s it had become customary to write off the Great Society as a failure, to contend that its policies had fostered dependence on the state, nurtured irresponsible behavior, and led to the overall deterioration of inner-city communities. Is this view correct? How far did the Great Society succeed in more fully including people of color in the American welfare state, solving major socioeconomic problems, and challenging the advantages of whites?

Poverty statistics offer the best means of answering these questions. Conservatives contend that the federal government's efforts to help the poor during the 1960s were almost unlimited; that despite these efforts, poverty became more severe; and that the reason poverty increased is that well-meaning government programs backfired, leaving their intended beneficiaries worse off. The best available evidence contradicts such claims.

First, despite the massive increase in funding of social programs during the 1960s, the actual spending remained modest in relation to the enormity of the problem. This was especially true of programs run directly by the OEO.

72. "Fulfilling the Great Society," 1617.

During the first year of the OEO's operation, when Mayor John Lindsay of New York said that his city alone needed $10 billion annually for five years to solve its welfare problems, Congress allocated around $750 million (or approximately $30 for each poor American) for the entire nation—and the figure never reached even $2 billion a year during the life of the program.[73] As Whitney Young, NUL director, suggested to the Senate in 1967, the "scale on which the war on poverty is being conducted is far too limited to do much more than act as a palliative. Two billion dollars per annum is not enough to do the job. Fifty billion dollars would be more like it."[74] More radical observers, such as the Chicago activist Saul Alinsky, were harsher. Alinsky attacked the program as a "macabre masquerade" and a "prize piece of political pornography." In what was probably the most influential book on welfare in the period, Frances Piven and Richard Cloward concluded that the reforms were little more than a political response to political disorder, a way of "regulating the poor," not solving their problems.[75]

Indeed, it is hard not to be reminded of the fate of the Freedmen's Bureau. Like the Bureau, the OEO—the lead agency in the War on Poverty— was given an initial lease on life of only a year, was underfunded and understaffed throughout its history, and moved to extinction very rapidly. Michael Brown argues that fiscal conservatism and the needs of Democrats, more than Republicans, to demonstrate to business interests that they understood the dictates of capital accumulation explain these results. Limited targeted benefits, Brown maintains, were chosen "not for their moral or political attraction, but rather because they cost less than comprehensive and universal social policies."[76] Others suggest that the rising costs of "that other war, Vietnam," and the need to secure business approval for it sharply diminished the funds available for the War on Poverty.[77] Still clearly it was a matter of prioritization. As Martin Luther King Jr. argued, if the nation can spend "35 billion dollars a

73. Walter I. Trattner, *From Poor Law to Welfare State: A History of Social Welfare in America* (New York: Free Press, 1989), 323.

74. Testimony of Whitney M. Young Jr. before Senate Committee on Labor and Public Welfare, Subcommittee on Employment, Manpower, and Poverty, *Examination of the War on Poverty,* hearings on S. 1545 (pt. 7), 90th Cong., 1st sess. (June 8, 1967), 2195.

75. Frances F. Piven and Richard A. Cloward, *Regulating the Poor: The Functions of Social Welfare* (New York: Pantheon, 1971).

76. Brown, *Race, Money, and the American Welfare State,* 4.

77. Quadagno, *Color of Welfare,* 105, 145.

year to fight an unjust, evil war in Vietnam, and 20 billion dollars to put a man on the moon, it [could] spend billions of dollars to put God's children on their own two feet right here on earth."[78] There was never nearly the dramatic spending suggested by the overblown rhetoric of a "war" on poverty.

Nonetheless, despite the limited appropriations provided, poverty declined significantly. Overall, the antipoverty programs managed to cut the poverty rate from double digits in the 1960s to single digits in the early 1970s. As Table 3.1 shows, poverty among blacks shrank from 55.1 percent in 1959 to 30.3 percent in 1974 and among whites from 18.1 percent to 8.6 percent before it began to move back upward. In the space of one generation, government programs combined with economic growth had reduced poverty among Americans in general by more than half and among African Americans by nearly half. No other period since the Census Bureau began recording these data demonstrates such large declines in poverty. In fact, Table 3.1 shows that poverty rates actually crept upward immediately after the Great Society and did not begin to decline again until the 1990s. Even during the booming economy of the 1990s, the rate of decline in poverty was very modest compared to the rate of decline during the Great Society.

Despite this fact, some have argued that the dramatic decline was the result not of the Great Society but simply of a growing economy. To be sure, economic growth played an important role. Even before the War on Poverty, the roaring economy created by World War II had lifted millions of Depression-injured citizens out of poverty, and the boom created by pent-up demand after the war had continued to boost the country into unrivaled prosperity. From 1959 to 1964 the poverty rate had already declined by 3.4 percentage points.

But faster economic growth was certainly not the only or even the primary reason poverty was reduced. As John Schwarz demonstrates, when one considers all income except that transferred to individuals through government programs, census evidence for 1965 indicates that about 21.3 percent of the public would have been living in poverty. In 1972, again considering all sources of income except that received from government programs, census figures show that about 19.2 percent of the public would have been living in poverty, only about one-tenth fewer than in 1965. That is, if the private sector in these times

78. Quoted in Katz, *Undeserving Poor,* 54.

Table 3.1.   Poverty status of people by race, selected years, 1959–2001 (numbers in thousands as of March of the followng year)

| Year | Below poverty level | | | | Black/white ratio |
| | White | | Black | | |
	Number	Percent[1]	Number	Percent[2]	
1959	28,484	18.1	9,927	55.1	3.04
1966	19,290	11.3	8,867	41.8	3.70
1967	18,983	11.0	8,486	39.3	3.57
1968	17,395	10.0	7,616	34.7	3.47
1969	16,659	9.5	7,095	32.2	3.39
1970	17,484	9.9	7,548	33.5	3.38
1971	17,780	9.9	7,396	32.5	3.28
1972	16,203	9.0	7,710	33.3	3.70
1973	15,142	8.4	7,388	31.4	3.74
1974	15,736	8.6	7,182	30.3	3.52
1975	17,770	9.7	7,545	31.3	3.23
1980	19,699	10.2	8,579	32.5	3.19
1985	22,860	11.4	8,926	31.3	2.75
1990	22,326	10.7	9,837	31.9	2.98
1995	24,423	11.2	9,872	29.3	2.62
2000	21,645	9.5	7,982	22.5	2.37
2001	22,739	9.9	8,136	22.7	2.29

[1]Percent of total white population.
[2]Percent of total black population.
Source: U.S. Bureau of the Census, *Current Population Surveys*, Historical Poverty Tables, Table 2 <http://www.census.gov/hhes/poverty/histpov2.html>.

of substantial economic growth reduced the percentage of Americans living in poverty by about one in every ten Americans, and exclusive of government programs, even by 1972 almost one in five Americans would still have been living in poverty. Thus the economy's growth during these highly prosperous years alleviated poverty only marginally. Now consider the influence of government programs on poverty levels. As a result of the antipoverty programs, more than half of the remaining 19 percent of impoverished Americans rose above the poverty line, leaving about 10 percent of the American people below the poverty line by 1972.[79]

Note, however, that the declines in the poverty rates for African Americans were absolute, not relative. That is, whites remained substantially less

79. John Schwarz, *America's Hidden Success: A Reassessment of Twenty Years of Public Policy* (New York: Norton, 1983), 47.

likely than blacks to be part of the nonpoor. As Table 3.1 indicates, in 1959 blacks were three times more likely to be poor than whites; in the early 1970s, they were more than three and one-half times more likely than whites to be poor. The War on Poverty had remarkably reduced the proportion of Americans of all races who lived below the poverty line, but even it was not strong enough to make serious inroads into white advantage.

Beyond poverty per se, the Great Society programs of the 1960s and 1970s improved the lives of millions of Americans in many ways. The food stamp program reduced flagrant hunger and malnutrition. Medicare and Medicaid improved health care dramatically. In 1963 one of every five Americans who lived below the poverty line never had been examined by a physician, and poor people used medical facilities far less than others. By 1970 the proportion never examined had dipped to 8 percent, and the proportion of poor people who visited a physician annually was about the same as for everyone else. Between 1965 and 1972, poor women began to consult physicians far more often during pregnancy, and infant mortality dropped 33 percent.

Gains among African Americans were particularly evident. Between 1950 and 1965, before the great expansion in the federal medical and nutritional programs, the infant mortality rate of African Americans barely fell, from 44.5 per 1,000 births in 1950 to 40.3 in 1965. After the expansion of the programs, the rate of African American infant mortality declined relatively quickly, from 40.3 in 1965 to 20.9 in 1970 (though it rose to 24.2 in 1975). Thus there occurred about a fivefold increase in the speed of reduction in the African American infant mortality rate after 1965, a change about twice as pronounced as that occurring in the white population.

Similarly, housing programs lessened overcrowding and the number of people living in substandard housing. In 1950, 16 percent of American households lived in overcrowded housing; by 1960 the figure was about 12 percent, by 1970 about 9 percent, and by 1976 less than 5 percent. The figure for African American families residing in overcrowded housing was reduced by more than 50 percent between 1950 and 1970.[80]

The achievements of some service-based programs also deserve recognition. Operation Head Start helped thousands of poor children prepare for school; Upward Bound prepared large numbers of adolescents for college; and

80. Ibid., 47–50.

financial assistance permitted many young people from families with low or modest incomes to gain higher education. Among young adults (those 25 to 29 years old), 4.2 percent of blacks had completed four or more years of college in 1959; by 1976 that figure had tripled. The figure for whites in the same age cohort, 11.9 percent in 1959, doubled in the same period. Gains were especially significant for white and black women. As with poverty statistics, however, college graduation rates stagnated for whites and actually declined for blacks until the mid-1990s (Table 3.2).

It already has been indicated that Legal Services enabled welfare mothers to win and maintain welfare. Through class-action suits, Legal Services also played a role in expanding the rights of the poor in other key areas as well: landlord-tenant relations, state housing laws, consumer credit, Medicaid.[81]

Table 3.2.   Percentage of people 25–29 years old who completed college, by race, selected years, 1959–1998

	White			Black		
Year	Both sexes	Male	Female	Both sexes	Male	Female
1959	11.9%	15.9%	8.1%	4.2%	5.6%	3.7%
1966	14.7	17.9	11.8	5.9	5.4	6.4
1967	14.6	17.2	12.1	5.4	4.2	6.3
1968	15.6	19.1	12.3	5.3	5.3	5.3
1969	17.0	20.6	13.4	6.7	8.1	5.5
1970	17.3	21.3	13.3	7.3	6.7	8.0
1971	17.9	21.3	14.6	6.4	6.4	6.5
1972	19.9	23.1	16.7	8.3	7.1	9.4
1973	19.9	22.8	17.0	8.1	7.1	8.8
1974	22.0	25.3	18.8	7.9	8.8	7.2
1975	22.8	26.3	19.4	10.7	11.4	10.1
1976	24.6	28.7	20.6	13.0	12.0	13.6
1980	23.7	25.5	22.0	11.6	10.5	12.5
1985	23.2	24.2	22.2	11.5	10.3	12.6
1990	24.2	24.2	24.3	13.4	15.1	11.9
1994	24.2	23.6	24.8	13.7	11.7	15.4
1995	26.0	25.4	26.6	15.3	17.2	13.6
1996	28.1	27.2	29.1	14.6	12.4	16.4
1997	28.9	27.2	30.7	14.4	12.1	16.4
1998	28.4	26.5	30.4	15.8	14.2	17.0

SOURCE: U.S. Bureau of the Census, *Current Population Surveys*, Historical Education Tables, Table A <http://www.census.gov/population/socdemo/educaton/tablea-02.txt>.

81. See Martha Davis, *Brutal Need: Lawyers and the Welfare Rights Movement, 1960–1973* (New Haven: Yale University Press, 1993); and Elizabeth Bussiere, *(Dis)Entitling the Poor: The*

Similarly, despite the disappointing record of some job training and employment programs, jobs provided by some Job Corps centers and the Comprehensive Employment and Training Act (CETA) were important forms of work relief.[82]

Other programs had indirect benefits. Although the intergovernmental transfers to cities in the period did not directly benefit the urban poor or even appreciably stem white flight to the suburbs, they provided national recognition of the special fiscal burden cities bore because of the concentrations of poor Americans within their borders and, more important, an economic cushion that allowed for high levels of public services such as libraries, police protection, and infrastructural maintenance to improve the quality of urban life. Finally, Community Action, for all the conflicts it engendered, nourished and intensified a growing citizens' movement, reshaped local politics, bolstered self-help efforts, and launched a new generation of black leaders, many of them women, into public life. Indeed, in many places throughout the South, OEO staff supported organizations favoring civil rights objectives and denied funding to those linked to the white male power structure. Bypassing the local racial state, OEO grants undermined the patronage-based system of party politics, empowered racially integrated community organizations, and created new distribution networks. These networks, fostered by CAAs, introduced a profusion of resources into southern and northern poor communities, including such basics as telephones, office staff, stationery, newsletters, meeting places, and access to legal advice. They also brought organization by founding affiliated agencies, which became sources of jobs open to African Americans. Many of the country's ablest black politicians, male and female, got their first opportunities for leadership in community action programs, and the political experience they garnered had nearly immediate payoffs in black electoral power. When Johnson signed the Voting Rights Act and declared the War on Poverty, there were no black mayors and fewer than 500 black elected officials at any level of government in the nation as a whole. Five years later there were 1,469 black elected officials and 48 mayors and vice-mayors; by 1979, there were 4,607, including 175 mayors.[83] Many of the newly elected officials had gained visibility as well

---

Warren Court, Welfare Rights, and the American Political Tradition (University Park: Pennsylvania State University Press, 1997).

82. Katz, *Undeserving Poor*, 111–14.

83. Data supplied in telephone interview of Alfred Baltimore, Joint Center for Political and Economic Studies, July 1, 1997.

as experience in community action programs, where they campaigned for poverty boards, chaired meetings, lobbied, litigated, and delivered speeches. Thus Community Action succeeded in bolstering the extension of political rights to African Americans.

In short, African Americans were key beneficiaries of many of the programs of the Great Society, since they were disproportionately represented among the ranks of the ill housed, the poorly educated, the un- and underemployed, and the recipients of inferior health care. Great Society programs had pronounced impact on the inner cities, heavily populated by African Americans, since almost all federally funded social services were delivered through state and local governments. As a result of higher spending at all levels of government in the 1960s and early 1970s, public employment (federal, state, and local) increased by 7.2 million jobs.[84]

A substantial proportion of those new jobs went to African Americans and white women.[85] Michael Brown concludes that "employment gains made by white women and blacks of both genders during this period were by and large concentrated in directly or indirectly publicly-funded human services and social welfare programs. Over half of the net gain in African American employment between 1960 and 1976 was in the public sector, largely in social programs."[86] In 1960, 13.3 percent of the total employed African American labor force were working in federal, state, and local government jobs combined; since 1970 more than 20 percent of all African American workers in the United States were on public payrolls. By 1970 government employed truly staggering proportions of college-educated African Americans: 57 percent of all African American male college graduates and 72 percent of all African American female college graduates. Since 1970, almost one-quarter of employment

84. Public sector employment grew from 7.4 million in 1955 to 14.6 million in 1974 but by only 4.5 million in the next two decades (1975–95). U.S. Bureau of the Census, *Statistical Abstract of the United States: 1977*, Table 489; ibid., 2002, Table 449. See also Bureau of Labor Statistics, "Class of Worker of Longest Job by Race and Sex," Current Population Survey, 1960, 1970, 1996, Pin-C-10; and Michael K. Brown, "The Segmented Welfare System," in Brown, *Remaking the Welfare State: Retrenchment and Social Policy in America and Europe* (Philadelphia: Temple University Press, 1988), 194.

85. By 1975, while blacks composed 11% of the total adult population, they accounted for 15.4% of full-time state and local government employees. By 1979, before the Reagan revolution, blacks composed 22% of full-time state and local employees. U.S. Bureau of the Census, *Statistical Abstract of the United States: 2001*, Table 452.

86. Brown, "Segmented Welfare System," 194.

growth for African Americans occurred in the public sector while only slightly over a tenth of employment growth for whites occurred there.[87] Many African American professionals found jobs in federal agencies; still more found employment at the local and state levels, administering social service and welfare programs largely in areas where African American workers were being displaced by automation and suburbanization.[88] In essence, the expansion of the black middle class (as well as more employment for white women) was virtually propelled by the growth of human service jobs. The result was sharp improvement in the conditions for a growing African American middle class who staffed the new public sector jobs created by the programs. Data on black employment in the economy as a whole bolster the conclusion that progress was made in the 1960s on a magnitude far greater than in the immediate post–Great Society era. For instance, blacks composed 2.5 percent of the total employed workers in the broad professional and managerial category in 1960; in 1970, their representation had grown to 5.4 percent, but by 1980 blacks had gained only half a percentage point in this occupational category.[89]

Higher education and better occupational deployment contributed to modest income gains for African Americans during the 1960s (or conversely a slight decline in white advantage). In 1947 white income was double that of blacks. Between 1950 and 1965, white income hovered around 1.8 times that of blacks, declining during the premier decade of the Great Society to roughly 1.6 times that of blacks (Table 3.3). The white income advantage rose again in the immediate post–Great Society era to pre-1966 levels, and did not decline again until the mid- to late 1990s.

Income levels were also helped in all probability by the expansion of cash transfers during the Great Society. Both cash and in-kind transfers brought hundreds of thousands of poor white women and people of color into the American welfare state. At the same time, the proportion of women on welfare in the labor force, either intermittently or steadily, rose by 28 percent between 1967 and 1973.[90] Since the stipends going to these newly covered beneficiaries

87. Bureau of Labor Statistics, "Class of Worker."

88. Rifkin, *End of Work*, 77–79.

89. U.S. Bureau of the Census, *Sixteenth Decennial Census, 1960*, Table 205, p. 544; *Seventeenth Decennial Census, 1970*, Table 223, p. 739; and *Eighteenth Decennial Census, 1980*, Table 278, p. 196.

90. Brown, "Segmented Welfare System," 195. See also Brown, *Race, Money, and the American Welfare State*, 333–44. For a general discussion of the feminization of poverty and related data, see Katz, *Undeserving Poor*, 66–78.

Table 3.3.   Median income of families in constant 2001 dollars, by race, 1947–2001

Year	White	Black	White/black ratio
1947	21,250	10,864	1.96
1950	21,453	11,638	1.84
1955	25,797	14,227	1.81
1960	29,553	16,359	1.81
1965	34,553	19,028	1.82
1970	40,411	24,789	1.63
1975	41,376	25,458	1.63
1980	44,569	25,788	1.73
1985	45,742	26,339	1.74
1990	48,480	28,135	1.72
1991	47,888	27,311	1.75
1992	47,814	26,093	1.83
1993	47,410	25,987	1.82
1994	48,304	29,180	1.66
1995	49,191	29,956	1.64
1996	50,275	29,792	1.69
1997	51,421	31,457	1.64
1998	53,168	31,890	1.67
1999	54,411	33,744	1.61
2000	54,509	35,146	1.55
2001	54,067	33,598	1.61

SOURCE: U.S. Bureau of the Census, *Current Population Surveys,* Historical Income Tables, Families, Table F-6D, <http://www.census.gov/hhes/income/histinc/fo6d.html>.

were not adjusted for inflation, however, the new cash transfers lost their influence in the post–Great Society environment.

In sum, the Great Society represented a turning point. For the first time since Reconstruction, American social policy did not turn a deaf ear to the needs of blacks. For the first time, African Americans were targeted for inclusion. For the first time, white advantage suffered a modest setback. The 1960s may have come to be identified by many as a time when American values grounded in the American ethos and general moral principles decayed, but these negative valuations did not describe the 1960s African Americans knew. For African Americans, many other people of color, and white women, the 1960s represented a time when America actually became a more moral nation—more devoted to its constitutional principles and democratic ideals, even if only moderately more. For African Americans, the truly immoral America was the one that had enslaved a substantial minority of its people, oppressed this minority for decades more, and institutionalized racism so thoroughly that even when policies that appeared neutral on their face were enacted, they had discriminatory results. That America was the country of truly corrupt values. The Great Society represented a momentary break with the old immorality and corruption, and the break had material and psychological effects. It gave rise to a tremendous sense of hope and optimism in black communities South and North. On the basis of the progress made and the belief that their own efforts could persuade government to deliver more, many African Americans identified strongly with Dr. King's dream.

Some American observers apparently are myopic when it comes to just how pervasive suffering and poverty were before the growth of Medicaid, AFDC, and food stamps. The key problem was not that the Great Society programs did too much for people and induced bad behavior, but rather that much too little other than public transfers was done in poor communities. Public investment in jobs, education, and neighborhoods was diminished after 1968—roughly the same time that corporate disinvestment sucked a vast number of jobs out of these same communities. "Transfers replaced public and private investment," says Michael Brown, "and perversely became the basis for a racially-loaded narrative about the debilitating effect of federal [social policies] and the bankruptcy of the Great Society,"[91] when the real tragedy was that programs had not been tried long enough and given enough resources to produce greater change.

So was the Great Society a total success? No. Obviously it did not obliterate white advantage; there were rip-off artists attracted by its pots of money, as there were (and are) by other, far larger pots of government money (HUD in the 1980s; the Pentagon in the 1980s, the 1970s, the 1960s, and on back; the savings and loan associations after Reagan-Bush deregulation; and the oft-sanctioned corrupt practices of the top twenty-five largest federal contractors). Yet the programs still did an enormous amount of good and provided fuller inclusion for women and people of color in the nation's social policy regime than ever before. While the Great Society definitely did not alter the structure of the American welfare state, its accomplishments belie contemporary conventional accounts that either ignore or belittle the impressive achievements of the era. Indeed, nearly all the racial progress that conservatives celebrate resulted disproportionately in the period of the Great Society and from its programs.

91. Brown, *Race, Money, and the American Welfare State,* 226.

The expansion of public social benefits from 1964 to 1976 transformed the lives of millions of Americans, especially among people of color, and demonstrated the capacity of government as an agent of social change. White skin privilege remained the order of the day, but the vast economic gap between whites and people of color began to close.

Their progress was not only material but ideological. In an era in which legal equality was achieved, old-style racism was vigorously challenged. More than in any previous era of American history, Americans were encouraged by leading white political actors of the day to overcome the ideology and reality of whiteness. If, as a result, the 1960s were a time of unprecedented optimism for African Americans, many whites saw their relative advantages begin to decline and interpreted black progress as a key challenge to their collective interests.

Legacies and the Great Society

Of course, there are less sanguine ways to read the evidence on the Great Society. Poverty remained unacceptably high. Millions of Americans still lacked health insurance. Housing remained a major problem. Hunger was still a national disgrace, and urban education continued to be a disaster.

Moreover, despite racial progress, white advantage remained palpable, as the social indicators in Tables 3.1 to 3.3 demonstrate. Even when black education and income were growing, the proportion of unemployment suffered by blacks increased. Even the War on Poverty contributed more to the nonpoor than to the poor. The gains welfare offered the poor were undercut by the reverse redistributive effects of the good, nonwelfare programs. In the mid-1970s, 80 percent of the social welfare budget went to the nonpoor.[92] Social insurance programs got steadily better; OAI benefits were increased, adjusted for increases in cost of living, and extended to more beneficiaries, especially dependents. Hidden welfare benefits (especially tax expenditures for fringe benefits such as health insurance and pensions and tax benefits such as the mortgage interest deduction) demonstrated an even more dramatic rise in the real value of federal benefits for middle-class families. By contrast, the real value of

92. Sheldon Danziger, Robert Haveman, and Robert Plotnick, "Antipoverty Policy Effects on the Poor and Non-poor," in Sheldon H. Danziger and Daniel H. Weinberg, eds., *Fighting Poverty: What Works and What Doesn't* (Cambridge: Harvard University Press, 1986), 66–67.

public transfers such as AFDC payments steeply declined as caseloads rose—a development not offset by food stamps. And as early as the late 1960s, eligibility criteria began to exclude more of the poor.[93]

To a large extent, limitations on the success of the Great Society can be explained by those three powerful legacies of the Freedmen's Bureau and Civil War veterans' pensions: segmentation, the liberal individualism ethos, and white skin privilege. Locked in by the segmentation that characterized the first two legs of the American welfare state as embodied in the Social Security Act of 1935 and hidden welfare in the 1940s and 1950s, the Great Society, too, developed separate policy tracks for the "deserving" and "undeserving." The best example, of course, is Medicare with its far more generous benefits for the "deserving" and Medicaid with its relatively stingy benefits for the "undeserving," but in general benefits to middle-class and upper-working-class (mainly white) men and their dependents were greater, absolutely and proportionately, than contributions to the poor. In effect, the Great Society did not challenge segmentation, but rather added a third leg—one that disproportionately targeted the poor and in action became an agent for extending equal opportunity to people of color and white women. As Attorney General Nicholas Katzenbach put it to HEW Secretary Joseph Califano in the Carter years, federal social policies during the Great Society were fashioned to help "all disadvantaged persons," but "would permit, and should permit, the concentration of these programs in areas in which the beneficiaries would be predominately [black]."[94]

Three relatively separate systems (social insurance, hidden welfare, and public transfers) disproportionately served different race and gender constituencies. White men were most likely to be beneficiaries of the first two legs of welfare and people of color and white women beneficiaries of the third. In short, while in the 1960s other Western welfare states were introducing universal programs that protected all vulnerable families against poverty and economic insecurity, the American welfare state not only continued its meager ways, not only wove the social safety net into the world of private-sector work, but also became more segmented and fragmented.

By strengthening the stimulus to class, race, and gender inequality, segmentation increased the potential for a politics of resentment. Although the

93. Linda Gordon, *Pitied but Not Entitled: Single Mothers and the History of Welfare* (New York: Free Press, 1994), 302.

94. Quoted in Brown, *Race, Money, and the American Welfare State*, 266.

advantages accruing to white middle-class families were actually greater than those going to the poor, mapping race to the public transfers of the Great Society conveyed the impression that people of color were being singled out for special help. This tended to reproduce and even expand the political isolation of racial minorities and leave the programs viewed as benefiting them vulnerable to attack. By 1968, polls showed that a large majority of whites held unfavorable opinions of the War on Poverty.[95]

Although some have argued that it was the militancy of the black movement in the late 1960s and the fact that relief in this period went disproportionately to African Americans that turned whites against blacks,[96] history indicates that it was more likely the reverse: white attitudes toward blacks and their opposition to providing help to African Americans influenced their opinions of the War on Poverty. Since the days of the Freedmen's Bureau, white antipathy toward federal social policy had been grounded in racial views. In the New Deal, a combination of silence on race matters, disproportionate black exclusion from the superior welfare programs, and state control of the inferior programs as a route to providing aid on a discriminatory basis was required to get around legislative impasse. As every Social Science 101 student learns, for something to be causal, it must at the very least occur first. Neither the Great Society nor black militancy produced whiteness as ideology and property value; instead the Great Society was constrained in conception and in what it could accomplish by necessarily having to operate within the playing field already established by the American ethos and white skin privilege. White antipathy to federal social policy in general had deep roots in the American ethos and white antipathy to helping blacks in particular had always been justified by designating blacks as unworthy of assistance.

Thus the more whites thought the civil rights laws and the Great Society programs had actually achieved equality of opportunity and the more African Americans still were in actuality disproportionately impoverished and living in demeaning conditions, the more whites not only opposed the Great Society but felt entitled to whatever measure of economic success they had attained.[97] In

95. Margaret Weir, Introduction to *The Social Divide: Political Parties and the Future of Activist Government,* ed. Weir (Washington, D.C.: Brookings, 1998), 17.

96. Ibid.

97. John H. Garvey and T. Alexander Aleinikoff, *Modern Constitutional Theory: A Reader,* 3d ed. (St. Paul, Minn.: West, 1994), 500–501.

this way, white skin privilege combined with the myth of equality of opportunity to provide a rationalization for racial oppression, making it difficult for whites to see the plight of people of color as illegitimate or unnecessary.

In this way, segmentation and equal opportunity mythology deepened cracks in the welfare state in the 1960s. The most destructive splits were those between beneficiaries of the first and second legs of the welfare state—upper-working-class and middle-class whites—and those who got welfare in the third leg. As people with jobs in the organized and professional sectors increasingly relied on hidden welfare, they demonstrated greater hostility to those who had neither stable jobs nor benefits. In addition, since most people who benefited from hidden welfare had no understanding of how government subsidized their benefits through tax expenditures, such workers and professionals became more appreciative of and loyal to private corporations, not the state—a development that undercut support for activist government more generally. The superior social insurance programs as well as the hidden welfare leg of the welfare state appeared as rights and deserved benefits that increased a citizen's self-esteem and feeling of entitlement. By contrast, those who received public assistance were cast as parasites. Both symbolically and practically, social insurance programs and hidden welfare extended the meaning of first-class American citizenship to include an economic shield against impoverishment, creating social citizenship alongside civil and political citizenship. By contrast, the expansion of public assistance programs during the Great Society, for all their merits, still placed the poor on a separate track that embodied a lack of national social citizenship.[98] Arguably the Great Society sought through community action to empower the poor, but from Jackson, Mississippi, to Newark, New Jersey, disproportionately white elites battled disproportionately black poor people, and community action was a short-lived phenomenon.

Thus segmentation in the American welfare state was reproduced and in some important ways expanded in the Great Society. In its wake, inequities of income, respect, and rights deepened political inequities. A detrimental political cycle emerged. Republicans increasingly appealed to staunchly conservative white voters, especially in the South. Meanwhile, just as blacks were gaining and using the vote as a result of the Voting Rights Act and the political sophistication some had gained from working in organizations such as the NWRO

---

98. Gordon, *Pitied but Not Entitled,* 302–3.

and CAAs, the party to which they gave the vast majority of their votes turned its attention elsewhere. Increasingly national Democratic politicians targeted the swing voters who did not recognize their dependence on the welfare state. As Democrats went after moderate and conservative white middle-class voters, especially in the North, the poor minorities who did support an activist government increasingly became nonvoters, political noncitizens. The situation became a downward spiral: the more Democrats sought to appeal to conservative voters, the more the poor did not vote; the more the poor did not vote, the more the Democrats sought to appeal to swing voters.[99]

Appeals to conservative voters, whether delivered by Democratic or Republican politicians, sounded a lot like the ones that surfaced as far back as Reconstruction to undercut the Freedmen's Bureau. The Great Society had gone too far; it interfered with states' rights and therefore was unconstitutional. It cost too much and was therefore fiscally imprudent. To the extent that it was needed, it had accomplished its task. It really was no longer needed because America was a land of opportunity; after all, whites had climbed their way up the economic ladder without government assistance. Providing public assistance to blacks would only encourage dependency, undermine the work ethic, and make welfare a way of life. What was needed was forced employment, not financial assistance.

It was the argument of a presumed black dependency that would have the longest political and policy life. Increasingly, however, the black dependency argument was set within a new template: "culture of poverty" theory, introduced most prominently by the anthropologist Oscar Lewis in the relatively liberalized political climate of the 1960s. Lewis's goal in discussing a culture of poverty was to provide a rich narrative and explanation of the dictates and results of Puerto Rican poverty.[100] Lewis targeted empowerment as the route out of the culture of poverty. As he saw it, when the poor became organized and politically active, the culture of poverty evaporated. His perspective was liberal and innovative because "the poor" had usually been constructed as lacking culture.

Despite Lewis's intention, however, policy analysts and many academics read accounts of the culture of poverty as evidence that the folkways, mores,

---

99. Ibid., 300–301.

100. Oscar Lewis, *La Vida: A Puerto Rican Family in the Culture of Poverty, San Juan and New York* (New York: Random House, 1966).

and norms of the poor were crude and irresponsible self-indulgence, the result of bad choices, not structural constraints. In an earlier period those who reached this conclusion would have cited natural inferiority as the cause. Culture of poverty theorists arrived at the same conclusion but argued that it was a negative culture that caused the economically disadvantaged to "misbehave" perpetually. Allegedly, the poor's commitment to live in disorganized hedonism and laziness was both a mark of poverty and what chained them to poverty, generation after generation. Just as those who opposed the Freedmen's Bureau ignored the impact of slavery on the life chances of blacks, so too did culture of poverty analysts deny or diminish the roles of racism, substandard education, housing, medical care, and job opportunities in creating and sustaining poverty. Poverty and the culture it supposedly spawned—the culture of dependency—were seen as outgrowths of individual and group irresponsibility.

Interestingly, this interpretation of the culture of poverty theory began to catch on at the height of the civil rights movement. For conservative white politicians and masses alike, culture of poverty arguments functioned as a justification for resisting the Great Society and for refusing to attach institutionalized racial inequality. Many politicians and policy makers translated culture of poverty arguments into sound bites to justify the position that it was deeply problematic to mount public policy initiatives aimed at ameliorating the lives of the poor, especially the black poor. After all, it was not structures of inequality but culturally determined bad choices of the poor themselves that led to lives of endemic and enduring poverty and dependency. "The fact that so many African American mothers remained poor in the United States sustained the popularity of culture of poverty theory, locking it into the heart of conservative politics for the rest of the twentieth century."[101]

The sociologist (later senator) Daniel Patrick Moynihan, in a report on the black family written for the Johnson administration in 1965, was the first to explicitly draw the connection between culture of poverty arguments and black mothers. Moynihan's concentration was on the disintegration of the black family and poverty "feeding upon itself." Thus from Moynihan's perspective, the central problem for African Americans was the culture of poverty, defined as one of degradation, deprivation, passivity, helplessness, and dependency. At the heart of the culture of poverty, Moynihan contended, was a crisis of family

---

101. Rickie Solinger, "Dependency and Choice," in Mink, *Whose Welfare?* 22–23.

structure. So long as this situation persists, "the cycle of poverty and disadvantage will continue to repeat itself." What must be attacked is a "tangle of pathology" resulting from individual behaviors.[102] In sum, even at the high point of the Great Society, family structure and individual behaviors were the central elements of not only the new explanation for poverty, especially black poverty, but the evolving ideology of whiteness. The problems of African Americans were individualistic and cultural rather than collective and structural.

Herbert Gans noted at the time: "The findings on family instability and illegitimacy can be used by right-wing and racist groups to support their claim that [blacks] are inherently immoral and therefore unworthy of equality. Politicians responding to the more respectable white backlash can argue that [blacks] must improve themselves before they are entitled to further government aid. . . . Worse still, the report could be used to justify a reduction of efforts in the elimination of racial discrimination and the War on Poverty."[103]

After the Moynihan Report, poor single women of color and their children moved into the foreground of public discussion about poverty. They increasingly were the main group accused of making bad choices and spreading the culture of poverty. When such charges were made, the argument was complex, reminiscent of arguments made during the Freedmen's Bureau experiment. It was often claimed that poor black women were at fault because they were unemployed. More often they were blamed for not marrying and having babies anyway. Just as often, the accusation against black women claimed that they had jobs while African American men did not, in effect depriving black men not only of jobs but of status. That situation, Moynihan contended, was a very consequential mistake, since it left black women presiding over families constructed as matriarchies, in defiance of the norm.

By transfusing the argument that bad culture inexorably led African

102. Daniel Patrick Moynihan, "The Negro Family: The Case for National Action," in Rainwater and Yancey, *Moynihan Report,* 39–125. For more discussion of the culture of poverty, see Oscar Lewis, "The Culture of Poverty," in Daniel P. Moynihan, ed., *On Understanding Poverty: Perspectives from the Social Sciences* (New York: Basic Books, 1969), 187–220; Frank Riessman, *The Culturally Deprived Child* (New York: Harper & Row, 1962), 2–3; and Oscar Handlin, *Boston's Immigrants: A Study in Acculturation* (Cambridge: Harvard University Press, 1959), 120–212.

103. Herbert Gans, "The Negro Family: Reflections on the Moynihan Report," in Rainwater and Yancey, *Moynihan Report,* 450.

American women into welfare dependency into the political dialogue and policy debates of the day, political actors updated the old arguments that blacks were unworthy of government assistance. Thus it was not, as some have argued, that white antipathy to the new social policies of the Great Society ascribed to African Americans the invidious stereotype of unworthiness, but rather that because whites already saw African Americans as unworthy, they concluded that programs addressing their needs were also unworthy. The popular misperception of the Great Society as identified with racial minorities meant that its programs in general would be slandered as serving the undeserving, because such hoary stereotypes of blacks had been prevalent among whites from the beginning of the nation. As these stereotypes had prevailed to undercut the Freedmen's Bureau and to help shape the New Deal, they resurfaced as a critical part of the attack on the Great Society and a limitation on how far its policies could go in overturning centuries of white skin privilege. In a time of legislated equality, however, whiteness as ideology took on a new set of clothes. Finally, it was accepted in principle that all men *and* women were created equal, but that natural equality had been betrayed by blacks' inferior culture and depraved values. Structure did not lead to culture, but rather culture to structure. If blacks would only become culturally more like whites (the new version of the "Ten Little Niggers" story's emphasis on "then there were none"), they would escape poverty and its related problems. There was no need for a fundamental shake-up in the nation's social, political, and economic orders.

Conclusion

It took unprecedented prosperity, technological change, economic modernization of the South, the concomitant out-migration of southern blacks from rural areas, ideological competition with the Soviet Union, the end of colonialism, the shrinkage of the New Deal coalition, the resulting new electoral needs of the Democratic Party, and most especially the Civil Rights Movement to begin to chip away at the edifice of white dominance and include people of color on a mass basis in the evolving American welfare state. Through the valiant efforts of an unprecedented socially disruptive interracial campaign led by African Americans, the large political shock of the Civil Rights Movement temporarily lowered the political-institutional and cultural barriers to reform. In this atmosphere, the decision was made to launch a racially targeted War on Poverty and to extend civil rights and other social protections to people of color.

These developments were clearly not the result of a consensual politics or without a heritage. To the contrary, ideological debates in Congress and the country over civil rights legislation and the Great Society's policies to help the poor had been foreshadowed as far back as the debates over the Freedmen's Bureau. Given the ideological construction many whites place on policies that benefit blacks, the Great Society's policies were almost immediately considered to be serving the undeserving simply because many saw them as serving blacks. This reaction proved once again how liberal individualism and white skin privilege institutionalize moral worthiness or desert according to race. Movement politics and a changing global context, however, made it nearly impossible for these debates to take place within the naked language of protection of white skin privilege as they once had done. Culture of poverty arguments surfaced as a new way to advance old arguments.

Still, as long as economic prosperity held and movement politics in the streets remained the order of the day, substantially more inclusive policies characterized the 1960s. In short, while the efforts of the Freedmen's Bureau and Reconstruction were short-lived and the New Deal failed to address the status of people of color in any fundamental way, the programs of the Great Society marked them for inclusion. Its programs resulted in sharp improvement in conditions for the small but growing black middle class through public-sector employment and significant growth in income maintenance for poor people of color. In respect to a number of key social indicators (poverty, income, and education, for example), black life in general improved at a faster rate than in any previous period of American history.

These developments clearly indicate that the American welfare state of the 1960s finally included middle-class, working-class, and poor clientele of all races on a mass basis. Yet just as certainly, the policy legacy left by the equal opportunity reforms of the 1960s and early 1970s nonetheless was a segmented welfare state that fused race and social policy in ways that continued to privilege whites. To be sure, each leg of the welfare state included some members of all classes and races, but segmentation remained tangible. The white nonpoor (especially white males) continued to be advantaged in the two legs of the welfare state (social insurance and privatized welfare) created before the 1960s while blacks, Latinos, Native Americans, and middle-class and poor white women were the primary beneficiaries of the new services and income-maintenance programs of the Great Society. At the same time, the gap between wealthy and middle-class whites on one side and everyone else on the other widened, largely as a result of the growth of tax expenditures and more favorable social insurance schemes. Ultimately the very race and class segmentation the Great Society reproduced—its focus on individual behaviors, its negligence in addressing structural problems and foreseeing major economic changes already on the horizon, and its failure to establish the institutions and coalitions needed to sustain it—foreshadowed its own dismantlement.

The most prominent national black leaders and civil rights organizations of the day understood the shortcomings of the Great Society and predicted a weak outcome.[104] In fact, many sought to promote an alternative social agenda, urging policy makers to address problems of poverty and inequality in comprehensive ways. Like A. Philip Randolph, leader of the Brotherhood of Sleeping Car Porters, most national black leaders understood that enemies of civil rights were also enemies of comprehensive social policy more generally. What was needed most, Bayard Rustin concluded, was full employment and effective measures to counter "structural unemployment"; thus the subtitle of the 1963 March on Washington—"A March for Jobs and Freedom." As the organizing manual for the 1963 march pointed out, there were two major categories of demands and two major foci of lobbying with members of the House and Senate during the march: civil rights demands and job demands. Similarly, testifying before a House committee only weeks before the march, Randolph explained: "Economic and civil rights are inseparable. . . . We cannot have fair employment until we have full employment. Nor will we have full employment until we have fair employment. National planning for jobs for all Americans is an urgent need of the hour. Government must take leadership in investment policies, tax policies, public works policies."[105]

Nor did 1963 exhaust the efforts of civil rights leaders to steer social policy on a path toward universality and comprehensiveness. To provide just four examples: King's last campaign, the Poor People's March, focused directly on

---

104. Dona Cooper Hamilton and Charles V. Hamilton, *The Dual Agenda: Race and Social Welfare Policies of Civil Rights Organizations* (New York: Columbia University Press, 1997).

105. Testimony of A. Philip Randolph before the House Committee on Employment and Manpower, July 25, 1963, in A. Philip Randolph Papers, FEPC, Box 36, Library of Congress, Manuscript Division.

economic uplift for all people who did not benefit from the status quo. The NUL's domestic Marshall Plan, the A. Philip Randolph Institute's Freedom Budget, and the heavy support of civil rights groups for full employment legislation were all instances in which the focus of civil rights leaders was predominantly on encouraging policy makers to address comprehensive social rights for all, not simply civil rights for African Americans.

For the most part, however, Washington turned a deaf ear to such urgings. The calls from black and other leaders to reorient the War on Poverty to create employment and more universal social programs found only limited support in the Kennedy and Johnson administrations, given the view of the postwar economy and the explanations of black disadvantage that prevailed.[106] Moreover, to address poverty in the terms urged by civil rights activists would have required something the nation never had—a tradition of social rights for all Americans bolstered by fiscal liberalism. Instead, refusing to increase the state's redistributive or regulatory capacities substantially or to confront class- as well as race-based inequalities directly, policy makers in the 1960s fashioned a new leg of a system based on the American ethos and the types of piecemeal targeted programs long familiar in a nation whose welfare system was heavily market oriented and fiscally conservative.

Still, even the targeted programs were major undertakings in the context of white politics in the 1960s. The new, more inclusive policies of the Great Society spawned a new politics in which conservatives of both major parties sought to take advantage of white resistance to change. Actually, there is ample evidence that LBJ understood the dilemma and anticipated the political impact of his administration's actions on behalf of racial minorities and the poor. In a speech for the annual meeting of the Leadership Conference on Civil Rights in 1987, Supreme Court Justice Thurgood Marshall revealed that Johnson had told him twenty years earlier: "It was not the Vietnam War that ruined me. I could lose the North, but not the South; and it was my role in civil rights,

---

106. Kennedy adopted the Council of Economic Advisers' plan to stimulate the economy by cutting taxes, supporting in rapid succession an accelerated depreciation schedule to recuse the taxes of large, capital-intensive corporations, an across-the-board investment tax credit, and finally a proposal to cut corporate and personal income taxes, with substantial benefits for upper-income earners. See James L. Sundquist, *Politics and Policy: The Eisenhower, Kennedy, and Johnson Years* (Washington, D.C.: Brookings, 1968), 48; and Margaret Weir, *Politics and Jobs* (Princeton: Princeton University Press, 1992), 70–76.

especially your nomination, that lost me the South."[107] Similarly, in more color-ful language, according to the veteran journalist Carl Rowan (then a speech writer for Johnson), LBJ commented before delivering a speech on the Voting Rights Act before a special joint session of Congress on March 15, 1965: "You want me to give this fuckin' speech and say the things you've written for me. Like 'we shall overcome.' And I'm going to do it, because I know it is right. But I ain't so goddamn sure as you are that 'we shall overcome.' You ever thought that we might be liberating some blacks and at the same time sound-ing the death knell of the Democratic party?"[108] Whatever his misgivings, however, then as well as later President Johnson urged the passage of measures that were inclusionary.

Nevertheless, when the crisis atmosphere subsided, LBJ's concerns over the fate of the Democratic Party proved prescient. Between 1944 and 1960, differences in the presidential voting choices of blacks and whites ranged from a low of 12 percentage points to a high of 40. Although black support for the Democrats jumped in 1964, racial voting differences were held to 36 points because a substantial majority of whites voted Democratic. But racial differ-ences jumped to 56 points in 1968 and until the end of the century never fell back to the levels of 1944 to 1960. Clearly, since 1964 blacks and whites (espe-cially white men) preferred different candidates and parties. Indeed, the Civil Rights Act of 1964, the Voting Rights Act of 1965, the Fair Housing Act of 1968, and the War on Poverty were premier factors in narrowing policy differ-ences between northern and southern Democrats and sharpening those between the Democrats and the Republicans. It is scarcely an exaggeration to conclude that the national party system of the last three decades of the twenti-eth century was shaped by these developments.

107. Author's notes, Annual Meeting of Leadership Conference for Civil Rights, dinner keynote speech by Associate Justice Thurgood Marshall, June 7, 1987.

108. Carl Rowan, *The Coming Race War in America: A Wake-Up Call* (Boston: Little, Brown, 1996), 43–44.

four
The Path Bends
Retrenchment from Nixon Through Reagan-Bush

The whole problem is really the blacks. The key is to devise a system that
recognizes this while not appearing to. Problem with overall welfare plan is
that it forces poor whites into the same position as blacks. . . . We have to get
rid of the veil of hypocrisy and guilt and face reality. There has never in history
been an adequate black nation, and they are the only race of which this is
true. . . . Africa is hopeless, the worst is Liberia which we built.
—*President Richard M. Nixon*

Like Andrew Johnson roughly a hundred years before him, Richard Nixon assumed African Americans were not like presumably hardworking poor whites but instead were inadequate, hopeless, lazy people dependent on the dole. In his view, the social policies of the 1960s had erred by seeking to treat poor whites and blacks of any class as equals. He was intent on turning back this trend.

Unlike Andrew Johnson, however, Nixon realized that his racial project had to proceed with caution and subterfuge. He understood that in an era of formal (legal) racial equality—the most significant product of the Civil Rights Movement and the Great Society—the operation of white privilege had to change. He could openly express racist views to his top advisers, but he could not, as Andrew Johnson had done, make public statements claiming blacks were inferior or refer to whites alone as "our people." He could not, as Johnson had done, declare the United States a country of, by, and for the white man and openly commit his government to making sure it remained so. The more racial equality came to be mandated by law and accepted in principle, the more subtle the defense of whiteness as property value and ethos had to be, manifesting itself among the populace as a nearly unconscious response. A people who considered themselves now free of racial bias, who were frustrated and embarrassed when accused of racism, but who nevertheless continued to prefer white skin and embrace its privileges needed a new justificatory rhetoric and politics of race.[1] Nixon's last two campaigns for the White House and his years as president provided the key building blocks for the new racial politics of the post–civil rights era. As time would tell, his racial project would produce fertile ground indeed for his party in the 1980s.

Even in the Nixon years, however, black leaders and most others sympathetic to equality of opportunity understood what was coming. As Martin Luther King Jr. explained it shortly before his assassination, "the line of progress is never straight. For a period a movement may follow a straight line and then it encounters obstacles and the path bends. . . . The inevitable counterrevolution that succeeds every period of progress is taking place."[2] And so it was. Building on the groundwork laid by Nixon, King's "I have a dream" was to become "I have a nightmare" in the minds of many African Americans by the end of the Reagan-Bush years.

The New Racial Politics and Social Policy in the Nixon Years

Acceptance of equality of opportunity as a principle by a majority of whites and the achievement of black voting rights set the stage for a new politics. Republicans and Dixiecrats faced an acute challenge. If nothing else, Goldwater's blistering defeat in 1964 had demonstrated that long gone were the days when such southern politicians as Theodore Bilbo, Eugene Talmadge, Harry Bird, "Cotton Ed" Smith, Strom Thurmond, Lester Maddox, George Wallace, and James Eastland found an open appeal to racism the way to certain victory, political longevity, and seemingly endless control of powerful committees of Congress or statehouses.[3] Similarly, in the North the wild-eyed conspiratorial rhetoric of the John Birch Society was unacceptable even to William F. Buckley

1. Maurice Berger, *White Lies: Race and the Myth of Whiteness* (New York: Farrar Strauss & Giroux, 2000).

2. Martin Luther King Jr., "Where Do We Go from Here: Chaos or Community?" in James M. Washington, ed., *A Testament of Hope: The Essential Writings of Martin Luther King, Jr.* (New York: HarperCollins, 1986), 562–63.

3. Carl T. Rowan, *The Coming Race War in America: A Wake-Up Call* (Boston: Little, Brown, 1996), 43.

Jr., whose *National Review* was the authoritative journal of the right. What was needed was a "New Right" that distanced itself (at least publicly) from several problematic sectors of the Old Right. Overt white supremacists, segregation-ists, and anti-Semites had to go or at least radically alter their rhetoric. Unvar-nished race appeals would have to be replaced with racial symbols and code words. No one played a greater role in shaping the new race-coded political strategy than Richard M. Nixon, perhaps the most complicated and duplicitous political personality of the twentieth century.

Nixon was helped along this path by Governor George Wallace of Ala-bama. Wallace was no simplistic ignoramus. He sought to develop a holistic new public philosophy concerning race and the welfare state. As Philip Thomp-son has argued, Wallace, during his presidential bid in 1968, sought first to develop a "moral" opposition to civil rights. Denying he was a racist, Wallace claimed to believe in equal opportunity but not racial favoritism. He portrayed civil rights and War on Poverty programs as the products of liberal Washington elites bent on helping African Americans at the expense of middle-class, work-ing-class, and poor whites.[4] When polls conducted during the 1968 presiden-tial race demonstrated that Wallace's message had struck a responsive chord among many white Americans, Nixon largely appropriated it as his own.

With the South looming as an electoral prize in 1968, Nixon not only exploited the race-coded symbolism and messages but expanded their reach. On the campaign trail, Nixon initiated practices and themes that would come to be part and parcel of every Republican presidential candidate's race for dec-ades. A day before the balloting for the Republican nomination in 1968, for instance, Nixon (the same man who had insisted on a strong civil rights plank in 1960) met with southern delegates to assure them that he was sympathetic to their racial situation. He promised to nominate "strict constructionists" for the Supreme Court, men who would be critical of federal intervention in their states. He endorsed a platform that made no mention of recently enacted civil rights statutes and did not include a full section on civil rights.

Nixon directly attacked the welfare system without specifying how he planned to change it. Since by 1968, polls confirmed that only 17 percent of

---

4. Philip M. Thompson, "Universalism and Deconcentration: Why Race Still Matters in Poverty and Economic Development," *Politics & Society* 26, no. 2 (June 1998): 187; and Thomas Byrne Edsall and Mary D. Edsall, *Chain Reaction* (New York: Norton, 1991), chap. 1.

whites believed the War on Poverty was doing a good job,[5] Nixon knew he had little to lose among white voters by attacking programs for the poor. The polls provided ample evidence that the seeds of massive white resistance, already well sprinkled, just needed to be watered. Thus it is hardly surprising that when he accepted the Republican presidential nomination, Nixon received a roar of applause when he told the audience: "I say it's time to quit pouring billions of dollars into programs that have failed. . . . Let us increase the wealth of America so that we can provide more generously for the aged, for the needy, and for all those who cannot help themselves. But for those who are able to help themselves, what we need are not more millions on welfare rolls, but more millions on payrolls."[6] As the epigraph to this chapter reveals, Nixon not only understood that there was a deep-seated racial animus attached to the issue of welfare, but subscribed to and set out to exploit it.

Yet it was not welfare but Nixon's call for "law and order" that proved to be his most skillful innovation in the use of race-coded messages for the coming war against the latest phase of America's welfare state. The riots of the late 1960s (Watts, Chicago, Springfield, Detroit, and many other cities) and the increasingly militant radicalism of such groups as the Black Panther Party provided the pretext. When the Panthers became an explicitly "nationalist, Marxist-Leninist political formation" (itself a contradictory ideology) challenging the legitimacy of the American state, and when Stokeley Carmichael declared "America is going to fall and I only hope I live long enough to see it"[7] at a meeting of communists and socialists from throughout the Americas (the Organization of Latin American Solidarity) held in Havana, Nixon's effort to link support for "law and order" with whiteness was facilitated spectacularly.

The results of the 1968 election revealed the immediate efficacy and far-reaching potential of race-coded messages. The worst fears of the Democratic Party's pragmatic faction were realized when its nominee, Hubert Humphrey,

5. Margaret Weir, "From Equal Opportunity to 'The New Social Contract': Race and the Politics of the American Underclass," in Malcolm Cross and Michael Keith, eds., *Racism, the City and the State* (New York: Routledge, 1993), 98.

6. Quoted in Dona Cooper Hamilton and Charles V. Hamilton, *The Dual Agenda: Race and Social Welfare Policies of Civil Rights Organizations* (New York: Columbia University Press, 1997), 177.

7. Quoted in Robert Smith, *We Have No Leaders: African Americans in the Post–Civil Rights Era* (Albany: State University of New York Press, 1996), 21.

won the bulk of the black vote but only 35 percent of the white vote nationally and lost virtually the entire South. George Wallace carried the Deep South states of Louisiana, Mississippi, Alabama, Georgia, and Arkansas, but Nixon narrowly won in Florida, South Carolina, North Carolina, Virginia, and Tennessee. The days when Democrats could win presidential elections through an alliance of northern liberals and southern conservatives were over. The next time the Solid South voted in unanimity was for Nixon in 1972. Nor was massive white resistance restricted to the South. Three out of ten northern whites who voted for Johnson in 1964 voted for Nixon or Wallace in 1968.[8]

What is perhaps most striking about the legacy of Nixon's success in 1968 is a twofold development. First, Nixon helped to transform Wallace's extremist views on civil rights, social welfare, and crime into mainstream views. It is this transformation, along with Nixon's Supreme Court nominations, budgetary priorities, and conflicts over busing for the purposes of school desegregation that earned him the enmity of leaders of civil rights organizations. Second, this transformation was so successful that it established a solid base for the Republican Party in the South and moved a majority of suburban white voters and many poor and working-class whites in the North into the Republican camp in national elections, while retaining the party's corporate elite core.

Nixon's Social Policies

Nixon's social policy agenda was driven by two main goals. First, Nixon sought to spread the distributional flow of social policy to working-class and poor whites and to contain liberal state-building by expanding social policies selectively.[9] His goal was to forge a conservative political base among the less affluent whites who had previously supported Democrats. Second, Nixon, ever the politician, was dead set on accelerating policies that would bitterly divide constituencies of the Democratic Party. His Family Assistance Plan is a vivid example of policies directed toward the first goal; the Philadelphia Plan exemplifies policies directed toward the second.

---

8. Edward G. Carmines and James A. Stimson, *Issue Evolution: Race and the Transformation of American Politics* (Princeton: Princeton University Press, 1989), 53–54.

9. Michael K. Brown, *Race, Money, and the American Welfare State* (Ithaca, N.Y.: Cornell University Press, 1999), 7.

The Family Assistance Plan

Nixon's Family Assistance Plan (FAP) promised a new approach to welfare. Claiming that his plan was designed to assist those left far behind the national norm and provide all with the motivation to work and a fair share of the opportunity to train, Nixon called for the elimination of AFDC in a nationwide radio and television address on August 8, 1969. In AFDC's place, Nixon proposed a guaranteed annual income for the working and nonworking poor. The FAP would provide $500 each for the first two members of a family and $300 for each additional member. Whereas AFDC penalized work, the FAP aimed at encouraging it. Under the plan, the head of a household could earn up to $720 annually and still receive the full FAP benefit. A household head who earned more than $720 would pay a 50 percent marginal tax. As earnings increased, benefits would decline 50 cents for each dollar until they reached zero and the family was supported entirely by earnings. In effect, a family of four headed by a person with a job would be substantially better off than a family receiving AFDC, since benefits combined with earnings could reach $3,810 annually while a family of four receiving AFDC would receive $1,600. Benefits would be denied to those who declined to work and beneficiaries could be compelled to work at jobs significantly below the minimum wage. Through the FAP the federal government would have intervened in the secondary labor market, subsidizing low-wage employers and ensuring a disciplined supply of workers.[10]

The proposed FAP generated both interest and opposition among liberals and conservatives alike. Its main features appeared liberal, and in some respects they were. The proposal for a federal minimum income standard and for wage supplementation would have blunted some of the worst poverty in the South. Both southern poor blacks and southern poor whites had the most to gain. States and localities stood also to be relieved of at least some of the burden of rising welfare caseloads, since the FAP would considerably expand the federal government's responsibility for the poor. It was these aspects of the proposal that attracted liberal support.[11]

10. Frances Piven and Richard Cloward, *Poor People's Movements: Why They Succeed, How They Fail* (New York: Pantheon, 1977), 340. The idea of a national minimum income standard had long been discussed. In 1967 LBJ established a Commission on Income Maintenance Programs, which called for a national minimum income standard; in 1968 the issue of income maintenance was endorsed by Eugene McCarthy in his quest for the Democratic presidential nomination and by Nixon (ibid., 319–20).

11. Ibid., 336.

In other respects the plan was regressive, particularly in its long-term implications. It would have wiped out the procedural and legal rights that AFDC beneficiaries had won through protest and litigation in the 1960s, especially the right to a hearing if one were terminated from the rolls. The work requirement, especially in jobs paying less than the minimum wage, threatened to lock poor blacks and Latinos in particular into being a permanent sub-minimum-wage labor force. The FAP's conservative potential was seen in the fact that it was being debated at the same time that the Nixon administration's fiscal policies were allowing unemployment to rise as a counter to inflation; indeed, by the end of 1970, the first year of debate over the FAP, the nation had been plunged into what was then the worst recession since World War II.[12]

In general, the FAP proposal reasserted views around since Reconstruction—that the key to reducing "parasitism" was to redesign relief arrangements so as to enforce work. It also viewed work as the panacea for other social problems. With the restoration of work discipline, family stability would be reinforced and various social ills (especially crime and civil disorder) curbed. In short, like the critics of the Freedmen's Bureau and like FDR when he faulted the effects of relief, the critics of the FAP focused on an allegedly overly permissive welfare system, not on defective socioeconomic and racially oppressive arrangements.[13] Finally, while the FAP would have put a floor under the income of the working poor, it would have eliminated equal opportunity from the agenda of the welfare state. While it was a costly plan, it stood to accomplish Nixon's goal of wooing poor whites to the Republican Party by spreading aid to the working poor and defusing the battle for equal opportunity.

The FAP was supported largely by congressmen representing the industrial states of the North, which were staggering under welfare caseloads and benefits. Southern congressmen, still trying not to undermine their low-wage economies, opposed the FAP. AFDC benefits in the South were so low that even an income standard of $1,600 for a family of four would have vastly increased benefits in most southern states and undermined the southern wage structure. As during the New Deal, southern members of Congress used their considerable power in the committee system to threaten the Nixon administration.

12. Ibid., 340.
13. Ibid., 339.

Some scholars believe that Nixon could have overcome the opposition of the South if he had persevered, but he did not. When compromises between liberals and conservatives seemed possible (mainly around issues such as raising the minimum income by a few hundred dollars and softening work provisions), Nixon refused to sanction them. Instead, on June 22, 1972—five days after the Watergate break-in—the president announced he would not support the liberal compromise, demonstrating the weakness of his commitment to passing the FAP. By this conjuncture, Nixon seemingly had realized that there was probably more political capital in exploiting the welfare issue than in enacting his FAP proposal.[14] Throughout the 1972 presidential campaign, Nixon harped on the "pathology-generating" features of welfare. As Frances Piven and Richard Cloward conclude, it is ironic that at a time when poverty had actually been substantially reduced and a step toward something like a national minimum income had already been taken, these gains became the object of "reform."[15]

The Politics of the Philadelphia Plan

Nixon's duplicity in exploiting the politics of race was demonstrated most directly in regard to affirmative action. His Philadelphia Plan, which required all contractors working on large federally funded projects to adopt "numerical goals and timetables" to ensure the desegregation of their workforce, is indicative. Ordered by Secretary of Labor George Shultz on June 27, 1969, the plan set a target range for minority hiring and timetables for meeting it for Philadelphia's construction contractors. Under the plan, if a racial imbalance existed in union membership, the employer could bypass the hiring hall and look elsewhere for workers. If the plan worked in Philadelphia, it would be instituted in nine other cities.

According to Nixon's aide John Ehrlichman, the main intent of the Philadelphia Plan was to generate dissension among core Democratic constituencies and keep them at odds. The administration understood that organized labor would not react kindly to any measure that cut into the unions' control over the supply of labor. This was particularly true in the construction industry,

---

14. Vincent J. Burke and Vee Burke, *Nixon's Good Deed: Welfare Reform* (New York: Columbia University Press, 1974), 185.

15. Piven and Cloward, *Poor People's Movements*, 343.

where by manipulating apprenticeships the skilled union workers had kept the labor supply low and thereby wages high. Losing the power to manipulate the numbers of trained workers for public-sector projects could set a precedent for private employers to reduce wage costs. For these unions, then, there was no way to disentangle race concerns from class ones.

Meanwhile, civil rights organizations understood that affirmative action could work only if it evaded the entrenched union power structure and its history of racial exclusion and discrimination. This made civil rights groups support goals and timetables as stridently as organized labor opposed them. What was at stake in the battle between building trades unions and the Civil Rights Movement was both the skin color of apprentices and arduously constructed mechanisms that protected wages and working conditions in a volatile industry in which the demand for labor fluctuated yearly and seasonally. For the Nixon administration this factor presented a win-win situation. As Ehrlichman explained it: "Nixon thought that . . . Shultz had shown great style in constructing a political dilemma for the labor leaders and the civil rights groups. The NAACP wanted a tougher requirement; the unions hated the whole thing. . . . Before long, the AFL-CIO and the NAACP were locked in combat over one of the passionate issues of the day, and the Nixon administration was located in the sweet and reasonable middle."[16] Thus Nixon's support for goals and timetables can be seen as a successful coalition-dividing attack. Indeed, when it served his purposes, Nixon characterized goals and timetables as "quotas," openly appealing to massive white resistance. "By the 1972 election," Thomas and Mary Edsall concluded, "Nixon was campaigning against the quota policies that his own Administration had largely engendered."[17] Some observers similarly see his efforts on behalf of black capitalism as an attempt to drive a class wedge among African Americans.[18]

Duplicity cropped up in other parts of Nixon's social policy agenda. When the Voting Rights Act came up for reauthorization in 1970, he tried

16. Quoted in Hamilton and Hamilton, *Dual Agenda*, 177, 183.

17. Thomas Edsall and Mary Edsall, "When the Official Subject is Presidential Politics, Taxes, Welfare, Crime, Rights, or Values . . . the Real Subject Is RACE," *Atlantic Monthly*, May 1991, 66.

18. See, e.g., arguments advanced by John David Skrentny, *The Ironies of Affirmative Action: Politics, Culture, and Justice in America* (Chicago: University of Chicago Press, 1996), 181–82; and Kenneth O'Reilly, *Nixon's Piano: Presidents and Racial Politics from Washington to Clinton* (New York: Free Press, 1995), 320–21.

unsuccessfully to substitute a weaker version. He sought to shift responsibility for school desegregation to the federal courts and then sought to stack those courts with southerners with pro-segregationist records. His Justice Department colluded with the FBI in a covert war against the Black Panthers, and his Omnibus Crime Control and Safe Streets Act of 1968 allocated huge revenues to riot control. Throughout his administration he refused to meet with so many black leaders that to demonstrate their ire, members of the newly formed Congressional Black Caucus boycotted his State of the Union address in 1970.[19]

Yet, although Nixon milked massive white resistance to maximum advantage, he was not free to totally ignore the pressures still flowing from African Americans and their allies. Memories of the riots of 1967 and the brazen activism of the Black Panthers and other militant groups fueled fears of more riots. Moreover, the growing number of black elected officials continued to pressure the administration, no matter how much Nixon sought to ignore them. Indeed, along with demands from local officials for fiscal relief, the FAP had been propelled onto Nixon's social policy agenda by the riots, just as rancorous demonstrations by local black grassroots organizations protesting discrimination in the construction trades had propelled the Philadelphia Plan.[20]

This was the context that persuaded Nixon, despite his overt appeal to massive white resistance, to pursue measures that were sometimes beneficial to people of color. He significantly expanded the EEOC's staff from 359 in 1968 to 1,640 in 1972 and its budget from $13.2 million to $29.2 million. His Labor Department provided for a doubling of OFCC checks from 22,500 in 1971 to 52,000 in 1973.[21] His Department of Housing and Urban Development (HUD) developed the Affirmative Fair Housing Marketing Regulations in 1972, requiring participants in HUD-assisted housing programs to conduct their marketing activities so as to attract those segments of the population least likely to apply.

Nixon also issued Executive Order 11625, directing federal agencies to develop comprehensive plans and specific program goals for a national Minority Business Enterprise program and to institute systematic data collection for the

---

19. Stephen Steinberg, *Turning Back: The Retreat from Racial Justice in American Thought and Politics* (Boston: Beacon, 1995), 99.

20. Ibid., 100–101.

21. Hugh Davis Graham, *The Civil Rights Era: Origin and Development of National Policy, 1970–1972* (New York: Oxford University Press, 1990), 448.

Office of Minority Business Enterprise Information Center. It was under Nixon as well that the Equal Employment Opportunity (EEO) Act of 1972, prohibiting discrimination in governments at all levels, became law. By requiring governments to maintain records on all employees by race and gender and to submit them to the EEOC, with the clear expectation that government would show improvement over time, the act also led to institutional changes. As EEO functions were established in each agency, recruitment and personnel practices changed in ways that benefited previously excluded groups, particularly in regard to recruitment of members of minority and immigrant communities. Moreover, the 1972 act provided minority employees with levers to act on more recalcitrant agencies, which they used with great effectiveness, especially in the uniformed services. Buttressed by Court findings of disparate impact, the 1972 act led to substantially greater employment of people of color in the public sector. The more conditions in the private sector offered native-born white workers a way up the hiring queue, the more jobs in the public sector opened up for people of color. With affirmative action regulations aiding this process of increasing access and with government employment rapidly expanding (especially through the creation of new, less skilled positions), government employment became nearly an occupational niche for women and blacks.[22]

There were other salutary developments in social policy during the Nixon years: expansion of the food stamp program and enhancement of its supplementation features; the Rehabilitation Act of 1973, according the physically disabled protection from discrimination; and the Comprehensive Employment and Training Act (CETA) of 1973, consolidating all major job training programs into a single administrative structure.[23] In 1974 the Supplemental Security Income (SSI) program was created. Nixon also supported the most generous increases in Social Security's history and added cost-of-living adjustments. Between 1969 and 1972 Congress raised benefits three times and finally in 1972 indexed benefits to inflation and maximum taxable wages to future wage movements. Assistance for poorer localities continued as a legiti-

22. Roger Waldinger, "When the Melting Pot Boils Over: The Irish, Jews, Blacks, and Koreans of New York," in Michael P. Smith and Joe Feagin, eds., *The Bubbling Cauldron* (Minneapolis: University of Minnesota Press, 1995), 265–79.

23. With the creation of CETA, job training was open to anyone who had been unemployed at least one week. At its height, CETA spent $10.2 billion and provided 739,000 public service jobs, 12% of the number of unemployed workers.

mate federal government responsibility. No-strings-attached revenue sharing and Community Development Block Grants enacted under Nixon used different approaches that benefited whites more than people of color but reflected the Great Society's sensibility that localities, especially cities, required special aid from the federal government. As a result, federal expenditures for cash and in-kind transfers directly targeted to the poor almost tripled from the end of fiscal year 1969 through fiscal year 1974, with most of the increase not in cash assistance but in programs such as food stamps, Medicaid, housing subsidies, and college student aid.[24] The chief result of these decisions was the vast expansion of a social welfare system of middle-income service beneficiaries and lower-income transfer and service recipients.

Thus the record of the Nixon administration with respect to race and poverty matters does not lend itself to a blanket verdict. To a large extent, the sensibilities of the Great Society continued in the Nixon years, in good part as a response to continued pressures from below. Perhaps the best way to understand Nixon's social policies is to remember that civic action can be effective and that it is possible to do right for the wrong reasons. Nixon the man was seriously flawed, but as president he was shaped both by the legacies of the Great Society and the movement politics of his years.

A key problem, however, was that the Civil Rights Movement was ebbing. Many of its leaders were moving into electoral politics, government bureaucracies, universities, businesses, and industry. Concomitantly, the ideology of protest began to take a backseat to the ideology of electoral politics.[25] "From protest to politics," Bayard Rustin put it, as the cadres of protesters waned. Behind diffusion of the Movement were other factors: the achievement of formal equality, the material concessions won, and the crisis in black leadership precipitated by the assassinations of King and Malcolm X. And so the cadres of organizers dwindled, their ranks diminished by the concessions won, the effective neutralization and repression of radical groups, and simply the drain of energy and financial resources of a movement under full steam for roughly twenty years.

With de jure desegregation generally accomplished, the Civil Rights Movement confronted far more ambiguous and difficult obstacles to racial

---

24. Michael K. Brown, *Remaking the Welfare State: Retrenchment and Social Policy in America and Europe* (Philadelphia: Temple University Press, 1988), 195–96.

25. Piven and Cloward, *Poor People's Movements,* 331.

progress. As social rights, not just civil and political rights, became the focal point, the task ahead was daunting. Bit by bit the idealism of the movement gave way to skepticism about the ability of America to change further and resolve gave way to resignation. The movement was rapidly running out of steam.

As the movement grew more bloodless, the nation and its political elites lapsed into their traditional mode of dealing with whiteness: evasion and denial.[26] Daniel Moynihan, now a Nixon aide, urged the president in February 1970 to adopt a policy of "benign neglect." "The issue of race has been too much talked about . . . ," he wrote, "too much taken over by hysterics, paranoids, and boodlers on all sides. We may need a period in which Negro progress continues and racial rhetoric fades."[27] Moynihan's recommendation—"benign neglect"—was, of course, an oxymoron: can neglect ever be benign? Yet it seemed to capture the political spirit of the post–civil rights era.

In general, by the early 1970s LBJ-style rhetoric that had once helped legitimize the African American struggle for equality gave way to rhetoric, policy, and action emphasizing law and order and the elimination of recently won benefits. In the presidential campaign of 1972, Republican-sponsored television advertisements warned Americans that if George McGovern, the Democratic nominee, won the election, he would put half of the population on welfare. In January 1973 Nixon exhorted Americans in his inaugural address not to ask what government could do for them, but what they could do for themselves, and then he rapidly popularized the slogan "workfare, not welfare." A mobilization against the poor, especially the black poor, was launched.[28] Nixon, however, would not preside over it. As a result of his own misdeeds in the campaign of 1972, he was forced to resign.

Between Nixon's resignation in the wake of the Watergate scandal and the Reagan years, action on social policy was minimal. The earned income tax credit (EITC), passed in 1976 over Gerald Ford's objections, targeted so-called forgotten Americans—stereotypically white male low-wage earners, not unemployed racial minorities. Jimmy Carter, more interested in curbing inflation than in addressing poverty or civil rights, is best remembered for ignoring the

26. Steinberg, *Turning Back,* 99–100.

27. Richard Nixon, *The Memoirs of Richard Nixon* (New York: Grosset & Dunlap, 1978), 540.

28. Piven and Cloward, *Poor People's Movements,* 332.

problems of the inner-city poor, despite the fact that African American voters were the pivotal factor in his slim margin of victory.[29] In fact, as a southern Democrat, Carter on the campaign trail was careful not to antagonize racially conservative whites and sympathetically spoke about those who sought to maintain the "ethnic purity" of their neighborhoods against "alien groups" and "black intrusion."[30] Although Carter appointed a record number of blacks to his administration and the federal bench, he did so little on civil rights that his own secretary of health, education, and welfare found it "remarkable that a Democratic President could go through almost all of his term without delivering a fervent, ringing, major public address on civil rights . . . after the setbacks of the Nixon years."[31] Carter showed just as little commitment, energy, and passion for other arenas of social policy. His proposed welfare reform package was reminiscent of Johnson's WIN program of 1967 and Nixon's FAP in that it proposed work requirements; what mattered most was that he devoted little or no attention to it. It was in this context of a near vacuum in social policy making that Ronald Reagan, elected president in 1980, would seek to perfect what Nixon had begun.

The Context of Reagan's Victory

To adequately understand both the racial politics of the 1980s and how it helped foster retrenchment in social policy in the Reagan years, one has to take into consideration discrete but interrelated economic, political, and social developments in the post–Civil Rights era. On the economic front, the end of the post–World War II boom, the high costs of the ill-fated war in Vietnam, and the concomitant fiscal pressures and business demands for tax relief combined to undercut the kind of innovation in social policy begun in 1964. By the mid-1970s the expected Keynesian relationship between prices and unem-

29. The Carter years did expand some social benefits. For example, during the stagflation crisis of the mid-1970s, unemployment benefits were temporarily extended and benefits to displaced workers were expanded under the Trade Expansion Act of 1962, but these measures benefited far more white male workers than racial minorities and white women. See Daniel Baumer and Carl Van Horn, *The Politics of Unemployment* (Washington, D.C.: Congressional Quarterly Press, 1985), 19, 110.

30. Jules Witcover, *Marathon: The Pursuit of the Presidency, 1972–1996* (New York: Viking, 1997), 302–9.

31. Quoted in O'Reilly, *Nixon's Piano*, 353.

ployment had virtually disappeared, and the nation found itself in a new situation: stagflation (high inflation and high unemployment).[32]

Stagflation shifted public psychology away from its relatively relaxed attitude toward the expansion of social welfare. Increasingly worried about downward mobility, their children's future, and even just plain survival, many Americans returned to an older psychology of scarcity. This was especially true for white men. Heretofore always the clearly advantaged in the labor market, white men became angry about their declining proportions in the civilian labor force and among full-time employees. Rising unemployment, however, was just the tip of the iceberg. Add to this the fact that the new jobs being created were in the low-paying sectors and often "contingent work" (part-time and temporary jobs without health and pension benefits) and one begins to get at the heart of the economic insecurities that characterized the American workforce by the 1980s.[33]

It did not matter that automation and globalization were the key forces behind these trends or that black and Latino men suffered far more from these processes than white men did. People of color became a convenient scapegoat as economic insecurities eventually translated into a preoccupation with gains made by people of color. Antoine Joseph refers to this development as "racial transference." He argues that as competition for shrinking opportunities (jobs, places in universities, good housing, and so forth) grows, those historically privileged scapegoat others for their own misfortunes. Without an adequate comprehension of the systemic causes of their plight, they transfer their frustrations onto historically oppressed groups. When politicians capitalize on such racial scapegoating through the use of code words and hostility toward equality of opportunity, a political atmosphere ripe for racial antagonism and animosity toward people of color grows.[34]

32. In the 1970s unemployment rose to 6.2%, and in the 1980s it averaged 7.3% for the decade, a sharp contrast to the 4 to 5% unemployment rates of the 1960s. For discussion, see Michael B. Katz, *The Undeserving Poor: From the War on Poverty to the War on Welfare* (New York: Pantheon, 1989), chap. 4.

33. According to Clinton's first-term labor secretary, Robert Reich, the average number of paid work hours in 75% of the jobs created in the 1980s was 27—indicating a phenomenal increase in contingent work. By the 1990s, Reich concluded, a quarter of the labor force was employed in contingent jobs.

34. Antoine Joseph, "The Resurgence of Racial Conflict in Post-Industrial America," *International Journal of Politics, Culture, and Society* 5, no. 1 (Fall 1991): 81–93. I thank Avis Jones Deweever for calling Joseph's work to my attention.

Economic change, then, sowed the seeds for a bend in the civil rights revolution, but economic change alone could not dictate the new racial politics or the policy reversals it facilitated. Much depended on political developments and how the political debate about reclaiming American prosperity was managed.

Among those attempting to come up with a new politics for the new economic context were, not surprisingly, America's corporate elites. The politics of equal opportunity in the 1960s had depended to a large extent on their confidence. With deficits rising and the economy in a tailspin, business interests lost confidence. Struggling to compete in an increasingly global market, business wanted to lower wages by reducing the influence of unions and cutting social programs that not only raised taxes but offered an alternative to poorly paid jobs. With the decline in movement politics—not just the antiwar and civil rights movements but the women's, students', senior citizens', gay rights, public-sector workers', and a long list of other movements—the situation became ripe for a mobilization of business interests and conservative politicians to bring expenditures into line with revenues by cutting the cost of social programs.

The organizations business had either founded directly or revitalized during the 1970s (for example, the Business Roundtable, formed in 1972 as a policy forum and lobbying agency for America's biggest corporations, and a reinvigorated Chamber of Commerce to organize and speak for small businesses) openly set out in the 1980s to turn back labor law reforms, defeat consumer protections, curb regulations in general, enact favorable tax legislation, and withdraw the relatively costly social policy concessions made during the Great Society. They were helped significantly by the conservative, pro-business intelligentsia they had nourished for at least a decade. For years, right-wing foundations such as those established by Lynde and Harry Bradley, Sarah Scaife, and John M. Olin had poured in millions of dollars to fund conservative research projects. By 1980, a blossoming network of Washington-based conservative think tanks and policy institutes (most notably the American Enterprise Institute, founded in 1970, and the Heritage Foundation, founded in 1973) as well as individual academics in elite universities had produced the means of presenting the conservative cause in a coherent and persuasive manner.[35] Much

35. John Myles, "Postwar Capitalism and the Extension of Social Security into a Retirement Wage," in Margaret Weir, Ann Shola Orloff, and Theda Skocpol, eds., *The Politics of Social Policy in the United States* (Princeton: Princeton University Press, 1988), 277.

of the work of the new pro-business intelligentsia centered on formulating, legitimating, and publicizing a political program linking race, "family values," crime, poverty, and cities. Developing nearly simultaneously with the revolution in communications, the new, highly funded conservative think tanks amassed and utilized a well-stocked arsenal of far-reaching means of communication, from computerized direct mail to fax broadcasts to electronic mail to satellite television and teleconferencing to electronic bulletin boards, networks, cable television, and talk shows on television and radio. The new communications technology gave them unprecedented speed in lobbying members of Congress and the administration and in influencing public opinion.

Of particular importance, these groups had expanded their political reach by forging shrewd alliances with elements of the populist right, especially leaders of the religious right, such as Jerry Falwell, Pat Roberts, and Paul Weyrich, who joined hands in the early 1980s to build broad and durable vehicles such as the annual Family Forum national conference.[36] While the religious right often focused on sex education, abortion, and school prayer, among its core values were also resistance to pluralism and diversity, demonization of feminism and working mothers, and objections to lesbian and gay rights—all increasingly important issues in the politics of civil rights and the coming cultural wars.[37] Meanwhile, open racial chauvinists such as Pat Buchanan and elements of white supremacist groups were part of the motley crew gathering on the right. Both the religious right and racial chauvinists became a link (even if unhappily) for business and the conservative intelligentsia to grassroots movements to support their agenda; and despite their considerable differences, business and the populist right had the same goal: to unite the various sectors of the right in a series of amorphous coalitions that scapegoated people of color, feminists, gays, and organized labor in order to roll back the limited social policy gains achieved in the 1960s.[38]

Finally, the political action committee (PAC) revolution that began in the 1970s provided a nearly direct route for business to influence candidates of both parties. As the sheer arithmetic of campaign finance became obvious to candidates at a time when political parties were waning, more and more candidates figured out that if organized labor and liberal PACs gave them every

36. Thomas B. Edsall, *The New Politics of Inequality* (New York: Norton, 1984).
37. Richard L. Berke, "Christian Group Offers Policy 'Suggestions,'" *New York Times,* May 18, 1995, B13.
38. Chip Berlet, "The Right Rides High," *Progressive,* Oct. 1994, 22–29.

allowable dollar, that was only about enough to hire competent fund-raisers to go after the big corporate money, not enough to run increasingly expensive campaigns. As a result, more and more candidates of both major parties jumped on the PAC bandwagon, which essentially meant running into the waiting arms of the newly mobilized business community. Republicans, not surprisingly, proved to be more successful in the battle for business PAC contributions, but Democrats were hardly slackers. In sum, by 1980 the secular, corporate, and religious branches of the right had spent hundreds of millions of dollars to build a solid national right-wing infrastructure that provided training, conducted research, published studies, produced educational resources, engaged in networking and coalition building, promoted a sense of solidarity and possible victory, shaped issues, provided legal advice, filed suits, suggested tactics, tested and defined specific rhetoric and slogans, and promoted candidates who would represent their interests.

With its national infrastructure in place and looking for both villains and ways to cut public spending, the Republican right set to work rebuilding the party, fashioning a new public philosophy, and capturing the national debate over such issues as taxes, abortion, sexuality, child-rearing, immigration, government spending, welfare, crime, and civil rights. Their first signal success was to convince a growing public that slow economic growth resulted from excess government and unproductive public expenditures, especially those aimed at helping the poor and racial minorities. Slicing benefits, they argued, would stimulate the economy, create jobs, and force poor people into an independence that in the long run would improve their lot. The second signal success was to tie "misguided" policies around the necks of blacks. Conservatives maintained that blacks were the main victims of so-called misguided welfare policies and that they would benefit from the stick of forced labor, which would end their dependence and in the long run make them happier and better off.[39] By the early 1980s, such conservative arguments not only set the terms of public debate over race, poverty, and social policy but dominated at the polls.

The Politics of Fear, Anger, and Division in the Reagan-Bush Years

In 1980 Ronald Reagan was the beneficiary of the new conservative mobilization. One way he sought to expand the party's electoral coalition was to build

39. At a meeting intended to recruit blacks to the Republican Party in May 1994, Patrick McSweeny, chairman of the Virginia GOP, told his black audience: "The Great Society has

on the national racial project set in place by Nixon. His task, consciously or not, was to advance what Michael Goldfield has called "the full fledged emergence of a dominating racist coalition."[40] Long-standing white racist sentiments, notions of individual liberties as old as the republic, and arguments about race, dependency, and the role of government around since the Freedmen's Bureau facilitated his task.

But 1980 was not 1880. Not only had formal equality been achieved, but far more Americans of all races rejected notions that some groups are naturally superior to others. In the post–civil rights era, racism and the politics of white skin privilege had to be camouflaged. The result was a politics of symbolism and race-coded messages that exploited hoary stereotypes of black culture.

Indeed, it is hard to exaggerate the importance of the cultural argument, emerging since at least the Moynihan Report, to the operation of modern racism. With biological arguments on the ropes as an explanation of white skin privilege, many whites readily embraced the notion that there are cultural characteristics that separate the "white race" from the black one. As the conservative social policy analyst Lawrence Mead put it, "The culture of black Americans is the most significant for an understanding of today's nonwork and poverty. Evidently the worldview of blacks makes them uniquely prone to the attitudes contrary to work and thus vulnerable to poverty and dependency."[41] In actuality, neither Mead nor other scholars nourished by conservative foundations adduced a body of evidence to support the conclusion that black and white Americans shared vastly different cultures, particularly at a time when the revolution in communications was homogenizing cultures not only domestically but worldwide. How it was that exposure to the same ethos, the same textbooks, the same religions, the same entertainment and news media and most other parts of popular culture could end up shaping white Americans to be hardworking, responsible, and sexually chaste and black Americans to be lazy, irresponsible, and sexually promiscuous was seldom, if ever, explicitly addressed. Had such scholars examined structures and the institutional matrix, they might have found a clue to the cause of racial inequality in America, but

---

done more harm to black Americans than 300 years of slavery." Quoted in Colbert I. King, "In Search of the Long-Lost Party of Lincoln," *Washington Post,* Nov. 11, 1995, A19.

40. Michael Goldfield, *The Color of Politics: Race and the Mainsprings of American Politics* (New York: New Press, 1997), 311.

41. Lawrence M. Mead, *The New Politics of Poverty* (New York: Basic Books, 1992), 148.

acting as if culture arose in a vacuum and were completely a matter of free choice, they produced analyses that led to a dead end. All that counted for the new race conservatives were unsubstantiated claims supporting a conclusion that blacks remained virtually an alien people whose values and behavior are markedly different from (and by implication inferior to) that of whites as a result of their culture. As old-style racism had depended on pseudo-scientific biological research, modern racism depended on pseudo-social-scientific cultural research.

Bad science, however, led to bad politics, for the cultural argument and the symbolism it propelled were key to Ronald Reagan's exploitation of racial symbolism as political capital. "I believe in states' rights," Reagan said as he kicked off his presidential campaign in Philadelphia, Mississippi.[42] The choice of this locale was hardly accidental, for it was here in the summer of 1964 that some local whites had brutally murdered three civil rights workers. This was just the type of act of white racism that the slogan "states' rights" had long been used to convey.

With this ominous beginning, Reagan expanded the use of racial symbols to win support from whites. The arguments were subtle and sophisticated, but every bit as divisive and invidious as old-style racism. Among the many tactics used to exploit racial symbols during the Reagan-Bush years, four were key.

The first prong was a continuation of Nixon's symbolic use of the "law and order" issue. Thus Reagan and his successor, George Bush, sought to win votes by linking crime to blacks and blacks to Democrats through a campaign of at best thinly veiled racial symbolism. At the heart of the nation's crime problem, the Republican message went, is a justice system that is soft on known perpetrators. The racial nexus was made vivid by ads focused on blacks who had committed crimes, particularly crimes against whites. Bush would prove to be more expert here than Reagan. In 1988, using a political ad based on William Horton Jr., an African American prisoner convicted of assaulting a white couple while on furlough from a Massachusetts prison, the Bush campaign sought to tie African Americans to crime and the 1988 Democratic nominee, Michael Dukakis of Massachusetts, to African Americans. To be sure, Horton's crime was reprehensible, but what made the case tailor-made for the Republicans was the racial aspect. The fact that Horton, a black man, used his

42. Lou Cannon, *Reagan* (New York: Putnam, 1982), 269–70.

furlough to rape a white woman made the racial nexus explosive. As Andrew Hacker notes, of all the offenses black men may commit, that one had the potential to stir truly primal fears. And thus Willie Horton moved to the center of the political campaign, cited repeatedly in speeches and advertisements to stoke white fears of "black crime."[43]

The second prong was to exploit widespread stereotypes of blacks as lazy and dependent, transforming Nixon's antiwelfare attack into a war on "big government." Throughout the 1980s, white prejudice against African Americans remained palpable. Indeed, one poll conducted by the National Opinion Research Center (NORC) found at the end of the decade that the majority of whites believed that African Americans were unintelligent, unpatriotic, and violent; did not want to work; and preferred public assistance to employment.[44] This latter stereotype in particular was used to undercut support for the welfare state. If blacks were to be made independent, the conservative message went, they must be made to work. Thus it became popular to promote a "new paternalism." Reagan used his bully pulpit to popularize these views. On the campaign trail and in office, he seemingly never tired of stoking white anger at black welfare recipients by recounting tall tales of "strapping young bucks" and Cadillac-driving "welfare queens" who abused the welfare system.[45] Watching these developments, undoubtedly many African Americans agreed with Rosalind Carter's conclusion that Ronald Reagan made "whites comfortable with their prejudices."[46] In fact, a 1985 *Washington Post*/ABC News survey found that 71 percent of African Americans thought that Reagan was "preju-

43. Andrew Hacker, *Two Nations: Black and White, Separate, Hostile, Unequal* (New York: Ballantine, 1995), 226–27.

44. Tom Smith, *Ethnic Images*, GSS Topical Report no. 19 (Chicago: National Opinion Research Center, December 1990). A poll conducted by the Anti-Defamation League in 1992 produced similar results. See National Conference of Christians and Jews, *Taking America's Pulse: The Full Report of the National Conference Survey on Inter-Group Relations* (New York, 1994), chap. 2. The NORC and ADL surveys may represent only the tip of the iceberg in racial stereotyping. As a methodological study by the Pew Research Center finds, standard polls conducted of a systematic sample in a few days may actually understate white hostility toward blacks and other racial minorities. See Charles S. Sugate et al., "Opinion Poll Experiment Reveals Conservative Opinions Not Underestimated, but Racial Hostility Missed," Pew Research Center for the People and the Press, Washington, D.C., Mar. 27, 1998.

45. Philip A. Klinkner and Rogers M. Smith, *The Unsteady March: The Rise and Decline of Racial Equality in America* (Chicago: University of Chicago Press, 1999), 300.

46. Quoted in David Broder, "The New Administration," *Washington Post*, Jan. 21, 1981, 24.

diced" against African Americans; 56 percent of black respondents in another poll thought he was actually "racist."[47]

The third and perhaps most important prong of the attack was exploitation of whites' economic insecurities by fanning their fears of affirmative action. Although the real goal was to reduce the effectiveness of virtually all antidiscrimination measures, affirmative action served as the key target in political propaganda. Like George Wallace and Richard Nixon before him, Reagan understood that the new racial politics in the era of formal equality had to be subtle. Thus, seeking to escape charges of race-baiting, Reagan set out to convince Americans that he was for civil rights but against unfair "preferences" and "quotas." Racial injustice no longer existed, he contended, and any past injustices were not at issue. He claimed that "civil rights leaders exaggerate the degree of racism to keep their cause alive."[48] Any racism that did exist was blacks' own fault: "There would be no racism if it weren't for black crime"; "we've created racism that wasn't there before affirmative action"; and "racism exists because whites are sick of paying higher taxes to take care of them" were typical refrains. As a consequence, according to Reagan, the problems facing contemporary blacks had more to do with their own inadequacies than racial oppression. Thus, if blacks are worse off than whites, it just indicates that those who should logically be on the bottom are on the bottom. There certainly is no need to change the entire system just because some are either unambitious, lazy, or inferior and get what they deserve.

In fact, Reagan claimed antidiscrimination policies had made blacks' problems worse. For one thing, policies such as affirmative action had deprived blacks of the self-esteem they need to progress in school and the workplace. Not only had such programs met with little success, according to Reagan, but in fact (along with welfare) had fostered dependence on the state, nurtured irresponsible personal behavior, and led to the overall deterioration of inner-city communities. What was needed, according to Reagan, were policies that would demand "personal responsibility," refocus entitlement programs, and increase the effectiveness of government services through competition. What

47. Richard Morin, "Black Views of President Reagan," *Washington Post,* Jan. 19, 1985, 1; Joint Center/Gallup Poll, Joint Center for Political Studies (now Joint Center for Political and Economic Studies), August 1986.

48. For an example of Ronald Reagan's views on this point, see "The Reagans," *Sixty Minutes,* CBS News, Jan. 15, 1989, 4 (transcript).

was needed, the story went, were "color-blind" policies that allocated rewards on the basis of "merit."

The color-blind argument, in particular, not only escalated the attack on affirmative action per se but in effect was the linchpin of the new defense of whiteness. It became a sophisticated way of playing the race card in an era in which formal equality was at its high point while class inequality was growing by leaps and bounds. For millions of white men not fortunate enough to have been born in the upper class, a belief that the United States was a "meritocracy" was their only connection to the American dream. Now these men were being primed to believe that affirmative action discriminated against them, cutting off that connection at the very moment their economic lives faced new challenges. It was a politically potent message, for what the right-wing attackers of affirmative action understood was that most white people resented both the old "special preferences" for the rich and what they were now being encouraged to believe were the new ones for blacks.

In the most cynical ploy of all, Reagan presented himself as the sort of color-blind person Martin Luther King Jr. dreamed about during the March on Washington. While King's whole message centered on encouraging America to overcome centuries of white privilege and current degradations of people on the basis of group differences by employing those very differences to transform the institutions and practices that made them matter, Reagan sought to (mis)-appropriate the color-blind imagery to avoid remedying the effects of difference by separating discourse and policy from their social and institutional matrix. By ignoring real conditions of inequality and deprivation, he distorted an America in which white men still ranked significantly higher on practically every imaginable desirable socioeconomic indicator into a world in which white men were the principal victims and sufferers. Up was down and down was up in Reagan's "New America."

Throughout it all, there was no mistaking the appeal to the voting bloc that mattered most to the Republicans. "If you happen to belong to an ethnic group not recognized by the federal government as entitled to special treatment," Reagan often said, "you are the victim of reverse discrimination."[49] Reagan understood that he had little to lose by such rhetorical extravaganzas:

---

49. Ronald Reagan, *A Time for Choosing: The Speeches of Ronald Reagan, 1961–1982* (Chicago: Regnery Gateway, 1983), 169.

the mass base he sought to appeal to was white and his political success depended on his ability to interpret white identity in positive political terms and reinforce white privilege, transforming people of color into "the other" in a white-dominated society. In essence, the color-blind argument sought to transform whites' legitimate class concerns into racial ones. If the spoken promise was to get the government off the backs of the middle and working classes, the unspoken promise was to get the "niggers" off the backs of whites, who had lost control over their schools and neighborhoods and bore the costs of the "rights revolution."[50] With color ever on the minds of Republicans, color-blind became the new code for protecting whiteness.

Blacks themselves might see the merits of his argument, Reagan apparently thought, if only their leaders helped them. Thus the last key prong of Reagan's attack was directed at black leadership itself. This attack generally began with the claim that black leaders no longer spoke for the black masses; they were "out of step." Highlighting poll data demonstrating black conservatism on moral issues such as school prayer, reproductive rights, and gay rights (but ignoring poll data demonstrating that these issues had little salience among blacks and that a veritable host of data continued to demonstrate that blacks were the most liberal constituency in America), conservatives in the 1980s portrayed black leaders as little more than pimps or shakedown artists who urged their followers to settle for excuses and handouts, thus encouraging the view that hard work and perseverance will not pay off since the deck is stacked against them.[51] Such self-pity, it was concluded, generated a "denial of individual responsibility," so not nearly enough black Americans are "taking possession of their lives."

Evidently what blacks needed, according to the conservative Republican administrations of the 1980s, was new leaders. Thus Reagan went eight years without meeting with a single traditional civil rights leader,[52] and Bush's single meeting with these leaders as a group was after the Los Angeles riots in the summer of 1992. Meanwhile, Reagan and Bush searched for their own brand

50. O'Reilly, *Nixon's Piano*, 366.

51. For the typical recitation of this argument, see J. C. Watts's response to President Clinton's State of the Union Address, on Feb. 4, 1997. Watts was the only black Republican member of the 105th Congress.

52. Rowan, *Coming Race War*, 55.

of black leaders to act as a political counterweight to the traditional cadre.[53] For example, even before his inauguration, prospective members of the Reagan administration held a conference of mostly black conservatives at San Francisco's Fairmont Hotel on December 12–13, 1980. The main representative of the administration at the conference was Edwin Meese III, already designated as counselor to the president with Cabinet rank and later to serve as attorney general. Black conservatives in attendance—for example, Clarence Thomas, who served as EEOC chair under Reagan and was later nominated by Bush to the Supreme Court, and Clarence Pendleton, who chaired the U.S. Commission on Civil Rights under Reagan, were long on record as challenging established civil rights groups on a range of issues, including school busing, social welfare, full employment, affirmative action, and in general the role of government in solving the nation's social problems. Summing up the meeting, Glenn Campbell, the president of the Institute for Contemporary Studies, which had sponsored the conference, suggested that the conference stirred "a national debate . . . on who speaks for blacks, and where future progress may be found."[54] While poll data confirmed there was little or no name recognition of black conservatives and they had no sizable constituency among blacks, what mattered most, as Charles Hamilton has argued, was symbolic politics—the "comfort level" black conservatives provided to white conservatives in their efforts to undo racial advances. "It is the whites who can and do feed off their speeches and writings, which is a cause for financing them," Hamilton concluded.[55]

Gluing the four-sided attack together were the stereotypes of deserving whites and lazy, irresponsible blacks who, masses and leaders alike, needed discipline. Eviscerating the welfare state was a necessary goal if progress was to be made. Ample data suggest that the more whites accepted the stereotypes of blacks, the less they supported government action on behalf of equality of opportunity. The more whites held misperceptions about the continuing inequalities suffered by blacks, the more formidable the obstacles to any government effort to equalize the social, economic, and political standings of the

53. "The Reagans" and Fred Barnes, "Inventanegro, Inc.," *New Republic,* Apr. 15, 1985, 9–10.

54. Glenn Campbell, preface to *The Fairmont Papers: Black Alternatives Conference* (San Francisco: Institute for Contemporary Studies, December 1980), xii.

55. Private communication.

races.[56] The more whites supported cutting back programs believed to serve blacks disproportionately, the more programs needed by nonaffluent whites, too, lost support. In the post–civil rights era, perhaps more than ever before, class and race interacted in ways that complicated the impact of the white racial project on poor whites even as they camouflaged continuing white privilege. Disinformation, distortion, and obfuscation on race played a large role in setting the stage for attempting to turn back the gains of the 1960s and eviscerate the American welfare state in the 1980s.

The Reagan-Bush Social Welfare Legacy

While constraints on the expansion of social policy had become fully evident during the Carter presidency, Ronald Reagan's election as president signaled an explicit retreat. Reagan had campaigned against the excesses of "big government," which to him included affirmative action goals and timetables, school busing, and antipoverty programs, as well as the Great Society bureaucracy. On the campaign trail, he promised to tame and roll back the welfare state.

True to his campaign promises, the policies and programs that suffered most during the Reagan administration were those created in the 1960s and early 1970s that had a disproportionately high black and Latino clientele and benefited the working poor in general.[57] For example, the Reagan-inspired 1981 Omnibus Budget Reconciliation Act ended the public service jobs program (CETA) altogether. CETA had been used by cities (unofficially) to bolster the ranks of municipal employees. To a substantial extent its total elimination reflected the lack of importance cities had for the Reagan administration. In CETA's place, a bipartisan agreement produced the Job Training Partnership Act (JTPA), which provided block grants to states. JTPA's administrative structure, which placed substantial control in the hands of governors and local business groups, was more in line than CETA with the ideological goals of the Reagan administration: to channel federal funds directly to private businesses and bypass local governments, a growing number of which were led by black and Latino mayors. In addition, general revenue sharing, which provided extra

56. See discussion of relevant data in the Introduction and in Richard Morin, "Misperceptions Cloud Whites' View of Blacks," *Washington Post,* July 11, 2001, A1.

57. For detailed data, analysis, and discussion, see House of Representatives, Committee on Ways and Means, *Overview of Entitlement Programs: 1993 Green Book* (Washington, D.C.: U.S. Government Printing Office, July 7, 1993), 1368ff.

funds for localities, ended in 1986. Urban Development Action Grants (UDAG) were also eliminated. Overall, grants for cities were cut almost in half during the Reagan years.

The 1981 Budget Reconciliation Act also legislatively removed 400,000 individuals from the food stamp program, and between 1980 and 1990 the number of food stamp recipient fell from 21.1 million to 20.1 million.[58] Similarly, in 1982 Reagan nearly terminated all funding for new construction of subsidized housing and required residents of public housing to pay 30 percent of their income toward rent instead of the previously required 25 percent. All told, subsidized housing was severely cut and public housing expenditures declined by more than 40 percent during the Reagan-Bush era.

Sharp cuts were also made in aspects of AFDC that benefited the working poor; for example, the amount of earned income that could be disregarded in benefit calculations was reduced; fewer deductions for work-related and child-care expenditures were allowed; and AFDC eligibility was limited to those with incomes below 150 percent of a state's standard of need. States gained leeway to impose work requirements; and the maximum monthly AFDC benefit for a family of four declined from $681 in 1980 to $486 in 1992, a nearly 30 percent reduction, attributable mostly to inflation rather than to reductions in nominal benefit levels (Table 4.1).[59] Although benefits had been falling since 1970 and continued to fall after Bush left office, they declined faster during the Reagan-Bush years than either immediately before or after. Spending on income security programs in general fell from 14.7 percent of federal outlays in 1980 to 11.7 percent in 1990.[60] Reagan also tightened eligibility for unemployment insurance. Along with demographic shifts and the decline in union membership, the new eligibility rules reduced the percentage of workers receiving unemployment benefits. By 1984, only 28.5 percent of the unemployed received unemployment benefits.[61] Medicaid benefits for the working poor were also cut and the minimum benefit for low-income Social Security recipi-

58. U.S. Bureau of the Census, *Statistical Abstract of the United States, 1999* (Washington, D.C.: U.S. Government Printing Office, 1999), 400.

59. The maximum benefit was literally cut in half between 1970 and 1996. Average family benefits fell by 40% during the Reagan-Bush era. See Committee on Ways and Means, *Overview of Entitlement Programs.*

60. U.S. Bureau of the Census, *Statistical Abstract of the United States, 1999,* 348.

61. Daniel P. McMurrer and Amy B. Chasanov, "Trends in Unemployment Insurance Benefits," *Monthly Labor Review,* Sept. 1995, 34.

Table 4.1.   Maximum benefits for a family of four in the median state, current and constant FY 1996 dollars, 1970–1996

Fiscal year	Current dollars	Constant dollars
1970	$221	$910
1975	264	793
1980	350	681
1985	399	582
1990	432	522
1992	435	486
1994	435	460
1995	435	447
1996	450	450

SOURCE: U.S. House Ways and Means Committee, *The Green Book, 1999*, 414.

ents was eliminated, the modest death benefit was ended, and the benefits for older children of deceased workers were phased out.

These changes had a substantial impact on poor people of all races, but especially black families headed by women; poverty grew. One study found that between 1979 and 1989, "among families with children, 63 percent of the increase in the poverty population could be attributed to governmental policy. For the total poverty population, this percentage was about the same for both single-parent and married couple families. . . . However, government policy accounted for 87 percent of the increase in poverty for black female-headed families."[62]

Those programs that disproportionately advantaged middle-class whites were more likely to be spared even when Reagan sought to cut them. For instance, the broad sweep of the Reagan agenda against both the unemployed and working poor slid through Congress and there was little or no public out-cry, but when Reagan proposed sweeping cuts in Social Security (a 10 percent cut in future benefits, a 31 percent cut in early-retirement benefits, and further narrowing of eligibility rules for disability), he was greeted by a storm of controversy. Reprisals were swift and harsh. Only days after the proposal appeared, Reagan's job approval rating dropped 16 points. Just as swiftly, Reagan retreated.[63]

Moreover, if Reagan had had his way, he would have sent two of the three

62. Committee on Ways and Means, *Overview of Entitlement Programs*, 1368.
63. Jill Quadagno, *The Color of Welfare: How Racism Undermined the War on Poverty* (New York: Oxford University Press, 1994), 162–63.

programs that had the greatest effect on the lives of the poor, AFDC and food stamps, entirely to the states, leaving only Medicaid to be paid for by the federal government. State and local governments would have had the option to reduce the scope of AFDC and food stamps or abandon them altogether. The historian Henry Steel Commager called the plan so bizarre that it was "a throwback to the Confederacy when the thirteen states claimed to be sovereign and the national government was all but impotent."[64] The plan won little support from either Republicans or Democrats and dissipated.

In sum, to a very real extent welfare state policies with more middle-class clientele fared well under Reagan, while those with working-class and poor clientele fared poorly. By the end of the Reagan-Bush years, it was nearly an article of faith among Republicans and most Democrats as well that federal spending on social programs should be cut, that no new public money was available, and that full employment would be inflationary and bad for financial markets.[65] In nearly any calculation, elites of both major parties focused on cutting those programs first and proportionately most that benefited people of color—that is, the equal opportunity programs of the Great Society.

The Reagan-Bush Civil Rights Legacy

It was not just spending on social welfare that suffered under Reagan's knife. Both Reagan and Bush also sought cutbacks in civil rights protections. The focal point was affirmative action.

In keeping with his 1980 campaign promise to dismantle affirmative action, Reagan sought to do so. What could not be accomplished legislatively, given the Democrats' control of Congress, he sought to do administratively. In 1981, for example, the Labor Department proposed revised OFCCP regulations to reduce the number of contractors covered, redefine the concept of underutilization, eliminate pre-award reviews, and lower standards in sex discrimination cases. In 1982, the Labor Department again proposed revised OFCCP regulations, this time to prohibit formula relief to victims of class-based discrimination, limit back-pay remedies to identifiable victims, and impose a two-year limitation on "make-whole relief."

64. Walter I. Trattner, *From Poor Law to Welfare State: A History of Social Welfare in America* (New York: Free Press, 1989), 366.
65. Robert Kuttner, "America Deserves a Raise," *Washington Post,* Apr. 14, 1992, C2.

In 1986 the Department of Justice accused the OFCCP of approving conciliation agreements enforcing "quotas," making the OFCCP reluctant even to use the word "goals." Also in 1986 the Federal Communications Commission, in an abrupt shift of policy, told a federal court in the District of Columbia that its practice of granting preferences to minorities and women seeking television and radio licenses was unconstitutional and should be eliminated.

These revisions and alterations were effective. All told, the Reagan and Bush administrations virtually eliminated the threat of sanctions for discrimination in employment. As a result, the contract compliance program ceased to have any general demonstrable positive effect on minority or white female employment. The absence of political leadership in support of the program reduced the perceived need to take affirmative action, and progress was mitigated.

Although compliance reviews increased during the 1980s, affected class findings, administrative compliance filings, back-pay awards, and debarments all fell into disuse. There were thirteen debarments (the ultimate sanction) during the Carter administration but only four each in the Reagan and Bush administrations. The Reagan administration's opposition to back-pay awards resulted in a decline in such awards from $9.2 million in fiscal 1980 to $1.9 million in fiscal 1986.[66] Moreover, measured in 1980 dollars, the OFCCP's budget appropriation fell from $53 million in 1980 to $33 million in 1986, and its authorized full-time employment fell from 1,454 to 906.[67]

Similarly, during the 1980s, other parts of the Reagan administration downplayed antidiscrimination policies. In Reagan's first year as president, Justice Department attorneys filed no cases under the Fair Housing Act of 1968. In 1982 they filed two. Under Nixon, Ford, and Carter, the department averaged thirty-two cases a year.[68] The pattern in employment discrimination followed that of housing. Although private lawyers brought cases that ultimately resulted in record-setting settlements and judgments under Title VII, the proportion of cases in which the EEOC found no cause roughly doubled, from about 30 to 60 percent, and direct beneficiaries of EEOC enforcement fell from

66. Women Employed Institute from OFCCP Quarterly Review and Analysis Reports, 1994. See also Edsall and Edsall, *Chain Reaction*, 188.

67. U.S. Civil Rights Commission, *Federal Enforcement of Equal Employment Requirements*, July 1987.

68. O'Reilly, *Nixon's Piano*, 369–70.

38,114 in 1981 to 29,429 in 1991. The proportion of class-action settlements also fell dramatically, from 45 percent in 1981 to nine percent in 1991.[69] Meanwhile, even in the administration's first two years, the budget of EEOC fell by 10 percent and the staff was cut by 12 percent.[70]

In short, under the Reagan-Bush assault on affirmative action, the threat of substantial legal sanctions or financial liability evaporated, as did affirmative action's effectiveness. Between 1980 and 1984, for example, both black male and female employment actually grew more slowly among firms covered by affirmative action than among noncontractors. In the 1970s, if an establishment grew by 10 percent, one could expect to see black male employment grow by 12 percent among noncontractors but 17 percent among contractors; after 1980, the comparable rates were 11 percent among noncontractors and 10 percent among contractors. The reversal for black females was even more marked. Clearly, in the case of affirmative action, Reagan's and Bush's actions had material effects on the progress of people of color and women. Indeed, as Jonathan Leonard concludes, the 1980s demonstrate an experiment in what would happen without affirmative action. The result of this experiment was the elimination of employment advances for minorities and women. Affirmative action, such as it was, no longer aided blacks, other people of color, or women.[71] As the New York City corporation counsel told the Supreme Court about the construction industry, "less drastic means of attempting to eradicate and remedy discrimination have been repeatedly and continuously made over the past decade and a half. They have all failed. Where affirmative action is ended, progress often stops."[72]

As already indicated, far more than affirmative action was at stake. The attack on affirmative action provided a smokescreen to cover attacks on civil rights protections more generally. In 1981, for instance, the assistant attorney general for civil rights, William Bradford Reynolds, testified before the House Subcommittee on Civil and Constitutional Rights that the Justice Department

69. Women Employed Institute from EEOC District Office Reports, EEOC Legal Services, EEOC Annual Reports, 1994.

70. Klinkner and Smith, *Unsteady March,* 301.

71. Jonathan Leonard, "Affirmative Action in the 1980s: With a Whimper Not a Bang," paper prepared for Glass Ceiling Commission, Department of Justice (Washington, D.C., 1995), 17–21.

72. Quoted in Herman Schwartz, "Affirmative Action," in Gertrude Ezorsky, ed., *Moral Rights in the Workplace* (Albany: State University of New York Press, 1987), 276.

would not seek involuntary busing as a remedy for state-imposed segregation but would seek voluntary student transfer programs. In fact, the Department of Justice began to enter school desegregation cases on the side of school districts facing desegregation orders. Virtually all pressure to use busing as a means of achieving desegregation was suspended. Higher education was also not exempt from the administration's attempt to defuse equal opportunity. In 1987 the Department of Education simply refused to begin enforcement of rulings to desegregate higher education systems in five states—Arkansas, Florida, Georgia, Oklahoma, and Virginia.

Even the Commission on Civil Rights, a relatively weak agency with virtually no enforcement powers, was not off limits. In late 1984 the Reagan administration recreated the commission in its own image. For the first time loyalty to the administration's conceptualization of civil rights became mandatory for appointment to the commission. In fact, several Republican commissioners who had been appointed by Reagan in 1982 were terminated because they had not supported the administration's positions on several civil rights issues. Studies of the commission in this period focused on "reverse discrimination" against white males and downplayed continuing discrimination against blacks, Latinos, other people of color, and women. The commission became so conservative that finally even Reagan rejected some of its draft proposals, such as freezing minority set-aside programs.

But Reagan and Bush achieved their greatest successes by stacking the federal courts, including the Supreme Court, with anti–civil rights justices. Perhaps the heaviest blows to the civil rights community were five Supreme Court rulings undercutting civil rights laws. The *Wards Cove* decision placed a high burden of proof on plaintiffs in cases involving unintentional discrimination.[73] The *Price Waterhouse* decision allowed employers to engage in intentional discrimination as long as there were other legitimate reasons for the decision.[74] In *Martin v. Wilks*, individuals were allowed to reopen consent decrees and settled cases, even where there had been every opportunity for those individuals to participate in the original litigation.[75] The *Lorance* case created an artificial time barrier for filing discrimination suits.[76] The *Patterson* case allowed racial harass-

---

73. *Wards Cove v. Antonio*, 109 S.Ct. 2115 (1989).
74. *Price Waterhouse v. Hopkins*, 490 U.S. 228 (1989).
75. *Martin v. Wilks*, 109 S.Ct. 2180 (1989).
76. *Lorance v. AT&T Technologies*, 490 U.S. 900 (1989).

ment on the job, saying that the 1986 Civil Rights Act prohibited discrimination only in the initial hiring decision, not on the job.[77] Other cases such as *Memphis Firefighters v. Stotts* in 1985 and *Wygant v. Jackson Board of Education* in 1986 also cut back civil rights protections.[78]

Most far-reaching of all—indeed, the biggest setback for affirmative action during the Reagan-Bush years—was the Supreme Court ruling in *City of Richmond v. J. A. Croson Co.,* striking down a Richmond, Virginia , program providing a minority business enterprise (MBE) set-aside in municipal construction contracts.[79] The Supreme Court held that the city had not proved that it served a compelling governmental interest in remedying past and continuing discrimination, and the means selected were not narrowly tailored to meet that interest. Writing the majority opinion, Justice Sandra Day O'Connor described such claims as amorphous and unsupported, and went so far as to speculate that blacks were simply uninterested in contracting work. In short, in the face of every public opinion survey on the subject demonstrating that opportunities in business were at the top of blacks' wish list,[80] O'Connor was predisposed to believe that African Americans and their culture rejected entrepreneurial life; thus black exclusion was rendered as both normal and just.

That *Croson* would have a dramatic impact on minority contracting was obvious almost immediately. Until 1978, black businesses in Richmond, where blacks accounted for more than 50 percent of the population, received only 1 percent of city contracts. Richmond had a long history of white racial domination. Blacks and their allies had sued the city on many occasions over voting, education, and housing; some of the cases had gone all the way to the Supreme Court. The old-boy network made sure that blacks were excluded from competitive bidding, and their efforts were reinforced by the bias of Richmond's lending institutions, In 1978 the city council, more than half of its members black, created a set-aside program requiring businesses owned by racial minorities and women to receive 30 percent of all city contracts. In 1990, one year

77. *Patterson v. McClain,* 491 U.S. 164 (1989).
78. *Memphis Firefighters v. Stotts,* 467 U.S. 561 (1984); *Wygant v. Jackson Board of Education,* 476 U.S. 267 (1986).
79. *City of Richmond v. J. A. Croson Co.,* 109 S.Ct. 706 (1989).
80. See, e.g., the JCPS/Gallup poll conducted in August 1989. When asked what was the most important goal for blacks, African American respondents chose "owning more businesses" over every other. Joint Center for Political and Economic Studies, Washington, D.C.

after the Supreme Court terminated the program, minority contractors again received only 1 percent of the city's business.

The *Croson* ruling was the first in which a majority of the Court used a "strict scrutiny" standard to evaluate an affirmative action program under the Equal Protection Clause of the Fourteenth Amendment. The Court's "strict scrutiny" indicates its suspicion of state policies that invoke racial classification—that is, its predisposition to view race-based state policies as violations of the Fourteenth Amendment's guarantee of equal rights for each person without regard to race. *Croson* obviously was a key step in the direction of not only ultimately eliminating affirmative action but reversing the focus on discrimination to claim white men were unfairly disadvantaged. In essence, in treating individual blacks and individual whites as equals, the Court obliterated the link between individual harm and harm done to individuals as members of a group, masking the different histories and meanings of blackness and whiteness in the United States. By asserting that white identity is identical to all other group identities, the Court denied that whiteness is based on racial exclusion and privilege. Thus the Court insulated historically accumulated white skin privilege— all the things that whites have been able to accrue over time to reproduce their advantages.

Not surprisingly, all these actions undercutting civil rights protections, along with cuts in social programs, gained Reagan the enmity of traditional black civil rights organizations. A multiracial civil rights umbrella group denounced Reagan for unleashing a full-scale assault on the legislative advances of the 1960s. The Leadership Conference for Civil Rights (LCCR) charged "that under the Reagan administration there have been no significant civil rights enforcement activities anywhere in the government."[81]

Throughout it all, Reagan acted like a man who, in the vernacular of the 1990s, just didn't get it. "Proportionally," the president claimed, "blacks benefited more than any other racial group from our economic policies."[82] It was a grave insult to the intelligence of a people who, as Tables 3.1 through 3.3 show, had suffered rising poverty and declining relative income and education during his presidency. Perhaps most galling of all was that despite the emphasis Reagan put on moving people from welfare to work, AFDC caseloads

---

81. Bob Pear, "Civil Rights Organizations Denounce Reagan," *New York Times,* Apr. 3, 1989, 1.
82. Ibid.

continued to swell and blacks lost ground to whites in employment. The black unemployment rate, always double that of whites since World War II, rose during the Reagan years to two and one-half times that of whites (Table 4.2). Blacks also composed a larger share of the poor, rising from 20 percent to 23 percent. And at the height of the 1982–83 recession, one of every five blacks was looking for work. Perhaps the most chilling statistic of all was the mortality rate: for the first time in a century, life expectancy for African Americans dropped while life expectancy for white Americans rose.[83]

Table 4.2.   Annual number and percent unemployed, by race, 1972–2001 (thousands)

| Year | Number unemployed | | Black percent of unemployed[1] | Percent unemployed | | Black/white ratio |
	White	Black		White	Black	
1972	3,906	906	18.6	5.1	10.4	2.04
1975	6,421	1,369	17.3	7.8	14.8	1.90
1980	5,884	1,553	20.3	6.3	14.3	2.27
1981	6,343	1,731	20.9	6.7	15.6	2.34
1982	8,241	2,142	20.1	8.6	18.9	2.20
1983	8,128	2,272	21.2	8.4	19.5	2.32
1984	6,372	1,914	22.4	6.5	15.9	2.45
1985	6,191	1,864	22.4	6.2	15.1	2.44
1986	6,140	1,840	22.3	6.0	14.5	2.42
1987	5,501	1,684	22.7	5.3	13.0	2.45
1988	4,944	1,547	23.1	4.7	11.7	2.49
1989	4,770	1,544	23.7	4.5	11.4	2.53
1990	5,186	1,565	22.2	4.8	11.4	2.38
1991	6,560	1,723	20.0	6.1	12.5	2.05
1992	7,169	2,011	20.9	6.6	14.2	2.15
1993	6,655	1,844	20.6	6.1	13.0	2.13
1994	5,892	1,666	20.8	5.3	11.5	2.17
1995	5,459	1,538	20.8	4.9	10.4	2.12
1996	5,300	1,592	22.0	4.7	10.5	2.23
1997	4,836	1,560	23.1	4.2	10.0	2.38
1998	4,484	1,426	23.0	3.9	8.9	2.28
1999	4,273	1,309	22.3	3.7	8.0	2.16
2000	4,099	1,269	31.0	3.5	7.6	2.17
2001	4,923	1,450	29.5	4.2	8.7	2.07

[1]Percent of total unemployed

Source: U.S. Bureau of Labor Statistics, Labor Force Statistics from *Current Population Survey*, Series ID: LFU21000010, <http://146.142.4.24/cgi-bin/surveymost>.

83. O'Reilly, *Nixon's Piano*, 376–77. According to the NCHS, black males experienced an unprecedented decline in life expectancy every year from 1984 to 1989 but an annual increase

As Reagan neared departure from office, at the Gridiron Club dinner of March 26, 1988, he told Carl Rowan, the club's first black president, "I tried hard to win friendship among blacks. But I couldn't do it . . . talked to black leaders after my election in 1980, and they went out and criticized me in horrible ways. . . . They attacked me at the outset, so I said to hell with 'em." Then he nodded at General Colin Powell and added this final comment: "Now there is one of the smartest black men I ever knew." Ronald Reagan left office no more color-blind than when he first began his push for the White House.[84]

Reagan's successor, George Bush, followed in his footsteps. Indeed, Bush showed little inclination to deal with the nation's domestic problems. As he ignored such issues as poverty, the number of poor Americans began to climb once again, going from about 31.8 million or 12.8 percent of the population in 1989 to nearly 33.6 million or 13.5 percent in 1990, then to approximately 35.7 million or 14.2 percent in 1991—the most in any given year since before the War on Poverty. Blacks, as small as their population in proportion to that of whites, accounted for a whopping 10 million of the poor in those years. Welfare applications soared.

Battered by caseloads, facing shrinking revenues and rising budget deficits, many states, in efforts to cuts spending, looked to welfare programs and either reduced their AFDC benefits or froze them. General assistance grants (aid going to the needy who did not qualify for AFDC) were especially hard hit, as states and county governments either terminated them or sharply reduced the amounts of benefits. As hundreds of thousands of former AFDC and general assistance beneficiaries and other poor citizens experienced renewed suffering and homelessness, a host of new measures that came to be known as the "new paternalism" arose. Through waivers received from the federal government, states moved to the forefront of developing paternalistic policies— applying "family caps" that denied additional benefits to AFDC mothers who

---

in 1990–92. In 1992, however, their life expectancy was still 0.3 years below their peak of 65.3 years in 1984. Before 1988, the life expectancy of black females fluctuated, but it increased from 1988 to 1992. Meanwhile, the largest gain in life expectancy between 1980 and 1992 was for white men (2.5 years), followed by white females (1.7 years), black females (1.4 years), and black males (1.2 years). See Kenneth D. Kochanek and Bettie L. Hudson, "Advance Report of Final Mortality Statistics 1992," *Monthly Vital Statistics Report* 43, no. 6(S) (U.S. Department of Health and Human Services, National Center for Health Statistics, Division of Vital Statistics, Mar. 22, 1995), 3.

84. O'Reilly, *Nixon's Piano,* 378.

had more children, linking benefits more directly to work and to children's school attendance, applying time limits for welfare eligibility, and so forth. Throughout the late 1980s, these were actions taken at the state and local levels of government, since as much as possible George Bush ignored social policy. Nonetheless, like Reagan, George Bush left the presidency as he entered it, promising in his reelection bid in 1992 to cut back the social policies of the Great Society. As an indication of Bush's insensitivity to poverty, race, and cities, Bush vetoed an urban aid package the day after the general election, "killing the only urban aid measure to emerge from Congress in the wake of the Spring 1992 riots."[85] Bush could have let the bill die by simply failing to sign it, because Congress had already adjourned, but he made a point of vetoing it, as he claimed to be opposed to some minor tax increases (several his administration had once proposed) included in the bill.

Also in an act of partisan politics in the last days before a new administration took office, the Bush administration's Justice Department filed legal briefs involving black voters in Alabama and Georgia that took positions opposed by its own civil rights division. In the Alabama case, the Justice Department told the Supreme Court that the state needed to create only one congressional district with a black majority, although the assistant attorney general for civil rights had said that there should be two such districts. In the Georgia case, the Justice Department concluded that blacks had no legal basis to challenge a form of local government under which one county commissioner, elected at large, exercises all legislative and executive power. The department's civil rights division had argued that this form of government in Bleckley County, Georgia, violated the Voting Rights Act because it denied black voters, who accounted for 22 percent of the population, the opportunity to elect even one candidate of their choice. "It is next to impossible for a black candidate to win an at-large county-wide election in Bleckley County," said a brief drafted by the civil rights division.[86]

The Limits of Conservative Efforts in the Reagan-Bush Years

Given the strength of the conservative movement in the 1980s and the power of the corporate elite, it is somewhat surprising that twelve years of Republican

85. Art Pine, "'92 National Elections," *Los Angeles Times,* Nov. 5, 1992. The riots broke out in the immediate aftermath of the first Rodney King verdict.
86. Robert Pear, "Justice Department Challenges Its Civil Rights Division," *New York Times,* Jan. 20, 1993, A18.

administrations did not achieve even more substantial cutbacks or elimination of more Great Society programs. To be sure, along with significant encroachments on long-agreed civil rights principles and social policies, the Reagan era's reduction of taxes for the rich, federal budgetary policies that increased defense spending at the expense of domestic spending, deregulation, and monetary policies that benefited the top 20 percent (and especially the top 5 percent) did abundant damage. Budgetary and monetary policies were especially detrimental to the working class of all races, who lost more through program cuts than they gained in tax cuts. Concomitantly, the gap between the highest and lowest incomes widened as the working and middle classes got poorer and the rich got richer.[87] What was true of the working class in general was truest for the black poor and working classes.

Yet Reagan hardly achieved the dramatic reversal in social programs he promised on the campaign trail. In fact, both the general features of the welfare state and antidiscrimination policy proved to have considerable staying power throughout the Reagan-Bush era.

Not that Reagan and Bush failed to attempt to deliver on their promises to achieve stark retrenchment in civil and social rights. Often both administrations had to be turned back by Congress or at times by their own conservative-packed courts. When Reagan threatened to veto the Voting Rights Bill of 1982, for example, Congress mustered enough votes not only to override his veto if necessary but to expand and strengthen the bill. Once it became clear that congressional support for the bill was strong, Reagan agreed to sign it. Reagan also initially opposed a national holiday honoring the birthday of Dr. Martin Luther King Jr. but relented when faced with a nearly united Congress.

Despite the many judicial setbacks, in other instances the federal courts, and the Supreme Court in particular, blunted the efforts of Reagan's Justice Department to do more damage.[88] For example, the Reagan administration sought to grant a tax exemption to the segregated Bob Jones University of Greenville, South Carolina.[89] A plank in the 1980 Republican platform had

87. Kevin Phillips, *The Politics of Rich and Poor: Wealth and the American Electorate in the Reagan Aftermath* (New York: Random House, 1990).

88. For a discussion of the role of the courts in sustaining civil rights from the viewpoint of an open opponent of affirmative action, see Robert R. Detlefson, *Civil Rights under Reagan* (San Francisco: Institute for Contemporary Studies, 1991), 4ff.

89. *Bob Jones University v. United States,* 461 U.S. 574 (1983).

promised to "halt the unconstitutional regulatory vendetta launched by Mr. Carter's IRS commissioner against independent schools," and Congressman (later Senator) Trent Lott of Mississippi wrote to Reagan in 1981 reminding him of it. As the case headed to the Supreme Court, Lott asked Reagan to take Bob Jones's side, and Reagan agreed to do so. As a result, the Justice Department, which previously had stood with the IRS, now switched sides and stood with the segregationists. In 1983, eight of nine Supreme Court justices (all except Chief Justice Rehnquist) ruled against Bob Jones University and the Reagan administration. Still trying to grab victory from the jaws of defeat, Reagan concluded: "[I] prevented the IRS from determining national social policy all by itself."[90]

Reagan refought the battle of *Bob Jones* in *Grove City College v. Bell* (1984),[91] in which the Supreme Court limited antidiscrimination sanctions to the specific program or programs that discriminated and not to the entire institution. Thus, if a university's political science department, for example, had discriminated, then the department would be ineligible for federal funds, but the university as a whole would remain eligible. When Congress undid *Grove City* with the Civil Rights Restoration Bill of 1988, Reagan vetoed it, claiming that it "vastly and unjustly expanded the power of the federal government over the decisions and affairs of private organizations." He then submitted his own bill, the Civil Rights Protection Bill of 1988, which also overturned *Grove City* but exempted from the sexual discrimination provision all educational institutions "closely identified with religious organizations." Congress overrode the veto and made the Civil Rights Restoration Act of 1988 the law of the land.[92]

Still the battle continued. In 1990 and 1991 the Bush administration sought to stop passage of a civil rights act dedicated to expanding protections for women and racial minorities against discrimination in employment as well as overturning a series of 1989 Supreme Court decisions limiting the scope of employment discrimination law. "The principal opposition tactic, as has become well known, was to paint the bill as 'quota' legislation," wrote James Forman Jr. in *The Nation*. "Opponents alleged that the bill would force employers to pay close attention to the race and gender of all job applicants, and in many cases hire minorities and women who were not as well qualified

90. Quoted in O'Reilly, *Nixon's Piano,* 370–71.
91. *Grove City College v. Bell,* 465 U.S. 55 (1984).
92. O'Reilly, *Nixon's Piano,* 376.

as whites under the employer's traditional method of determining merit."[93] This effort on the part of the Bush administration also met with defeat. When a veto override threatened, the Bush administration retreated and agreed to a measure very close to one it had denounced as a "quota" bill. The Civil Rights Act of 1991 not only overturned a raft of Supreme Court decisions that had made it harder for women and people of color to sue over job discrimination but for the first time in history allowed punitive damages in sex discrimination cases.

Reagan and Bush also had to be rebuffed in regard to fair housing and the Commission on Civil Rights, which Reagan had packed with ultraconservatives. In 1983 Congress passed a fair housing act over the White House's opposition, and in 1986, when the civil rights community called for defunding the Commission on Civil Rights, the House and Senate agreed to reduce its funding from $12 million to $7.5 million in 1987.

Civil rights for the physically and mentally challenged were expanded. In 1992, Section 503 of the Rehabilitation Act was amended to provide that the standards of Title 1 of the Americans with Disabilities Act would apply to determining violations of non–affirmative action employment discrimination under Section 503. In all, twenty civil rights bills favored by the civil rights community were passed during the Reagan-Bush era. Even in an era of substantial loss, then, some gains were made.

Even affirmative action, though substantially made more difficult by *Croson* and underenforced by the Reagan and Bush administrations, nonetheless remained the law of the land and both administrations were rebuffed on several occasions. For instance, in 1985 the attorney general proposed to amend Executive Order 11246 to prohibit the use of goals and timetables; and in 1991 the Bush White House circulated to federal agencies and departments a sweeping directive that would have eliminated all policies seeking to implement affirmative action for women or people of color in hiring or promotion. Neither change was adopted.

Nor, ultimately, did either Bush or Reagan issue anti–affirmative action executive orders. Despite all the rhetoric about "reverse discrimination," neither president proposed a new civil rights bill to "protect" whites from it. Instead Reagan weakly announced that smaller companies under contract with

93. James Forman Jr., "Saving Affirmative Action," *Nation,* Dec. 9, 1991.

the United States government did not have to file written affirmative action plans. Although Reagan appointed the black conservative Clarence Thomas to chair the EEOC, no changes were made to the EEOC's *Guidelines on Affirmative Action*. Instead Thomas informally told the general counsel not to approve agreements with goals and timetables in them. Reagan thus used affirmative action more to exploit white fears and resentment and thereby ratchet up whiteness than to actually eliminate it. For the rest, his and Bush's court appointees would have to do the job.[94]

In sum, Reagan's and Bush's efforts to erode civil rights protections in schools, hiring, firing, and business contracting proved harmful to further progress by women and people of color. Their main tactics were deliberately failing to enforce the laws, withholding operating funds, and installing anti–civil rights justices and other appointees. Still the Reagan-Bush years represented something less than dire fundamental change. From the perspective of the late 1980s, the change in rhetoric was considerably larger than the change in drastic programmatic alternatives.

Similarly, Bush's and Reagan's attempts to alter social welfare either failed to effect structural change or were subsequently reversed even before they left office. As we have seen, the most politically successful welfare reform initiative during the Reagan years was the Family Support Act (FSA) of 1988, and Reagan signed it with great relish. The legislation, he argued, would "lead to a lasting emancipation from welfare dependency."[95] More realistically, the FSA was nothing more than an incremental piece of legislation that was full of compromises between liberals and conservatives. To be sure, most of the provisions favored by liberals—cash benefit increases, minimum national benefit standards, incentives for states to increase cash benefits for single-parent families—were left out of the bill. Nor did it provide the money that would be needed to make a major commitment to training and providing jobs for AFDC recipients. The total federal funding increase of the FSA for 1989–93 was only $3.3 billion, with added state and local costs estimated at $700 million for the same period.[96] Yet the FSA, signed October 13, 1988, also had some liberal

94. Skrentny, *Ironies of Affirmative Action*, 226–29.
95. Quoted in James Barnes, "Waiting for Clinton: The Politics of Welfare Reform," *National Journal*, Mar. 5, 1994, 516.
96. R. Kent Weaver, "Ending Welfare as We Know It," in Margaret Weir, ed., *The Social Divide: Political Parties and the Future of Activist Government* (Washington, D.C.: Brookings, 1998), 370–71.

tendencies: states had to set up education and training programs; at least 55 percent of funds had to go to long-term recipients or those under age twenty-four in danger of becoming long-term dependents; states had to provide aid for transportation to jobs and other services; the family income not counted in determining welfare eligibility was increased from $75 to $90; Medicaid benefits had to be provided for at least a year for those moving into low-paying jobs; and all states had to adopt programs to help two-parent families (AFDCUP programs). Given the FSA's ambiguous goals and low funding, it is small wonder that within four years Reagan's rosy forecast that the FSA would end welfare dependency was turned on its head: by 1992 the average monthly enrollment of people covered by AFDC had climbed from 11 million to 13.6 million.[97]

Meanwhile, under both Reagan and Bush, Congress expanded and indexed the earned income tax credit. Under Reagan the expansion came as part of the administration's huge tax-reform effort in 1986 and represented a modest attempt to provide tax relief for those near the very bottom of the American income structure, since massive tax relief was being provided to people in higher tax brackets. Under Bush the earned income tax credit was expanded after Congress appeared to be stalemated over passage of a bill to aid state support for child care. Instead of putting most of the money into direct aid to the states for child care, Congress put it into direct tax relief to poor families with at least one worker.[98]

In fact, by the time Bush left office, Congress had actually increased spending for some safety-net programs and reversed Reagan-initiated changes in programs such as AFDC by liberalizing eligibility, restoring very modest work incentives, and allowing individuals who lost AFDC benefits to remain eligible for Medicaid. Moreover, targeted women, infants, and children's assistance (WIC) and Head Start grew more than any other social programs in the 1980s, and the principal Medicaid cuts expired after 1984, after which Medicaid expanded, as did food stamps and SSI. By 1984, change in federal social welfare policy had shifted very modestly in the other direction. In addition, in contrast to the preferences of the Reagan administration, AFDC and most

97. Barnes, "Waiting for Clinton," 516.
98. Sandra Hoferth, "The 101st Congress: An Emerging Agenda for Children in Poverty," in Judith Chafel, ed., *Child Poverty and Policy* (Washington, D.C.: Urban Institute, 1994), 203–43.

other means-tested programs won exemption from the automatic cutbacks of the Gramm-Rudman statute, a signal that Congress really did consider them part of the social safety net despite the political weakness of their clientele. Most important of all, Congress did not act on the Reagan administration's more radical 1982 "New Federalism" proposal, which would have transferred jurisdiction over AFDC and food stamps to the states in exchange for a federal takeover of Medicaid (in part because the administration failed to come up with a concrete bill). Ultimately, as Barbara and Peter Gottschalk contend, cuts in programs for poor Americans during the Reagan-Bush era were largely a continuation of trends that started during the Ford and Carter administrations, not a sharp break with the New Deal legacy, even in its Great Society rendition.[99]

In sum, there was very real retrenchment with substantial negative impacts on the poor, African Americans, and Latinos. The inevitable counterrevolution King saw as far back as the late 1960s was taking place. But as regards both civil rights and social welfare, embedded in the mixed record of the Reagan-Bush years was stagnation, the end of progress, not obliteration. The question that begs to be asked is: If conservative Republicans were so formidable in the 1980s and liberal Democrats so politically weak, why were the Reagan and Bush administrations unsuccessful in fulfilling their promises to fundamentally cut back social provisions, eliminate affirmative action, and dramatically transform the American welfare state?

Impeding Reagan and Bush

The answer stems in part from political forces rooted in the legacies of past policy and thereby the state itself. Just as the equal opportunity and antidiscrimination policies of the 1960s paved the way for massive white resistance and the politics of retrenchment in the 1980s, dialectically the 1960s policies also stimulated the growth of institutions and politics for their defense.

For instance, bureaucrats within the welfare state, especially through their unions (AFSCME, the American Federation of State, Municipal, and County Employees, and AFGE, the American Federation of Government Employees) defended social welfare against further cuts and affirmative action against elimination. In addition, the numerous state, county, municipal, and

---

99. Barbara Gottschalk and Peter Gottschalk, "The Reagan Retrenchment in Historical Context," in Brown, *Remaking the Welfare State,* 67.

special district agencies, initiated or expanded as a result of the growth of welfare programs in the 1960s and affirmative action in the 1970s, mounted campaigns to limit destruction of the programs they administered. Associations of mayors, county officials, and governors became some of the most vocal groups in the nation in resisting slashes in social programs. After all, they would have been on the front line where the pain would be felt and people's hostilities might be released. Similarly, the vast array of offices set up to implement affirmative action from federal to local levels acted in its defense. To take just one vivid example, within a year after the *Croson* decision in 1989, sixty cities spent more than $30 million to conduct disparity studies in an attempt to demonstrate that racial discrimination was ongoing, and that their cities were therefore constitutionally allowed to maintain minority set-aside programs.

Moreover, a wide range of civic organizations mobilized. For example, in defense of welfare, hundreds of thousand of "private sector" charities (a heavy majority created after the 1960s and dependent on national, state, and local government welfare financing to deliver services)[100] joined in the mobilization. Social workers' organizations heavily participated in the struggle. Welfare recipients themselves reinvigorated such organizations as the NWRO, and other activists formed new organizations, such as the Coalition for Human Needs, to educate the public and organize lobbying campaigns. These groups joined with older civil rights and children's rights organizations (such as the Children's Defense Fund) as well as senior citizen groups (such as the American Association of Retired Persons) to fight cuts in welfare on national, state, and local levels.

In defense of affirmative action, historic civil rights organizations and minority business associations joined a long list of university administrators and corporate officials who favored affirmative action and reported that the policy was good for American education and American business.[101] Taken together, this set of diverse groups provided a level of concentrated support for affirmative action that tended to dwarf their diffuse opposition. While they did not represent a force capable of expanding affirmative action policy, they made the

100. Lester Salamon, "Partners in Public Service," *Foundation News,* July–August 1984.
101. R. Kent Weaver and Bert A. Rockman, eds., *Do Institutions Matter? Government Capabilities in the United States and Abroad* (Washington, D.C.: Brookings, 1993).

status quo, not program elimination, the more likely outcome in the 1980s.[102] Indeed, in at least one instance, affirmative action was further institutionalized: the Business Opportunity Report Act, passed near the end of Reagan's second term, created the Commission on Minority Business, whose primary responsibility was to step up the implementation of minority set-asides. Regarding both welfare and affirmative action, the existence and mobilization of an institutional support network was able to protect programs under attack during the Reagan-Bush years.[103]

It also did not help the Reagan and Bush administrations' efforts at retrenchment that public opinion was not clearly supportive of the dramatic changes they sought. To be sure, Americans of all races, classes, parties, and ideologies and of both genders wanted the welfare system to be "fixed," but polls throughout the 1980s showed that for strong majorities of voters the goal of welfare reform was to get people to work, not to limit benefits or punish recipients.[104] Only if children were protected and there were jobs for their parents was majority support for reform certain and unambiguous in the 1980s. The context of relatively high unemployment (especially in Reagan's first term) doomed these prospects and weakened support for change. For the Reagan and Bush administrations to have gone further than they did in trashing welfare would have put them on the defensive over the "fairness" issue at a time when various national surveys repeatedly reported a widespread impression that Republican policies harm the poor and benefit the rich.[105]

102. In *Policy Paradox and Political Reason* (New York: HarperCollins, 1988), Deborah Stone points out that whenever a policy struggle is marked by concentrated opposition and diffuse support, the status quo is the most likely outcome.

103. Weir et al., *Politics of Social Policy,* 357–80.

104. See analysis of polls in the early 1980s by Seymour Martin Lipset, "The Elections, the Economy, and Public Opinion," *PS: The Journal of the American Political Science Association* 18, no. 1 (Winter 1985): 28–38. As late as the early 1990s, a majority polled still prized welfare reform that provided jobs. When asked to name the top goal for reforming welfare in November 1993, 52% of voters selected "helping people get off the welfare rolls and into the work force," placing it well ahead of such goals as "strengthening families and family values" (32%), "ending long-term dependence on welfare as a way of life" (29%), "eliminating fraud and abuse" (28%), and "saving taxpayers money by reducing spending on welfare" (7%). See Geoffrey Garin, Guy Molyneux, and Linda DiVall, "Public Attitudes toward Welfare Reform: A Summary of Key Research Findings," Peter D. Hart Research Associates and American Viewpoint, Washington, D.C., 1, 3–4.

105. Lipset, "Elections, the Economy, and Public Opinion," 28–29.

The public's view was even more complex and uncertain. A sharp bipolar pattern existed in regard to affirmative action, with nearly half of Americans supportive of the policy and half not. Indeed, depending on the way questions were worded, polls showed a slight majority of Americans continuing to support affirmative action during the 1980s.[106]

Not only did the general public narrowly split, but both parties increasingly were divided internally regarding affirmative action. Throughout the 1980s, two key factions made up the Republican Party: fiscal conservatives who favored the limited state but took great pains to avoid being known as nativists bent on protecting white privilege; and ultraconservatives who actually preferred a strong state when it came to race, abortion, school prayer, gay rights, and the death penalty. This second wing of the party would have eliminated not only affirmative action but nearly every other antidiscrimination policy, but they did not have clear and unchallenged ascendancy. Splits in the Republican electorate were mirrored in the Reagan and Bush administrations, where both wings of the party were well represented. The ultraconservatives, including Reagan's attorney general, Edwin Meese, and assistant attorney general for civil rights, W. Bradford Reynolds, sought to terminate affirmative action, but fiscal conservatives such as Donald Regan and Bill Brock sought to circumvent them. One tool often used by the fiscal conservatives was to leak the ultraconservatives' plans to the press. The resulting outcry from protected groups (especially from white women's organizations, which Republicans still had some dreams of capturing) would stymie plans to end affirmative action. Much the same process worked in the Bush years. At the same time, there were relations with Congress to be managed, and here too splits in the Republican Party played an influential role in preventing extreme retrenchment.

Arguably, at least, most of the establishment—Democratic and Republican alike—accepted affirmative action as a genuine part of the American political landscape in the 1980s. Similarly, there was still support for the core of the Great Society's War on Poverty. One reason Reagan never sent Congress his "New Federalism" proposal was that Congress seemed highly unlikely to enact it.

Key Republicans such as Senators Robert Dole and John Danforth

106. See annual polls conducted from 1984 through 1988 by the Gallup Organization for the Joint Center for Political Studies, Washington, D.C., and the NBC/*Wall Street Journal* polls in March–April 1995, conducted by Hart-Teeter.

strongly supported affirmative action in the 1980s. When Dole's wife, Elizabeth, was secretary of labor, she held a ceremony celebrating the twenty-fifth anniversary of Executive Order 11246. Had Reagan or Bush done away with affirmative action in the 1980s, moderate Republicans and Democrats (who still controlled both houses of Congress throughout most of the 1980s)[107] might well have coalesced to pass legislation endorsing at least the broad principle of affirmative action (which some argue is precisely what the Civil Rights Act of 1991 did).

As long as Democrats controlled Congress, the full dismantling of affirmative action was unlikely, particularly in view of the slow but steady growth of blacks, Latinos, and women as Democratic members of the House of Representatives and their elevation to prominent positions in committees and subcommittees. The new caucuses formed by racial minorities and women tended to work in concert with the express objective of moderating proposals initiated by conservatives.

In general, the Democratic-controlled Congress pursued two main strategies to thwart Reagan and Bush. First, party members joined together to create a relatively solid congressional voting bloc that strongly opposed bills containing provisions to limit or reduce social service programs and fundamentally alter affirmative action. The Democratic coalition gained limited Republican support. The second strategy was directly successful. Democrats attached programs and agencies that were in danger of elimination or severe cutback to Republican bills that were sure to pass. Since Reagan and Bush did not have the option of a line-item veto, many, but not all, Democratic provisions designed to retain entitlement programs passed. While Democrats were usually not successful in their attempts to expand or refine existing entitlement and social service programs, they were able to stop conservatives from abolishing them and redirecting all funds to business-oriented policies. Hence as long as the Democrats controlled Congress, Republican successes were constrained and the core Great Society programs survived. These struggles were part and parcel of the heightened atmosphere of partisanship in Congress.

In addition, the Reagan administration was hampered by what Lowi and Ginsberg call the R.I.P. (revelations, investigations, prosecutions) process,

---

107. The Republicans won control of the Senate in 1986, but it reverted to the Democrats in 1988.

which seemingly has become a fixture in the American political process.[108] That is, with Reagan's last years in office increasingly filled with the Iran-Contra scandal, the administration had little time to break new ground on the racial front or any other.[109] In sum, understanding the limits on Reagan's and Bush's ability to fundamentally transform the nation's social policy regime requires comprehending links among the American economy, culture, constitutional structure, policy legacies, public opinion, and political processes. Liberal politicians, journalists, some large corporations, and an array of pro–civil rights organizations stubbornly defended existing policies against the assaults of the Reagan and Bush administrations. There is perhaps a political lesson in the fact that there were both some gains and successful defenses of some equal opportunity programs under Nixon, Reagan, and Bush: less may depend on who occupies the White House than on exerting sufficient pressure to force the hand of government.[110]

Finally, perhaps more than any other single factor, changes in the operation of white skin privilege acted as a bulwark against fundamental reversals of gains in civil rights. Despite skillful manipulation of racial symbols on the part of Republican administrations, formal equality, the acceptance of the principle of racial equality, and growing access of racial minorities not only to the vote but also to political office combined to moderate retrenchment. The shifting ideology of white privilege was found in examples of substantial opposition of businessmen and some other Republicans (as well as the slew of elites from local governments to academia) to an outright repeal of affirmative action during the Reagan-Bush years. This opposition cannot be explained on the basis of self-interest alone but rather also reflects changes in the ideology of whiteness unthinkable before the Civil Rights and Great Society years.

Conclusion

In the vacuum created by economic stress and liberal capitulation, a genuinely conservative public philosophy gained easy ascendancy and strong electoral support in the 1980s. Confirming E. E. Schattschneider's conclusion that new

108. Theodore J. Lowi and Benjamin Ginsberg, *American Government,* 4th ed. (New York: Norton, 1996), chaps. 6–7.
109. O'Reilly, *Nixon's Piano,* 375.
110. Steinberg, *Turning Back,* 103.

policy produces new politics,[111] conservatives responded to the equal opportunity policies of the Great Society with a new politics of race carried on through pejorative code words and labels embedded in a new public philosophy. That new philosophy blamed the social policies of the 1960s (and ultimately those of the New Deal), rather than new economic processes at work, for problems such as growing unemployment, underemployment, inequality, deepening poverty, and stagnating productivity and wages. The Great Society was castigated as actually advantaging African Americans over whites and women over men and generating unacceptable rates of crime, violence, unwed motherhood, and dependency.

The goal of Republican politicians was to stoke the fires of white resentment encouraged by economic insecurity by scapegoating people of color. Nixon pandered to white interests so openly that he inherited the Wallace vote, which contributed to his landslide victory over George McGovern in 1972. He became the first Republican ever to sweep the South and carry large numbers of northern blue-collar white voters as well. After the short-lived, uneventful presidency of Gerald Ford, the Democrat Jimmy Carter, propelled into office by the Watergate scandal on the one hand and the black vote on the other and widely regarded as sympathetic to people of color, actually delivered little on the social policy agenda, including civil rights. Reagan shamelessly appealed to the ideology and reality of whiteness. Although he professed to be opposed to virtually all "big government" aid programs, he left untouched those that disproportionately assisted middle-class whites, especially Social Security and Medicare. Instead he focused on those programs most identified in white minds with blacks, especially welfare and food stamps. Bush followed in his predecessor's footsteps, leaving a host of problems in his wake. Most of all, the Reagan-Bush administrations sought to associate whiteness with unfair *dis*advantage. Ironically, the Republican administrations of the 1980s claimed that the only thing that could fix white "disadvantage" was color-blindness. In actuality, color-blindness in a country in which white privilege continued to prevail meant disregard of color and power. Avoiding any serious discussion of the real advantage white men still held and the structural reasons for it, Republican administrations of the 1980s encouraged working -class whites to ignore the

111. E. E. Schattschneider, *The Semi-sovereign People* (New York: Holt, Rinehart & Winston, 1960).

class nature of their problems in the new global economy and to transfer their frustrations to people of color—blacks, Native Americans, and "immigrants.". There was never another era in which those who disavowed the advantages of whiteness more firmly predicated their lives on its privileges. As Hodding Carter summed up the Reagan years: "It is a new America, Ronald Reagan's America, and at times it smells a lot like the old Mississippi. . . . The Reagan presidency has given new hope to America's bigots and renewed legitimacy to the sly slogans of white supremacy. If it is not precisely a return to the time of Redemption . . . it is not because the President and his men have not tried."[112]

In Reagan's "new America," it became customary to besmirch the America of the 1960s and to look with nostalgia at the America of the 1950s or before. In this supposed morality play, the 1960s were cast as beginning a period of great cultural and moral decline. The attempt was to rewrite the decade as having been all about "flower power," sexual freedom and promiscuity, drugs and crime. The hard-fought battle to make the nation a full democracy was either forgotten or assigned an insignificant role in characterizations of the 1960s.

But was America really a moral society before the 1960s? How moral was it to enslave a people and then oppress and exploit them for a hundred more years through Jim Crow? How moral was it to deny the most basic of democratic rights on the basis of race? How moral was it to confine women, more than half of the population, to jobs paying either the lowest or unequal wages for the same work or to the sphere of domesticity?

Conversely, was it moral to privilege white men simply because they were just that—white and men? Was it moral to save for white men virtually all the valued positions in society whether they "merited" them or not? Was it moral to provide white men access to property ownership when women were denied the right to accumulate property for a very long time and blacks and Asians even longer? Was it moral for white men to be property owners and blacks to be property? Arguably, behind the smoke and mirrors used to castigate the 1960s and the Great Society programs it spawned was really the bemoaning of the period's challenge to white power.

Electoral outcomes and public opinion surveys show that in the 1980s a strong majority of whites bought the conservatives' view of the reforms of the

112. Hodding Carter III, *The Reagan Years* (New York: Braziller, 1988), 108.

1960s. The result was frayed support for a social policy apparatus that had developed in relatively unbroken fashion from the New Deal through the Great Society.

Concomitantly, there was real retrenchment with substantial negative impacts on the poor and people of color in the years from Nixon through Bush. The inevitable counterrevolution King prophesied had begun. Yet, as a result of actions of political forces created and nurtured by movement politics and many of the policies of the Great Society, splits within the Republican party, Democratic control of Congress, and the mobilization of opposition by groups that would have been dramatically affected by change, the most potentially devastating assaults on civil rights and social policy were averted during the 1980s. The question was what the 1990s would bring.

five

Racially Charged Policy Making

Crime and Welfare Reform in the Clinton Years

All of us, we know all about race baiting. They've used that old tool

on us for decades. And I want to tell you one thing: I understand this

tactic and I will not let them get away with it in 1992.

—*Bill Clinton*

When Bill Clinton was elected president in 1992, to most African Americans it was evidence that the nation had finally emerged from the long dark tunnel of the Reagan-Bush years. Whatever other Americans in the 1980s and 1990s thought of the administrations of Ronald Reagan and George Bush, and however history ultimately judged the two presidents, for African Americans the two administrations had meant a period of waning social policy and significant setback.

To be sure, some affluent African Americans experienced improvement in their living standards under Reagan-Bush, but most blacks did not. The downward plunge for African American and Latino men was especially acute. While the decline in year-round, full-time employment of white men fell by 4 percentage points from 1979 to 1992, the comparable decline for African American men was 6 percentage points and for Latino men a whopping 13 percentage points. Even among college-educated African American men the negative trend was unmistakable. In 1979 an African American male college graduate working year-round, full-time, earned 81 percent of his white male counterpart's salary; in 1992; after twelve years of Reagan-Bush, African American male college graduates earned only 74 percent of the salaries of white male graduates. Although the media in the late 1980s and early 1990s concentrated on an "angry white men" phenomenon, if there was ever a group of men whose shrinking opportunities justified anger, it was men of color.

A host of studies throughout the Reagan-Bush era showed discrimination on the basis of race to be alive and well in America. Researchers at the Urban Institute, for example, found significant levels of discrimination against African Americans and Latinos in labor and housing markets.[1] The Federal Reserve Bank found "dramatic disparities in loan rejection rates" by race, a fact attributed to discrimination in the finance industry against people of color.[2]

It was not only Reagan's policy actions that infuriated African Americans. Reagan's seemingly endless petty insults and racial gestures made him anathema in virtually every African American community. His refusal to meet with the Congressional Black Caucus; his jokes about "welfare queens," "pimps," and "chiselers"; his inability to remember the name of the only African American in his cabinet; his red-baiting attacks on the memory of Dr. Martin Luther King Jr.; and his visit to a Nazi burial ground in Germany—all contributed to the massive contempt African Americans felt for him.[3]

The affronts continued at the Republican National Convention of 1992. From Pat Buchanan, Ronald Reagan, and Pat Robertson to Newt Gingrich, Marilyn Quayle, and George Bush, intolerance became the Grand Old Party's not so grand old theme as speaker after speaker hid behind religious values as the raison d'être for making ugly concessions to the far right. Attacks on citizens living in inner cities, gays, and women were relentless; even many Republicans found the convention repugnant.[4] The convention only added to African Americans' reasons for exultation when George Herbert Bush lost to William Jefferson Clinton, even though Clinton was not extraordinarily popular among African Americans in 1992.

Despite his promise not to let "them" get away with a campaign predi-

---

1. Margery Austin Turner, Michael Fix, and Raymond Struyk, *Opportunities Denied, Opportunities Diminished: Discrimination in Hiring* (Washington, D.C.: Urban Institute, 1991), 91–99; Michael Fix and Raymond Struyk. *Clear and Convincing Evidence: Measurement of Discrimination in America* (Washington, D.C.: Urban Institute, 1993).

2. Cited in Julianne Malveaux, "The Parity Imperative: Civil Rights, Economic Justice, and the New American Dilemma," in *The State of Black America: 1992* (Washington, D.C.: National Urban League, 1992), 283.

3. Clarence Lusane, *African Americans at the Crossroads: The Restructuring of Black Leadership and the 1992 Elections* (Boston: South End Press, 1994), 132.

4. E. J. Dionne, "Some Republicans Also Object," *Washington Post*, Aug. 4, 1992, 23, and Lusane, *African Americans at the Crossroads*, 133.

cated on the politics of racial division, Clinton rankled some key African American leaders when in January of the election year he authorized and oversaw the execution of Ricky Ray Rector, a brain-damaged African American man so mentally incompetent that he did not know who he was, and at his last meal asked for his desert to be saved so he could eat it after his execution.[5] Tensions erupted in February 1992 when Clinton, told erroneously by an aide that Jesse Jackson had endorsed Iowa Senator Tom Harkin for the Democratic nomination without first informing him, had some angry things to say about Jackson in remarks recorded on videotape and ultimately broadcast to millions.[6] In March 1992, Clinton's decision to golf at an Arkansas country club that had no black members set off a firestorm of criticism and raised anew questions about the depth and sincerity of his commitment to bridging the nation's racial divide.[7]

In June 1992 anger flared again when, in what his staffers came to term "counter-scheduling" (that is, giving unpopular centrist speeches to left-of-center groups to demonstrate his independence from "special interests"), Clinton sharply criticized the National Rainbow Coalition for inviting the rap musician Sister Souljah to speak at its national leadership summit, after she was accused of making racist remarks in the wake of the riots that followed the acquittal of the police who had been videotaped as they brutalized Rodney King.[8] To many African Americans, Clinton's remarks were little more than a public attempt to show his distancing from Jackson in particular and blacks in general, part and parcel of the New Democratic version of playing the race card. And throughout the campaign Clinton's most popular campaign promise, "to end welfare as we know it," was viewed by many African Americans as a race-coded message that the Democrats were breaking from supporting programs and policies that could be seen as beneficial to them. In short, despite Clinton's oft-

5. Lusane, *African Americans at the Crossroads*, 158–59.

6. Howard Kurtz, "In Instant Replay, Clinton's Unvarnished Emotion," *Washington Post*, Feb. 29, 1992.

7. "Clinton to Boycott All-White Club," *Washington Post*, Mar. 20, 1992.

8. Mark Miller, "'Manhattan Project,' 1992," *Newsweek*, Nov. 6, 1992, 55. As Clinton's campaign strategist, James Carville, concluded, what Clinton got out of the Sister Souljah and other "distancing" affairs was white votes, particularly the votes of the so-called Reagan Democrats, such as the North Philadelphia electrician who said, "The day he told off that fucking Jackson is the day he got [mine]" (quoted in Kenneth O'Reilly, *Nixon's Piano: Presidents and Racial Politics from Washington to Clinton* [New York: Free Press, 1995], 415).

repeated pieties about "racial healing," in the eyes of many African Americans he was far from above doing a little race-baiting of his own.

Yet if African Americans were not elated by the Clinton candidacy, just as surely his election signaled to the 82 percent who voted for him in 1992 a new beginning and a new hope. Unlike many national white politicians (including the Democratic presidential nominees who preceded him in 1984 and 1988), Clinton grew up around African Americans, and the economic hardships of his youth often placed him in the company of poor ones. Although never on the front lines as a civil rights advocate in the 1960s, Bill Clinton had spoken out against racism since he was a boy. When he was sixteen years old, he fought for a civil rights plank in the platform of his party at the American Legion Boys Nation. As early as 1969 he cited his passionate opposition to "racism in America" in his ultimately famous letter to the head of the University of Arkansas's ROTC program. His campaigns for governor led him to many African American churches in many small towns. From time to time as candidate and governor he recalled being repulsed by the segregation of his youth and vowing to fight discrimination and prejudice at every opportunity.

Moreover, Clinton had recently demonstrated the continuing fire of his commitment to civil rights. In 1987 he testified against the nomination of Reagan's conservative nominee Robert Bork to the Supreme Court, a man most civil rights groups concluded would turn back the clock on racial progress. Despite the fact that Judge Bork had been Clinton's constitutional law professor at Yale, Clinton stated that he was uncompromisingly opposed to the nominee, given Bork's anti–civil rights record, his right-wing views, and the potential of his nomination to reopen racial wounds.[9] In addition, unlike President Bush, who saw no connection between the response to the verdict in the first Rodney King trial and conditions of life faced by inner-city blacks and called the riots "the brutality of a mob, pure and simple,"[10] Clinton spoke of the injustice of the verdict and how it tapped into feelings of hurt and frustration, especially for the forgotten and left behind. "The people in the other America deserve the same law and order that the rest of us demand," Clinton concluded.[11] Thus when Clinton accused the Republicans of neglect, selfish-

9. W. John Moore, "On the March Again?" *National Journal,* Dec. 12, 1992, 2824.

10. Linda Greenhouse, "NAACP Chief Assails Bush as Graduates Cheer," *New York Times,* May 10, 1992, 1.

11. E. J. Dionne Jr. and Maralee Schwartz, "Clinton Issues Plea for Racial Harmony; Candidate Plans to Visit L.A. Today," *Washington Post,* May 3, 1995, A1.

ness," and divisiveness and explained his empathy with society's victims because of his own experience in overcoming poverty,[12] he scored high points among African Americans.

More, however, than Clinton's empathy and symbolic politics made African Americans feel a greater "comfort level" (to borrow Jesse Jackson's term). His campaign promises were key. Bush, who had claimed to be the "education president," had cut thirty-two education programs, proposed a voucher system that had the potential to exacerbate the crisis of the public schools, and never fully funded successful programs such as Head Start. By contrast, Clinton called for $65 billion for public education, increased opportunities for college students, and full funding for Head Start. Under Reagan-Bush, federal spending on the cities fell from $37 billion to $13 billion, and Bush's answer to the crisis in the cities in 1992 was mostly a call for more law and order and budget cuts. Clinton, by contrast, proposed an "investment strategy" that included a $50 billion urban rescue plan that theoretically would create jobs and begin to attack some of the entrenched economic and social problems of inner cities.[13]

Indeed, Clinton's policy pledges, if implemented, would have a positive impact on many African Americans. He pledged to raise caps on damages in workplace discrimination cases; support statehood for the District of Columbia; sign the Motor Voter Bill, which would ease access to voter registration; and appoint more people of color and women to top-level administration positions. He promised to end tax incentives that encourage and allow companies to export their plants and jobs and to raise the minimum wage—two initiatives heavily supported by most African American leaders. Given the escalating crisis in African American health care, Clinton's pledge to create a fair, affordable, and quality universal heath care system also was well received among African Americans. His promise to finance his program of reform by raising taxes on the rich and cutting the military budget were steps long sought by African American activists.[14] In sum, when Clinton spelled out how he would reorient social policy and simultaneously end "a dozen years of racial and social divisiveness,"[15] there were lots of reasons for African Americans to believe that his

12. David Broder, "For the Democrats, a Beginning," *Washington Post,* Oct. 9, 1991, A25.

13. Lusane, *African Americans at the Crossroads,* 141–42, 169–79, 177–79.

14. David Broder, "Clinton's Pledges," *Washington Post,* Jan. 20, 1992, A1.

15. Quoted in Dan Balz, "Gov. Clinton Enters Presidential Race," *Washington Post,* Oct. 4, 1991, A1.

promised restructuring of politics, markets, and society would have at its heart a fundamental commitment to addressing the greater hardships faced by the vast majority of people of color.

Clinton wanted to reduce the political salience of race as a central cleavage and at the same time retain strong African American and Latino political support. After all, the electoral arithmetic of the Democratic party since 1968 amply demonstrated that the Democrats in the 1990s had no more hope of winning national elections without a nearly unanimous bloc of highly motivated African American voters and a strong majority of Latino voters than they did without securing a substantial minority (at least 40 percent or so) of white voters. The question for Clinton, then, was how to avoid a key challenge that other Democrats had faced: how to signal whites (especially white men) that the party was not a captive of so-called special interests (increasingly perceived by key sectors of America as allied or interrelated and pressing the claims of "minorities"—not only African Americans and Latinos but also trade unionists, feminists, gays, AIDS victims, and so forth) and yet claim to be enough of a party of inclusion to discourage a popular African American candidate from opposing him, maintain African American and Latino leadership support, and inspire people of color to turn out to vote in large numbers.

The challenge for the Republicans, of course, differed from that of the Democrats. Long the benefactors of race being politically salient, Republicans faced an entirely different set of questions. With the sole exception of 1976, the party whose most illustrious leader was the "Great Emancipator," Abraham Lincoln, won the White House with less than 15 percent of the African American vote in every election since 1968.[16] The party's stock in trade, in the eyes of many voters, was a politics permeated by race, which played on anxieties of white Americans. Thus the Republicans, with an obviously more racially homogeneous base, could play the race card in a way Democrats could not. Their challenge, however, was to escape their growing image as the party of whiteness with all the concomitant vulnerability to charges of racism and sexism.

Democratic Party Dilemmas and Racial Politics

Clinton's choice of tactics for managing the politics of race was grounded in the struggle between the two major wings of his party that began as far back

---

16. David Bositis, "Blacks in the 1996 Republican National Convention," Joint Center for Political and Economic Studies (Washington, D.C., 1996), 16; and Marjorie Connelly, "Portrait of the Electorate," *New York Times*, Nov. 10, 1996, 28.

as 1968 and escalated throughout the 1970s and 1980s. By the 1990s, once submerged differences surrounding issues of race and social policy vied openly for dominance. Two main dramatically different explanations of racial politics competed against each other; both were concerned with explaining why whites had been leaving the party in droves.

On one side, liberal Democrats (or populists) argued that Republicans had consciously and aggressively spread the politics of divisiveness, seeking to convince whites that the causes of their problems were Democratic-sponsored social programs aimed at people of color. According to liberals, the Republican story was little more than an incendiary fairy tale. What was needed for the Democrats to win the presidency in the 1990s, liberals posited, was not desertion of social policies that worked and a strong defense of civil rights but a more intense focus on the pocketbook issues that had once guaranteed the party success. Working-class whites, liberals maintained, had been out of sync with the party for decades on issues involving race. There had been no prior racial compatibility; the New Deal coalition was never a multiracial garden of Eden; rather the white working and middle classes had sided with the party only because of its vision on the central questions of economic security and jobs. It had been the failure of the party since the 1970s to provide answers to the declining economic plight of workers and the "meltdown" of the middle class that accounted for the Democrats' political misfortunes. What was needed was to see to it that the working and middle classes' economic needs were met.

Thus, instead of joining Republicans in a rightward drift, the most liberal elements of the party (disproportionately black and increasingly centered in Jesse Jackson's Rainbow Coalition) took the argument a step further, concluding that the Democratic Party should move leftward and educate, organize, and register the vast segment of the potential electorate of all races that neither benefited from Republican policies nor voted in large numbers. To force the party to do so, they advocated mobilization outside of the party as a first step. Once organized, they would enter the party to transform it from within. That transformation would involve seeing to it that the party took up a renewed economic populism that set new priorities and investments in people— especially universal health care, education, children's programs, and job creation. "Corporate responsibility," the stark reduction of tax expenditures and subsidies to unproductive corporations, and a sharply downsized military budget were identified as the chief means to pay for the new social investments.

To be sure, these suggestions bore potential and deserved far more careful consideration than they received. But the problem for liberals and progressives was not only that they had lost a substantial amount of political muscle, but that they ended up sounding as though they were proposing little more than a big laundry list of new and costly spending programs, vague with regard to purpose. Rather than having what President Bush once called the "vision thing," a coherent response to the conservatives' interpretation of events, Rainbow progressives fell somewhat short of a new pro-active public philosophy replete with a moral core and justificatory rhetoric about the role of government and the proper relationship of state, market, and society. Without providing their own new worldview, progressives were forced to fight a battle they could not win.

One even more basic problem for Jackson's Rainbow Coalition was that no long-term coalition ever materialized. From the start the "rainbow" was identified primarily with blacks, and it remained so throughout the 1990s. In addition, structurally the Rainbow remained little more than an election-year mechanism for a candidate who was charismatic (especially to blacks, a much smaller but important segment of Latinos, and members of the white left). While the Rainbow needed to build a grassroots infrastructure spanning the nation that would precede and outlive Jackson's candidacies, some close to Jackson, such as Jack O'Dell and Manning Marable, maintain that Jackson's grip on the Rainbow was so strong that he set out after 1988 to put in place rules that stripped local Rainbow chapters of any power to act on their own and virtually even a reason to exist. Rather than digging in and doing the hard work of building at the grassroots level and either running stealth candidates or endorsing candidates only after they met the Rainbow's agenda (much as the Christian Coalition did successfully on the Republican right), Jackson's Rainbow remained mainly an organization inside the Beltway for all practical purposes. With little more than a national office working exclusively on the issues and activities that Jackson himself deemed critical, Jackson's influence was limited in the 1990s to whatever resulted from his considerable media and networking skills.

One thing the challenge of the progressive wing of the party provoked, however, was a vigorous response from moderates and conservatives, particularly southern ones. In 1985 moderate and conservative Democrats created the Democratic Leadership Council (DLC) to "revitalize the Democratic Party and lead it back into the political mainstream."[17] By 1992 the DLC had more than

17. "About the DLC," *Mainstream Democrat*, Mar. 1991, 25.

3,000 members (most elected officials) in twenty-seven states.[18] This gave the DLC, unlike the Rainbow, not only key players in place across the nation but institutional structures as well that could be activated in campaigns.

From its inception the DLC made it clear that it intended to publicly disassociate the party from Jackson and the liberals. In their attack on liberalism, the DLC theorists Bill Galston and Elaine Kamarck declared, "The public has come to associate liberalism with tax and spending policies that contradict the interests of average families; with welfare policies that foster dependence rather than self-reliance; with softness toward perpetrators of crime and indifference toward its victims . . . and with an adversarial stance toward mainstream moral and cultural values. . . . Jesse Jackson's 1984 and 1988 campaigns . . . were the purest version of liberal fundamentalism."[19] Dubbing themselves "New Democrats," the DLC essentially counseled a deemphasis on race at least as dramatic as Moynihan's "benign neglect" during the Nixon years. Yet the DLC also wanted to reinvigorate the coalition under the New Deal and Great Society banners.

To do so, the DLC told the story that the Democrats in the 1960s had been hijacked by a band of small-minded black militants and "champaign liberals" who insisted on race-targeted programs and censored public discussion of the social pathologies among the black poor. This resulted in failure to give proper weight to the concerns of the beleaguered white working and middle classes. In turn, whites—especially white males—were affronted by the civil rights agenda of the party. In this lament, progressive agendas lost credibility and Democrats lost the White House because they deviated from the old New Deal coalition's focus on universal programs and became identified with "special interests." This alienated the Democratic Party's white working- and middle-class constituencies, who carried the fiscal burden for the programs, many of which offended their own "traditional values."[20]

Conspicuously missing from New Democrat formulations were discussions of the explicitly racial stratification within the working class and a history of white working-class antagonism toward blacks. Forgotten was the reason

18. Donald Lambro, "Insurgent DLC Sees Victory within Its Grasp," *Washington Times,* May 4, 1992, A1.

19. William Galston and Elaine Ciulla Kamarck, *The Politics of Evasion: Democrats and the Presidency* (Washington, D.C.: Progressive Policy Institute, September 1989), 4–5.

20. For discussion and critique of these views, see Adolph Reed and Julian Bond, "The Assault on Equality: Race, Rights, and the New Orthodoxy," *Nation,* Dec. 9, 1991, 4–6.

there was a need for aggressive antidiscrimination efforts in the first place. Long gone was any account of why the New Deal virtually excluded blacks from many of its social policy initiatives and was silent on civil rights. Neither Joe Sixpack nor Suzy Yuppie was directly implicated as a beneficiary of a racist structure. Instead, it was as if history began in 1964. In the rhetoric of the DLC, white working-class and middle-class hostility to black aspirations was presented as a post–Civil Rights Movement phenomenon even as the old New Deal coalition was romanticized as neutral with respect to distinctively racial stratification. What was needed, then, from the New Democrat point of view, was a return to the political mainstream. As the Democratic pollster Stanley Greenberg saw it, this meant not only abandoning many Great Society programs, but first and foremost, that "the plight of the poor and the unfinished business of civil rights [were] no longer the first principles of Democratic politics."[21] In short, from the New Democrats' perspective, race was at the center of the party's dilemma. The party's identification with blacks had virtually destroyed the Democrats' coalition and put it at risk of becoming a permanent minority in presidential elections.[22] To rebuild, New Democrats counseled, the party should deemphasize issues of racism, poverty, and civil rights (especially affirmative action) and instead focus on the concerns of the white middle class in terms of lower taxes, opposition to "quotas," and a tough approach to welfare and crime.[23] Many of the New Democrats also advocated their own explicit version of the GOP's southern strategy, arguing that a moderate southerner would be the party's ideal presidential standard bearer. "Such an individual not only might attract middle-class voters in the North but also might lead southern whites, who had defected to the Republicans in presidential elections, to return to their Democratic roots."[24]

In 1992, Governor William Jefferson Clinton of Arkansas, aided by another southern moderate as vice presidential candidate, Senator Albert Gore of Tennessee, sought to provide a real-life answer to the question of reducing

21. Stanley Greenberg, *Report on Democratic Defection* (Washington, D.C.: Analysis Group, 1985), 13, 18, as quoted in Thomas Byrne Edsall and Mary Edsall, *Chain Reaction* (New York: Norton, 1991), 182.

22. See Harry McPhearson, "How Race Destroyed the Democrats' Coalition," *New York Times,* Nov. 20, 1988.

23. Edsall and Edsall, *Chain Reaction.*

24. Benjamin Ginsberg and Martin Shefter, *Politics by Other Means: Politicians, Prosecutors, and the Press from Watergate to Whitewater* (New York: Norton, 1999), 54.

the political salience of race as a central cleavage while retaining strong black and Latino political support. Clinton had learned from the efforts of Michael Dukakis, the party's presidential nominee in 1988, that it was not enough to pose as a pragmatic centrist. Thus he decided to carefully stake out his claim to represent a new kind of Democrat. His attempted solution relied on three interrelated strategies.

The first strategy was to seek to control racial symbols. Thus as a candidate in 1992, Clinton attempted to distance himself from his party's image of being "soft on crime" by promising to get tough on crime while posing for photographers with a formation of mostly black convicts providing the backdrop. His opponent in the California Democratic primary, Jerry Brown, concluded that Clinton looked like a "colonial master' in the photograph.[25] To reinforce his claim to be tough on crime, Clinton assured the nation, "[Bush] won't streamline the federal government and change the way it works; cut 100,000 bureaucrats and put 100,000 new police officers on the streets of American cities, but I will."[26] Advocating funding for police while failing to address racial bias in the criminal justice system and ignoring police brutality fulfilled a dual purpose: it demonstrated that Clinton had moved away from identification with racial minorities and rhetorically posited that his administration would spend more on activities such as policing than on social programs.

The second strategy was to emphasize responsibility over rights. Thus Clinton's 1992 campaign manifesto, *Putting People First* (co-authored with Al Gore), was thin on civil rights. In a chapter on civil rights race rated less space than sexual preference or physical disability and did not make the thirty-one "crucial issues" listed and addressed in alphabetical order, from agriculture to women.[27] By contrast, Clinton was much less reticent in his calls for "personal responsibility." Often addressed to exclusively black audiences, the message of personal responsibility allowed the candidate to play off many whites' highly negative perceptions of racial minorities as "irresponsible," lazy," and "violence prone."

25. Quoted in Susan Yochum, "Civil Rights an Issue in Spirited Democratic Debate," *San Francisco Chronicle,* Mar. 6, 1992, A1.

26. William J. Clinton, speech accepting the Democratic presidential nomination, July 16, 1992, in *1992 Congressional Quarterly Almanac,* 55-A.

27. O'Reilly, *Nixon's Piano,* 410. The candidates pledged to "actively work to protect the civil rights of all Americans," but they also vowed to "oppose racial quotas." See Bill Clinton and Al Gore, *Putting People First: How We Can Change America* (New York: Times Books, 1992), 32, 63–66.

Clinton's third strategy for managing the politics of race was to empha-size universal social policies instead of race-specific or -targeted ones. Thus he pledged to create a universal health care system, to provide increased opportu-nities for college students, and to raise the minimum wage. By contrast, *Putting People First* sidestepped the increasing spatial concentration of poverty in inner cities and, eschewing "federal handouts," it emphasized the primary impor-tance of national economic expansion.[28] This was clearly a retreat from Lyndon Baines Johnson's understanding that two centuries of slavery and a third of Jim Crow required compensatory actions to level the playing field.

On the campaign trail in 1992, these strategies, merged with Clinton's economic populist message,[29] apparently bore sweet fruit. Although Clinton's core votes in November 1992 came from the traditional Democratic base—union households (55 percent), Latinos (61 percent), liberals (68 percent), Jews (78 percent), and African Americans (83 percent)—Clinton won in many sub-urbs that Democrats had lost badly in previous presidential contests.[30] In gen-eral, he improved the Democrats' showing among whites, winning even 42 percent of the southern white vote, a significant leap over Walter Mondale in 1984 and Dukakis in 1988, both of whom did not carry 30 percent.[31] In fact, it was the first time since 1976 that a substantial enough minority of white

28. John Mollenkopf, "Urban Policy at the Crossroads," in Margaret Weir, ed., *The Social Divide: Political Parties and the Future of Activist Government* (Washington, D.C.: Brookings, 1998), 473.

29. There is substantial evidence that economic populism was Clinton's best selling point. According to exit polls, more than two out of five voters (43%) said that the state of the economy was the issue that had determined their vote. Of these 43%, 53% voted for Clinton, 24% for Bush, and 23% for Perot. Among the quarter of the electorate who felt that their economic situation was better—disproportionately more affluent voters—Bush beat Clinton by 60 to 25%; but for the one-third of the voters who felt that their economic situation had worsened, Clinton defeated Bush by a whopping 62 to 13%. In short, after twelve years of *upward* redistribution during the Reagan-Bush era, repairing the social safety net, alleviating pressures on families, and having concerns for those who had lost ground resonated with renewed vigor in the 1992 presidential campaign. With economic issues taking the fore, the so-called wedge issues—such as affirmative action, abortion, and crime—did not emerge as critical or decisive concerns among voters. See William Schneider, "A Loud Vote for Change," *National Journal*, Nov. 7, 1992, 2542; and Kevin Phillips, *The Politics of Rich and Poor: Wealth and the American Electorate in the Reagan Aftermath* (New York: Random House, 1990), Introduc-tion, chaps. 3–4.

30. Marjorie Connelly, "Portrait of the Electorate" *New York Times*, Nov. 11, 1996; Lusane, *African Americans at the Crossroads*, 169–70.

31. "1992 Presidential Results in Southern States," *Southern Political Report*, Nov. 1992, 4.

male voters (37 percent compared to Bush's 40 percent and Perot's 22 percent) joined white women (who voted 41 percent for Clinton, 41 percent for Bush, and 19 percent for Perot) and people of color to elect a Democratic president.[32] Thus while Clinton clearly owed a debt first and foremost to the traditional Democratic base and white women, his improved showing among white men sealed his narrow victory. In essence, Rector, Souljah, and other efforts at racial inoculation allowed this New Democrat to distance himself enough from "liberal fundamentalism" to narrowly split the white vote.[33] Meanwhile, with only minimal effort, Clinton overwhelmingly won the African American vote. Black voters composed 8 percent of the total electorate on election day (down, however, from 10 percent in 1988) and 15 percent of Clinton's total vote (down from 20 percent of Dukakis's vote).[34] Still there were enough of the largely taken-for-granted black voters to provide the margin of victory for Clinton in such key states as Illinois, Michigan, Ohio, and New Jersey.[35]

Despite heavy black support, however, it was certain in 1992 which side had won in the sustained two-decade-long ideological struggle for the heart and soul of the Democratic Party. As the veteran journalist Thomas Edsall concluded, "a factional struggle between center and left has been won by the center." Even when Clinton was nominated, Jackson's Rainbow Coalition, who had sought to make the Democratic Party respond to the core victims of economic change, white skin privilege, and urban decay, issued its own 1992 platform, which declared on the last page, "In the middle of a national economic crisis, we have three conservative candidates running for president," effectively lumping Clinton together with President Bush and Ross Perot.[36]

The question was what would happen once Clinton was in the White House. What would his New Democrat strategy entail and how well would it work? Would his administration be, as Jackson predicted, little more than a continuation of conservatism, or would the New Democrat break new ground? What would be the new administration's strategies toward key racially targeted and racially charged social policies in particular?

32. Connelly, "Portrait of the Electorate."
33. O'Reilly, *Nixon's Piano,* 416.
34. Connelly, "Portrait of the Electorate."
35. O'Reilly, *Nixon's Piano,* 416.
36. Thomas B. Edsall, "Show of Party Unity Masks Scars of Ideological Battle: Center Wins Day in Democrats' Tug of War," *Washington Post,* July 13, 1992, A1.

The Deficit, Race, and Class

In a capitalist system, parties, candidates, and administrations must all be sensitive to business concerns. One immediate concern for Clinton was the vast and growing budget deficit. The deficit, Paul Pierson persuasively argues, "fundamentally altered the politics of national policymaking. It shifted attention away from the merits and limitations of individual programs to broader, more abstract arguments about the appropriate scope of government; it altered the nature of legislative politics, as massive budget bills became the major instrument for producing policy change; it gave preexisting policy commitments a formidable political advantage over any new policy initiatives; and it helped generate an atmosphere of austerity" conducive to timidity in the social policy arena.[37]

From the administration's inception, then, it was questionable how much of his promised new investments Clinton could actually deliver. Unless some dramatically new policy strategies, entailing some hard decisions regarding budgetary priorities, were tried, the budget deficit would function as a very effective lid on new public initiatives. Moreover, among the populace, the deficit had become a virtual metaphor for what was wrong in American government. Given trends in taxes, spending, and the deficit—either as facts or as the subjects of public debate—it was clear from the start of the Clinton administration that the more the president prioritized deficit reduction, the more he would have to downplay his campaign's theme of "investment" policies—particularly those targeted toward cities and racial minorities. With the deficit casting a long shadow on the incoming administration, Clinton's choice was clear: (1) placate financial markets, establish his bona fides as a "New Democrat," work with conservative Democrats in Congress to deal with the deficit; or (2) deliver to the Democrats' loyalists, establish that he could be counted on to keep his promise regarding "investments," and work with liberal Democrats in Congress to create new public initiatives.

There were a number of reasons Clinton was from the start likely to choose the former course. First, both to cut the deficit sharply and to provide new or expanded public initiatives without a substantial change in policy strategy or budgetary priorities required new revenues. Republicans were unusually

---

37. Paul Pierson, "The Deficit and the Politics of Domestic Reform," in Weir, *Social Divide*, 127.

committed to not raising taxes since they believed Bush's flip-flop on his 1988 promise of "no new taxes" had contributed to his loss to Clinton in 1992. This meant that Clinton would have had to do something no Democrat in post–World War II America had done before: pass major new social policy legislation with virtually no support from Republicans. Second, it was unlikely that enough Democrats would have gone along with Clinton. Risk-adverse, the party did not want to be solely accountable for any new taxes. Third, Clinton, unlike FDR and LBJ, could not claim an electoral mandate, and conservative Democrats held the balance of power in Congress.

This was the political-economic context that encouraged restraint in Clinton's first budget proposal. To be sure, the proposal was significantly different from those of Reagan and Bush. The administration asked for $160 billion over the four years 1994–97 in additional spending for infrastructure, health care, education, and tax incentives for the private sector.[38] Redistribution relied on increases in taxes on the wealthy and new investments (mainly in regard to the earned income tax credit, which was for the working poor, not for the jobless), but the economic magnitude of these efforts was relatively small, and in the case of the latter built upon trends in the Bush years.

The most important early budgetary request for the nonworking poor (and the disproportionate share racial minorities composed among this group) was a supplemental request (which came to be known as the "economic stimulus" package) in 1993 for funds to create jobs for those who were not benefiting from what was then dubbed a "jobless recovery." The supplemental appropriation sought "emergency" funds of $16.3 billion as a supplement to the 1993 budget. Included in the proposal was money to create jobs (particularly summer jobs for youth and infrastructure construction projects), to fully fund Head Start and infant nutrition, to extend the unemployment benefits period due to expire in April 1993, to support the small business loans program, and to fund research and development work by businesses, colleges, and universities. The administration justified the overall package not only as social investments designed to help the unemployed but as necessary for continued long-term economic growth. No explicit reference was made to people of color and the programs would obviously apply to all racial groups, but civil rights groups hailed programs that would obviously help the unemployed and underemployed,

38. Viveca Novak, "Spending Spree?" *National Journal,* Feb. 17, 1993, 510.

given the huge share of African Americans and Latinos in these groups. So too was additional funding for preschoolers and youth greeted with cheer.

However, this test of the hidden agenda failed, killed by a Republican filibuster in the Senate. The few portions that survived—some funding for construction projects, summer jobs, and college loans and the extension of unemployment benefits—hardly favored the "truly disadvantaged." For the most part, the surviving package helped those already covered by social insurance in the labor market but did little for those outside that sphere. As the original Clinton proposal went down to defeat in the Senate, Senator Robert Byrd (D-Va.) summed up the results aptly: "Billions for unemployment, but not one cent for jobs."[39] After the failure of the stimulus package, the Clinton administration avoided further proposals for significant spending increases.

Clearly Clinton had been dealt a bad hand on the budget. The budget deficit nearly foreclosed the possibility of progress on social policy. But could things have worked out differently? Was there a path not taken, what Barrington Moore called a "suppressed historical alternative?"[40]

Two Roads Not Taken

Two suppressed alternatives, recommended sequentially by Clinton's first labor secretary, Robert Reich, were an attack on tax expenditures as a way of increasing revenues and introduction of a capital budget as a way of justifying investments. Both had potential, however, for infringing on the privileges of whiteness.

Tax expenditures, having underwritten the hidden welfare state since the 1940s, had by the 1990s come to compose a very large proportion of the federal budget. In 1993 the revenue loss to the government totaled $78.2 billion from the mortgage interest deduction and other tax breaks for homeowners, $46.9 billion for employer-provided health insurance, and $49.4 billion for corporate retirement pensions, the three leading but hardly only tax expenditures. Seemingly, at least, tax expenditures have a number of characteristics that

39. Quoted in Jon Healey, "Democrats Look to Salvage Part of Stimulus Plan," *Congressional Quarterly Weekly Report,* Apr. 24, 1993, 1004; and Dona Cooper Hamilton and Charles V. Hamilton, *The Dual Agenda: Race and Social Welfare Policies of Civil Rights Organizations* (New York: Columbia University Press, 1997), 241.

40. Barrington Moore, "Revolution in America?" *New York Review of Books,* Jan. 30, 1969, 4.

make them key targets for a Democratic administration: they are costly and their reduction would ease budgetary problems; they have grown phenomenally since the 1950s, with little or no consideration of whether they serve any important public purpose; they provide the vast majority of their benefits to affluent whites, so the costs of reform would fall most heavily on Republican constituencies.[41] Had the administration sought to cut back tax expenditures, it might have freed up enough resources for new initiatives needed by racial minorities and the poor.

Alternatively, the capital budget concept is an accounting approach in which the federal government (like most state governments, private corporations, or just plain parents sending their children to expensive private schools) would distinguish between consumption and investment expenditures. According to the capital budget idea, it is appropriate to borrow for investment in anticipation of future economic returns. Introducing a capital budget would have highlighted one of the administration's main arguments for government activism: the need to invest in the physical and human capital required to compete in the rapidly changing global economy.

At the same time, "introducing a capital budget would have reframed the deficit issue, calling into question the apocalyptic scenarios associated with government borrowing. Loosening this constraint might have created the opening for Clinton proposals that would cost money in the short run."[42] Like cutting back tax expenditures, the capital budget option would have eased the government's fiscal constraints while providing enough resources to create or expand programs serving Clinton's key electoral constituents. However, the administration—fearful of alienating Wall Street and the widespread antideficit mood—rejected the capital budget concept outright. Similarly, fearful of provoking opposition from affluent whites who are disproportionately beneficiaries of private health insurance, pensions, mortgage interest deductions, and so forth, the administration refused to put cutbacks in tax expenditures on the agenda.

41. Pierson, "Deficit and the Politics of Domestic Reform," 147. See also Christopher Howard, *The Hidden Welfare State: Tax Expenditures and Social Policy* (Princeton: Princeton University Press, 1997).

42. Pierson, "Deficit and the Politics of Domestic Reform," 147. For a full discussion of the capital budget conception, see Robert Eisner, *How Real Is the Federal Budget Deficit?* (New York: Free Press, 1986).

The suppression of these alternatives highlighted not only the administration's narrow room to maneuver and not only the real direction regarding investments in social initiatives it would pursue, but also the powerful continuing constraint of whiteness. The growth of the hidden welfare state with its unacknowledged, untouchable, and massive subsidies for primarily upper-middle-class whites is now a decisive constraint on American social policy. As even social insurance programs became increasingly vulnerable to charges of being poorly targeted and inefficient, criticism of hidden welfare, the programs most deserving of such challenges, remained (pun intended) beyond the pale. Mentioning the huge tax expenditures that benefited middle class over poor, white over people of color, remained taboo.[43]

Having rejected these alternatives, Clinton found his path clear by the end of his first year in office. The administration's only modestly activist first budget ultimately passed by only a single vote in each chamber after a ferocious six-month battle, and then only when spending cuts were increased, new revenues were rolled back, and deficit reduction goals were raised. That development, along with the debacle over the stimulus package, signaled the failure of the administration's budget strategy to move the congressional center of gravity even modestly to the left. By early 1994, it was nearly certain: any major new policy initiatives would continue the rightward drift, now a crucial characteristic of the post–Great Society years.

Hard-Liner on Crime

The nation's retreat from liberal social policies and an activist government was promoted by victim-blaming social theories and laissez-faire leadership. In place of a public philosophy supporting the welfare state, what Stuart Hall has called "authoritarian populism" emerged.[44] Building on growing fears among the populace that society was spinning out of control, authoritarian populism sought to impose a new regime of social discipline from above. Groups increasingly frightened, plagued by economic insecurity, and disillusioned with political leaders became yet more vulnerable to racist, sexist, and fundamentalist

43. Pierson, "Deficit and the Politics of Domestic Reform," 147–48.
44. Stuart Hall, *The Hard Road to Renewal: Thatcherism and the Crisis of the Left* (London: Verso, 1988).

appeals that used social divisions to build support for repressive policies. Conservatives preached that the wider social order was threatened by disorder at the bottom (Willie Horton and dysfunctional welfare mothers) rather than self-interested economic decisions and behavior at the top. In this context, two areas conservatives and moderates of both major parties promoted for drastic reform were crime and welfare.

Crime became the first policy area confirming the rightward drift of the Clinton years. Indeed, Clinton sought to establish his conservative credentials nowhere more than in the area of crime. To do so required not only altering his party's image on crime but also on exploiting the politics of race.

From the 1960s to the 1990s, national Democrats and Republicans had sought to sell sharply differing views of the crime problem that paralleled their stands on race and civil rights. Democrats had generally argued that the crime problem was rooted in broader structural forces, a symptom, not cause, of joblessness, urban decay, lack of education, and lack of hope. Institutional racism and its result, racial inequality, made these general societal problems worse for African Americans and generated higher crime rates in black communities. National Democrats also often pointed out that Republican diatribes against crime were little more than smokescreens for attacking African Americans. This was true ever since Republicans raised the "law and order" issue as a justification for going after civil rights protesters. To solve the crime problem, Democrats had typically concluded, required taking a number of preventative actions, for example, improving education, job training, and employment opportunities (especially for youth), creating more drug-treatment programs, providing antigang grants, and furnishing social counseling. It also involved the identification of bias crimes and protecting freedom of speech and other civil liberties for protesters and, by corollary, the accused more generally.

Republicans had made a mantra of calls for "law and order," race-coding this theme by tying it to the protest politics of the 1960s, especially civil rights protest. Those who saw the Civil Rights Movement and other protests of the 1960s as a threat to and unwelcome disruption of the social order had gravitated in droves to the Republican Party. For Republicans and their growing host of supporters on the issue, crime was a result of social pathology and individual irresponsibility, and perhaps genetic proclivity. In the conservative view, what was needed was a far more punitive criminal justice system. To solve the crime problem, Republicans called for capital punishment for more offenses, longer sentences, prosecution of youthful offenders as adults for certain violent crimes, victims' rights, and so forth.

From the 1960s to 1990s, Democrats were increasingly tagged as not taking crime seriously enough. By the late 1980s, Republicans had come to own the crime issue. Democrats were accused of being "soft on crime," especially "black crime," and Republicans as being "tough on crime," the latter apparently being the more appealing approach to many Americans. In 1988, 40 percent of respondents to a Gallup poll indicated that the Republicans were better able to handle crime, while only 24 percent thought the Democrats were.[45] The racial overtones of the crime debate were clear. By 1993, while only a third of whites thought that racial prejudice motivated law-and-order politicians, over half of blacks reported they did.[46]

Despite his heavy black support, however, Bill Clinton was intent on becoming his own kind of law-and-order president. To do so, he elevated the crime issue, and as it rose on the governmental agenda, so it did on the public agenda. Indeed, the real jump in crime on the public agenda in the 1990s occurred alongside Clinton's emphasis on the issue. For example, from 1982 to 1991, the proportion of Americans who said crime was the nation's most important problem remained fairly steady (4 percent in 1982, 5 percent in 1991). In 1992, this percentage rose very slightly to 7 percent, but by 1993 it had risen to 13 percent and a year later to 39 percent.[47] In fact, after Clinton endorsed "three strikes you're out" in his January 1994 State of the Union address, the figure rose to a whopping 49 percent, topping the list of most important problems facing the nation.[48]

Clinton's goal in focusing on crime was to appear to be a tough guy on

45. Ann Chih Lin, "The Troubled Success of Crime Policy," in Weir, *Social Divide*, 323.

46. Ibid., 314; Leslie McAneny, "Americans Discouraged by Government's Ineffective War on Crime," *Gallup Poll Monthly*, Dec. 1993, 29ff.

47. *Gallup Poll Monthly*, Aug. 1994.

48. To be sure, the rise of crime on the public agenda was helped along by a series of state and local events, including high-profile mayoral elections in New York and Los Angeles and a governor's race in New Jersey, all of which focused on crime; the highly publicized murder of Polly Klaas, a young girl in California, by a released white felon; a successful "three strikes you're out" referendum in Washington State; and the gunning down of a carful of commuters on the Long Island Rail Road by Colin Ferguson, a black immigrant. But Clinton's own public rhetoric also reinforced and helped elevate the issue of crime. See discussion in Lin, "Troubled Success of Crime Policy," 312–18.

the issue without totally alienating black voters and black leaders. To do so, he would be a man of the center, apparently interpreted by the president as the midpoint between the ideological right represented by conservative Republicans and the ideological left represented by liberal Democrats, especially those in Congress. This meant he would master a politics of accommodation, not compromise. While compromise would have required standing on some first principles even if it required standing alone and staking out a position based on careful examination of the foundations and arguments of opposing positions that supported these first principles or priorities, accommodation simply required letting every claimant leave the table with some part of its loaf in hand.

As Ann Lin argues, Clinton's politics of accommodation in the debate over crime was based on two main strategies: (1) redefining the crime issue as gun control and police funding; and (2) challenging liberals over their support for civil liberties and their opposition to the death penalty. The first strategy, Clinton's redefinition of what it meant to be tough on crime, struck at the Achilles' heel of the Republicans' crime image. As advantaged as the Republicans had become on the issue in the perceptions of a crime-fearing public, the party was threatened by rising support for gun control. By the early 1990s, about two of every three Americans supported stricter gun-control laws.[49] Growing support for gun control among both the public and the police provided an opportunity for partisan repositioning on crime.[50]

Meanwhile, by supporting the death penalty and tougher federal sentencing and simultaneously downplaying civil liberties, Clinton sought to demonstrate that he had moved away not only from the party's image as "soft on crime" but from the party's most loyal constituencies, such as African Americans and civil liberties activists.[51] In this regard, criticism from liberal groups could, like the Souljah affair in the 1992 campaign, invigorate the president's image as a new kind of Democrat. While it may not have been calculated, a group such as the Congressional Black Caucus (CBC) rising to the bait to oppose the president on crime was not necessarily a negative development for the administration's political purposes. All the administration had to do was sit

---

49. David W. Moore and Frank Newport, "Public Strongly Favors Stricter Gun Control Laws," *Gallup Poll Monthly*, Dec. 1993, 27; Lin, "Troubled Success of Crime Policy," 315–16.

50. Lin, "Troubled Success of Crime Policy," 316.

51. Ibid., 313.

back and let the CBC do the heavy lifting in portraying Clinton's actions on crime as one more move of the administration to distance itself from blacks.

To an important extent, this is precisely what happened. The critical factor here was Clinton's crime proposal in his first administration's grand escalation of recent trends federalizing crime. Indeed, more than any other factor, it was the federalizing of death penalty cases that produced an explicit battle in Congress over rights.

Since 1976, when the death penalty was reinstituted, nearly 40 percent of those who have been executed have been black, despite the fact that blacks compose only about 11 percent of the adult population.[52] As studies by the Sentencing Project and the American Civil Liberties Union (ACLU) have documented, those, especially blacks, whose victims were whites were much more likely to receive the death penalty than those whose victims were black. Since 1977, although blacks are disproportionately likely to be victims of homicides, 85 percent of all people who have been executed had killed a white person; only 11 percent had killed a black.[53] Moreover, federal courts found reversible constitutional error in 40 percent of death-penalty cases since 1976, even after multiple layers of review by state courts.[54] In short, suspected racism in the application of capital punishment made the attempt to broaden its use both problematic and emblematic of racial concerns.

Responding to the perceived threat, Representative John Conyers (D-Mich.), a member of the Judiciary Committee and of the CBC, promised, on the day Clinton announced the crime bill in the summer of 1993, that "without the Congressional Black Caucus signing off on this legislation, it is not going anywhere. Period."[55] By September 1993, the CBC was even more committed to opposing the president's bill. At its hearings on the Clinton bill at the CBC Foundation's annual legislative weekend, Kweisi Mfume (D-Md.), chair of the CBC, said that to prevent the crime bill's passage the caucus would, if neces-

---

52. Committee on the Judiciary, Subcommittee on Civil and Constitutional Rights, *Racial Disparities in Federal Death Penalty Prosecutions, 1988–1994,* Staff Report, 103d Cong., 2d sess. (March 1994), 6.

53. Erika Eckholm, "Studies Find Death Penalty Tied to Race of the Victims," *New York Times,* Feb. 24, 1995, B1.

54. David Cole, "Strict Scrutiny: Destruction of the Habeas Safety Net," *Legal Times,* June 19, 1995, 33; and Lin, "Troubled Success of Crime Policy," 320.

55. Holly Idelson, "An Era Comes to a Close: Costly Victory on Crime Bill Exposes Democratic Weakness, Foreshadows GOP Takeover," *Congressional Quarterly Weekly Report,* Dec. 23, 1995, 3872.

sary, "bring the government to a stop," and Craig Washington (D-Tex.). who chaired the hearings, promised the bill would pass only over the caucus's "political dead bodies."[56]

In the aftermath, several black interest groups formed a coalition that included the NAACP and its Legal Defense Fund, the National Conference of Black Lawyers, and the National Black Police Association. Staffers of the CBC and representatives of civil libertarian groups (especially the ACLU and the Sentencing Project) met with the coalition dozens of times over nearly a year. One proposal to grow out of the coalition was the Racial Justice Act of 1994 (RJA). Supported by the CBC, the Congressional Hispanic Caucus, and the Progressive Caucus, the RJA proposed that defendants subject to the death penalty would be allowed to use statistical evidence to demonstrate whether race was a significant factor in the decision to invoke capital punishment. A defendant who offered such a study would have been able, under the RJA, to force state or federal prosecutors to explain to the court's satisfaction any apparent pattern of racial bias. Only strong, unexplained evidence would suffice to set aside a death sentence. Even then a court system could later reimpose the death penalty on proof that the system had reformed its jury selection or cured the case of its race-based capital sentencing.

Supporters of the death penalty and conservatives went after the RJA provision from its inception. Senate Republicans, led by Orrin Hatch of Utah, threatened to filibuster the entire crime bill if it was brought to the floor with the RJA included. Many House Democratic members, who initially voted for the provision, soon conceded that it was not worth the fight with Republicans and excluded the RJA from the version of the House bill that passed.

The CBC, realizing that it did not have the votes to get its own bill passed, decided to concentrate on winning inclusion of the RJA in Clinton's bill.[57] To do so, they chose to negotiate with the Clinton administration rather

56. Quoted in Robert Smith, *We Have No Leaders: African Americans in the Post–Civil Rights Era* (Albany: State University of New York Press, 1996), 221.

57. The black interest groups were so concerned about the highly punitive provisions of the Clinton crime bill and their likely disproportionate impact on minorities that at first they wrote their own alternative bill, the Crime Prevention and Reform Bill, introduced in October 1993 by Craig Washington (D-Tex.). The alternative bill, supported by the CBC, the Hispanic Caucus, and the Progressive Caucus, argued that addressing the root causes of crime would do more to reduce crime than increasing penalties and building more prisons. Their bill called for funding a wide range of crime-prevention efforts.

than mobilize mass support. The CBC's goal was to get the Clinton administration to lobby senators to support the RJA. The decision to negotiate caused a split between the CBC and black interest groups, who up to this point had been central in drafting and promoting the RJA.

As the CBC concentrated more and more on negotiating with the White House, its staffers began to drop off from meeting with the coalition. This strategy also isolated the CBC from the Progressive Caucus, comprising the House's most liberal Democrats, who continued to fight for a fully alternative bill to Clinton's crime proposal. By the late spring of 1994, the coalition had fallen apart.

Meanwhile, the White House had its own strategy. It was preparing to outflank the CBC on every front. For months the president refused to meet with the CBC, obscuring his own inclinations. Asked about the RJA in April, he did not endorse the specific provision in the bill, but added obliquely in Clintonspeak: "We think that you can absolutely have a racial justice provision that will do some good."[58] When he finally met with the CBC in late June 1994, the caucus, which had to accept all the bill's new death penalties, thought it had a deal with the administration.[59] The president who had signed death warrants in Arkansas would say publicly that the RJA was a desirable part of a balanced crime bill and would lobby for it. Caucus members and civil rights forces would join the lobbying. But as late as mid-July, not a sound came from the administration to advance or defend the racial justice provision.

In fact, the administration was lobbying; just in the opposite direction: Clinton was courting black interest groups and local elected officials for his version of the bill, which did not include the RJA. The White House turned to two main sources. First it successfully lobbied the United States Conference of Black Mayors, which included the ten big-city mayors, to support its version of crime reform. It appealed to this group on the basis of the prevention programs included in the bill (such as community development corporations, drug treatment programs, midnight sports leagues, antigang grants, and programs aimed at ending violence against women and seniors).[60] The black mayors in turn sent

---

58. Quoted in Dan Balz and Ronald Brownstein, *Storming the Gates: Protest Politics and the Republican Revival* (Boston: Little, Brown, 1996), 93.

59. Interview with Craig Washington, June 21, 1994.

60. Clarence Lusane, "Interaction and Collaboration between Black Interest Groups and Black Congressmembers in the 103rd Congress: A Study in Race-Conscious Policy Innovation" (Ph.D. diss., Howard University, 1997), 326–52.

Mfume a letter urging the caucus "not to oppose a crime bill which includes so many vital provisions for the people of our cities because it may not include the Racial Justice Act." With the exception of Baltimore's Kurt Schmoke and Washington's Sharon Pratt Kelly, every big-city black mayor signed the letter. The CBC never formally responded to the mayors' letter, but as Representative Robert C. Scott (D-Va.) noted in a fax to Mfume, the date of the mayors' letter, July 14, 1994, indicated that the "White House was busy getting signatures," while the CBC thought that "everything was still on the table for negotiation."[61]

Second, the president lobbied black ministers to pressure the CBC to drop its opposition to his version of the bill. Speaking at a black church in the District of Columbia, Clinton portrayed the passage of the crime bill as a "morally right thing to do" and "the will of God."[62] Later he invited twenty-five black clergymen to the White House and urged them to pressure CBC members to vote for the bill. After this meeting, Representative Charles Rangel (D-N.Y.), one of the most outspoken critics of the president's bill, curiously announced that he would consider switching his position if "religious leaders" persuaded him that the bill's sweeping anticrime provisions could outweigh his opposition to the death penalty. As if on cue, Clinton produced a statement signed by forty black clergymen supporting the bill.[63] Indeed, as Reagan-Bush tried to create their own black leaders as a tactic for managing racial politics, Clinton-Gore often sought to recruit black clergymen to be the stalking salesmen for their brand of playing the race card. These tactics led the CBC to accuse the White House of failing to negotiate in good faith and circumventing them in order to pass the bill.[64]

By then the White House was totally in charge of the ground rules for negotiation with the CBC. Ignoring the RJA, the White House began to incorporate many of the prevention programs supported by black interest groups in its omnibus proposal. For example, the National Conference of Black Lawyers helped to draft the provision on antigang grants and drug courts; the National

61. United States Conference of Mayors to the Honorable Kweisi Mfume, July 14, 1994; and Bobby Scott to Mfume, July 15, 1994 (fax), Congressional Black Caucus Archives, Congressional Black Caucus Foundation, Washington, D.C.

62. National Rainbow Coalition, "It's Still a Crime (Bill)," *JaxFax,* Aug. 18, 1994; and Lusane, "Interaction and Collaboration," 341.

63. Interview with Charles Rangel, Oct. 27, 1994.

64. Interview with Kweisi Mfume, Oct. 10, 1994.

Black Police Association contributed to the provisions regarding midnight sports leagues.[65]

Black interest groups and CBC members continued to argue, however, that the prevention provisions did not offset the harm that would come from other provisions in the bill. Thus the president also offered to issue an executive order barring discrimination in federal executions. The CBC and key black interest groups rejected that offer, noting that since 1976 only 1 percent of death-penalty cases occurred at the federal level. Instead, contrary to wishes of black interest groups such as the NAACP and the National Conference of Black Lawyers, the CBC counteroffered to allow the RJA to be dropped if the White House would drop the sixty-odd federal death-penalty provisions that were now in the bill. The White House response was an unequivocal no. A commission to study racial discrimination in death sentencing offered by the White House was also rejected by the CBC, leading one White House aide to lament, "The payoff isn't working."[66]

Then the CBC threatened to launch a protest vote against the procedural rule that would bring the conference version of the bill to the House floor, an action that is usually extremely partisan. In response, Clinton called a July 25 meeting at the White House, finally admonishing the CBC that he could and would get the bill passed even if all the black voting House Democrats stood in the way—an unlikely scenario in any case. Mfume summed up the meeting with Clinton as "very, very frank," indicating that the president had called the caucus's bluff.[67]

Not surprisingly, however, the White House never intended to let all the CBC members vote against its bill. Even as the CBC began to raise the volume of its objection to the removal of the RJA, the administration was picking off CBC members one by one. Within days of the White House meeting, at least four members (Bobby Rush of Illinois, Walter Tucker of California, Sanford Bishop of Georgia, and Harold Ford of Tennessee—all Democrats) were prepared to vote for the procedural rule as well as for the bill.[68] In the end, despite the deletion of the racial justice provision in the House-Senate conference, the

65. Interview with Greg Moore, legislative director for John Conyers (D-Mich.), Oct. 24, 1994.

66. Bob Cohn, "Buying Off the Black Caucus," *Newsweek*, Aug. 1, 1994, 24.

67. "Hill Briefs," *Congress Daily*, July 26, 1994, 4.

68. Mary Jacoby, "Black Caucus Acts to Kill Crime Rule," *Roll Call*, July 18, 1994, 20.

Clinton crime bill not only passed the House 235 to 195, but the vast majority of CBC members, 24 of the 39 members in the House, voted for the bill; 12 voted against it, and 3 did not vote.[69] As Clarence Lusane concludes, theoretically, CBC unity could have made the difference. Only 20 votes separated passage and failure on the crime bill. Had the CBC's 24 members who voted for the bill joined the 12 who voted against it, the vote would have been 211–219 to defeat the bill. The influence of CBC unity would have been decisive. But instead, CBC disunity meant that a bill excluding the RJA and including dangerous portents for African Americans became law. Clinton's strategy had clearly worked: he had divided and conquered.

The crime bill demonstrated not only how easily the CBC could be had, but made apparent for all to see both the disintegration of its ties to the grassroots and the emerging problems for the black working class in depending on black elites to challenge whiteness. Neither the CBC nor black interest groups mobilized their constituents in opposition to the crime bill. No mass phone calling or letter writing was organized; no public education campaign was planned or implemented. Not even one press release was issued by the CBC outlining its position. Interest groups produced no new research arguing their case. The testimony of black interest groups and floor speeches of black members of Congress received little or no coverage in the black press. Few op-ed articles appeared in the white press. In the end, not only were CBC members left to split off willy-nilly in support of the bill, white members of Congress received almost no pressure from blacks at all. Thus the broad public education and developed networks that would have enabled the black community to live to fight another day failed to materialize. Instead the 1994 National Election Study (NES) found that an overwhelming majority of blacks (83 percent) reported favoring the Clinton crime bill; this was more than the 73 percent of whites who also favored it.[70] By the time the Republicans gained control of Congress in 1994, there was not even enough of a residue of organization among African Americans to begin to fight for preserving the prevention funding.

Ironically, however, Bill Clinton had handed the Republicans an issue

69. Roll Call 416, *Congressional Record,* daily ed., Aug. 21, 1994, H9005.

70. National Election Studies and Inter-University Consortium for Political and Social Research, Institute for Social Research, *American National Election Studies, 1948–1994* (CD-ROM, May 1995).

(which proved to be highly successful for their party) in the 1994 campaign. Clinton's own rhetoric reinforced and helped elevate the crime issue precisely at the time data from the National Criminal Victimization Survey, widely viewed as the most accurate national measure of crime rates, showed crime rates to be level or declining. He had patently ignored the CBC and demonstrated that he risked little in alienating black voters. Yet conservatives gave him no points for courage. They exploited the general lack of coherence in the legislation, painting it as full of "failed Great Society programs," and labeling the prevention programs as "pork barrel," apparently a much more creative coup with white voters in 1994.[71]

When the Republicans took control of Congress in 1994, they sought even more punitive measures (warrantless searches and seizures and weakening the exclusionary rule, limiting appeals of death sentences, eliminating funding for community policing and prevention activities, and so forth). When in April 1995 domestic white terrorists bombed the Alfred Murrah Federal Building in Oklahoma City, attention was diverted from street crime and a bipartisan bill passed on April 24, 1996, supporting habeas corpus reform to limit death-row appeals and streamlining the deportation of criminal aliens. The bill weighed in so heavily on expanding the death penalty that its name was changed from the Comprehensive Anti-Terrorism Act of 1995 to the Effective Death Penalty and Public Safety Act of 1996.[72] By signing the 1996 act, Clinton once again demonstrated that those who opposed the expansion of the death penalty and limiting habeas corpus reform were expendable. He managed to preserve community policing funding by drawing on money already appropriated to the Justice Department, but the prevention programs became victims of the appropriations and budget battles in Congress.

Only a horrific act of domestic terrorism made crime explode again onto the national scene during Clinton's second term. That act was the killing of a teacher and fourteen schoolchildren (including the two suburban white student terrorists, who committed suicide) at Columbine High School in Littleton, Colorado. The suburban terrorists had booby-trapped the school with bombs, hop-

---

71. Rep. Dick Armey, speech delivered at the signing of the "Contract with America," Sept. 27, 1994, Republican National Committee. See discussion in Lin, "Troubled Success of Crime Policy," 321–23.

72. Holly Idelson, "Crime Provisions in Anti-Terrorism Bill, *Congressional Quarterly Weekly Report*, Mar. 16, 1996, 703.

ing to kill far more people. As an indicator of growing bigotry, perhaps, the Columbine youths had represented themselves as neo-Nazis and had sought out one of the school's few black students, Isaiah Shoels, for murder. Coming as it did on the heels of other recent acts of terrorism committed by white youths in rural and suburban areas and presaging widespread threats of similar violence on high school campuses across the nation as well as the shooting of six youths by a lone white youth terrorist in an affluent suburb of Atlanta, the attack spurred the administration and Congress to turn their attention to gun control. Although no strong gun-control legislation was forthcoming during the Clinton years, it was striking that now that youth violence had been brought home to the suburbs, the White House, Congress, and the white public picked up the issue. Meanwhile racial minority youths had been murdered on the streets of America in growing numbers every day during the 1990s without inspiring action. Nor did issues such as police misconduct, racial profiling, the prison industrial complex[73]—all issues on the agendas of many black organizations—produce much more than lip service and studies by "commissions." They never commanded sustained attention from either the administration or Congress. African American interests were patently ignored in the fight over crime in both of Clinton's terms.

Meanwhile, black men occupied more than half the nation's prison cells and each year found the prison population increasingly blacker and browner, especially as a result of drug arrests. Moreover, since most states deprived felons of the right to vote ever again, some pointed to felony conviction as "the new disenfranchisement." In effect, the crime legislation during the Clinton years simply built upon trends begun under Reagan. By the end of the 1990s, the drug war had become focused so overwhelmingly on racial minority men that on roadways from New Jersey to California, black and Latino drivers were subjected to such frequent, unjustified traffic stops and searches that they complained of a new, unwritten violation in traffic codes, "driving while black." As the century ended, some courts ruled that police had engaged in "de facto racial profiling." In at least one state, New Jersey, under sustained pressure from civil rights activists, racial profiling was grudgingly acknowledged; the state was

73. Katha Pollitt, "Gunned Down and Fed Up," *Nation,* Mar. 15, 1999, 9; Alexandra Marks, "NYPD as Lab for Reducing Police Brutality," *Christian Science Monitor,* May 13, 1999, 3; Jennifer Gonnerman, "Prison Politics: Angela Davis Takes On the Criminal Justice System," *Village Voice,* Sept. 29, 1998, 51.

forced to revamp its narcotics strategy of selective enforcement; and a federal judge was put in charge of monitoring the police force.[74]

Summing up the Clinton approach to crime-fighting, Philip Heyman, Clinton's first deputy attorney general, concluded: "None of it is accidental. It's been the most careful political calculation, with absolutely sublime indifference to the real nature of the problem."[75] Whites continued to be treated in the superior manner by law enforcement officials that Du Bois had written of nearly a century ago.

The Case of Welfare Reform

The racial politics of welfare played out somewhat differently. In the summer of 1994, congressional Republicans, expecting significant gains in the November elections, sought to delay consideration of welfare reform altogether until the next Congress, so they could deny the Democrats credit for a legislative victory and increase the prospects of getting a more conservative version of welfare reform. It proved to be a fortuitous decision for their party and its position on welfare reform. To the surprise of most observers, the Republicans did not just gain a significant number of new seats; they actually took control of both the Senate and the House for the first time in forty years. Their victory represented the end of an era and bad news for all people who favored progressive social policy.

More than any other action, it was Clinton's monumental and exceedingly complicated health care reform plan that allowed Republicans and the press to cast him as a big-government liberal who was part of the "inside the Beltway" problem. But once the Republicans controlled Congress, they did not focus on health care; their eyes were on welfare reform.

The choice of welfare was hardly race-neutral, of course. Despite the fact that children composed roughly three of every four welfare beneficiaries and that blacks composed fewer welfare beneficiaries in 1993 than at any time since 1960, the stereotypical image of a welfare recipient continued to be that of a poor black woman living in a big city, abusing drugs, and spawning a criminal class. The fury in the election of 1994, which *USA Today* dubbed "the revenge

74. David Kocieniewski and Robert Hanley, "An Inside Story of Racial Bias and Denial," *New York Times*, Dec. 3, 2000.

75. Quoted in David Johnston and Tim Weiner, "Seizing the Crime Issue, Clinton Blurs Party Lines," *New York Times*, Aug. 1, 1996, A1.

of the white male,"[76] built directly on racist, sexist stereotypes. Meanwhile, the passage of California's Proposition 187, which would sentence children who live in the United States illegally through no fault of their own to a perpetual underclass status by denying them education and health services, further demonstrated the public's nativist, racist, and nearly hysterical mood.

Clearly the time was ripe for a sustained assault on the welfare state, and controlling the deficit provided an immediate excuse for it. Thus, in the wake of their unexpected victories, congressional Republicans mobilized to try to do what Reagan and Bush had failed to accomplish. Taken as a whole, their legislative plan—titled the "Contract with America"—represented an unusually aggressive effort to redistribute who gets what from government.[77] Proposed spending cuts in education, training, employment, housing, and antipoverty programs were to fall very heavily on traditional Democratic constituencies, especially the poor, racial minorities, and cities. The reductions in planned expenditures on low-income programs were to be much larger than anything even the Reagan administration had proposed. By contrast, rather than concentrating on lower tax rates per se, the Contract's budget proposals were full of tax expenditures for businesses and hidden welfare for the affluent—activist government in conservative clothing. For instance, sharp cuts in on-budget spending were to be accompanied by new subsidies for "American Dream" savings accounts, adoption, long-term care insurance, elderly dependent care, and the costs of child rearing. The well-to-do elderly were to get more favorable treatment of their earnings, and the "marriage penalty" was to be reduced. These new benefits not only were overwhelmingly regressive and therefore highly favorable to important Republican constituencies, but could be disguised as "tax cuts" that simply restored people's money rather than as instances of government largesse. Thus Republicans stood to get credit for introducing these benefits and yet voters were unlikely to attribute their good fortune to government. In effect, Republicans stood to reap the political gains of what was in actuality new social spending without encouraging public support for activist government.

Direct proposed tax cuts were even more likely to help affluent people in contrast to the poor and working classes. Given the link between class and race,

76. *USA Today,* Nov. 9, 1994, A1.
77. Pierson, "Deficit and the Politics of Domestic Reform," 153.

few people of color would benefit from proposed tax cuts. Fewer than 2 percent of black households stood to gain from the Contract's proposed capital gains tax cut, fewer than 10 percent from the back-loaded IRA, and fewer than 5 percent of black seniors from tax reductions on social security benefits In sum, the effects of proposed tax expenditures and direct tax cuts were highly favorable to important Republican constituencies. On the one hand, the combination of deep cuts in on-budget spending and the tax subsidy packages promised a sweeping redistribution of the costs and benefits of government to primarily affluent whites. On the other, the Contract's welfare reform proposal targeted particularly those groups that were heavily black: teenage mothers, long-term recipients, and children whose paternity had not been established. The block grant proposals would result in substantial reduction of a host of other antipoverty programs, from public housing to Medicaid to food and nutrition.

The revival of racial symbolism and code words was central to the Republican strategy in passing the Contract.[78] Speaker of the House Newt Gingrich's oft-repeated refrain evoked racially linked stereotypes to attack the entire welfare state: "No civilization can survive for long with 12-year-olds having babies, 15-year-olds killing one another, 17-year-olds dying of AIDS, and 18-year-olds getting diplomas they can't read. Yet every night on the local news, you and I watch the welfare state undermining our society."[79] The Speaker, who fancied himself not only a historian but a futurist, pointed out that in some other time, some other civilization, these people may have been tolerated, but no more.

Undergirding Gingrich's coded messages were works of conservative authors, many of whom now take credit for welfare reform and who openly implicated blacks. According to Lawrence Mead, for example, "today's poor blacks function poorly because their parents did and their parents did, a pattern that ultimately goes back [to slavery]. . . . Group memories of slavery and Jim Crow inculcate hopelessness more powerfully than any bias blacks are likely to meet at present."[80] For Mead and other conservative scholars, the belief in an

---

78. For an excellent study of the use of racial stereotypes in undercutting support for progressive social policy, particularly regarding welfare, see Kenneth J. Neubeck and Noel A. Cazenave, *Welfare Racism: Playing the Race Card against America's Poor* (New York: Routledge, 2001).

79. Newt Gingrich, *To Renew America* (New York: HarperCollins, 1995), 8–9.

80. Lawrence M. Mead, *The New Politics of Poverty: The Non-Working Poor in America* (Washington, D.C.: Brookings, 1997), 114.

intergenerational transmission of hopelessness, like intergenerational poverty and welfare use, meant that government needed to impose behavioral standards on blacks. Poor black women were singled out to be especially likely to be "dependent" and "unwilling to work." Mead's evidence for this conclusion included data showing that many fewer black women worked as domestics in 1980 than in 1950. For Mead, this "selfish resistance to menial jobs" must stop.

In 1995, Republicans set about fashioning a plan (dubbed the "new paternalism," but sounding a lot like the old paternalism advocated as far back as Reconstruction) to restructure the welfare state that actually codified Mead's and other Republican academic spokespersons' views into law. The racial subtext in the proposal was so thinly veiled that people of color, blacks especially, could hardly escape the recognition that they were under attack. Thus it was hardly surprising that blacks were far more likely than whites to disapprove of House Republican proposals. In fact, large majorities of African American respondents were opposed to Contract proposals such as cutting spending on food stamps, replacing school lunch programs with block grants, cutting the national service program, ending direct student loans for college education, cutting off welfare to teen mothers, and cutting welfare spending in general (Table 5.1). When asked whether they agreed or disagreed with most of what the Republicans in Congress were proposing, 80 percent of African Americans, compared with 39 percent of whites, disagreed. Indeed, the Contract with America soon became known in black circles as the Contract on Black America.

Extreme right-wingers, too, understood the racial subtexts of the Contract. On the campaign trail in New Hampshire in 1996, Patrick Buchanan, a candidate widely known for his racist and anti-Semitic appeals, declared: "I can win because it is clear to the point of transparency that the ideas of the Buchanan camp of 1992 took root in America. Indeed, they may now even be heard raucously championed in the well of a Republican House. Our campaign may have lost, but our cause triumphed." David Duke, a Republican presidential candidate in 1992 and a former Ku Klux Klansman, was more blunt: "That Contract with America of Gingrich's—that's mine."[81]

To a substantial extent, Clinton was not well positioned to lodge a coun-

81. Quoted in Robert Pear, "The Contract in Review," *New York Times,* June 19, 1996, A1.

Table 5.1.   Which Republican proposals are a step in the right direction/step in the wrong direction? (percentage) Hart-Teeter, April 1995

	Blacks	Whites
Cutting spending for the Department of Education		
Right direction	8%	15%
Wrong direction	90	79
Replacing the school lunch program and other federal nutrition programs with block grants		
Right direction	16	41
Wrong direction	79	44
Cutting the national service program, which gives stipends and college tuition credits to young people in public-service jobs		
Right direction	29	35
Wrong direction	69	57
Ending direct lending of student loans by the government, and having banks make all student loans		
Right direction	18	41
Wrong direction	69	47
Ending the federal food stamp program and giving the money directly to the states		
Right direction	28	54
Wrong direction	42	35
Making unwed mothers under the age of 18 ineligible for welfare		
Right direction	32	54
Wrong direction	56	38
Cutting spending on Medicare in order to reduce the budget deficit and lower taxes		
Right direction	6	26
Wrong direction	86	61
Cutting spending on welfare		
Right direction	34	56
Wrong direction	64	41
Cutting spending on food stamps		
Right direction	18	46
Wrong direction	81	51
Cutting welfare for parents who have more kids		
Right direction	48	70
Wrong direction	51	27
Placing a two-year limit on welfare		
Right direction	57	78
Wrong direction	41	20

Source: Unpublished data from Hart-Teeter proprietary poll conducted April 3–5, 1995, for *Wall Street Journal.*

terattack. On the campaign trail in 1992, Clinton had promised to "end welfare as we know it" by stressing time limits and work requirements, but also by job training, job creation, supportive child care, health care, transportation services, and enforcement of child support. Such reforms, however, would cost far more than the much-criticized AFDC program, generically known as "welfare." In 1993, $22 billion were spent on AFDC, roughly 1 percent of the federal budget and only 2 or 3 percent of most state budgets; but reforms of the kind Clinton promised would cost tens of billions more, and his ambitions for welfare reform shrank considerably once he was in office. A plan drafted in February 1994, which would have provided most of the supportive services the public favored, placed the cost of the new welfare system at an additional $58 billion in spending over ten years; a later version came in at $35 billion; and Clinton's June 1994 bill had whittled the cost to $30 billion. Each time the dollars contracted, the services and the job-opportunity side of the plan shrank and opposition from key Democratic constituencies grew.

The June bill proposed a work-oriented welfare reform plan with relatively soft time limits, financed by cuts in entitlements for other relatively unpopular and weak constituencies (mainly legal immigrants and persons disabled as a result of drug and alcohol abuse). The bill also included very limited aid for child care and other ancillary services. While Republicans denounced the president's plan as "weak on work," black and Latino organizations criticized its failure to address job creation and its proposed cutback in immigrant benefits.[82]

At any rate, Clinton, who had decided to focus the administration's attention on achieving health care reform first,[83] never really pushed the plan in Congress. In fact, the most prominent impact of his proposal was that it helped to push Republicans to shift their own welfare reform stance further

82. Conclusions based on author's participant observation in meetings of constituency groups with the Clinton working group on welfare reform.

83. But then health care reform never passed. For an explanation of the failure of health care reform, see Theda Skocpol, *Boomerang: Health Care Reform and the Turn against Government* (New York: Norton, 1997). For an explanation of the actions and responses of civil rights activists in the health care reform debate, see Hamilton and Hamilton, *Dual Agenda*, 244–54. According to David Ellwood, one of the administration's three aides in charge of welfare reform, "welfare was always seen as something that was likely to divide the party, to make things more difficult, and the president wanted to avoid alienating liberal votes he needed to pass health care. It was also believed that spending on welfare would look better in light of health care reform" (interview, Mar. 17, 1994).

rightward to avoid losing the issue to Clinton. Thus the administration's acceptance of time limits with a work requirement pushed Republicans in a more
punitive direction (notably time limits with no work guarantee) in order to
demonstrate that they would be tougher than the Democrats on welfare
reform. In effect, Clinton's June proposal succeeded mainly in opening the door
to changes far more conservative than those he initially envisioned.

Now in control of Congress, Republicans walked through that door in
1995 and achieved much of what they had proposed regarding welfare. Their
success was made less surprising by the president's own further accommodation
to Republican themes. Almost immediately after the Democrats' stunning
defeat in 1994, the president hyped the (very real) "common ground" between
his welfare reform plan and the Republican plan. A year later (November 1995)
the president declared that he had been too "soft and weak" on welfare reform,
raised taxes too much on corporations and the very rich, and sought to do too
much in education reform. He promised to move rightward.[84]

To be sure, the House Republicans did not get everything they originally
proposed. The initial proposal in the Contract, the "Personal Responsibility
Act," also consolidated food and nutrition programs such as food stamps, the
Supplemental Nutrition Program for Women, Infants, and Children (WIC),
and school lunch and breakfast programs into one block grant, stripped their
entitlement status, and cut the total funding by 5 percent. In addition, it
required states to exclude permanently from AFDC eligibility almost all children whose paternity had not been established. Indeed, the most controversial
provision of all in the Contract's initial plan was to use savings achieved by
eliminating the children of teenage parents and those whose paternity could
not be legally established from AFDC rolls to establish orphanages for the destitute—a proposal that earned Gingrich the name "Scrooge" in December
1994.[85] The bill also forbade abortion counseling and required single parents

84. Ann Devroy, "Clinton Says Welfare and Education Plans Flawed, Pledges to Move
Right," *Washington Post,* Nov. 2, 1995, A13.
85. The orphanage proposal set off a firestorm of criticism—some even coming from the
right. Administrators who ran orphanages and foster care institutions, such as Gingrich's own
example of Boys' Town, argued that they already could not meet the demand and that their
first priority was keeping families together. The National Council on Adoptable Children as
well as some scholars at conservative think tanks, such as Douglas Besharov of the American
Enterprise Institute, countered that the costs of placing over a million children of current welfare recipients in orphanages would be astronomical compared to the costs of AFDC. Adding
all benefits together (food stamps, public housing subsidies, Medicaid, and AFDC), Besharov
concluded that while the total government support for a typical welfare family with three chil-

to work at least thirty-five hours a week if they had been receiving AFDC assistance for at least two years. Nonwork assistance was limited to two years. States were required to have an escalating proportion of their caseloads in jobs or face penalties. All told, the bill (excluding nutrition components) was expected to save the federal government about $30 billion over five years, with more than half of those savings coming from exclusion of legal resident aliens from means-tested benefits.

Some highly visible Republican governors opposed parts of the initial plan. These governors favored block grants with no strings attached. As John Engler, Republican governor of Michigan, put it, "Conservative micro management is just as bad as liberal micro management."[86] Other Republican governors, such as George W. Bush of Texas and Pete Wilson of California, opposed the cut-off of aid to legal immigrants, viewing it as a costly transfer from the federal government to their states.

In the light of these differences, House Republican leaders and Republican governors negotiated and came up with a replacement welfare bill with more flexible work requirements in exchange for a block grant with a decline in real funding for five years. When Clinton and congressional Democrats attacked the bill as "weak on work" and "tough on kids," work requirements were stiffened again. The revised Personal Responsibility Act passed the House of Representatives on a largely party-line vote near the end of the first hundred days of the 104th Congress. Only nine Democratic members voted for the bill; only five Republican members voted against it (and two of those were Cuban exiles who represented districts in South Florida).[87]

Yet although the vast majority of Democrats voted against the bill, many supported a conservative Democratic alternative (sponsored by Nathan Deal of Georgia, who later became a Republican). The Democrats' conservative bill also contained hard time limits but won Clinton's backing—indicating that the president had backed away from his bill with more flexible limits introduced in the 103d Congress. Clinton's capitulation provided additional leverage for House Republicans to insist on hard time limits in welfare reform. The question

---

dren is about $15,000 annually, putting those children in an orphanage would cost at least $72,000.

86. Quoted in Lori Montgomery, "In Welfare Debate, Engler Is Both a Model and a Maverick," *Detroit Free Press,* Jan. 20, 1995, 1A.

87. Kent Weaver, "Ending Welfare as We Know It," in Weir, *Social Divide,* 396.

was what would happen in the Senate, where the Republican majority was much slimmer.[88]

Presidential politics complicated the task in the Senate. Majority Leader Robert Dole of Kansas, a 1996 presidential candidate and ultimately the Republican nominee, was committed to achieving legislation to demonstrate that he could be effective. In order to garner support from moderate Republicans and Republican governors and achieve enough Democratic support to pass welfare reform, Dole criticized the evolving House Republican bill in January 1995 as being overly radical, particularly in its ban on cash benefits to teen mothers. Later Dole introduced a bill, endorsed by twenty-six of the nation's thirty GOP governors, similar to the House GOP bill in most respects, save requiring states to end cash assistance to unwed teenage mothers and eliminating family caps. Dole's bill also did not cut off aid to legal immigrants. Dole's bill would have cut $43.5 billion over five years or $70 billion from the amount that would have been spent in the next seven years. Most of the savings would come from AFDC, food stamps, and SSI. Those programs would be cut by about 10 percent.

Facing competition from Phil Gramm and other more conservative candidates in the Republican primaries, however, Dole began to move rightward to appeal to conservative activists, who have a high turnout rate in Republican primaries. Dole eventually carved out a majority for a bill including work requirements and hard time limits.

At that point, what was expected, at least by welfare advocacy groups, to be the key point of battle between Clinton and the Republicans was the proposal to eliminate the individual entitlement through block-granting welfare, ending a sixty-year guarantee that all poor children who qualified for assistance would be able to get it. The president had previously argued that block grants were unnecessary because the federal government could already give states great flexibility, and that he had streamlined the process through which states could get waivers for their own welfare plans. Block grants, Clinton argued, would lead state governments to engage in a "race to the bottom" in providing for the needy since state legislatures are not known for giving programs for the poor high priority. Thus block-granting welfare without requiring states to maintain their own efforts was an open invitation to welfare cutbacks, the administration had contended.

88. Ibid., 388–89.

Yet, as the debate ensued in the 104th Congress, the administration's plan, which would have replaced AFDC with a new cash welfare program conditioned on a recipient's willingness to take certain steps toward self-sufficiency but retaining a federal guarantee of cash benefits to eligible recipients who followed the rules, was barely part of key discussions. Both Senate Democrats, who had introduced the president's plan, and the White House had relatively little to say on the issue of ending the individual entitlement status of welfare. By September 1995, Bill Clinton endorsed the Senate Republican bill in principle and most Senate Democrats followed suit. Indeed, when the Senate bill, modestly less stringent than the House bill but ending the guarantee of welfare benefits to the poor,[89] came to a vote, 35 Democratic senators voted for it and only 11 against it. The bill was passed 87 to 12, opposed by only the Senate's most liberal Democrats (and one exceptionally conservative Republican, Lauch Faircloth of North Carolina, because the bill was not far enough to the right for him).

As Kent Weaver concludes, the heavy support of Senate Democrats and Clinton's general endorsement fundamentally altered the nature of the debate over welfare. From then on, only exceptionally conservative proposals had any chance of passage. According to the White House aide George Stephanopoulos, the White House staff and the Cabinet were bitterly divided over whether Clinton should sign the Republican welfare bill. Donna Shalala, secretary of Health and Human Services (HHS), passionately argued that "the objective reality is that people are going to get hurt."[90] Secretary Henry Cisneros of Housing and Urban Development (HUD) joined Shalala in urging a veto of the measure, as did Labor Secretary Robert Reich, Treasury Secretary Bob Rubin, Economic Security Adviser Laura Tyson, and aides Harold Ickes and Leon Panetta.

Dick Morris, the president's pollster, disagreed, saying his polls predicted that a veto of welfare reform would transform Clinton's projected reelection victory in November 1996 into a 3-point loss. Rahm Emmanuel and Mickey Kantor sought to be more substantive and less political in their advice to the

89. Unlike the House bill, the Senate bill would have retained cash assistance for children of unwed teenage mothers and families on welfare that had additional children, provided limited assistance for child care, and added penalties for states that cut their spending on welfare by more than 20%.

90. George Stephanopoulos, *All Too Human: A Political Education* (Boston: Little, Brown, 1999), 419.

president to sign the bill. They argued that vetoing the bill would cause more harm by perpetuating a failed system. It would be irresponsible to do nothing. New Democrat Bruce Reed went so far as to call the measure "a good welfare bill wrapped in a bad budget bill," reminding the president that the time limits and work requirements were close to his own original proposals. He, like Morris, also warned the president of the political potential. A (third) veto, Reed said, would turn off voters who had taken Clinton seriously when he promised in 1992 to "end welfare as we know it." Finally, Vice President Gore also urged the president to sign the bill.[91]

Whether Clinton just followed his own mind or listened to his New Democrat advisers more intently than to his liberal Democrat ones, the result was a decision to sign into law in July 1996 a new welfare system. The final bill, the Personal Responsibility and Work Opportunity Reconciliation Act (PRWORA) of 1996 brought stunning changes in family assistance for the poor. AFDC was abolished, replaced by a block grant to the states called Temporary Assistance to Needy Families (TANF). For the first time in sixty years, there was no individual entitlement to cash assistance. Each state's share of the block grant was based on its historical allocation of AFDC funds. Limited contingency funds were provided for recessionary periods. States were required to maintain 80 percent of their current spending to obtain their full share of block grant funds, though states that met work requirements needed to maintain only 75 percent. As for work requirements, strict quotas were established for the percentage of adult recipients who must be participating in "work-related activities," starting at 25 percent of the targeted caseload working twenty hours a week in 1997 and rising to 50 percent of the caseload working thirty hours a week by 2002. The law's definition of "work-related activities" was also quite narrow, limiting education and training to no more than one year, after which time only taking a job or completing community service work could count toward fulfilling this requirement. In addition, subsequent legislation limited the number of recipients in education and training programs to no more than 20 percent of those counted as fulfilling the work quota. The 1996 law prohibited states from spending TANF funds on recipients who had received assistance for more than two years and were not working. A five-year time limit on adults' receipt of cash assistance was set, although states were

91. Ibid.

provided the option to set lower limits. States were also provided permission to exempt up to 20 percent of their caseloads from time limits. Teen parents were required to live with parents or in an adult-supervised setting. States were given the option to establish family caps or teen parent exclusions. To appease the Christian right, states were also provided the opportunity to compete for bonuses of up to $20 million a year for as many as five states if they successfully reduced "illegitimacy." Although the act provided additional funding for child care, it did not provide an entitlement to that care. To pay the bill, there was a sharp reduction of benefits to legal immigrants and changes in the food stamp and SSI programs, including tightening eligibility for disabled children.[92] Nonetheless, a case could be made that even these restrictions did not impose great new burdens because many states were already experimenting with these and other limitations. In that spirit, the law most significantly allowed states to set even stricter limitations and to impose tough sanctions on recipients, including termination for failure to comply. States could set a time limit on the receipt of assistance that was shorter than five years; they could require work sooner than two years, even immediately if they so chose. By 1997, twenty-one states had adopted a time limit shorter than five years and twenty-six states adopted a work requirement sooner than two years, with thirteen states choosing to adopt an immediate work requirement.

The 1996 law also allowed states to choose a variety of other options, including mandatory drug-testing of all recipients, denial of aid to persons convicted of drug felonies, requiring community service as a condition attached to the receipt of aid, and denial of additional aid for a child born while the mother is receiving assistance; twenty-one states chose that highly controversial last option. Finally, one of the most significant changes under the law is associated with what legislation refers to as "individual responsibility plans" that states can require adult recipients to sign as a condition for receiving assistance. An individual responsibility plan includes steps that the recipient promises to take to get off welfare, most especially taking paid employment. States can adopt procedures to penalize recipients who do not fulfill the steps in their "individual responsibility plans" or are otherwise deemed negligent under the new welfare regime. For instance, failing to keep an appointment with your case manager (now often called a job coach or counselor) can be grounds for the imposition

92. Weaver, "Ending Welfare as We Know It," 395–96.

of a sanction. Sanctions normally involve reductions in benefits and they can be imposed initially or after a number of violations. They can involve only the recipient's part of a family's assistance check or they can be what are called "full family sanctions."[93]

Although the new welfare reform clearly had important racial implications, throughout the debate race was the proverbial pink elephant, never officially acknowledged but always casting a long shadow. Perhaps the most notable factor in the debate over welfare was the inaction of people of color; they were barely visible among the key players either proposing alternative legislation or even responding to the Republicans' bill. To be sure, the CBC held one press conference decrying the bill's potential effects on poor children and many of its members made eloquent, haunting speeches on the floor of the House, but by and large the caucus was anything but an influential contender in welfare reform.

Given the Republicans' tight control of the House and the CBC's related inability to affect legislation through the normal legislative process, the caucus might well have been influential only if it had reverted to its original status as a protest lobby, as it had done on major proposals as late as the Carter administration, and undertaken such dramatic action as staging a strategic walkout or other disruption of normal affairs in the House, or drawing a line in the sand and withholding support from the Clinton administration if it compromised. The caucus also might have resuscitated a tactic from the late Congressman Adam Clayton Powell's old playbook and insisted on adding racial-justice riders to the welfare reform bill (and perhaps to every other measure that came before the Republican-led House). The point of this kind of action would not be to persuade the House or the Clinton administration to attend to black citizens' needs. Rather it would be to use public office as a bully pulpit. But the CBC proved unwilling to pursue such a course. Its members, now a diverse lot, were constrained not only by the idiosyncratic politics of their districts but by their official leadership positions and individual ambitions. Some apparently genuinely supported the White House's policies and some had to toe the administration's line because they needed its support for one thing or another in their districts. Hence, if Clinton appeared willing to compromise on welfare reform,

93. Joe Soss, Erin O'Brien, Sanford Schram, and Thomas Vartanian, "Predicting Welfare Reform Retrenchment: Race, Ideology, and Economy in the Devolution Revolution," article emailed by Schram, Sept. 9, 1999.

a substantial number of members of the CBC willingly followed him. In fact, some CBC members were unwilling not only to oppose the president with their votes but even to voice criticism of him. Still others, such as Harold Ford of Tennessee in his role as the ranking Democratic member of the leading sub-committee on welfare reform, scrambled for a compromise with Republicans in order to show he still retained at least some relevance. Ford put together a task committee in which selected liberal advocacy group staffers were encouraged not to worry about the plan to end the entitlement status of welfare but rather to come up with a plan to provide "awards" to poor children in families receiving welfare if they made good grades in school, did not get pregnant, and did not break the law. Internally, Ford argued that the Republicans were more serious about welfare reform, and he concluded that black interests might be better served by compromising with Republicans.[94]

Finally, even if the CBC had been able to determine its own position on welfare reform, no chairperson of the caucus, no matter how politically persuasive, could impose discipline on its members in 1996. This had been demonstrated not only regarding the crime bill but also on a growing number of occasions involving other legislation. For example, the caucus went on record as opposed to the balanced budget amendment, but three of its members voted for it. Given the Republicans' abolition of the office, staff, and financial support of the CBC, imposing discipline proved even more difficult in the 104th Congress than in the past. Several members stopped attending the weekly CBC meetings altogether and many more attended only sporadically. Thus, with the CBC becoming less cohesive in the 104th Congress, the organization squandered the opportunity to at least introduce its own plan. Nor did it play a role in mobilizing popular political action against the key plans before the House. Only during the week before the House vote on the Personal Responsibility Act did the CBC take to the airwaves with radio ads against the Republican plan, and then only because one prominent philanthropic foundation provided a small grant for the Joint Center for Political and Economic Studies to conduct research to develop an alternative plan and for CBC members to air paid advertisements. Although members of the CBC lined up to make radio ads to be aired in their districts, there was never an active black coalition involving the

94. Participant observation of meetings in February–May 1996 with Rep. Harold Ford of Tennessee and civil rights groups.

CBC that proposed an alternative bill on welfare reform. In the end, like the last cohort of black southern legislators waiting to be driven out of office after the restoration of white supremacy a century before, some members of the CBC pathetically sought to fashion compromises with an increasingly obdurate tyranny, a poignant reminder that at times the greatest danger lies in not standing on principle.

In the vacuum created by the lack of leadership in the CBC, it fell to the Progressive Caucus to seek to organize an opposition in Congress. Yet they were not supported by or even encouraged by a strong lobby among black organizations. Despite the fact that 16 percent of the total black population (the vast majority of them poor children) were recipients of AFDC, Capitol Hill faced only minimal lobbying from African American leaders, organizations, and individuals.

In a very real sense, black, Latino, and women civil rights activists and leaders never prioritized welfare reform. Organizations such as the NAACP, the NUL, and LULAC (the League of United Latin American Citizens) had little or no visibility in the welfare reform debate. What was left among liberals to lobby on behalf of the poor was Washington-based intergovernmental lobbies (such as the American Public Welfare Association) and research or advocacy groups (such as the Center on Budget and Policy Priorities, the Center on Law and Social Policy, and the Children's Benefit Fund [CDF])—all groups that relied mainly on their policy expertise and the media to gain entree into the policy-making process. Even these groups exhibited extreme caution in criticizing Clinton. Throughout the Clinton administration, they were very mindful that they were "FOBs"—Friends of Bill. More important, none of these groups had a mass political base.[95]

In the mid-1990s, it was this lack of leadership, this failure of organizational connectedness to the grassroots, that provided the open space for the Nation of Islam's controversial leader, Louis Farrakhan. In the midst of the debate over welfare, hundreds of thousands (if not a million) of black men marched on Washington on October 16, 1995, in what was billed as "a day of atonement."[96] Perhaps more than any other development, Farrakhan's appeal reflected the failure of the black political elite to connect to the black poor. In

95. Weaver, "Ending Welfare as We Know It," 376.
96. Jerry Watts, "The Trap of Imagery," *Common Quest,* Fall 1996, 57–58.

short, in the absence of a genuinely popularly based leadership organized around deliberative processes and issues that concretely connect with people's daily lives and concerns, Farrakhan was able to project himself as leader of the black masses.

Farrakhan's rise and the relative silence of traditional black leaders in the welfare reform debate perhaps demonstrate more about the increasing significance of class and the negative views a growing proportion of the black middle class has of the black poor than they do about black leadership's interest in either mobilizing on behalf of the black poor or encouraging the poor to mobilize for themselves. Indeed, the predominantly middle-class "million" black men who marched behind Farrakhan apparently were not turned off by a message concentrating on the "irresponsibility" of black men (read *poor* black men), validating the right's explanation of poverty and inequality.[97]

In fact, the central implication of the Million Man March (MMM) for issues such as welfare reform was exceptionally consistent with the PRWORA, so much so that much of the march's propaganda could have come directly from the bill's preamble, concentrating as it did on the behavioral problems of black men and the deficiencies of individuals and social pathology, not lack of opportunity, white skin privilege, unemployment, underemployment, inherent contradictions and crises of capital, the intensification of slow-growing low-wage jobs in the new high-tech global economy, or any other impersonal, structural, or racist forces. The problem of poor black families instead was viewed as a result of bad behavior and poor choices; the solution, "personal responsibility" and black community self-help, like the politics of George Bush, was to be achieved through "a thousand points of light," not public policy.

Black leaders were not the only predominantly liberal faction missing in action from the welfare debate. Female members of Congress also exercised little or no influence. In the Senate, most women Democratic members even refused to meet with women's organizations seeking their opposition to the

97. For data on the class composition of the marchers, see Mario A. Brossard and Richard Morin, "Leader Popular among Marchers," *Washington Post,* Oct. 17, 1995, A1, A23; and Lorenzo Morris et al., "Million Man March: Preliminary Report on the Survey," Howard University, Department of Political Science, 1995. According to the Howard University poll, three out of four were under the age of 45; two out of three had household incomes of $30,000 or more, with nearly one in five making more than $75,000 a year; and nearly three of four attended at least a year of college and more than a third were college graduates. The march sought to exclude black women and largely succeeded: only 9% were women.

most extreme aspects of the Republicans' welfare bill. In fact, with the exception of Carol Moseley Braun of Illinois, all the Democratic women senators voted for the worst provisions in the bill.[98] The absence of liberals in general from the welfare reform debate was so remarkable that for months Senator Moynihan complained that while his office was crowded with lobbyists when the issue was health care, he could look from his office window "clear across to the Supreme Court" without seeing one group lobbying for welfare reform.[99]

Meanwhile, conservative get-tough-on-welfare groups such as the Christian Coalition, the Eagle Forum, the Family Research Council, and the Traditional Values Coalition became heavily engaged in welfare reform. Some of these organizations, by contrast to the liberals, have a mass political base and engage in techniques of modern mass politics such as the issuance of voter guides and letter-writing campaigns. The conservative groups also had a clear research arm to turn to in their attempt to marshal "evidence" for their right-wing views of welfare reform: the ultraconservative Heritage Foundation, for instance, heavily funded by right-wing zealots such as Joseph Coors and Richard Scaife. Under the leadership of Robert Rector of Heritage in particular, a strong coalition was built among right-wing organizations that were in turn linked to Republican members of Congress and their caucuses.[100] The influence of Rector is best summed up by Ron Haskins, staffer of the U.S. House Human Services subcommittee. According to Haskins, the opening section of the PRW-ORA, laying out its underlying premises, was drafted by Rector: "Rector wrote it and we just edited it," Haskins said.[101] Those underlying premises promote marriage as "the foundation of a successful society" and only thinly disguise attacks on black men as the premier group rejecting marriage and threatening society. In short, right-wing groups found their interests addressed in the legislation's hard time limits, restrictions on teen mothers, and competitive bonuses for reducing illegitimacy.

Looking over the course of the debate over welfare reform, one can see that Clinton had relatively little pressure from the left and a great deal from

98. Interview with Heidi Hartmann, executive director of the Institute for Women's Policy Research, Washington, D.C., June 4, 1997.

99. Quoted in Peter Kilborn and Sam Verhovek, "Welfare Shift Reflects New Democrat," *New York Times,* Aug. 2, 1996, A1.

100. Weaver, "Ending Welfare as We Know It," 376–77.

101. Quoted in Kevin Merida, "The Ideas behind Welfare Reform," *Washington Post,* July 27, 1996, A1.

the right. His response was to move from being the president who proposed to increase welfare spending by an additional $30 billion in his June 1994 proposal to signing and seeking to take credit for a Republican welfare bill that promised to cut $56 billion in spending, end welfare as an entitlement, and give states vast new powers to remove people from welfare rolls whether there were jobs for them or not. The bill deeply cut food stamp spending and achieved nearly half (44 percent) of its projected savings by sharply restricting benefits to legal immigrants. As a result, it was predicted that over half a million legal immigrants would lose SSI benefits and a million would lose food stamps, and Medicaid as well as AFDC.[102] In fact, when the PRWORA and a 1996 immigration measure (forcing sponsors of immigrants to meet income requirements; making it harder for the government to sue employers who discriminate against immigrants; and stripping immigrants of some of their most important legal protections) are taken as a group, it is clear that the Clinton administration endorsed the most punitive measures toward immigrants in decades.[103] It was a remarkable retreat, not only from the vision the president had outlined in 1992 but from the domestic social policy regime of sixty years.[104] It was also an overhaul that was all but unimaginable during twelve years of Republican control of the White House.

Seeking to placate the liberal wing of his party (particularly racial minorities) for signing what Senator Moynihan predicted would ultimately prove to be "the most brutal act of social policy since Reconstruction,"[105] Clinton campaign strategists constantly declared in 1996 that the president had already moved ahead on several elements of his plan to raise more people out of poverty by increasing the minimum wage, expanding the EITC, and stepping up ways to force parents, mostly fathers, to pay child support. By contrast, both government agencies and private-sector research institutes projected that ultimately more than a million more children (disproportionately black ones, given the bill's focus on long-term welfare recipients and children of teenage parents) would be thrown into poverty. In response, the president promised he would

102. Judith Havemann, "Gore Proposes Restoring More of Legal Immigrants' Benefits," *Washington Post,* Jan. 26, 1999, A7.

103. Eric Schmitt, "The Clinton Record: Milestones and Missteps on Immigration," *New York Times,* Oct. 26, 1996, A1.

104. Kilborn and Verhovek, "Welfare Shift Reflects New Democrat."

105. Ibid.

try to fix the bill by restoring some aid to legal immigrants and spending an additional $13 billion on efforts such as job creation. In short, the president sought to have it both ways: he deserved credit for finally "ending welfare as we know it"; he deserved to be reelected precisely because he needed to fix the mess he had just helped create.

Apparently this strategy worked well in November 1996. After his successful fight with Congress over the budget in 1995 and raising the minimum wage in 1996,[106] the president staged a remarkable political comeback, pushing his job-approval rating to the highest sustained level of his presidency. As in 1992, African Americans, Latinos, Jews, organized labor, and white women contributed heavily to Clinton's electoral success. Exit polls showed that the Republican presidential nominee, Robert Dole, actually won narrowly among whites (46 percent compared to Clinton's 43 percent, with 9 percent of the white vote going to Perot), but Clinton was pushed over the top by winning the plurality of the white women's vote, winning 84 percent of the black vote (compared to Dole's 12 percent) and 72 percent of the Latino vote (compared to Dole's 21 percent).[107] Given his support among racial minorities, Clinton certainly had not been hurt by signing the patently conservative welfare reform bill. Instead, on election day 1996, the Voter News Service exit poll found that Clinton did very well among those who reported the new federal welfare law "cuts too much." He won 69 percent of their votes compared to 55 percent of those who thought the cuts were "about right" and 34 percent who thought the cuts were "not enough." These data demonstrate that Clinton knew he stood to lose nothing politically by signing the Republicans' bill. Where else were the poor and their allies to turn?

The Implementation of Welfare Reform and Racial Disparities

While the nation awaits the ultimate verdict on the 1996 welfare reform, the initial deliberations paint a complex picture. To be sure, the most dire predictions of the PRWORA's opponents have not materialized. Overall caseload

106. With more than eight of every ten Americans supporting an increase, 93 of 237 Republican members of the House voted to raise the minimum wage from $4.25 an hour to $4.70 on July 1, 1996, and to $5.15 a year later. The bill passed in the House by a lopsided 318 to 144. See John E. Yang, "House Approves 90-Cent Boost in Minimum Wage," *Washington Post,* May 24, 1996, A1.

107. Voter News Service, *New York Times,* Nov. 10, 1996.

declines have been dramatic, falling from 12.3 million in 1996 to 5.4 million by June 2001, or a 57 percent drop.[108] While AFDC was received by 4.8 percent of the nation's total population in 1996, only 2.1 percent of the population received TANF in June 2000. Many former welfare recipients were finding and maintaining jobs (or at least circulating in and out of the labor market). According to the Department of Health and Human Services (HHS), in 1999 "56 percent of TANF recipients lived in families with at least one family member in the labor force. That is up from 43 percent in 1993."[109] For fiscal year 1999, every state had met its work participation target.[110]

Yet despite these glowing reports, some developments are far from salutary. First, many scholars have contended that a strong economy deserved more credit for declining welfare caseloads than did programmatic change. After all, data demonstrated that the decline began before the 1996 reform. Concomitantly, these studies predicted that an anemic economy could not only reverse progress but leave the poor without a safety net. By the fall of 2002, there were signs that this was precisely what had happened. For the year from June 2001 to June 2002, a period of recession, data on TANF showed that caseloads increased in the majority (29) of states. These increases were fairly large, averaging over 9 percent. While the remaining states and the nation as a whole continued to experience small declines in caseloads, the missed picture of caseload trends fluctuating among states and across time challenged the view that the long-term impact of TANF will draw applause.[111]

Second, even as TANF caseloads dropped, poverty was at best declining at a far slower rate and at worst increasing. Certainly the latter was the case in 2001. The number of people living in poverty rose by 1.3 million between 2000 and 2001, from 31.6 million to 32.9 million. African American families were particularly hard hit; their poverty rate increased from 19.3 percent in

108. Cheryl Wetzstein, "Welfare Reform Halves Rolls, Recipient Families," *Washington Times,* Sept. 3, 2000, 3.

109. U.S. Department of Health and Human Services, Administration for Children and Families, "Change in TANF Caseloads since Enactment of New Welfare Law," <http://www.hhs.gov/news/stats/Aug–Dec.htm>.

110. "TANF Reports All States Meet Overall Welfare to Work Participation Rates," *HHH News* (Department of Health and Human Services), Aug. 22, 2000.

111. "New Data Show Most States Had TANF Caseload Increases in Last Year," Center for Law and Social Policy, Washington, D.C., June 17, 2002; and "TANF Caseloads Declined in Most States in Second Quarter, but Most States Saw Increases over the Last Year," ibid., Oct. 1, 2002.

2000 to 20.7 percent in 2001, while changes in the poverty rate were not statistically significant for most other demographic groups. In 2001, blacks were 3.6 times more likely to live in poverty than non-Latino whites. Moreover, the poor became poorer. The average amount by which people who were poor— and children who were poor—fell below the poverty line reached their highest levels on record: $2,707 per poor person in 2001. Blacks were disproportionately likely to experience the poverty deficit.[112]

Poverty rates tend to rise when unemployment increases significantly, and unemployment was much higher in 2002 than it was in 2001. Meanwhile the number of unemployed workers who had run out of unemployment benefits before finding work was also much higher in 2002 than in 2001. More than a million workers exhausted all of their unemployment benefits before finding work in 2002. Blacks were three times more likely than whites to be among the long-term unemployed who had exhausted their benefits.[113] Without the backup of either unemployment benefits or TANF, many families apparently lived more precariously in 2002 than in 2001.

Third, perhaps the truest test of the 1996 reform began only on August 22, 2001, which marked not only the fifth anniversary of the PRWORA but also the end of the five-year time limit for many poor people. It is probable that some of the observed decreases in TANF caseloads are attributable to time limits taking effect. For instance, among the eight states that reached a time limit for the first time in the first half of 2002, seven experienced a caseload decline between April and June 2002.[114] National data remain sparse about those former TANF beneficiaries who have hit the time limit. Their forcible entry in a sagging labor market is unclear.

Fourth, a growing number of state- and city-level studies find that racial disparities in welfare receipt are growing under the PRWORA. African Americans and Latinos have been less likely to "move from welfare to work," and even when they do, their fates in the labor market have differed from those of whites. Indeed, even if African Americans and Latinos are only slightly more likely to be left behind on welfare rolls, as national statistics suggest, the PRW-

---

112. U.S. Bureau of the Census, "CPS Annual Demographic Supplement (2001 Poverty)," http://ferret.bls.census.gov/macro/032002/pov/tod.htm.

113. "Census Data Show Increases in Extent and Severity of Poverty and Decline in Household Income," ibid., Sept. 24, 2002.

114. "TANF Caseloads Declined in Most States."

ORA has done nothing to produce relative gains for people of color. They remain more likely than whites to be represented in the nation's least generous welfare program.

State-level studies have provided the most important evidence regarding the fourth argument. Almost consistently these studies have found that welfare reform is not working equally for whites and people of color.[115] Several studies conclude that blacks and Latinos in particular face a double whammy: they are disproportionately likely to live in states that have the harshest and most punitive policies, which cause many to leave welfare before they are equipped with the skills to support their families. As the best prepared exit welfare, the unskilled face increasingly heavy odds.

Studies have found that states where blacks compose a higher proportion of the welfare population have adopted stricter sanctions, particularly shorter time limits and family caps. Whether there are jobs waiting for them or not, beneficiaries in these states are pushed off TANF as a result of harsh sanctions.[116] For example, a study of caseloads declines in New York City and fourteen states in 1998 (an aggregation of areas containing 70 percent of all welfare beneficiaries in the nation) found that white beneficiaries are leaving the system much faster than African American and Latino beneficiaries, pushing the minority share of the caseload to the highest level on record. According to the study, blacks now actually outnumber whites on welfare, and the Latino share

115. Maria Cancian, Robert Haveman, Thomas Kaplan, and Barbara Wolfe, "Post-Exit Earning and Benefit Receipt among Those Who Left AFDC in Wisconsin" (Institute for Research on Poverty, University of Wisconsin–Madison, Oct. 30, 1998); Claudia Coulton and Nandita Verma, "Employment and Return to Public Assistance among Single Female-Headed Families Leaving AFDC in Third Quarter, 1996, Cuyahoga County, Ohio" (Cuyahoga Work and Training, May 1999); Michael E. Foster, "Amended Quarterly Progress Report: Outcomes for Single Parent Leavers by Cohort Quarter" (Atlanta: Georgia Department of Human Resources, Evaluation and Reporting Section, January–March 1999); Susan T. Gooden, "All Things Not Being Equal: Differences in Caseworker Support Towards Black and White Welfare Clients," *Harvard Journal of African American Public Policy* 4 (1998): 23–33; Welfare and Child Support Research and Training Group, School of Social Work, University of Maryland–Baltimore, "Life after Welfare: Fourth Interim Report" (Baltimore: Family Investment Administration, Maryland Department of Human Resources, October 1999); and Karen L. Westra and John Routley, "Cash Assistance Exit Study: First Quarter 1998 Cohort" (Phoenix: Arizona Department of Economic Security, Office of Research and Evaluation, May 5, 1999).

116. Soss et al., "Predicting Welfare Reform Retrenchment." For a conservative perspective with some similar empirical findings, see Robert E. Rector and Sarah E. Yousef, "The Determinants of Welfare Caseload Decline," Report no. 99–04 (Washington, D.C.: Heritage Center for Data Analysis, Heritage Foundation, May 1999).

of welfare rolls is growing the fastest, so that blacks and Latinos together outnumber whites by about 2 to 1. New York's record is indicative. By midsummer 1998, New York's welfare rolls were 5 percent white, 33 percent black, and 59 percent Latino. Other states, including Illinois, Ohio, Pennsylvania, Florida, and Michigan—all states with large welfare populations—have also seen the number of whites on welfare declining faster than those of racial minorities, as have other states with still more significant caseload declines (for example, Wisconsin, Massachusetts, and New Jersey).[117]

A growing number of national studies support these disturbing conclusions. According to an Urban Institute study in May 2001, "the share of TANF families that reported their race as white dropped from 42 to 33 percent; the share of TANF families that reported their race as black rose correspondingly from 34 to 46 percent." In general, all available data suggest that blacks are leaving the TANF rolls far more slowly than whites and more are returning. Those still on TANF are less likely to live in homes where there is an adult in the paid labor force. Even HHS's highly salutary study shows that among persons receiving TANF, blacks are far less likely to have a family member in the labor force than other groups. According to HHS, 38.3 percent of whites and 42.1 percent of Latinos receiving TANF in 1998 had no one in the labor force, but 53.4 percent of blacks had no one in the labor force.[118]

Other studies indicate that even when blacks and Latinos leave welfare, their experiences differ from those of whites. When Susan Gooden studied several counties in Virginia, she found that former black welfare recipients earned less than whites, even when they had higher levels of education; were less likely to be employed full-time; were more likely to work in lower-paying occupations; suffered more negative treatment from employers; benefited more from individual job search and job readiness courses than whites; and were not informed by caseworkers of available ancillary services, such as transportation assistance. Gooden attributes the differential impact of welfare reform to prevalent discrimination in the labor market and cultural differences.[119] Similarly, a

117. Jason DeParle, "Shrinking Welfare Rolls Leave Record High Share of Minorities," *New York Times,* July 27, 1998, A1.

118. U.S. Department of Health and Human Services, "Indicators of Welfare Dependency, 2001: Indicators of Dependence," Table IND 2a, <http://aspe.hhs.gov/ hsp/indicators01/ ch2.htm>.

119. Gooden, "All Things Not Being Equal."

study of California's "immigrant" women's experiences of seeking to move from welfare to work concluded that "in most instances, immigrant women are forced to apply for jobs even if their English or job skills are poor. As a result, they're unable to secure work or wind up in temporary and low-paying jobs that offer no promise of long-term stability."[120] With states emphasizing immediate job placement, however, almost no emphasis is being placed on training, especially in basic language skills.[121]

Although there is little understanding of the phenomenon of the deepening coloration of welfare, since post-1996 welfare reform outcome studies fail to address its differential outcomes for whites and people of color, a combination of factors seemingly lies at its roots: racial discrimination by employers and by landlords in neighborhoods near jobs; the greater disadvantages in education, skills, incomes, health, and number of children; and the higher rates of extreme poverty shared by African Americans and Latinos than by other racial groups. Black women in particular had fewer opportunities to leave welfare rolls as a consequence of marriage. and both blacks and Latinos are heavily concentrated not only in inner cities but in neighborhoods least likely to offer jobs. According to the Census Bureau, in 1998 only 31 percent of white welfare families lived in central cities, but 63 percent of Latino welfare families and 71 percent of African American welfare families lived in job-starved inner-city neighborhoods. Supporting this contention are census data showing that 64 percent of black recipients in 1994 lived in census tracts where at least a fifth of the population was poor. The figure for Latino recipients was also very high (55 percent); but for whites it was a comparatively low 21 percent. That not only suggests that blacks and Latinos live farther from jobs, but "it may also mean they have less work experience and fewer contacts to help them find jobs."[122] In general, research shows that big cities are lagging behind states in welfare caseload declines.[123]

Case studies also indicate that people of color and whites who leave welfare do so for different reasons and suffer different fates. In Illinois, for example,

120. Barbara Harris, " 'Welfare-to-Work' Not Working for Immigrant Families, Study Shows," *San Jose Sentinel,* Apr. 13, 1999, A1.

121. DeParle, "Shrinking Welfare Rolls."

122. Ibid.

123. Bruce Katz and Kate Carnevale, "The State of Welfare Caseloads in America's Cities," working paper, Center on Urban and Metropolitan Policy, Brookings Institution, Washington, D.C., May 1998, 4–19.

among white welfare "leavers," 40.1 percent left the rolls because they earned enough money to become independent, compared to 27.4 percent of blacks and Latinos. Moreover, 54.3 percent of cases involving racial minorities closed because recipients did not comply with state welfare rules. Among whites, 39.1 percent fell into this category."[124]

Arguably, the paradox of blacks living in states with stricter sanctions and greater caseload declines and still becoming more, rather than less, of the welfare population is explained by accumulated white skin privilege. Not only have centuries of racial discrimination played a key role in leaving people of color stuck in low-wage, high-unemployment cores of metropolitan areas, but access to educational attainment retains the scars of racial bias.[125] Even though more blacks are cast out of TANF as a result of stricter sanctions, so many reflect a heritage of disadvantage in skills that a greater racial coloration in caseloads results.

Data collected for the nation as a whole demonstrate less dramatic change in the racial/ethnic makeup of welfare caseloads than most of the state caseload studies, but the pattern is the same. The representation of blacks and Latinos has crept upward while the representation of non-Latino whites has declined (Table 5.2). In more than two-thirds of the states, the white rate of decline in welfare caseloads outpaced both the black and Latino rates by at least 10 percentage points. The result was that whites accounted for a smaller percentage of welfare beneficiaries in 1999 and 2000 than at any earlier time since the government began compiling figures in 1973. While blacks accounted for 39 percent of the nation's welfare caseload nationally in 2000 and Latinos accounted for 25 percent, whites accounted for just 31 percent of the rolls. The situation was even worse for children of color. In 2000, black children composed 41.4 percent of all beneficiaries, Latino children 17.7 percent, and white children only 33.1 percent.[126]

This disproportion has altered the racial balance in a program long rife with racial stereotypes and conflicts—a development that could ultimately be

124. Sarah Karp, "Work Preparation Falters: Minorities Off Welfare Get Few Jobs," *Chicago Tribune,* Jan. 11, 2000.

125. Factors identified in Pamela J. Loprest and Sheila R. Zedlewski, "Current and Former Welfare Recipients: How Do They Differ?" discussion paper, Urban Institute, Washington, D.C., November 1999, 6.

126. Department of Health and Human Services, 2001 TANF Annual Report to Congress, "Exhibit II: Trend of AFDC/TANF Characteristics, FY 1990–FY2000." <http://www.acf.dhhs.gov/programs/opre/characteristic/fy98/tab24r_98.htm>

Table 5.2.   Distribution of AFDC/TANF families by race, 1983–1998 (percent)

Fiscal year	White[1]	Black	Latino	Asian	Native American	Unknown/ other
1983	36.5	38.3	10.5	1.3	0.9	12.6
1984	36.6	36.7	10.7	1.8	0.9	3.9
1985	40.8	41.6	13.6	2.4	1.2	2.2
1986	39.7	40.7	14.4	2.3	1.3	1.4
1987	38.8	39.8	15.5	2.6	1.3	2.0
1988	38.8	39.8	15.7	2.4	1.4	1.9
1989	38.4	40.1	15.9	2.7	1.3	1.5
1990	38.1	38.8	16.6	2.8	1.4	1.5
1991	38.1	38.8	17.4	2.8	1.3	1.6
1992	38.9	37.2	17.8	2.8	1.4	2.0
1993	38.3	36.6	18.5	2.9	1.3	2.2
1994	37.4	36.4	19.9	2.9	1.3	2.1
1995	35.6	37.2	20.7	3.0	1.3	2.2
1996	35.9	37.2	20.7	3.0	1.3	2.2
1997[2]	34.5	37.3	22.5	3.3	1.3	1.1
1998	32.7	39.0	22.2	3.4	1.5	1.3

NOTE: Race is determined based on the race of the adult recipient; in child-only cases, race is determined based on the youngest child in the unit.

[1]White, non-Latino.
[2]October 1996–June 1997 only, due to the transition from AFDC to TANF.

SOURCE: Department of Health and Human Services, Administration for Children and Families, Characteristics and Financial Circumstances of TANF Recipients, 1998, and earlier reports. Statistics for 1999–2000 are from Department of Health and Human Services, 2001 TANF Annual Report to Congress. "Exhibit II: Trend of AFDC/TANF Characteristics, FY1990–FY2000."

used to make beneficiaries seem even more "undeserving" and propel further cuts in welfare spending. More to the point, given the legacy of stereotyping of black women as the ultimate welfare recipients even during the long years when whites outnumbered racial minorities among welfare caseloads, it is likely to become even more difficult to maintain political support for any type of welfare, including TANF, in the current economic climate. If, in an era of disinformation and misinformation about who actually made up the welfare rolls, whites were so easy to mobilize against welfare, what will happen when racial minorities actually are the bulk of welfare beneficiaries, seemingly confirming stereotypes? Will politicians use welfare, once again, as the ultimate wedge issue?[127]

127. See Martin Gilens, *Why Americans Hate Welfare* (Chicago: University of Chicago Press, 1999), 71; and Gerald C. Wright Jr., "Racism and Welfare Policy in America," *Social Science Quarterly* 57, no. 3 (December 1976): 718–30.

In sum, welfare reform is not working equally across race and ethnic boundaries. Studies suggest that the 1996 welfare reform law, in its implementation, has once again reproduced racial stratification, not alleviated it.

Conclusion

In the 1990s many whites became frankly tired of the pursuit of racial justice. Roughly 130 years had passed since the enslaved were liberated and more than thirty since the passage of major civil rights legislation. While many whites claimed to hold in esteem those blacks who worked hard and "played by the rules," they expressed exasperation with poor blacks, whom they stereotyped as lazy, promiscuous, criminal, and demoralizing the entire nation.

Although class was increasing in significance both within and among racial groups, race was not necessarily decreasing in significance. For instance, many whites viewed white welfare mothers as women who had gone through a messy divorce and needed a little time to get their lives together, and viewed young white criminals as alienated youths who had stumbled into the wrong "clique," but they had a different image of black beneficiaries of AFDC and black youths convicted of crimes, who belonged to "gangs." While the proponents of "family values" thought a wealthy white woman to be admirable for giving up her career to stay home with the children, they thought a poor black woman to be morally corrupt if she wanted to stay home and care for her children. The old-style honorific of "homemaker" was reserved for white women only. Recasting "welfare as we know it" meant forcing poor women into the workforce even if it meant return to a form of servitude of which black women held vivid memories.[128]

In this social and political atmosphere a clarion call was heard for tougher measures to curb dependency and irresponsible behavior. To be sure, policy makers heeding the call were careful to claim that the proposed policies were "race-neutral"; the drive to make single mothers work would apply to everyone on the welfare rolls; the new prisons being built would be filled by whatever people the courts decided belonged there. Yet despite these assurances, there can be little doubt that the chief targets of the crackdown were members of

128. Andrew Hacker, "Malign Neglect: The Crackdown on African Americans," *Nation*, July 10, 1995, 45.

communities of color, particularly those in the country's principal minority race.

Indeed, the tone of public rhetoric throughout the debates over crime and welfare was eerily similar to that of the Reconstruction era. Constant cries rose up demanding that authority over social welfare be given back to the states. The focus on denying benefits arose out of the fear of discouraging work and encouraging dependency. A new paternalism was needed to curb blacks' tendency toward not only dependency but criminality. The happy-go-lucky Sambo and the black beast were still prevailing images. The fervor for devolution and its twin, states' rights, and the claims that the federal government was actually advantaging blacks through reverse discrimination were enough to have made Andrew Johnson proud. In sum, the politics of race in reforming welfare during the Clinton years was, once again, shaped by underlying patterns of discrimination and white accumulation, working to the disadvantage of African Americans.[129]

Of course, there are important differences between the conservative politics of the Reconstruction era and the retrenchment of the 1990s. In the 1990s, few claimed dependency to be a result of biological inferiority. Yet the cultural explanation seemed also to be little more than a smokescreen. Most surveys that oversampled poor people of color in the 1990s found they do not differ from more affluent whites in valuing education, work, and family structure, but differ in their expectations of achieving them. Indeed, these surveys show that poor people of color tend to place less value on leisure than do the more affluent.

Meanwhile, in the cultural explanation of the 1990s, the strong correlation between family structure and economic variables such as income is usually assumed to indicate that marriage (and a presumed lack of desire for it among the poor) is both cause and solution of the problems of poor female-headed households. But of course, correlation does not causation make. In fact, the causal relation may run in the opposite direction: no or low income leads to less likelihood of marriage or the breakdown of marriage. Although it is well established that most divorces are precipitated by disagreements over money, little research has unequivocally demonstrated what is cause and what is effect

---

129. For a book that lays "bare the 'dirty little secrets' of a new order of social policy and its relation to race and gender, see Sanford F. Schram, *After Welfare: The Culture of Postindustrial Social Policy* (New York: New York University Press, 2000).

in regard to the relationship between the income and marital status of poor families. Thus there appear to be serious conceptual as well as empirical flaws in the cultural argument that in effect leads to the same policy recommendations that flourished in the era of biological explanations of racial inequality.

This similarity should not be ignored. The resemblance between social policy recommendations flowing from biological arguments before the civil rights era and cultural arguments since then reveals what may be the most formidable roadblocks to the realization of egalitarianism and full democracy in the United States. Despite the tremendous changes that occurred during the civil rights era, narratives that fit the American ethos and white supremacy remain powerful.

The crackdowns on crime and welfare in the 1990s revealed that both the Democratic administration and congressional Republicans could ignore the interests of racial minorities, demonstrated that two dominant belief systems continued to undermine the development of altruistic social policies, and cast in bold relief the lack of grassroots mobilizing capacities of established black and Latino interest organizations. Actions in both issue domains uncovered the dilemma that confronted minority leaders and voters: despite their differences with Clinton, their opposition to Republican proposals was still greater. Most ironic of all is that by the end of the Clinton years, the center of political gravity had shifted farther to the right in crime and welfare debates.[130] Although congressional Republicans achieved far less than they set out to achieve[131] and

130. Other areas also bore the brunt of setbacks that disproportionately harmed people of color. The 1996 Omnibus Budget Reconciliation act, according to Robert Reischauer, former director of the Congressional Budget Office, was "historically unprecedented" in its disproportionately negative impact on city government, city economies, and the urban poor (Mollenkopf, "Urban Policy at the Crossroads," 490). When the Republicans considered abolishing HUD in early 1995, Secretary Henry Cisneros saved it only by deregulating public housing authorities and transforming the FHA into an independent government-owned corporation. As a result, spending on urban and housing programs was significantly reduced. The immigration reform bill, signed Sept. 30, 1996, gutted antidiscrimination rules protecting immigrants in the workplace, raised new barriers to the granting of asylum, and stripped most courts of their power to block potentially illegal government policies. See Schmitt, "Clinton Record."

131. With the exception of welfare reform, very little of the Contract with America actually became law; the notable exceptions were a bill to make Congress follow federal laws just like the rest of the nation and another to bar Congress from imposing unfunded mandates on the states. These were very limited victories, given that both bills were left over from the 103d Congress and had substantial backing from Democrats. One other measure, the line-item veto, passed both houses of Congress and was signed by the president, but the Supreme Court declared it unconstitutional in 1998.

some liberal advances were made (especially in regard to expanding the EITC and raising the minimum wage),[132] there is no gainsaying that by the time the Clinton years ended, the nation had witnessed the most conservative changes in social policy it had experienced in sixty years. With the elimination of entitlement of every citizen to at least a modicum of economic security independent of the market and inheritance, not only the Great Society but the Social Security Act of 1935 was overturned. The role of "government as we knew it" since the days of FDR was pummeled by conservative Republicans with substantial assistance from moderate/conservative Democrats in Congress and the White House. Perhaps more revealing, the new agenda of liberals was no longer new programs and additional spending to meet pressing needs of the less affluent and racial minorities, but trying to hold on to programs and contain the extent of retrenchment and cutbacks. Thus, by the end of the Clinton years, the nation had virtually come full circle. More than at any point since the 1960s, poverty and racial discrimination, once seen as problems requiring state action, were now seen as the results of state action. What was once the solution (activist social policies) had now become the problem (dependency); and what was once the problem (the lash of poverty) had now become the solution (market forces).

---

132. For discussion, see Margaret Weir, "Wages and Jobs: What Is the Public Role?" in Weir, *Social Divide,* 294–98.

six
Addressing "America's Constant Curse"
The Politics of Civil Rights in the Clinton Years

Anybody who looks at my entire public life can see that it's been dominated

by three things: economics, education, and race. . . . If there is any issue I

ought to have credibility on, it is this one {civil rights} because it is a part

of who I am and what I've done, and I don't feel the need to defend myself.

—*President William Jefferson Clinton*

While establishing his conservative credentials on crime and welfare, Clinton came across as nearly a Great Society liberal on matters such as administrative appointments and enforcing civil rights laws. He promised and largely delivered a race- and gender-balanced cabinet that would "look like America," and he substantially increased funding for civil rights enforcement.

Appointment Politics and Stronger Enforcement of Civil Rights

Even before Republicans took control of Congress in January 1995, Clinton stayed away from Congress on matters of race. Indeed, the only piece of legislation he signed in his first two years that civil rights activists fought for was the National Voter Registration Act of 1993. Seen as a benefit to the poor because it allowed citizens to register to vote while they were renewing their drivers' licenses, applying for welfare, or joining the military, the Motor Voter Bill, as it was called, was proposed long before Clinton was elected. When finally passed and signed into law, it was a relatively weak form of the original proposal. Congressional Democrats had joined Republicans in deleting portions of the bill that were most likely to maximize registration among the poor, such as providing automatic voter registration to all clients at welfare offices.[1] Still, it was one gain that flowed to people of color and the poor of all races from having a Democratic administration, because both Reagan and Bush had opposed the bill.

Instead of new policy proposals to appeal to minority constituencies, Clinton chose to make numerous appointments while delegating most civil rights responsibilities to the Justice Department's civil rights division, with the Departments of Housing and Urban Development (HUD), Education, and Labor playing subsidiary roles. As much as possible, a wall of silence surrounded the work of these departments' civil rights actions.

This meant that Clinton looked most like a traditional Democrat overtly when making appointments. His first cabinet included five African Americans, two Latinos, and four women. Even using the appointments process, in the tradition of John Kennedy and Jimmy Carter, to reach out to minority constituencies was too much for many New Democrats. For example, Bill Galston and Elaine Kamarck, two DLC policy analysts who joined his White House staff, urged him not to prioritize appointing minorities or anyone else from the party's liberal wing, but rather to send a firm message of his sincerity as a New Democrat through his appointments. The president, they wrote, should use the appointments process "to continue his break with the past and to avoid being captured by the very forces he has undertaken to reform."[2] The two New Democrats urged Clinton to create what Galston later called "a government of national reconciliation" by offering top jobs to independents and centrist Republicans. Both Galston and Kamarck believed that appointing Republicans and independents would give Clinton a strong base from which to seek support from the moderate voters he needed to enlarge his plurality electoral victory into a lasting majority political coalition.

But on the campaign trail, Clinton had promised a government that "looked like America," and in the transition he was barraged with demands from Democratic interest groups to name women and people of color to top jobs. Substituting patronage for policy, Clinton obliged. As a result, Clinton

1. Benjamin Ginsberg and Martin Shefter, *Politics by Other Means: Politicians, Prosecutors, and the Press from Watergate to Whitewater* (New York: Norton, 1999), 22.

2. Quoted in Dan Balz and Ronald Brownstein, *Storming the Gates: Protest Politics and the Republican Revival* (Boston: Little, Brown, 1996), 81.

and administration spokespersons were fond of noting that the nation had "never seen an administration as diverse as this one at high levels."[3]

Clinton also was true to his campaign pledge to appoint judges of more diverse race, ethnicity, and gender to fill a slew of vacancies he found waiting for him as the first Democratic president in twelve years. One of his two choices for the Supreme Court—the first Court appointments by a Democratic president in twenty-six years—was a woman, Ruth Bader Ginsburg; and by the end of his first term, "more than half of Clinton's 196 appointments [were] women or . . . minorities or both" (30 percent women, 20 percent blacks, and 7 percent Latinos), almost twice the proportion among those chosen by Bush.[4] Judicial appointments, too, set a new record (Table 6.1). The percentage of federal judges who were minorities grew from 11 percent in 1993 to 15 percent in 1999, and the percentage who were women grew from 13 percent to 20 percent.[5]

Some interpreted this as a direct challenge to white male privilege. Burt Soloman wrote in the *National Journal* that Clinton's record of minority appointments had "eclipsed Jimmy Carter's previous standard for slighting white men."[6] Yet the numbers masked an appointment system that continued

Table 6.1.   Clinton's judicial nominees compared to those of other recent presidents (percent)

	Carter	Reagan	Bush	Clinton
Sex				
Male	84.5	92.4	80.5	71.0
Female	15.5	7.6	19.5	29.0
Race/Ethnicity				
White	78.7	93.5	89.2	74.8
Black	14.3	1.9	6.5	16.7
Latino	6.2	3.1	4.3	6.8
Asian	0.8	0.5	0	1.4
Native American	0	0	0	0.3

Source: *USA Today*, Aug. 22, 2000, 11A.

3. Stanley Greenberg, speech at the DNC Black Leadership Summit, June 28, 1994. Even as Clinton left office, he was still touting the "most diverse administration. It even looks like America" (speech at DNC, Aug. 14, 2000).

4. Neil Lewis, "In Selecting Federal Judges, Clinton Has Not Tried to Reverse Republicans," *New York Times,* Aug. 1, 1996, 20.

5. Administrative Office of the U.S. Courts, August 2000.

6. Burt Solomon, "Clinton's Gang," *National Journal,* Jan. 16, 1993, 16.

to advantage white men significantly and was so "dominated by politics and paybacks" that racial minority nominees remained "twice as likely to be rejected as whites."[7] While nearly half (48 percent) of Clinton's nominees were women or minorities, 35 percent of minority nominees were not confirmed by the Senate, compared with a 14 percent failure rate among whites. Blacks and Latinos who supported affirmative action were singled out for defeat by the Republican-led Judiciary Committee. It was only after the 2000 presidential election that Clinton, as he left office, nominated a black to the appeals court for the Fourth Circuit, covering five Mid-Atlantic states—a circuit that had a larger percentage of black residents than any other, about 25 percent. (This act set the stage for the Bush administration either to support confirmation for the appointee or oppose him.)

In addition, as Gerald Horne noted, "the administration's rainbow of hues [was] not . . . matched by a rainbow of views." All of the minority Cabinet members and judges were considered to be political moderates,[8] chosen perhaps because they would not challenge the president when he betrayed his base. Moreover, despite the importance of not "ghettoizing" black appointees in those Cabinet positions traditionally held by blacks, it was nevertheless ironic that none of Clinton's black Cabinet appointees led the departments that could represent black interests on issues such as poverty and civil rights.

Appointment politics were hardly a complete success. Missteps in the appointments strategy engendered as much anger as goodwill. The most spectacular case angering civil rights activists was the jettisoning of the nomination of Lani Guinier for assistant attorney general for civil rights.[9] Other criticisms from minority groups arose over the administration's tortoise-like pace in filling civil rights positions. For more than a year after Clinton was elected, important vacancies at Justice, Labor, and the EEOC left on hold a variety of issues affecting women, people of color, and the disabled.[10] For instance, it was not until

7. Joan Biskupic, "Politics Snares Court Hopes of Minorities and Women," *USA Today*, Aug. 22, 2000, 1.

8. Geoffrey Horne called this "a superficial multiculturalism": "Race: Ensuring a True Multiculturalism," in Richard Caplan and John Feffer, eds., *State of the Union 1994: The Clinton Administration and the Nation in Profile* (Boulder, Colo.: Westview, 1994), 186.

9. For fuller discussion, see Kenneth O'Reilly, *Nixon's Piano: Presidents and Racial Politics from Washington to Clinton* (New York: Free Press, 1995), 415, 417–20.

10. Stephen Labaton, "Administration Leaves Top Civil Rights Jobs Vacant," *New York Times*, Oct. 31, 1993, 18.

February 1, 1994, almost fourteen months after the president took office, that the civil rights position at Justice was finally filled. It was nearly two years after his election before the Senate confirmed Gilbert F. Casellas, a Latino attorney, as head of the EEOC, the last major unfilled civil rights position in the administration. Five weeks later the Republicans won control of both houses of Congress. From then on, the administration was on the defensive.

The president's judicial appointments became a particular sore point with many civil rights activists. While running for office in 1992, Clinton promised to reshape the character of the federal courts, reversing the trend to the right under the Reagan and Bush administrations.[11] In fact, however, Clinton made selections that were not expected to change the ideological nature of the bench, although they won high praise for their diversity and quality. While the Bush and Reagan administrations fundamentally changed the courts by nominating highly ideological conservative judges, according to legal scholars, Clinton's judges had no discernable ideology. One statistical analysis demonstrated that the ideology of Clinton's appointees fell somewhere between the conservatives selected by Bush and the liberals chosen by Carter.[12]

A second aspect of Clinton's balancing act on issues of race was stepped-up enforcement of civil rights laws. The Civil Rights Division, under the leadership of Assistant Attorney General Deval Patrick, was the site of most action. Activities ranged from limited place-based initiatives such as targeting jurisdictions with minority language populations in order to provide more effective assistance in voting to winning major financial awards in discrimination cases.[13] As for issues with direct financial implications, the department reached a $54 million settlement with Denny's restaurant chain, which had been accused of

11. Stephen Labaton, "President's Judicial Appointments: Diverse, but Well in the Mainstream," *New York Times*, Oct. 17, 1994, A15.

12. Study reported in *Legal Times*, Dec. 17, 1996, A1.

13. As co-chair of the National Church Arson Task Force, Patrick also headed up investigations into the black church arsons that were sweeping the country in the mid-1990s. The task force's work led to the arrest of more than 100 suspects in more than 80 fires since 1995. When Patrick found no evidence of a widespread conspiracy, however, many blacks, given their historical experience with law enforcement, were skeptical. Particularly pastors of burned-out churches complained to Attorney General Janet Reno and Treasury Secretary Robert Rubin that investigators were harassing them or their congregations rather than vigorously pursuing the possibility that white hate groups were setting the fires. It did not help that two ATF agents were assigned to the investigation at the same time they were facing potential disciplinary action for taking part in the racist shenanigans at a highly publicized so-called Good Ol' Boys Roundup in May 1995.

racially discriminatory practices. Similarly, it reached an agreement with a subsidiary of the Fleet Financial Group, resulting in the payment of $4 million in damages to African Americans and Latinos who had been charged higher interest on home mortgage loans than comparably qualified whites.[14] As a result of this success, Justice broadened its coverage to include the huge portion of the lending industry that is unregulated, including finance companies, direct mortgage lenders, and others often used by poor and low-income people. Just as the Denny's settlement had ripple effects throughout the restaurant industry, the Fleet settlement began to alter mortgage-lending bias in the industry. As a result of such actions, a record volume of lending to minority borrowers occurred during the Clinton years.[15]

In other action, HUD tackled the task of desegregating public housing projects, most visibly in Vidor, Texas, a small town known for its racism and whose local Klan vowed they would continue to "run off" African Americans who moved into housing projects. Yet, although the administration doubled the budget for fair housing enforcement and attempted to crack down on mortgage discrimination, little actually changed in respect to housing desegregation or the creation of more public housing to accommodate the hundreds of thousands of families backlogged and waiting for housing in cities. In some instances, HUD tried to produce more change, but was rebuked by the then Democratic-controlled Congress. Perhaps the most spectacular demonstration of this result was HUD Secretary Henry Cisneros's attempt to enable public housing families to use Section 8 certificates to move to suburban jurisdictions. Following a modestly successful development of such a program in Chicago (the Gautreaux housing program),[16] Cisneros proposed a $235 million demonstration project to use 3,000 Section 8 certificates each year for two years to enable public housing families in Baltimore, Boston, Los Angeles, and New York to move to the suburbs. If these demonstration projects worked well, HUD hoped to extend similar practices to the entire base of Section 8 vouchers

14. James S. Hirsch, "Fleet Agrees to Pay $4 Million to Settle Complaints of Bias," *Wall Street Journal,* May 8, 1996, A4.

15. Interview with Susan Patterson, federal bank examiner, Charlotte, N.C., Oct. 27, 1996.

16. For a brief discussion and evaluation of the Gautreaux experiment, see "The Promise of Housing Mobility Programs," *Urban Institute Policy and Research Report* 25 (Winter 1995–96): 4–6.

and certificates.[17] The proposal quickly generated a firestorm of protest in the conservative press, most notably the *Wall Street Journal,* where a columnist attacked it as "sowing chaos in suburban neighborhoods, rewarding those who are dependent on the state, and alienating middle-class Americans, who end up paying for apartments that they themselves could not afford."[18] When residents of a couple of white blue-collar towns east of Baltimore protested against what they believed would be the arrival of tens of thousands of black public housing tenants in their neighborhood, Barbara Mikulski, the ranking Democratic member of the Senate Banking, Housing, and Urban Affairs Committee, expressed strong reservations about the program, and Congress eliminated its funding.[19] Meanwhile hundreds of thousands of families with small children continued to be unhoused or poorly housed. As one HHS staff person put it to the political scientist John Mollenkopf: from start to end, the administration "compartmentalized urban issues to one small set of programs."[20]

Finally, at the Department of Labor, the Office of Federal Contract Compliance Program (OFCCP) stepped up compliance reviews and complaint investigations during the Clinton administration. Financial settlements for victims of discrimination, debarments, and back-pay awards soared compared with the record during the Reagan-Bush years.[21] In sum, while Clinton officials did not make new antidiscrimination policies, at least there was a return to more fully enforcing current civil rights law and not substantially undermining inner cities.

How much the White House was behind the renewed enforcement and urban efforts, however, is unclear. Most not only appeared to be departmental initiatives, but in some instances seemed to depend on the initiative of individual staff rather than their departments as a whole. For example, just how

17. John Mollenkopf, "Urban Policy at the Crossroads," in Margaret Weir, ed., *The Social Divide: Political Parties and the Future of Activist Government* (Washington, D.C.: Brookings, 1998), 485–86.

18. James Bovard, "Clinton's Wrecking Ball for Suburbs," *Wall Street Journal,* Aug. 4, 1994, A12.

19. Karen DeWitt, "Housing Voucher Test in Maryland Is Scuttled by a Political Firestorm," *New York Times,* Mar. 28, 1995, B1; and Mollenkopf, "Urban Policy at the Crossroads," 486.

20. Quoted in Mollenkopf, "Urban Policy at the Crossroads," 486.

21. Linda Newborn, "OFCCP: Back in Business," *Black Collegian* 25 (February 1995): 107–11; Gary Glaser and Edmund Cooke Jr., "The Scrutiny Intensified," *HR Focus* 73 (April 1996): 5; and "OFCCP 1994 Enforcement Data," *Labor Law Journal* 46 (January 1995): 64.

aggressively the federal government should enforce affirmative action was the subject of a simmering debate among Justice Department officials. Patrick (who left at the end of Clinton's first term) was a tough, staunch defender of affirmative action. When he took on reverse discrimination cases in places like Piscataway, New Jersey, and conservatives furiously criticized him (calling him a "quota lover" and mispronouncing his first name as "devil"), both Clinton and Attorney General Janet Reno publicly gave him a lukewarm endorsement. Behind the scenes, Reno is reported to have been unhappy that Patrick chose to take a stand on the New Jersey case.[22]

Reno's number two at Justice, Jamie Gorelick, was assigned to search for a compromise standard. Gorelick defined her views to the media as moderate to conservative, concluding that her personal goal was a "race-neutral society. I don't like numbers games."[23] According to media reports, Gorelick would not have chosen to intervene in the New Jersey case.

One piece of anecdotal evidence indicates the strain in Patrick's relationship with the White House. When Patrick learned that the president planned to speak at Martin Luther King Jr.'s birthplace in Atlanta in January 1995 without mentioning civil rights, he quietly refused to appear with him. The joke at Justice was that the administration was eager to have civil rights laws aggressively enforced—as long as no one knew about it.[24]

The problem was, however, keeping Clinton's enforcement initiatives in particular and civil rights in general in the closet. This became more difficult once the Republicans took control of Congress, and it soon became clear that eliminating affirmative action, though not a formal plank of the Contract with America, was one in effect.

Affirmative Action and the "New" Whiteness

To be sure, the storm clouds that surrounded affirmative action in the 104th Congress had been gathering for decades. Open racists sometimes played a role

22. Lincoln Caplan, "A Civil Rights Tug of War," *Newsweek,* Feb. 13, 1995, 34. The administration subsequently pulled back its support. In 1997 the case was settled before the Supreme Court could rule on it. A coalition of civil rights groups, believing the case was weak, raised funds to settle it out of court. Joan Biskupic, "Rights Groups Pay to Settle Bias Case," *Washington Post,* Nov. 22, 1997, A1.

23. Caplan, "Civil Rights Tug of War," 34.

24. Ibid.

far beyond their numbers by funding more "respectable" organizations in the war against affirmative action. For example, Clint Bolick's Center of Individual Rights (CIR), a conservative law firm devoted to ending affirmative action and an important lobbying group on Capitol Hill, maintained links to openly white supremacist groups on the far right. The CIR's federal tax returns reveal contributions from the Pioneer Fund, founded in the 1930s by a millionaire who advocated sending blacks to Africa, and currently supporting research asserting the genetic superiority of whites. The fund's charter sets forth its mission as "racial betterment" and aid for people "deemed to be descended predominantly from white persons who settled in the original 13 states prior to the adoption of the Constitution." Its recent grant recipients include Arthur Jensen and Roger Pearson. Famous for his attack on Head Start, Jensen argued in the *Harvard Educational Review* that black children test at an IQ of 85 and urged "eugenic foresight" as the only solution. Pearson, director of the Institute for the Study of Man and publisher of *Mankind Quarterly* (described by *The Independent* of London as having links to former Nazi geneticists), has written, "If a nation with a more advanced, more specialized, or in any way superior set of genes mingles with, instead of exterminating, an inferior tribe, then it commits racial suicide." Other funders and bedfellows of CIR include the usual right-wing foundations: Bradley, Carthage, Olin, Scaife, and Smith-Richardson. In turn, CIR has represented those openly expressing racial animus—for example, it represented Michael Levin, the philosophy professor at the City University of New York Graduate School who taught that blacks are less intelligent and more criminal than other races and therefore should have to ride in separate subway cars, in his dispute with City College. CIR is the law firm that won its greatest victory so far representing Cheryl Hopwood in her precedent-setting case that led to a decision ending affirmative action at the University of Texas. "Other CIR clients include the sponsors of California's anti–affirmative action Proposition 209 and Katuria Smith, a rejected student who sued the University of Washington Law School claiming discrimination. CIR is the firm which also represented plaintiffs in a similar suit against the University of Michigan and, for good measure, Jessie Thompkins, an African American student protesting diversity scholarships for whites at overwhelmingly black Alabama State University."[25] In effect, the war against affirmative action not only includes a highly coordinated broad right wing but is heavily financed by open racists.

25. Laura Flanders, "Affirmative Racism," *Nation*, Mar. 8, 1999, 7–8.

By the 1990s, the vast majority of whites, upwards of 70 percent, opposed affirmation action at least when viewed as dictating "preferences" or "quotas." But arguably most whites who are increasingly vocal in their opposition to affirmative action are not bigots in the traditional sense.[26] Indeed, some statistical analyses demonstrate that the most important factor determining white support or opposition to affirmative action is their view of black progress. The more whites perceive blacks to have made progress since the 1960s, the more they oppose affirmative action.[27]

But in the face of a barrage of data demonstrating stark racial inequalities, why do whites believe people of color have made so much progress, much less reached parity with whites? A series of concurrent ideological and structural changes that have characterized the United States since the mid-1970s help explain this development and reify whiteness. These changes include the virtual elimination of de jure discrimination; the rise of conservative political forces exploiting racial fears in the light of challenges to racial hierarchies; increasing economic insecurity as a result of restructuring in the form of automation, corporate downsizing, and globalization; and concomitantly the dwindling of trade unionism and other embryonic forms of class politics that encourage Americans to look across identity groups.

The result of all these trends has been an increased sense of solidarity among whites based on their skin color or their common Euro-American identity. As part of this growing racial solidarity, whiteness as ideology was bolstered in the 1980s and 1990s by a set of attitudes emphasizing innocence, disadvantage, cultural superiority, and victimization—all of which heightened white hostility to affirmative action. It is small wonder that many politicians began to see affirmative action as the ultimate wedge issue.

The Congressional Republican Attack on Civil Rights

Although conservative politicians of both major parties sought to appeal to white voters, especially white males, by tapping into white feelings of inno-

---

26. For an excellent argument regarding the complexities in the affirmative action debate, see Christopher Edley Jr., *Not All Black and White: Affirmative Action and American Values* (New York: Hill & Wang, 1996).

27. Celeste Lay, "Sources of White Opposition to Affirmative Action: Lessons from Public Opinion Analysis," paper presented at the American Association for Public Opinion Research Conference, May 19–21, Portland, Ore., 9–10, 20; and James R. Kluegel and Eliot R. Smith, "White Beliefs about Blacks' Opportunity," *American Sociological Review* 47 (1982): 518–32.

cence, disadvantage, cultural superiority, and victimization, Republican conservatives took the lead by targeting affirmative action for complete elimination. As long as the Democrats controlled Congress, however, Republican presidents could not totally wipe out the policy, and in any event, many congressional Republicans supported aspects of affirmative action. The situation in the 104th Congress, however, bore more ominous portents. The opponents of affirmative action now dominated.

Even before the new Congress convened, Senator Orrin G. Hatch of Utah, chair of the Judiciary Committee, talked about his intention to review every civil rights law since *Brown v. Board of Education* in 1954; and at the very start of the new Congress, in January 1995, the House Economic and Educational Opportunities Committee held hearings on the Clinton administration's civil rights agenda. Despite the fact that the administration had, at most, pursued a very limited strategy regarding civil rights and then only through stealth action, the oversight hearings attempted to orchestrate the charge that Clinton's civil rights policies far exceeded the original intent of Congress. Those hearings, according to the committee's chair, William F. Goodling (R-Pa.), might lead to amending or writing new civil rights laws. On February 5, 1995, appearing on NBC's *Meet the Press,* Majority Leader and presidential candidate Bob Dole queried: "Has it [affirmative action] had an adverse or reverse reaction? . . . Slavery was wrong. But should future generations have to pay for that?" Dole, once a firm supporter of affirmative action, now requested a review. Concomitantly John Boehner of Ohio, chairman of the Republican Conference, announced in early February 1995 that both the House and Senate would review affirmative action laws.[28] By February 21, 1995, the first product of retrenchment was realized. The House voted to abolish a set of tax breaks given to communication corporations that sold their companies to minority group members.[29]

To win their battle against affirmative action, Republicans understood that they had to keep the focus on "preferences" and "quotas," for polls showed that the more people of all races thought of affirmative action in these terms, the more likely they were to oppose it. By comparison, when affirmative action

28. Transcript of *Meet the Press,* NBC News, Feb. 5, 1995, 12; and "Affirmative Action Will Be Examined in Senate, Dole Says," *New York Times,* Feb. 6, 1995, A15.

29. Paul Farhi and Kevin Merida, "House Rejects Tax Break: Viacom Sale to Minority Group Spurred Vote," *Washington Post,* Feb. 22, 1995, A1.

was asked about in a straightforward manner or when a justification was given for the policy, support increased among whites as well as blacks. In March 1995 polls, for example, a focus on preferences reduced support for affirmative action among whites by more than 30 percentage points—thus the importance of the Republicans' constant invocation of "preferences," "special rights," and "quotas" in their framing of the debate. Polls also showed that when asked about affirmative action for women rather than for minorities, white support tended to rise by more than 10 percentage points.[30] Thus it was also clear that the Republicans' effort to eliminate affirmative action would benefit them most if they kept the focus on blacks. If they did, Republican strategist Bill Kristol predicted, affirmative action would not only be the ultimate wedge issue, it would blow the Democratic party "completely apart."[31]

In the Senate, Dole opened the attack on affirmative action. Releasing a report he had requested the Congressional Research Service (CRS) to prepare, he claimed to have found 160 federal preference programs, and he promised to introduce legislation to eliminate every one of them.[32] In fact, only 42 of the programs listed made any reference to giving "preference" as a means of outreach to minorities and women. Since quotas are illegal, none included them, a fact that reportedly surprised politically naive freshman Republican members of Congress.[33] Even goals and timetables were rare, with fewer than one out of every four programs on Dole's list either specifying or directing agencies to establish them. Nonetheless, Dole's claim to have found 160 preference programs became the object of pack journalism, repeated over and over as if it were an accurate portrayal of the CRS list.

In the House, Charles Canady (R-Fla.), chair of the Judiciary Committee's

30. Hart-Teeter and Princeton Survey Research Associates proprietary polls, March 1995. For additional discussion and polls, see Lawrence Bobo and Ryan A. Smith, "Antipoverty Policy, Affirmative Action, and Racial Attitudes," in Sheldon Danziger, Gary D. Sandefur, and Daniel H. Weinberg, eds., *Confronting Poverty: Prescriptions for Change* (New York: Russell Sage Foundation, 1994), 378–79; and Charlotte Steeh and Maria Krysan, "The Polls: Trends, Affirmative Action, and the Public, 1970–1995," *Public Opinion Quarterly* 60 (Spring 1996): 128–58.

31. George Stephanopoulos, *All Too Human: A Political Education* (Boston: Little, Brown, 1999), 195–107.

32. David Maraniss, "Campaign '96—With Roots in the Middle, Dole Shifted Uneasily on a Racial Issue," *Washington Post*, Oct. 31, 1996, A1.

33. Interview with Vin Weber, co-director of Empower America, May 14, 1995.

Constitution Subcommittee, promised to move legislation parallel to Dole's through the subcommittee. Because he exercised tight control over witness lists, the African Americans and Latinos who were called to testify read like a who's who of the party's minority conservatives. It did not matter that the black conservatives represented the views of very few blacks. What mattered most was that they provided a comfort level and political cover to white conservatives in the latter's efforts to undo racial advances. Meanwhile, a large number of requests from traditional civil rights groups and liberal research institutes that supported affirmative action were turned down.[34]

During the same period, the Supreme Court was reviewing a bumper crop of cases that had the potential to alter substantially the course of affirmative action decrees on topics including awarding federal contracts, providing federal oversight for school desegregation, and creating majority-minority districts. Other cases percolating their way up to the Court included cases involving minority scholarships at universities, affirmative action in university admissions, and the pursuit of faculty diversity.[35]

The Republican challenge and the actions of the courts threatened the delicate balance on racial issues that was central to Clinton's political strategy. Republican use of affirmative action as a wedge issue threatened to be fatal to Clinton, and the legal climate suggested that the ground was shifting away from affirmative action. The president responded by ordering an "intense, urgent review" of affirmative action, telling the Democratic congressional caucus, "Let's see what we can defend and what we can't."[36]

34. Interview with Sherille Ismail, House Judiciary Committee staff assistant to Rep. John Conyers (D-Mich.), Apr. 7, 1995.

35. *Adarand Constructors, Inc. v. Pena,* 515 U.S. 200 (1995), involving a white subcontractor whose low bid was rejected; *Missouri v. Jenkins,* 515 U.S. 70 (1995), involving the scope and duration of federal oversight of the Kansas City metropolitan school district's desegregation efforts; *U.S. v. Hays,* 515 U.S. 737 (1995), 94–558, involving the constitutionality of drawing a second majority-black district to provide Louisiana's poorest section of blacks the opportunity to elect the representative of their choice; *Podberesky v. Kirwan,* 38 F.3d 147 (4th Cir., 1994), cert. denied, 115 S.Ct. 2001 (1995); and *Piscataway Township Board of Education v. Taxman,* cert. granted June 27, 1997, 117 S.Ct. 763 (1997) (case later settled out of court).

36. Quoted in Elizabeth Drew, *Showdown: The Struggle between the Gingrich Congress and the Clinton White House* (New York: Simon & Schuster, 1996), 290. For accounts of the review, see ibid., 289–96; and Steven A. Holmes, "On Civil Rights, Clinton Steers Bumpy Course between Left and Right," *New York Times,* Oct. 20, 1996, 16; see also the analytic account in Christopher Edley Jr., *Not All Black and White: Affirmative Action and American Values* (New York: Hill & Wang, 1996).

According to the White House aide George Stephanopoulos, White House staffers were sharply split from the start over what the response to affirmative action should be. African American staffers such as Alexis Herman, then director of public liaison, later labor secretary; Maggie Williams, the first lady's chief of staff; and Thurgood Marshall Jr., senior adviser to the vice president, vigorously supported affirmative action and urged the president to make a strong defense, which they insisted was not only the morally correct but also the politically expedient thing to do. Equally passionate in their arguments to move in the opposite direction were the New Democrats. According to Stephanopoulos, Bill Galston, deputy domestic policy adviser; Joel Klein, deputy counsel; John Smith, associate attorney general; and Vice President Gore argued that affirmative action was a correct idea that had gone wrong over time. The New Democrats contended that affirmative action increasingly was being implemented in a rigid and inflexible manner. It was becoming just another form of discrimination and was both morally and politically the wrong thing to do. Quite obviously the New Democrats echoed the themes of innocence, disadvantage, and victimization rampant among the white public. "Being honest meant that we had to address the legitimate resentments of whites who felt punished for past wrongs that they didn't condone and hadn't committed. Presidential leadership, they insisted, required straight talk about where affirmative action had failed and how it needed to be fixed."[37] In general, according to Elizabeth Drew, White House officials coming out of the DLC "urged a phasing out of set-asides—the reserving of certain contracts for minorities [and women]—and their replacement with programs encouraging economic empowerment."[38]

Meanwhile, civil rights activists greeted Clinton's review with skepticism, especially when the president declared at a conference in Ottawa on February 25, 1995, "What we need to guarantee is genuine equality of opportunity. We shouldn't be defending things we can't defend."[39] He expressed doubts about whether some of the programs were needed and whether criteria other than race, such as class and place, ought to be used. "So the question is: How do we now go forward? And let me tell you the questions I've asked my folks to

37. Stephanopoulos, *All Too Human*, 362–63.
38. Drew, *Showdown*, 292.
39. Quoted ibid., 290.

answer. I've said, first of all, how do these programs work, and do they have a positive effect? . . . Secondly, even if they work, are they sometimes, at least, unfair to others? Could you argue that in some cases there is reverse discrimination, and if so, how? Thirdly are there now others in need who are not covered by affirmative action programs?"[40]

Stephanopoulos, generally regarded as a liberal in the White House, oversaw the review and recruited Christopher Edley Jr., a Harvard Law School professor who had just left the Office of Management and Budget, to coordinate the operation.[41] The questions about possible changes to affirmative action were wide-ranging. Not only was there consideration of replacing race and gender with class and place as the bases for affirmative action; other questions included how broad affirmative action protections should be: Should they continue to include women? What about Latinos?[42]

Divisions among Cabinet heads mirrored divisions among the White House staff regarding the way these questions should be answered. Cabinet members sparred over whether the president should defend affirmative action, modify it in some way, or abandon it altogether. Chief of Staff Leon Panetta, whom ironically Richard Nixon fired as director of the Office of Civil Rights at the Department of Health, Education, and Welfare for being too aggressive on busing, reportedly wanted the president to disavow affirmative action so thoroughly that he should back Proposition 209, the California ballot initiative banning affirmative action programs in the state and its local governments.[43]

On the other side of the debate were HUD Secretary Henry Cisneros, HHS Secretary Donna Shalala, Attorney General Janet Reno, Labor Secretary Robert B. Reich, Commerce Secretary Ronald Brown, and Energy Secretary Hazel O'Leary. Key elements of the Democratic base, they argued, benefited from affirmative action; without their enthusiastic support, Democrats would be doomed in the next election.[44]

---

40. "Remarks to a Question-and-Answer Session with the College Press Forum," *Weekly Compilation of Presidential Documents*, Mar. 27, 1995, 460.

41. According to Stephanopoulos, *All Too Human*, 363, Edley was chosen explicitly because he was black, so that whatever side the president decided to come down on, people would believe the result was "not rigged."

42. See Drew, *Showdown*, 291.

43. This was Panetta's position, according to Rep. Maxine Waters (D-Calif.). According to Waters, while Edley did not support Proposition 209, he did support stiff new restrictions on minority set-asides. Waters said she had stopped returning phone calls from Edley and Panetta. Interview with Maxine Waters, May 10, 1995.

44. See Drew, *Showdown*, 293.

Reno's and Reich's departments played critical roles in affirmative action's defense. At Justice, both Reno and Patrick made calls on the CBC in particular and progressive members of Congress in general, encouraging them to help Justice make the fight to maintain affirmative action. Reich's Labor Department supplied new research findings to arm affirmative action's defenders. For instance, a major report of Labor's Glass Ceiling Commission had been in the works for months; now the commission issued a preliminary version of the report, which detailed how white women and people of color were still excluded from the nation's top posts.[45] The substantial media coverage that followed release of the report highlighted its conclusion that although white men composed only 37 percent of the nation's adult population, they occupied 95 percent of the top positions in *Fortune* 500 companies. Stories also emphasized the continuing stark differences in wages and wealth between white men and everyone else. The clear indication was that affirmative action had produced the limited progress that had occurred since 1970 and was still desperately needed, given continued inequality. A few weeks later, Labor issued a second report that would play a marked role in the debate. The report pointed out that of the 90,000 complaints of employment discrimination based on race or gender that the federal government received in 1990–94, fewer than 3 percent were for reverse discrimination and a "high proportion" of the claims brought by white men were "without merit."[46]

Minority and women's groups and their congressional allies used these reports in their counteroffensive. On the same day the Glass Ceiling Commission issued its preliminary report, leaders of women's organizations and minority organizations headed by women, such as the Lawyers' Committee on Civil Rights and the NAACP's Legal Defense Fund, held a press conference declaring their opposition to cutting back affirmative action, followed by a march to the White House and a meeting with White House officials. For the Leadership Conference on Civil Rights, Ralph Neas arranged for the views of prominent global businessmen who favored affirmative action to be heard at the White House. Civil rights groups organized a briefing for Democrats on the House Judiciary Committee that incorporated their views in a position paper issued

45. Federal Glass Ceiling Commission, *Good for Business: Making Full Use of the Nation's Human Capital* (Washington, D.C.: U.S. Government Printing Office, March 1995).

46. Alfred W. Blumrosen, "Draft Report on Reverse Discrimination Commissioned by Labor Department," no. 56 (Washington, D.C.: Bureau of National Affairs, 1995), E1.

by Richard Gephardt (D-Mo.). The CBC organized an affirmative action task force (co-chaired by Maxine Waters of California and Kweisi Mfume of Maryland) that held a press conference each week throughout May, June, and July. The issue of affirmative action was so important to the CBC that members vied to chair the task force. It was a far cry from their relative inaction on welfare reform, an indication of differing class constituencies in regard to the two measures.

The National Rainbow Coalition also held a series of press conferences in which Jesse Jackson suggested that his decision on whether to launch a race for the presidency in 1996 hung on the president's decision on affirmative action. In fact, Stephanopoulos points out that Jackson's threat was direct. When Stephanopoulos and Clinton's aide Harold Ickes tried to feel out Jackson regarding his intention to run in 1996, Jackson, "sitting beneath a huge wall map of the United States marked with each state's filing deadline for an Independent slot on the presidential ballot, issued his bottom line: 'If we can use goals, targets, and timetables to get fair trade with Japan, we can use goals, targets, and timetables to get a fair shake for our own folks. . . . That's what affirmative action is all about . . . [and] I'm not moving one inch on set-asides.' "[47] Jackson confirms Stephanopoulos's interpretation of events: "There is no question about it. My position on it was quite public, and I stated it to [Clinton]. I had no inclination to run. My choice was, rather, to support him. But if he had taken away that program for equal opportunity, he would have crossed the line."[48]

When the *New York Times* published a story about a leaked draft of the anticipated White House review indicating that the president was going to sharply stiffen the rules governing minority set-asides and might even fully replace them by a system of race-neutral incentives for businesses to locate in poor neighborhoods, a firestorm broke out among black groups.[49] While vowing to battle GOP attempts to gut affirmative action policies, Representative Mfume warned on June 5, 1995, that White House efforts to date had left

---

47. Stephanopoulos, *All Too Human,* 370.

48. Quoted in Holmes, "On Civil Rights, Clinton Steers Bumpy Course."

49. Robert Pear, "Report to Clinton Has a Mixed View on Minority Plans," *New York Times,* May 31, 1995, A1, B6. According to Stephanopoulos, *All Too Human,* 371, Clinton was intrigued by these ideas. To dissuade Clinton, Stephanopoulos said he had to organize meetings between Clinton and such civil rights leaders as John Lewis and Vernon Jordan and Cabinet secretaries Shalala, Cisneros, Ron Brown, and Dick Riley.

black members of Congress concerned and that "the President runs the risk of permanently losing large segments of his base."[50] He promised economic boycotts and street demonstrations if the president curtailed affirmative action. Meanwhile, the staff of the Congressional Black Caucus Foundation (CBCF) was instructed to begin to identify the particular companies to boycott—ones where black employees were disproportionately underrepresented and black consumers overrepresented.

A group of the nation's top 100 black businessmen, responding to the threat to eliminate or seriously alter minority set-asides, organized a political action committee (MOPAC). In early June 1995, leaders of MOPAC met with Clinton to press their demands, but the *New York Times* also reported that one Clinton official said there might be a political benefit to black businessmen criticizing the president's eventual proposal. "We want black businessmen to scream enough to let angry white males understand that we've done something for them," said the unnamed official.[51]

Note how much more organized black leadership was when the black middle class's interests were threatened than when those of the poor were threatened by welfare reform. There had been no threats to leave the party by members of the CBC, no threats by Jackson to run if Clinton signed the PRW-ORA, no organization of black businessmen seeking a meeting with Clinton. Instead a rather tepid response was given to opposing the 1996 welfare reform bill before it passed, and in the aftermath of its passage not just a few black elected officials campaigned for Clinton on the basis that he was needed to "fix" the bill. To an extent, the question "Is there a black community anymore?" gained new relevance during the Clinton years as traditional black leaders became more openly attentive to the needs of the black middle class and by comparison downplayed those of the black working and poor classes. Even as white privilege remained the order of the day, class privilege was having a greater impact on the politics of black leaders.

In short, the two wings of the Democratic party were flying in different directions, with Jackson threatening a primary challenge if Clinton did not "stand firm" on affirmative action and Connecticut Senator Joe Lieberman of the DLC declaring that racial preferences were "patently unfair" and endorsing

50. Remarks of Kweisi Mfume, co-chair of Congressional Black Caucus (CBC) Task Force on Affirmative Action, CBC press conference, June 5, 1995.
51. Pear, "Report to Clinton Has a Mixed View," B6.

California's Proposition 209. The divisions in the party were so stark that some in the administration even disagreed over whether a Jackson race for president would be a good or bad thing for Clinton. According to Stephanopoulos, while White House staffers such as he and Ickes worried about how many voters Clinton would lose to a Jackson candidacy, Dick Morris wanted Jackson to run for president as an independent. "Claiming he 'polled it,'" Morris argued: "'If Jesse runs it will cost us three points with blacks but open up 15 percent of white voters' who would never even consider voting for Clinton without Jackson in the race." Morris urged Clinton to replace affirmative action with a system based on "class not race."[52]

Meanwhile, a possible run for the Republican presidential nomination by Colin Powell in 1996 only ratcheted up tensions. If Clinton abandoned affirmative action, it would put him to the right of Powell on race issues.

Throughout the five-month review period, Clinton acted much as he did in the fight over the racial justice provision in the debate on the 1994 crime bill. Despite the CBC's persistent requests for "dialogue," the White House delayed consulting or meeting with the group. It was late June 1995 before the president dispatched Stephanopoulos and Edley to meet with the caucus. Both White House aides listened to the CBC's concerns but provided few insights into the president's position. Meanwhile, Clinton had Panetta making the rounds on Capitol Hill to see what fellow Democrats would do if the administration signaled its support for California's Proposition 209.[53] The president also engaged in Clintonspeak. For instance, at the April 1995 convention of the California Democratic Party, he argued both sides of the affirmative action debate: "We need to defend, without apology . . . anything we're doing that is right and decent and just that lifts people up," he stated, but he also concluded that we Democrats must also empathize with the "so-called angry white males" and "have to ask ourselves: Are they [affirmative action programs] all working ? Are they all fair?" Similarly, at a meeting with the CBC, when Eleanor Holmes Norton of the District of Columbia tried to pin the president down about the conclusions his review drew, Clinton vaguely responded,

52. Stephanopoulos, *All Too Human,* 370–71.

53. At a meeting of the CBC on June 28, 1995, Bennie Thompson of Mississippi, Carrie Meek of Florida, and Maxine Waters of California discussed Panetta's meetings with members of Congress regarding Proposition 209 (author's notes). See also "Affirmative Action on the Edge," *U.S. News & World Report,* Feb. 13, 1995, 32.

"I don't think I'll cause high anxiety. You'll find what I do interesting but not troubling." After the CBC left, Chief of Staff Erskine Bowles explained to Clinton that probably the CBC interpreted Clinton's answer and nods of agreement with them as meaning he would fully support affirmative action. Clinton responded, "I didn't say that."[54]

The Supreme Court weighed in on June 12, 1995, ruling in *Adarand*, as in *Croson*, that federal affirmative action programs are subject to the most rigorous level of review; that is, strict scrutiny. The decision appeared to cast doubt on many federal programs, although the justices did not actually strike down any programs and a majority said that affirmative action may indeed be appropriate in some circumstances.

As it turned out, Clinton and the Democrats were able to capitalize on the Court decision. Even before the president issued his review, House Democrats cited *Adarand* as a basis for their unwillingness to consider new anti–affirmative action legislation in 1995. As Representative James E. Clyburn, a member of the CBC and the Democratic task force on the programs, put it in late June 1995: "We have a Court decision and that ought to guide us."[55]

In fact, as Steven A. Holmes concluded, the decision carried "a silver lining" for the administration. "In effect, the Justices had said, mend it, don't end it." Thus, "the decision allowed the administration to modify affirmative action programs in ways that preempted the criticism raised by Republicans while fending off blacks, Latinos, women, and other liberals by saying the changes he made were mandated by the Supreme Court."[56] It also gave the president a way to sound principled by not having to openly break with his well-known, long-held views supporting antidiscrimination and equal opportunity.

On July 18, 1995, Clinton delivered his long-awaited speech on affirmative action. By then Dick Morris had called (the weekend before the speech) with the convenient news that a new poll he had commissioned showed that a Jackson candidacy would turn the presidential race from a 38–38 tie with Bob Dole to a 30–38 loss.[57]

The heart of Clinton's speech endorsed affirmative action. He asserted that the record of the past thirty years shows—"indeed screams"—that "the

54. Reported in Stephanopoulos, *All Too Human*, 370.
55. Interview with Rep. James E. Clyburn (D-S.C.), June 30, 1995.
56. Holmes, "On Civil Rights, Clinton Steers Bumpy Course."
57. Stephanopoulos, *All Too Human*, 372.

job of ending discrimination in this country is not over." "When affirmative action is done right, it is flexible, it is fair, and it works. . . . Let me be clear: affirmative action has been good for America." "Mend it, don't end it," the president said. Yet he also argued that "some people are honestly concerned about the times affirmative action doesn't work, when it's done in the wrong way." He vowed that when the administration found such cases, it would fight them in court, by filing reverse discrimination suits if necessary. But pointing to research data and the Glass Ceiling Commission report, Clinton argued that there is little evidence to back up Republicans' assertions that whites are being broadly discriminated against and minorities unfairly rewarded in government employment and the awarding of contracts and other benefits. Clinton concluded that "most of these [discrimination] suits . . . affect women and minorities for a simple reason—because the vast majority of discrimination in America is still discrimination against them." Hence most of the current backlash, Clinton said, comes not from cases of reverse discrimination but from "sweeping historic changes" taking place in the global economy that have left many lower- and middle-income whites struggling to keep pace. "Affirmative action did not cause the great economic problems of the American middle class," Clinton said. "If we're really going to change things, we have to be united."[58] It was a strong speech and one in which Clinton sought to move Americans from race to class concerns.

But there were also arguments in the review directly devoted to reassuring his centrist supporters. Especially in the case of set-asides, the review focused on how these programs could be reformed.[59] The review recommended that an interagency group should come up with ways to tighten the test of who is economically disadvantaged, develop new standards for when any individual firm no longer needs special help in receiving government work, establish more stringent safeguards against front firms, and establish measures to reduce the concentration of set-asides in certain business fields. It also called on Vice President Al Gore to find a way to expand government set-aside programs to firms located in economically disadvantaged areas, regardless of the race or gender of their owners. In short, the new standard being promoted for set-asides was

58. President William Jefferson Clinton, "Remarks by the President on Affirmative Action," Office of the Press Secretary, White House, July 19, 1995.
59. George Stephanopoulos and Christopher Edley Jr., *Affirmative Action Review: Report to the President* (Washington, D.C.: U.S. Government Printing Office, 1995), 74.

place-based, not race-based, affirmative action.[60] In the end, it was the classic Clinton balancing act. His "mend it, don't end it," gave comfort to both camps of his party. As Drew noted, "He managed to please a large segment of the party's base without driving away its center."[61]

This conclusion, however, perhaps applied more to the Democratic centrist part of the electorate than to Democratic centrist politicians and thinkers. Over at the DLC, long on record as urging phasing out affirmative action, there was considerable hand-wringing. Within two weeks of the president's address, the organization's centrist think tank, the Progressive Policy Institute (PPI), published a proposal to radically overhaul affirmative action, phasing it out from government hiring and contracting and making it voluntary in the private sector but retaining it on college campuses. At the same time, the DLC, which constantly equates trying to be somewhere just about in the middle of liberal Democrats and conservative Republicans as saying something "new," directly criticized Clinton for "failing to address the public's doubts about the basic fairness of race-conscious policies."[62] In particular, the PPI report concluded, all "160" programs allotting "10 percent or more of federal contracts to businesses owned by minorities or women" should be "ended within five to 10 years." In their place, the DLC counseled, should be "empowerment initiatives" such as tax incentives for businesses to invest in low-income communities. Then in what must have come as a cynical joke to the civil rights community, the PPI report called for grants to be given to community groups that could conduct audits of racial bias, for example, by sending blacks and whites to apply for the same job. If discrimination is found, such groups could invoke consumer boycotts or other forms of public suasion, rather than litigation. In short, government-financed inspiration for protest was to replace government policy promoting equality of opportunity. To act upon the PPI report, Senator Lieberman promised to introduce legislation that would totally repeal affirmative action, proving that the DLC was ever more indistinguishable from conservative Republicans on matters of race.

Yet, despite the criticisms from the right wing of his own party, the overall response to Clinton's address was better than either politicians or pundits

60. See discussion of place-based affirmative action in Paul M. Barrett and Michael K. Frisby, "Politics and Policy: 'Place, Not Race,' Could Be Next Phase in Government's Affirmative Action Programs," *Wall Street Journal*, Oct. 19, 1995, B16.

61. Drew, *Showdown*, 296.

62. Paul Taylor, "Affirmative Action Overhaul Is Urged," *Washington Post*, Aug. 4, 1995, A6.

predicted when the review began. Polls taken after the president's address showed that a majority of the public agreed with Clinton.[63]

The Republican Response to Clinton's Review

Outflanked by Clinton, Republicans on the presidential campaign trail condemned the president's message and promised to continue to move full steam ahead on eliminating affirmative action. Dole promised he would still introduce his bill, but the scramble for the nomination complicated his aim. Trying to beat Dole to the punch and claim the mantle as the one who had eliminated affirmative action, Senator Phil Gramm of Texas, another contender for the Republican presidential nomination, offered an amendment to an appropriations bill that would prohibit the government from giving "preference" to female- or minority-owned companies for contracts funded by the bill. Not to be beaten, Dole engineered the defeat of Gramm's measure, encouraging the Senate to wait for his own bill.[64]

In the House, Gary A. Franks, then one of only two black Republicans in Congress, was blocked in late July from bringing an amendment similar to Gramm's to the floor. On July 27, 1995, shortly before Dole resigned from the Senate to pursue the presidential race full-time, he and Representative Canady introduced their legislation. Emphasizing the code words that produce opposition to affirmative action, Dole claimed his bill would end any "preferential treatment" of minorities and women in federal contracts or employment. He said that such programs, designed as temporary remedies, had wrongly become permanent and amounted to a ridiculous "quota tokenism."[65]

63. For instance, a late July–early August *Wall Street Journal*/NBC News poll found that by a margin of 57 to 26%, respondents reported that federal programs giving preference to women and minorities "should continue with reforms." Also by a 47–41% margin, respondents thought that the current national debate over affirmative action was "a divisive and negative development." Ronald G. Shafer, "Washington Wire: The Wall Street Journal/NBC News Poll," *Wall Street Journal*, Aug. 4, 1995, A1.

64. Meanwhile Governor Pete Wilson of California, another Republican presidential contender, was claiming he deserved the mantle of "first to eliminate affirmative action," since his leadership had engineered the policy's elimination from the University of California system. Indeed, every 1996 Republican presidential contender except Sen. Arlen Spector of Pennsylvania opposed affirmative action.

65. Bob Dole and J. C. Watts Jr., "A New Civil Rights Agenda," *Wall Street Journal*, July 27, 1995, A10; and Steven A. Holmes, "G.O.P. Lawmakers Offer a Ban on Federal Affirmative Action," *New York Times*, July 28, 1995, A17.

But by then it was clear that there would be no action on affirmative action in either chamber before the 1996 elections. What had brought about this remarkable shift?

From the start of the 104th Congress, it was clear that eliminating affirmative action could not be placed on the fast track in the Senate, given that body's rules, greater Democratic unity, and more moderate Republicans; but the House, by passing nine of the ten planks of the Contract with America in its first 100 days, had proved that it could act swiftly. Why was it unable to do so on affirmative action?

The answer is to be found not only in Clinton's actions, helped along by the Supreme Court, but in splits within the Republican party on affirmative action. Concerned about their image as the rich white men's party, some Republicans wanted to play a balancing act of their own. Gingrich and the Civil Rights Working Group (a collection of conservative legal advocates and several Republican congressmen and their staff headed by the CIR's Bolick) favored not eliminating affirmative action, but rather rewriting affirmative action laws so they favored the poor instead of certain racial and ethnic groups.[66] As Gingrich put it in April 1995: "I'd rather talk about how do we replace group affirmative action with effective help for individuals, rather than just talk about wiping out affirmative action by itself."[67] Thus this group talked about "retargeting" affirmative action.

These ideas were not universally shared. Other Republicans sharply opposed any idea of class-based preferences, viewing them as even worse than race and gender "quotas."[68] This group wanted simply to eliminate affirmative action once and for all. There were yet others, Republican moderates—including many prominent governors—who opposed "quotas" but supported

66. "Republicans Retreat on Key Issues: Education, Environment, Quotas," *Human Events,* July 7, 1995. This group talked about creating "a 'socio-economic index,' based on a myriad of factors including family income, quality of education, and general childhood background. Using this index, the government would enforce preferences for the 'economically disadvantaged' throughout society, in college admission, the awarding of government contracts, and even private hiring."

67. Quoted in Will Marshall, "From Preferences to Empowerment: A New Bargain on Affirmative Action, Executive Summary," Progressive Policy Institute, Washington, D.C., Aug. 3, 1995, 2.

68. See the comments of Roger Pilon of the Cato Institute and Linda Chavez, president of the Center for Equal Opportunity, in "Republicans Retreat on Key Issues."

retaining "goals and timetables" as part of race- and gender-based affirmative action.[69]

Dole's presidential campaign camp reflected these divisions. When the Dole-Canady bill was submitted, an adviser commented that "no one was going to get to the right of Dole on this subject." But according to the veteran journalist Bob Woodward, Senator Alfonse D'Amato of New York, another key Dole adviser, lectured other Dole advisers that opposing affirmative action would hurt Dole politically. "You're going to lose this election! You may have cost Bob Dole this election. I cannot believe you guys are giving him this advice and getting him to do this," D'Amato reportedly shouted. "Are you letting your speechwriter, that Mari Will woman, drive the issues and the intellectual side of the campaign?" Mari and her husband, the conservative columnist George Will, were strongly opposed to affirmative action. They were running the campaign, D'Amato charged. "If you're doing that, you're crazy."[70] Unable to agree on a positive program to replace affirmative action, many in Dole's campaign, just as many Republicans in Congress, felt they would be vulnerable to charges of racism if they eliminated it.

Also, as Dole's selection of Jack Kemp as his running mate indicated, Republicans had some intention of going after some of the black vote in 1996. Representative J. C. Watt, a black Republican from Oklahoma, and Representative James M. Talent, a white Republican of Missouri, had been working to produce a package of legislation designed to help the inner cities, including enterprise zones and school choice. According to one Republican aide, "They were afraid that the publicity raised by an assault on [affirmative action] would interfere with their efforts."[71] Indeed, the split between Watt and Franks, the only two black Republicans in Congress, and their public sparring over affirmative action on the floor of the House perhaps best symbolized the ambivalence and division in the party over the policy.

Republican governors were also divided. While many were opposed to affirmative action, many of the best known (among them John Rowland of

69. See Steven A. Holmes, "Preferences Are Splitting Republicans," *New York Times,* July 29, 1995, 6; and Michael A. Fletcher, "Losing Its Preference: Affirmative Action Fades as Issue," *Washington Post,* Sept. 18, 1996, A12.

70. Quoted in Bob Woodward, *The Choice* (New York: Simon & Schuster, 1996), 226.

71. Quoted in "Republicans Retreat on Key Issues."

Connecticut, George V. Voinovich of Ohio, Jim Edgar of Illinois, George Pataki of New York, Tom Ridge of Pennsylvania, William Weld of Massachusetts, Christine Todd Whitman of New Jersey, and Tommy Thompson of Wisconsin) were in favor of the policy. This group told the press they had no plans to become recruits in the war because they objected both substantively and politically to the attack on affirmative action. Voinovich's comments were typical: "A lot of us believe [affirmative action] is good for America. . . . Making this an issue is not good for the country—or the Republican party." Tommy Thompson put it even more boldly: affirmative action is "a divisive issue that is counterproductive" for Republicans. "We're doing well with a whole variety of economic and family issues, why be divisive," he said. Ridge added, "There has been racial and gender discrimination; there continues to be racial and gender discrimination." Weld declared that in a country "where black unemployment is twice that of white unemployment" and "95 percent of the top corporate jobs in America are held by white men, affirmative action is still needed."[72] Many of the businesses that were heavy contributors to the Republicans were also in favor of affirmative action. An impressive number of CEOs issued statements saying they valued and remained fully committed to affirmative action.[73]

Finally, Republican attempts to eliminate affirmative action were frustrated in part by the nature of the issue. In many ways affirmative action is an issue like reproductive choice: those who feel strongly about it are deeply committed to their positions and tightly knit into opposing camps. But the issue had little salience in 1996. Unlike welfare reform, which ranked among the top three or four "most important" issues in polls, affirmative action was seldom named as an important issue. An October 1996 poll conducted for *U.S. News & World Report* found only "one half of one percent of respondents chose ending the policy as the top political priority. On the list of major issues, it ties for 30th, after reforming the tax code and abolishing the IRS."[74]

To be sure, references to "quotas" or "preferences" tap into economic

72. David S. Broder and Robert A. Barnes, "Few Governors Join Attack on Racial Policies," *Washington Post*, Aug. 2, 1995, A1, A21.

73. Alan Farnham, "Holding Firm on Affirmative Action," *Fortune*, Mar. 13, 1989, 87–88; and James P. Pinkerton, "Why Affirmative Action Won't Die," *Fortune*, Nov. 13, 1995, 191–98. See also Federal Glass Ceiling Commission, *Good for Business*.

74. Lincoln Caplan, "The Hopwood Effect Kicks In on Campus," *U.S. News & World Report*, Dec. 23, 1996, 26.

worry and feelings of victimization, and so sway white opinion to the negative, but the more economic worries subside, the less interest whites show in affirmative action. In 1996 the economy appeared healthy, with inflation low and unemployment declining. It was not the time for Republicans to try to make affirmative action the ultimate wedge issue. The policy's detractors among the public proved to be diffuse, its supporters vocal and united. In this political environment, "mend, not end" proved to be the silver bullet, enabling Clinton to put the Republicans on the defensive. Although Dole introduced his bill, neither he nor any other Republican pressed it, and the 104th Congress ended without having enacted any broad-based ban on affirmative action.

The End of Affirmative Action as We Know It?

Despite the fact that the 104th Congress did not act, it became common in the late 1990s for the policy's foes and allies alike to refer to a "post–affirmative action era." Much of the reversal of fortune continued to be attributable to federal court actions. In July 1998 a federal appeals court voided a government requirement that radio and television stations seek minority job applicants. The ruling expanded the strict-scrutiny standard, for the first time, to programs that simply use special efforts to recruit racial minorities.[75] Partly as a result of this ruling and partly as a result of tax laws and the deregulation brought about by the Telecommunications Act of 1996, substantial new barriers have meant that companies controlled by minorities and women are far less likely to win government licenses for radio or television stations or telephone services, even if they are qualified to run these operations. Thus increasingly these groups are left out of the new economy, as they were of the old.

Another blow came when the Supreme Court refused in March 1999 to review a case involving recruitment of minority firefighters in Dallas. By refusing to hear the case, the high court ensured that Dallas would no longer be able to employ an affirmative action program it had adopted a decade earlier to help diversify the ranks of its firefighting force.

Indeed, by 1999 rulings against affirmative action and their negative impacts on opportunities for racial minorities had become common. In 1997 the Supreme Court refused to reconsider California's Proposition 209. Even ear-

75. Steven A Holmes, "FCC Requirement on Minority Hiring Is Voided by Court," *New York Times,* Apr. 15, 1998.

lier, after the Supreme Court refused to hear *Podberesky v. Kirwan,* the University of Maryland was forced to eliminate its race-based Banneker scholarship program. In the following year, the number of merit-based scholarships going to blacks at the University of Maryland dropped by half.[76] The Court's decision to leave intact the federal appeals court decision in *Hopwood v. Texas,* which ruled against affirmative action for purposes of diversity (including training or recruitment conducted in what could be construed in a race-conscious way), sent ripples throughout higher education, as one institution after another began reviewing its affirmative action program.[77] The effect at the University of Texas was dramatic. Three years after the *Hopwood* decision, there were all of 8 African American students in the University of Texas Law School's first-year class of 455, a smaller percentage than in 1950.[78] Meanwhile, evidence mounted that the state was still spending substantially more on its predominately white higher education institutions (particularly their professional schools) than on predominately black ones.[79]

Yet the die was not yet cast. Several more recent federal court rulings favored affirmative action, at least modestly. For example, in *Hunt v. Cromartie*—the third time the Supreme Court heard a case relating to the redistricting of North Carolina's twelfth district—the Court offered a bit of restraint on what was seemingly the inexorable movement away from affirmative action. The justices ruled unanimously on May 17, 1999, that judges must look deep into the evidence before deciding that state lawmakers had unconstitutionally used race as a major factor in drawing legislative districts. This ruling made it harder for lower courts to summarily strike down election districts that concentrate racial minority voters.[80] Also in early December 2000, two federal court rulings came down on the side of affirmative action in university admissions as a means of promoting diversity. The Ninth U.S. Circuit Court of Appeals ruled that the University of Washington Law School did not violate the Constitution when it carefully considered race in admissions decisions—a ruling in conflict

76. The number of blacks receiving merit-based scholarships at the university fell from 38 in 1994 to 19 in 1995. Roland King, Office of University Relations, University of Maryland, College Park, citing data from the university's Office of Institutional Relations.

77. *Hopwood v. Texas,* cert. denied July 1, 1996, 861 F.Supp. 551, 78 F.3d 932.

78. "Living without It," *Economist,* Mar. 13, 1999, 34

79. "Law Professors Sue Texas, Claiming Discrimination," Associated Press, May 15, 1999.

80. Joan Biskupic, "N.C. Redistricting Gets Another Chance," *Washington Post,* May 18, 1999, A8.

with the *Hopwood* decision, which struck down affirmative action in Texas, Louisiana, and Mississippi. A week later, a federal judge in Detroit also upheld the use of race as a factor in college admissions, ruling that the University of Michigan's affirmative action program was justified by the educational benefits of racial diversity. Both courts accepted a key contention of affirmative action proponents: that race-consciousness in admissions enhances the educational experiences not only of minority students but of whites too, amplifying an argument made by Justice Lewis F. Powell a quarter century earlier in the 1978 landmark case *Bakke v. Board of Regents* that integration is a compelling state interest and therefore constitutional.[81] Perhaps these two rulings provided advocates of affirmative action a guidepost to the future. Most of the justification for affirmative action has concerned righting past wrongs, something the courts have made more difficult to prove by requiring a demonstration of local "intent." But if racial diversity is considered in the state's interest because it improves conditions for everyone, then racial preferences would be defensible. Businessmen in support of affirmative action, for example, have increasingly argued that diversity is good for American business in a more and more globalized world.

However, the fact that the Michigan and Washington rulings conflict with *Hopwood* is likely to be a factor in the Supreme Court's decision to hear an affirmative action case, and there may lie the rub, for the trend in the Supreme Court is a restrictive view of racial considerations in most recent rulings. In short, although the Supreme Court had not rejected affirmative action altogether by the turn of the new century, both opponents and proponents of affirmative action agreed that recent rulings had sent the federal district and appeals courts the unmistakable message that affirmative action is a dying and disfavored policy.

A raft of challenges to affirmative action continued to make headway in the states. Buoyed by their victory, Proposition 209's supporters kept up the momentum they had gained with its passage. Ward Connerly, the best-known black supporter of the initiative, launched a national organization to promote similar challenges in other states. Washington State became the next site of their victories. In Washington, by a 58 percent majority, voters in November

---

81. Jacques Steinberg, "Defending Affirmative Action with Social Science," *New York Times,* Dec. 17, 2000.

1998 approved Initiative 200, which banned most state-supported forms of affirmative action.[82] Other states targeted for anti–affirmative action efforts by Connerly and his allies were Michigan, Colorado, Florida, Nebraska, Nevada, Massachusetts, Texas, and Oregon. Florida's Governor Jeb Bush already has administratively eliminated affirmative action in his state.

Meanwhile, the Clinton administration did a great deal of "mending." Three months after Clinton issued his review, the Department of Defense (DOD) suspended a major contracting rule, known as the "Rule of Two," which had been applied to all defense contracting since 1987.[83] Under the Rule of Two set-aside program, a DOD prime contract was reserved for a small disadvantaged business—usually minority-owned—whenever two or more such firms were available and qualified to bid. Its suspension was especially important because the Pentagon was by far the biggest federal player in the realm of affirmative action contracting. Since 1972, Defense contracting with women and racial minorities had risen steadily from only slightly more than one-quarter of 1 percent to a high of 6.3 percent in 1996, the year of the review. Since that time progress has stalled. By 1998 Defense contracting with women and racial minorities, at 6.0 percent, had already started to decline.[84]

It did not help when in May 1996 the administration announced new federal procurement rules toughening participation standards in all federal con-

---

82. Sam Howe Verhovek and B. Drummond Ayres, "Washington State Voters Approve Initiative Limiting Affirmative Action," *New York Times,* Nov. 4, 1998. As a result of passage of Initiative 200, a federal judge ruled that a reverse-discrimination lawsuit against the University of Washington Law School could no longer have the status of a class-action suit, undercutting its value as a precedent-setting law applicable constitutionally and reducing its likelihood of becoming a major Supreme Court case on affirmative action. For discussion, see Eric St. John, "Not a Class Action: Judge Rules that Passage of Washington State's Initiative 200 Downgrades Status of Reverse Discrimination Lawsuit," *Black Issues in Higher Education,* Mar. 4, 1999, 20–21.

83. In 1994 the Rule of Two alone resulted in $1 billion in federal business for minority firms. Also in 1994, DOD set aside $2.8 billion in contracts for minority-owned firms through the SBA and $1.4 billion more through military programs. The Rule of Two had been used most aggressively to steer work to minority builders, partly because there are many more of them than of minority-owned high-tech companies. All told, in 1994 DOD paid minority firms $6.1 billion (roughly 8 or 9% of all its contracting, far exceeding DOD's benchmark 5% of procurement to go to disadvantaged firms) for construction work, maintenance, landscaping, and other services, in large part because of set-asides and other race-related goals. As a result, minority-owned companies in construction and other relatively low-tech fields have been hard-hit. See Ann Devroy, "Rule Aiding Minority Firms to End: Defense Department Move Follows Review of Affirmative Action," *Washington Post,* Oct. 22, 1995, A1, A8.

84. Data provided by Federal Procurement Data Systems, June 1999.

tracting. As the Justice Department put it: "We are proposing significant reforms and changes in the whole range of federal affirmative action in procurement."[85] Changes included using race-neutral alternatives as frequently as possible, ending exclusive set-aside programs for two years, and tightening eligibility requirements for minority firms. Under the new rules, members of specified protected groups must identify the particular group membership that entitles them to be judged as socially and economically disadvantaged, ending the automatic presumption that all minorities are disadvantaged and moving closer to the requirement for individualized inquiry into the economic disadvantage of participants.

As a result of a Justice Department review (prompted by the *Adarand* decision) of the legality of federal programs that grant breaks exclusively to minorities and women, the Clinton administration eliminated or altered at least seventeen affirmative action programs by 1999 and dollars going to minority contractors fell sharply. For instance, in 1997, after the Energy Department changed the requirements for its national laboratories to subcontract with women- and minority-owned companies, the dollars spent with such companies dropped by a whopping $150 million in two years, from $215.8 million in 1996 to $66.1 million in 1998. Among federal minority set-aside programs that have been sharply scaled back are those in the Federal Highway Administration, the Environmental Protection Agency, and the National Aeronautics and Space Administration, as well as programs aimed at increasing the numbers of Foreign Service officers, racial minority teachers and scientists, and managers of public radio and television stations. Indeed, although losses in defense contracting as a result of the elimination of the Rule of Two may represent a big change, declines in minority contracting across all federal agencies may have been even more dramatic. Only 5.8 percent of federal contracts were performed by minority- and female-owned firms in 1995, and the proportion had already declined to 4.2 percent of federal contracting dollars by 1998, according to the Office of Management and Budget (Table 6.2).

The new rules are expected to speed up the decline. Changes in federal procurement already have been sweeping, and departments such as Commerce, Justice, and the Small Business Administration have already proposed "a more

85. Paul M. Barrett, "Affirmative Action for U.S. Contracts Is Limited in Ruses Using 'Benchmarks,'" *Wall Street Journal*, May 23, 1996, A4; and Steven A. Holmes, "In New Guide, U.S. Retreats on Contracts for Minorities," *New York Times*, May 23, 1996, A26.

Table 6.2. Percentage of federal contracting dollars awarded to minority-owned businesses, 1994–1998

Year	Total contracts (thousands)	Minority-owned businesses[1] (thousands)	Percentage of total
1998	$180,914,794	$7,541,579	4.2%
1997	172,720,914	10,278,903	6.0
1996	178,607,943	10,292,619	5.8
1995	180,851,975	10,519,469	5.8
1994	174,687,952	9,059,488	5.2

[1]Includes businesses owned by white women.

SOURCE: Federal Procurement Data System.

flexible set of considerations." One major new "flexible consideration" has resulted in the extension of benefits of affirmative action efforts to "disadvantaged" whites, and has made it easier for white men to prove they are disadvantaged on the basis of income and other factors, and as a result are eligible for preference.[86] In minority contracting, more than any other area, the transformation of affirmative action into a class- rather than race-based program is well under way.

The decline in federal minority contracting opportunities will in all likelihood be ultimately devastating to minority businesses. Such opportunities serve as a major point of entry for socially and economically disadvantaged minority entrepreneurs and small business concerns into the mainstream of American enterprise. Thirty-two of the 100 largest African American firms and 17 of the 100 largest Latino firms were or had been in the Section 8(a) program of the Small Business Administration in 1994. Moreover, 68 of the 100 largest black businesses were federal government contractors in 1994.[87] In sum, although the Clinton administration continued to defend federal affirmative action programs in Congress and the courts, it conducted the most sweeping reduction of those measures since they were instituted during the Nixon administration, and these reductions have begun to have a material impact.

State and local anti–affirmative action efforts have spread what is happening in contracting to other arenas. For instance, after implementation of California's Proposition 209, admissions of African American, Native Ameri-

86. Steven A. Holmes, "Administration Cuts Affirmative Action while Defending It," *New York Times*, Mar. 16, 1998.
87. Stephanopoulos and Edley, *Affirmative Action Review*, 114.

can, and Latino students to the state's system of higher education declined dramatically. By 2000, the number of black and Latino freshmen admitted to the University of California system had rebounded to the level it was when race and gender-based affirmative action was still in place, but most of the recovery can be attributed to the fact that more blacks and Latinos were being admitted to lesser-known campuses. The number at the flagship Berkeley campus was still well below 1997 totals, as it was at the prestigious Los Angeles campus. In addition, most of the general rebound was due to a rise in Latino admissions, while black students remained 7 percent below the level of 1997, the last year of affirmative action.[88] The institution of class-based preferences did not stop this slide. When administrators at the University of California at Berkeley substituted family income for race/ethnicity in 1998, only 29 percent of the 5,200 applicants with family incomes below $30,000 were African Americans, Latinos, and American Indians. In the fall of 1998, enrollment of black freshmen plummeted to 122 from 252 the previous year.[89]

In sum, there can be no gainsaying the fact that "affirmative action as we knew it" no longer exists. Colleges and universities are being propelled toward policies—especially "class, not race" plans—that are touted as the new answer to problems of inequality but are, on the basis of early evidence, almost certainly being oversold. While a policy of affirmative action based on socioeconomic status sounds appealing, and its proponents argue that because minorities are more likely than whites to be poor, minorities would be more likely than whites to benefit, most systematic studies show that whites get the lion's share of the slots. Not only do low-income whites have access to better preparation for college in better high schools than low-income blacks and Latinos; not only do low-income whites score higher than low-income blacks and Latinos on standardized college admission tests; but the white poor outnumber the black and Latino poor by 2.5 to 1. In short, the pool of poor whites to draw from is significantly larger than the pool of poor racial minorities.[90]

Despite the fact that affirmative action had suffered the most severe set-

88. Michelle Locke, "California's Minority Enrollment Is Up, but That's Only Part of the Story," *Black Issues in Higher Education,* Apr. 27, 2000.

89. David L. Marcus, "Whatever Happened to Minority Students? Universities Try Risky New Steps to Diversify," *U.S. New & World Report,* Mar. 22, 1999, 28–30.

90. Robert Bruce Slater, "Why Socioeconomic Affirmative Action in College Admissions Works against African Americans," *Journal of Blacks in Higher Education,* Summer 1995, 57.

backs of its roughly thirty-year history and conservatives in both parties remained committed to demolishing the policy stone by stone if necessary through new legislation, judicial challenges, and administrative action, apparently President Clinton still longed to be remembered as the president who substantially contributed to ending what he once called "America's constant curse," racism in America.[91] Toward that end, he proposed a year-long dialogue on race.

The President's Initiative on Race (PIR)

Speaking at the University of California at San Diego's commencement ceremony on June 14, 1997, the president announced: "Today, I ask the American people to join me in a great national effort to perfect the promise of America for this new time as we seek to build our more perfect union. . . . That is the unfinished work of our time, to lift the burden of race and redeem the promise to America." Pledging both to lead a dialogue and to encourage public officials and citizens to take action based on the conclusions reached in these conversations, Clinton indicated the import of these efforts to his legacy: "If ten years from now people can look back and see that this year of honest dialogue and concerted action helped to lift the heavy burden of race from our children's future, we have given a precious gift to America." Yet always seeking to reach out to moderates and conservatives, the New Democrat president also stressed: "Beyond opportunity, we must demand responsibility from every American. Our strength as a society depends upon both—upon people taking responsibility for themselves and their families, teaching their children good values, working hard and obeying the law, and giving back to those around us. . . . No responsibility is more fundamental than obeying the law. It is not racist to insist that every American do so."[92] And thus Clinton began his initiative on race, ever trying to play a balancing act between New and Old Democrat, both calling race a burden and linking it to irresponsibility and crime.

Clinton was not prompted by a crisis to establish a commission on race, such as those spawned by white riots in the 1940s and black ones in the 1960s. There had been no major riot since he was elected president, and the only big

91. "A Polite Kind of Race War," *Newsweek,* Jan. 26, 1998, 29.
92. William Jefferson Clinton, "Remarks by the President at University of California at San Diego Commencement," June 14, 1997, "Weekly Compilation of Presidential Documents," <http://frwais.access.gpo.gov>.

march of African Americans on Washington during the Clinton years, the Million Man March, made zero policy demands. As one Clinton associate put it, "Nothing's forcing Clinton to react." He added, "There's not a whole lot of forward-looking pressure on the race issue."[93]

One immediate question about the potential productivity of the president's initiative flowed precisely from this setting: Was the relative quiescence on race that characterized the late 1990s infertile ground for the PIR? In an age of the "public" presidency,[94] could a president inspire a national conversation on a subject as complex as race without a coinciding crisis to call citizens' attention to the issue and coalesce opinion around specific policy alternatives?

Most scholarship on the public presidency suggested that the answer to these questions was a resounding no—that is, that the PIR, designed in large part to elicit a response from the public, was likely to fail. Woodrow Wilson's argument that presidents should mold existing public opinion and partially formed policy preferences by "interpreting" them in public addresses and using these interpretations as leverage in legislative battles with Congress did not suggest that a president could spur the formation of policy preferences in the absence of public concern over an issue. He also did not contend that public opinion should be discerned by direct feedback from small groups of witnesses at hearings.[95]

Richard Neustadt explicitly pointed to the difficulties for a president who seeks to take on the role of teacher, educating the public on important issues of the day. According to Neustadt, the public is generally inattentive unless an event occurs to stimulate concern. While presidents can sometimes manufacture such events, Neustadt maintained, "no matter how cooperative the press, a president needs quiet from competitive events if what he does is to be noticed as happening."[96] In addition, quasi-experimental media research finds that whether citizens believe political leaders should take responsibility for solutions to a problem such as racial inequality depends on whether media coverage of

93. James Bennet, "As His Legacy, Clinton Seeks to Improve Race Relations," *New York Times,* Apr. 9, 1997.

94. George C. Edwards, *The Public Presidency* (New York: St. Martin's Press, 1983); and Jeffrey Tulis, *The Rhetorical Presidency* (Princeton: Princeton University Press, 1987).

95. Woodrow Wilson, *Constitutional Government in the United States* (New York: Columbia University Press, 1908).

96. Richard E. Neustadt, *Presidential Power and the Modern Presidents: The Politics of Leadership from Roosevelt to Reagan* (New York: Maxwell Macmillan, 1990), 74–79.

actions taken by the leader is episodic (focusing on discrete events) or thematic (focusing on events within their societal and historical contexts).[97]

Just how hard it would be for Clinton to overcome these difficulties was soon demonstrated. Large segments of both the general public and political activists on left and right simultaneously revealed they were turned off by the PIR. Conservative Republicans declared the time for dialogue had passed. What was needed was conservative action, especially directed toward eliminating affirmative action. Thus Jack Kemp and J. C. Watts Jr. announced shortly after Clinton's San Diego speech that they had a plan superior to affirmative action. They then trotted out the old Republican favorites: public school choice, tuition vouchers, enterprise zones, and privatization of public housing—the latter two already largely appropriated by the Clinton administration.[98]

Many members of the civil rights community, for their part, viewed the PIR as symbolic politics at its worst. Charles Kamasaki, vice president of the National Council of La Raza, the oldest Latino advocacy group, commented that little was clear about the White House plans except that "the President wants to leave a legacy of being a real nice guy on these issues."[99] What was needed was "the courage to lead," not another study, added Roger Wilkins, a history professor at George Mason University and an assistant attorney general during the Johnson administration. "Why not turn attention to the backlog of nearly 75,000 discrimination cases at the Equal Employment Opportunity Commission or the assistant attorney general for civil rights vacancy, or the staff director vacancy at the U.S. Commission on Civil Rights?" Wilkins asked. "This man has been President for four and one-half years, and now he is trying to make civil rights part of his legacy. Isn't it kind of late?"[100] In fact, to many

97. Shanto Iyengar, *Is Anyone Responsible? How Television Frames Political Issues* (Chicago: University of Chicago Press, 1991), 61–74; and Renee M. Smith, "The Public Presidency Hits the Wall: Clinton's Presidential Initiative on Race," *Presidential Studies Quarterly* 28, no. 4 (Fall 1998): 780–85.

98. Jack Kemp and J. C. Watts Jr., "Better than Affirmative Action," *Washington Post*, July 8, 1997, A15. See also Steven A. Holmes, "Gingrich Offers His Own Program to Promote Racial Healing," *New York Times*, June 19, 1997.

99. James Bennet, "Clinton Plans Moves Aimed to Improve Race Relations," *Washington Post*, June 5, 1997.

100. Michael A. Fletcher and Dan Balz, "Race Relations Initiative May Pose Risks for Clinton," *Washington Post*, June 12, 1997, A1. When asked about widespread skepticism among civil rights leaders that his initiative would go beyond mere talk, Clinton responded that his commitment to solving the race problem was beyond reproach. See Alison Mitchell, "Clinton Feeling Sure-Footed on Tightrope of Race," *New York Times*, June 16, 1997.

on the left, talk about reconciliation was the death blow to the spirit of confrontation that had forced the nation to face up to its racial dilemma in the 1960s and to initiate a process of racial reconstruction.[101] In sum, practically the highest praise the PIR generated in the civil rights community was that it was better than nothing.

Meanwhile, public opinion polls showed that most Americans had little hope for the initiative. In April 1998, only small majorities of whites (54 percent) and people of color (59 percent) agreed that the initiative was needed.[102] Only sustained attention from Clinton to his PIR had a chance at altering these views.

Missteps in the Structure, Focus, and Goals of the PIR

To conduct his conversation on race, the president held a series of "town meetings." He also appointed a board charged with overseeing the year-long effort to solicit and gather research on the racial problems that have affected the United States since World War II and then to forecast how to improve race relations in the first half of the twenty-first century. The PIR advisory board was instructed to produce its findings in a report that would serve as the basis for Clinton's own report on how to improve race relations. Selection of advisory board members was completed soon after the San Diego address. A racially diverse group (save for the striking absence of Native Americans), the PIR's advisory board was headed by the esteemed historian John Hope Franklin.[103]

In all, the advisory board held eight public meetings in five states and the District of Columbia. The meetings covered topics ranging from education and housing to employment and the administration of justice. Board members also attended meetings held by federal agencies on topics including health and immigration. Board members individually participated in approximately 300 meetings with a wide cross section of communities and constituencies. Cabinet secretaries and other officials took part in more than 140 race relations dialogues in more than forty cities.[104] In addition, to engage a wider set of academ-

101. Stephen Steinberg, *Turning Back: The Retreat from Racial Justice in American Thought and Politics* (Boston: Beacon, 1995), 99.
102. Gallup Poll, "Special Reports: Black/White Relations in the U.S.," June 10, 1997.
103. Phil Hall, "A Flawed Race Panel," *New York Times,* June 13, 1997.
104. Steven A. Holmes, "Clinton Staff Starts to Put Race Policy into Practice," *New York Times,* Feb. 1, 1999, A4.

ics, the PIR commissioned the National Research Council (NRC), the research arm of the National Academy of Sciences, to coordinate studies by prominent researchers on a range of topics related to race, including demographic trends. The NRC held an invitation-only research conference in October 1998 to air findings to yet a wider set of academics and researchers. The PIR also published *One America Dialogue Guide,* a manual to assist groups in holding constructive dialogues on race in their communities. In sum, the PIR engaged in a very substantial array of activities.

However, there was a large time lag in getting started. The board did not meet publicly until September 30, 1997, a third of the way into the president's allotted year. Staffing was especially slow. The board had no staff until Judith Winston became its executive director at the beginning of August 1997, and it took Winston another month to hire and train additional staff.[105] Throughout that period, board members struggled to determine the panel's charge. To what degree was the advisory board able to act independently? Which racial groups were to be the focus of the PIR? To what extent should the board seek the views of conservatives? That the board had to hash out these questions in the public eye demonstrated not only the lack of forethought that had gone into creating the PIR but also the potential for more heat than light to be the outcome of it.

One of the earliest debates among board members was over which racial populations would be at the center of its work. Should the focus be on the old black/white issues or equally on Latinos (nearly as large a population as African Americans, 11.2 percent and 12.1 percent, respectively, in 1998) and Asians/ Pacific Islanders (3 percent and the fastest-growing racial population). Especially given the often fractious competition among racial/ethnic minorities,[106]

105. Peter Baker, "Four Months after Clinton Began Effort, Panel Finally Puts Its Staff in Place," *Washington Post,* Oct. 5, 1997, A6.

106. See Paula McClain and Joseph Stewart Jr., *Can We All Get Along? Racial and Ethnic Minorities in American Politics* (Boulder, Colo.: Westview, 1995), 127, chaps. 7–8. See also Romesh Ratnesar, "The Next Big Divide? Blacks and Hispanics Square Off over Bilingual Education—and for Control of Public Schools," *Time,* Dec. 1, 1997; Thomas Hardy, "Black Activists Downplay Rift with Hispanics over Remap Plan," *Chicago Tribune,* June 5, 1991. *Inside Edition,* Jan. 19, 1998, discussed negative portrayals of blacks in Latin American advertising and entertainment media. For how these stereotypes as well as experience within Latin America discourage thinking of blacks and Latinos as coalition partners, see William W. Sales Jr. and Roderick Bush, "Black and Latino Coalitions: Prospects for New Social Movements in New York City," in James Jennings, ed., *Race and Politics* (New York: Verso, 1997). For discussion of Asian American views of affirmative action, see Kenneth Lee, "Angry Yellow Men,"

Angela Oh, an Asian American on the board, urged her colleagues to move beyond the "black-white paradigm." While they were all well aware of the history of slavery, she said, "we can't undo this part of our heritage. . . . Where we can affect is where we're going from here." Oh's comments drew a response from the two African American members (Franklin and the Reverend Susan Cook), who argued that it was important to remember that racism in America was born out of slavery and bias against African Americans. "There is a black-white dialogue that cannot be overlooked," said Cook. "This country cut its eyeteeth on racism with black-white relations," added Franklin. "They learned to do this to other people at other times because they'd already become experts" by doing it to blacks.[107]

The controversy over focus resurfaced often in board proceedings and spread into administrative politics. When in the fall of 1997 Chief of Staff Erskine Bowles started meeting separately with minority aides about the impact of policies on different racial groups, and black staffers cautioned him that the president's push for mandatory educational-standards testing might alienate African Americans, Bowles authorized a black staff member to attend all White House meetings on the issue. Latino staffers asked for and got equal time. Latinos also often complained that they were not adequately represented as panelists in board meetings. For instance, at a televised advisory board meeting held in Houston on April 14, 1998, on the role of race in sports—widely considered to be an attempt to involve white men in the race dialogue—Latino representatives claimed their group interests were not fairly represented. With only one Latino, the St. John University basketball star Felipe Lopez, on the

---

New Republic, Sept. 9, 1996, 11. For discussion of the impact of affirmative action on college admissions of diverse racial and ethnic groups, see Theodore Cross, "Suppose There Was No Affirmative Action at the Most Prestigious Colleges and Graduate Schools," *Journal of Blacks in Higher Education,* Spring 1994, 50–51; Norman Matloff, "How Immigration Harms Minorities," *Public Interest,* Summer 1996; Emily MacFarquhar, "Fighting over the Dream," *U.S. News & World Report,* May 18, 1992, 34; Bill Piatt, *Black and Brown in America: The Case for Cooperation* (New York: New York University Press, 1997); James Johnson Jr. and Melvin Oliver, "Interethnic Minority Conflict in Urban America: The Effects of Economic and Social Dislocations," *Urban Geography* 10 (1989): 449–63; Antonio H. Rodriguez and Carlos A. Chavez, "Perspective on Racial Tensions: The Rift Is Exposed; Let's Bridge It," *Los Angeles Times,* July 24, 1992; Stephanie Chavez, "Racial Tensions over South L.A. Jobs Grow," *Los Angeles Times,* July 22, 1992, B1; E. San Juan Jr., "Multiculturalism vs. Hegemony: Ethnic Studies, Asian Americans, and U.S. Racial Politics," *Massachusetts Review* 21, no. 3 (Fall 1992): 467–78.

107. Peter Baker, "A Splinter on the Race Advisory Board: First Meeting Yields Divergent Views on Finding 'One America,'" *Washington Post,* July 15, 1997, A4.

ten-member panel, one questioner from the audience noted that "not once have I heard you mention Hispanics." Lopez agreed: "People really have to realize that we are making a great contribution to this country." Before the broadcast, Latino groups had threatened to protest the meeting and were dissuaded only by the president's agreement to meet privately with them beforehand.

Perhaps, however, it was the lack of representation of a Native American on the board that was the stiffest challenge. At the outset, Native Americans protested the absence of any member of their group on the board or as a consultant to the dialogue.[108] These concerns festered and grew. On March 25, 1998, an advisory board meeting in Denver descended into chaos and incoherence as a vocal group of Native American advocates loudly and repeatedly disrupted the proceedings. Many in the group, which made up about a third of the more than 500 people who had gathered in a university student center, wore red bandannas and ski masks, chanted and beat drums, and shouted down speaker after speaker, including Franklin when he tried to explain that he did not have the power to appoint additional board members. "How can you have a dialogue on race without one American Indian on your board?" one man shouted at Franklin. "Dialogue! Dialogue!" other protesters chanted derisively. Although Franklin sat down and did not try to speak again, in what was a moment that could only be described as incongruous given the many times African Americans had demanded to know why they were being excluded from official panels and events, African American staff of the commission added insult to injury by lecturing Native Americans to be "civilized." Moreover, behind the scenes, black staff negotiated with white Denver police officers to throw out the Native Americans.[109]

After the meeting, Franklin and other board members said that, despite the lack of Native Americans on the board, they had bent over backward to solicit their views. They noted that they had hired a special consultant, Laura Harris, a Comanche and the daughter of former Senator Fred Harris of Oklahoma, to work with Native Americans. They also pointed out that they had held special meetings with tribal leaders in Santa Fe, Phoenix, and Denver, something the board said it had yet to do with representatives of other racial groups. Native American leaders countered that whatever the board may have

108. Phil Hall, "A Flawed Race Panel," *New York Times,* June 13, 1997.

109. Telephone interview June 18, 1998, with Joe Feagin, professor of sociology at the University of Florida and a member of the race panel at the Denver meeting.

done did not make up for the absence of a representative. "Not having an indig-enous person on the board is a slap in the face," said Steve Newcomb, head of the Indigenous Law Center, a Native American civil rights group.[110] In what was perhaps the most curious attempt of all to show that Native Americans were not excluded, President Clinton announced in the midst of his third town hall meeting, a televised panel discussion on race, that he is part Cherokee—his grandmother was a quarter Indian. That makes him one-sixteenth Indian. This news was as much a surprise to the nation's two million Native Americans as it must have been to the federal prosecutors who thought they knew everything about the president's personal life. The press joked that the first American Indian had been elected president and no one even knew about it.[111]

In short, one thing the PIR evoked was just how increasingly complex and contentious the subject of race had become as various racial/ethnic popula-tions grew in size, identity, and demands. Ultimately the president weighed in on the issue of which groups would be the focus. Apparently he agreed with Oh and others who wanted a more "multicultural" focus, since he announced at an annual convention of the NAACP that the focus of the board would be on "multiracialism," not black-white relations, as Franklin had recommended. By that time, Franklin had already criticized Clinton for delivering his first major address on his race initiative to a black audience. In an interview with the Asso-ciated Press, Franklin noted: "The white side has been in control of virtually everything, so they're the ones who need educating on what justice and equal-ity mean."[112] It would not be the last time that the president and the chair of his board openly disagreed.

Clinton and Franklin also publicly disagreed over whether the charge of the board was to hear only from those with proven sympathies for civil rights or include those who were actually enemies of civil rights, at least "as we knew them" since the mid-1960s. Franklin's position was clear: When conservatives charged that the board's membership was ideologically one-sided—composed of liberals and moderates only—he declared that the critics of affirmative action had "nothing to contribute."[113] White House aides reportedly cringed. In

110. Steven A. Holmes, "Indians Are Latest to Disrupt Race Panel," *New York Times,* Mar. 25, 1998.

111. Richard Williams, "The Part-Cherokee President," *New York Times,* July 16, 1998.

112. Ibid.

113. Peter Baker, "Reaching Out to Revitalize Race Panel, Clinton Scouts for More Voices to Spur Reconciliation Dialogue," *Washington Post,* Nov. 20, 1997, A14.

response, Clinton again publicly disagreed with his board chair and invited a group of conservatives to the Oval Office to share their views on race in an encounter session on December 19, 1998.[114] Indeed, as a result of Republican complaints, the panels were increasingly composed of roughly equal numbers of conservatives and liberals—which severely constrained the probabilities of a clear mission, purpose, and policy potential.[115] In effect, the work of the board was plagued by continued interference by White House officials who feared the political consequences of its work.[116]

Finally, it did not help that White House aides acknowledged that the PIR's "goals were not clearly defined."[117] This lack of clarity extended even into Clinton's third and final town hall meeting in July 1998, at which Clinton and the participants spent most of their time "talking about talking bluntly about race."[118] But lack of focus and clear goals were only one problem; there were many others.

Strategy and tactics proved to be a second set of problems. The advisory board was required to meet in public by law—a setting that hampered the ability of board members to speak candidly about divisive and sensitive issues. Additionally, since the discussion was promoted as a "dialogue," the advisory board was often criticized for spending too much time listening to the reports of "experts" on race and not enough time allowing "average Americans" to express their views.[119] Whether experts or common citizens, however, there was far more "serial monologue" than dialogue.[120]

At the same time, the president's choice of a town meeting format in

114. For a discussion of the transcript of the meeting released by the White House, see Charles Devarics, "Clinton, Affirmative Action Opponents Meet," *Black Issues in Higher Education,* Jan. 8, 1998, 4–5. See also Baker, "Reaching Out."

115. Peter Baker, "With Outburst at Fairfax Forum, Race Initiative Finally Hits a Nerve," *Washington Post,* Dec. 18, 1997, A1.

116. Steven A. Holmes, "Clinton Panel on Race Urges Variety of Modest Measures," *New York Times,* Sept. 18, 1998.

117. Michael A. Fletcher and Peter Baker, "Clinton Sees Today's Town Hall Meeting as Turning Point in His Race Initiative," *Washington Post,* Dec. 3, 1997, A9.

118. Jim Lehrer, quoted in "Clinton at Race Forum Is Confronted on Affirmative Action," *New York Times,* July 9, 1998, 23.

119. The early meetings (late 1997–early 1998) could best be described as a parade of polite and harmonious academic talking heads providing detailed evidence of what many policy makers already knew about the progress of race relations and the importance of diversity. See discussion in Baker, "With Outburst at Fairfax Forum." See also Steven A. Holmes, "President Nudges His Race Panel to Take Action," *New York Times,* Oct. 1, 1997, 23.

120. Felicia R. Lee, "The Honest Dialogue That Is Neither," *New York Times,* Dec. 7, 1997, 5.

which he promised to solicit direct feedback from the audiences also failed to generate dialogue about racial issues. Instead these meetings produced discussions in the press about Clinton's performance and willingness to listen to all points of view. Moreover, the town meeting approach all but guaranteed that media coverage of the PIR would be episodic. Indeed, news reports of both advisory board and town meetings tended to center on spectacles, as when on December 18, 1997, at a board meeting in Fairfax County, Virginia, a photographer with ties to the white supremacist David Duke grabbed a microphone and shouted, "There's no one up there that's talking about the white people! We don't want to be a minority in our own country!"[121] or when in San Jose, California, on February 11, 1998, a woman, claiming she was a former Secret Service agent, insisted that Clinton was dead and the government was covering it up; or when at the same meeting a man suddenly rose and bellowed: "What about the Gypsies."[122]

Issues of discrimination, racism, and oppression in their historical and societal contexts got lost because news reports focused on Clinton as a media performer. Journalists dubbed him the "first conversationalist" and "chief talker," and referred to his initiative as "a national gabfest," "the jaw, jaw approach," and "governing by therapy."[123]

To the extent that coverage was episodic and focused on the dramatic, the complex causes of and solutions to racial problems were ignored by the media, and hence by citizens.[124] Both Board Chairman Franklin and President Clinton apparently came to understand the mistake of the public commission. In his evaluation of the PIR at the end of its year, Franklin commented: "We have learned how difficult it is to hold productive discussions about race under the glare of television lights and cameras, in large meetings among relative strangers, and among people who expect more than an advisory board can reasonably deliver."[125] And Bill Clinton concluded, "It's very hard to pierce through the public consciousness and to do a sustained public education cam-

121. Ibid.

122. Holmes, "Indians Are Latest to Disrupt Race Panel."

123. Lee, "Honest Dialogue"; Walter Goodman, "Where Image Prevails, Talk about Race Turns Bland," *New York* Times, Dec. 9, 1997, E2; Russell Baker, "We've Got to Talk," *New York Times,* June 17, 1997, 21; Skip Thurman, "Next Clinton Focus: Healing Racial Rifts," *Christian Science Monitor,* June 3, 1997, 1; Glenn C. Loury, "Why Talk about Race? Welfare and Crime Demand More than Feel-Good Chat," *Washington Post,* Dec. 7, 1997, A24.

124. Smith, "Public Presidency Hits the Wall," 780.

125. John Hope Franklin, "Talking, Not Shouting, about Race," *New York Times,* June 13, 1998, 15.

paign in the absence of some great conflict."[126] Neustadt concluded, "The president as teacher needed real, rather than manufactured, events to raise citizens' awareness."[127]

The Distraction of Presidential Misconduct and the PIR Board Report

In the absence of a real-life racial crisis, only the most sustained effort by the president could have made a difference. But Clinton was ill positioned to provide such effort. Not only was there the usual panoply of domestic policies requiring presidential action; not only did the president have to focus on a potential war in the Middle East; but especially after allegations surfaced that he had had sexual relations with Monica Lewinsky, a young White House intern, and may have perjured himself when he denied it, neither Clinton nor administration officials had time to push the race initiative. In March 1998, a news report on Clinton's upcoming second town meeting in Houston with sports officials and athletes noted: "The national dialogue has been eclipsed in recent months by the possibility of war with Iraq and the accusations of sexual impropriety against Mr. Clinton, who has devoted little public time to promoting the initiative."[128]

By the time the board's report was issued, most people were too busy reading Independent Counsel Kenneth Starr's report (replete with lurid tales of sexual escapades) to notice it. Indeed, the day after the president's board released its long-awaited recommendations, the *Washington Post* carried the story on page 8. The big headline on page 1 that day was "Clinton Videotape Set for Release."[129] In short, the Lewinsky scandal hampered publicity about the board's final report and its consideration.[130]

Moreover, to the extent that stimulating a constructive dialogue on race required moral leadership, perhaps the most noteworthy irony of the Lewinsky scandal was that it left the president in an extremely weak position. Here was a president who had gotten lots of political mileage from belaboring the virtues

126. Steven A. Holmes and James Bennet, "A Renewed Sense of Purpose for Clinton's Panel on Race," *New York Times,* Jan. 14, 1998, 1.

127. Neustadt, *Presidential Power,* 74–79.

128. Steven A. Holmes, "Race Forum Will Seek New Focus," *New York Times,* Mar. 20, 1998, 21.

129. See discussion in Francine Kiefer, "Why White House Pushes Race Initiative," *Christian Science Monitor,* Feb. 24, 1999, 2

130. Holmes, "Clinton Panel on Race."

of taking "personal responsibility" for one's own life and actions and who signed punitive crime and welfare reform laws to show that he would reward only those who "played by the rules," and that he could get tough on those who were "irresponsible"—a theme, recall, the president emphasized in his announcement of the PIR. Here was a president who repeatedly sought to convey a message that he was a "new" morally invigorated Democrat who stood for good, "traditional," stern values, but who ended up being revealed in the most humiliating way of recklessly playing fast and loose with settled notions of personal responsibility when it came to his own life.[131]

As Randall Kennedy noted, Clinton's personal failings had far-reaching public consequences. "For one thing, to the extent that Clinton really desired to assist racial minorities in a systemic, lasting fashion, the scandal caused by his misconduct handicapped substantially his ability to do so. . . . Tragically . . . his deeply ingrained moral weakness delayed even modest progressive reforms on the racial front."[132]

Yet it was not just presidential misconduct that reduced the impact of the report. The tepid report (produced in fifteen months, not twelve) of his Initiative on Race offered no road map toward the president's lofty goal of fostering a new climate of "racial reconciliation." The four major recommendations—the creation of a permanent presidential council on race; the development of an education program to keep the public informed about race; a presidential "call to arms" to leaders of the public and private sectors to "make racial reconciliation" a reality; and the engagement of youth leaders in an effort to build bridges among the races—as well as the calls for tighter enforcement of civil rights laws, an end to sentencing disparities for crimes involving crack versus powder cocaine, greater spending on teacher training and school construction in minority areas, and reaffirmation of support for affirmative action were hardly bold new ideas that needed a year-long study to develop.[133]

Indeed, perhaps nothing better illustrates the modesty in both substance and rhetoric of the Clinton panel's report on race than a comparison with the

131. For discussion, see Barbara Ransby, "Feminists and Black Leaders Need to Stop Defending Clinton," *Miami Herald,* Sept. 14, 1998.

132. Randall Kennedy, "Is He a Soul Man? On Black Support for Clinton," *American Prospect,* March–April 1999, 30.

133. Holmes, "Clinton Panel on Race."

Kerner Commission's report issued thirty years earlier. Where the Kerner report focused on action, the Clinton report focused on study; where the Kerner report made straightforward and explicit recommendations, the Clinton report was ambiguous and vague; where the Kerner report identified white racism as the key cause of continuing problems, the Clinton report failed to identify any main cause of problems; and where the Kerner report predicted dismal prospects unless fundamental structural changes were made, the Clinton report celebrated racial progress. The presidential statements that opened the two reports were starkly different. Lyndon Baines Johnson's introductory statement to the Kerner report was virtually a call to war: "The only genuine, long-range solution from what has happened lies in attack—mounted at every level—upon the conditions that breed despair and violence. All of us know what those conditions are: ignorance, discrimination, slums, poverty, disease, not enough jobs. We should attack these conditions—not because we are frightened by conflict, but because we are fired by conscience."[134] Bill Clinton's opening remarks were considerably more ambiguous and equivocal. Indeed, Clinton simply repeated remarks from his San Diego speech urging Americans to join him in seeking to build a "more perfect union" by "lifting the burden of race."

The key routes proposed to lift this burden were also starkly different in the two reports. Where the Kerner report called for "strategies for action that will produce quick and visible progress"; the PIR called for "a language or vocabulary that respects differences." Where the Kerner report was detailed and candid in its recommendations for opening up opportunities to the excluded, the PIR focused on improving data collection on race and convening meetings. Where the Kerner report proposed to create uniform national standards for welfare recipients that were at least as high as the poverty level, the Clinton report proposed to "examine" income inequality. Where the Kerner report proposed to reorient federal housing policy in order to locate more low- and moderate-income housing outside of the ghetto, the Clinton report was silent on scatter-site housing. Finally, where the Kerner report warned about the dangers of increasing separation and inequality and called for crucial government action—including substantial new spending to be supported, if neces-

134. Steven A. Holmes, "Word for Word/1968 and 1998, the Fire Wasn't This Time: Two Race Reports," *New York Times,* Oct. 4, 1998.

sary, by tax increases—to address the problems of America's inner cities, the Clinton report recommended a presidential council on racial disparities.[135]

In short, the Clinton report was anything but a brave contribution to dialogue on the politics and policy of race. Save for affirmative action, the PIR report sidestepped the highly contentious racial issues of the day. The issue of racial profiling is a case in point. The PIR report only called for the Justice Department to *consider* restricting the use of racial profiling by federal law enforcement agencies and urging local police departments to do the same. Thus the report stopped far short of calling for the practice to be outlawed, as most civil rights advocates had hoped. On other hot-button issues, such as school vouchers to allow poor children to attend private schools and busing to achieve school desegregation, the PIR board report made no concrete recommendations at all.[136]

To be sure, the rhetoric of the Kerner Commission report remained just that, rhetoric. As Anthony Downs has pointed out, no one took seriously the broad programs suggested by the Kerner Commission, much less tried to implement them. He points out that whites understood that such a charge would have cut into their privileges of sending their children to the best schools, saving the best neighborhoods for their occupancy, and saving the best jobs for their employment. Politicians of the late 1960s also understood the potential consequences if they had tried to implement the Kerner Commission's recommendations. Thus the Kerner Commission Report did little but call white people's attention to their privilege and its consequences, but even egalitarian rhetoric was more than the PIR was willing to risk.

Apparently some members of the PIR's board agreed that the Clinton report was pretty tame and obsequious. Thomas Kean, former Republican governor of New Jersey, concluded: "Race is very divisive. As the year wore on, people became—not the Board, but people in the Administration—became concerned. We were not encouraged to be bold." Kean, who was especially concerned about the pernicious effects of racial stereotyping in the media, added: "My recommendations were much bolder than anything contained in this report."[137]

135. Ibid.
136. Holmes, "Clinton Panel on Race."
137. Ibid.

The Impact of the PIR

It was not that the PIR had no impact at all. From his announcement of the PIR onward, the president indicated that he would propose new spending to encourage stricter enforcement of civil rights laws. In November 1997 at the University of Maryland, the seven-member PIR board also suggested that federal antidiscrimination efforts should be expanded. Responding, the administration announced in January 1998 that it was seeking an $86 million increase in financing for the EEOC, the fair housing program in HUD, the civil rights division of Justice, and other agencies that investigate complaints of bias—the largest single spending request to enforce civil rights laws in nearly two decades.[138] A spending bill approved by the House and Senate in the immediate aftermath, however, fell substantially short of the administration's request. As a result, civil rights organizations, including the NAACP, the National Organization for Women, the National Council of La Raza, and the American Association of Retired Persons, criticized Congress's unwillingness to appropriate adequate funding for civil rights enforcement as hypocritical, since many Republican lawmakers who opposed affirmative action said what was needed was vigorous enforcement of civil rights laws rather than the extension of "preferences" to minorities and women.[139] Aided by the pressure groups, in successive budget proposals the administration sought still higher levels of spending on civil rights enforcement, and money specifically targeting racial discrimination increased by more than 15 percent during the Clinton years.

Other White House initiatives in response to the board's recommendations included requests for funding of a comprehensive action plan to promote educational achievement of Latino students, development of new approaches to address racial and ethnic health needs, new grants to help Native American tribal governments, and higher Small Business Administration goals for African American, Latino, and other disadvantaged small businesses. The president also requested $10 million to gather new kinds of data on racial discrimination, including anecdotal accounts, in order to create a kind of annual discrimination index. In February 1999 the president opened a White House office on race

138. The president's 2000 budget proposed still more funding for civil rights enforcement; $312 million for the EEOC, for instance, 12% more than in 1999, and $47 million for HUD's Fair Housing initiatives, $7 million more than in 1999.

139. Steven A. Holmes, "Federal Anti-Bias Spending Is Inadequate, Groups Say," *New York Times,* Oct. 8, 1998.

relations. (While its announced purpose was to make sure race-related issues found their way onto the president's agenda and to coordinate Cabinet action and policy making, it was substantially less than the kind of permanent presidential council on race modeled along the lines of the president's economic council that the PIR board recommended.) Additional actions included sponsoring seminars within executive branch agencies and including sections on the status of racial minorities in routine government reports, such as the *Economic Report of the President*.[140] Naturally these efforts were decried by conservatives.[141]

Nonetheless, these were fairly modest achievements. For the most part, the dialogue on race never really seemed to take off; never really seemed to break new ground; never seemed enough to shake up the bulk of Americans, complacent about race relations or indifferent to them; never seemed enough to arouse what Martin Luther King had termed "creative tension" in thoughtful people; never seemed enough to challenge the views of even those who were explicitly and openly racist.

Indeed, just months before the race commission's report was issued, several exceptionally warped white Americans issued a report of their own. They picked up a forty-nine-year-old African American man, James Byrd Jr.; took him for a ride in the small town of Jasper, Texas; beat him bloody and senseless, then chained him to the rear bumper of their truck and dragged him to his death, decapitating him in the process. The three white racists arrested in the killing of Byrd had little in common with the students at the University of California, San Diego, where Clinton announced his PIR. Unlike the San Diego graduates that day in June 1997, the three racist killers were prison graduates, poorly educated, and just plain poor. Their crime was as stupid, as hideous, as barbaric as any that occurred in the nation some thirty years earlier, when the Civil Rights Movement flourished. The racists arrested then were often Klansmen. The racists arrested in Jasper had links to neo-Nazi groups and a racist prison gang. Their crime revealed that not only institutional racism but even the most cruel and bigoted acts of racism were not relegated to the past.[142]

Nor was racism rearing its ugly head just in the cowboy culture of the

---

140. See, e.g., *Economic Report of the President* (Washington, D.C.: U.S. Government Printing Office, February 1999), 107–12. According to administration sources, this was the first time this report had contained a separate section on racial minorities.

141. Kiefer, "Why White House Pushes Race Initiative," 2

142. Editorial, *New York Times,* Mar. 19, 1998, A27.

Southwest. In 1999, New York City authorities investigated police who fired forty-one bullets at an unarmed immigrant from West Africa. In Boston, federal officials examined longstanding complaints by blacks and Latinos of racial violence in public housing; and in the suburbs of Chicago the actions of one white bigot affiliated with the white supremacist World Church of the Creator left one African American and one Korean dead and several other racial and religious minorities wounded in July 1999.[143] New Jersey first denied but ultimately admitted that racial profiling thoroughly infused police practices in conducting the drug war. It was hard not to conclude that the PIR had barely dented either institutional or individual racism

Finally, the Gallup polls showed that the president's call for dialogue had no discernible effect on citizens' opinions. In January 1997 racism was not a major public concern—only 4 percent of all responses to a survey question about the nation's most important problem dealt with racism and race relations. That percentage remained statistically constant in the ensuing Clinton years. In April 1998, 2 percent cited racism and race relations as the "most important problem facing this country today," and in June 2000, this figure stood unchanged despite the work of the PIR.

Nor did the president ever take to the bully pulpit on matters of race in the aftermath of the PIR. Although he had promised to redeem the PIR by writing a substantial book on race, that project too soon became mired in delay and White House disputes between New Democrats and traditional ones, making it increasingly unlikely that the overall initiative would ever produce the bold conclusions and proposals Clinton once promised. By the time Chris Edley, chosen as the ghost writer for the task of writing Clinton's book, reportedly left in frustration in the early summer of 1999, it appeared that Clinton's hopes of leaving a legacy of producing courageous means of improving race relations in America had been torpedoed.[144] Ultimately, the president left office without his promised treatise on race ever seeing the light of day and having failed to make racial discrimination a high-profile issue.

Assessing Clinton's Impact on White Skin Privilege

Throughout his years as president, William Jefferson Clinton was enthusiastically received at black meetings and conventions, whether they were civil rights

143. AP and Reuters news services, "White Supremacist Calls Dead Suspect a 'Martyr,'" July 5, 1999.

144. Charles Babington, "Like Commission, Clinton's Book on Race Languishes," *Washington Post,* June 20, 1999, A2.

organizations, minority media associations, the Congressional Black Caucus, or commencement addresses at HBCUs. Indeed, it became practically anathema to criticize Clinton for anything among blacks. Poll data corroborated Clinton's strong support. Around the time Clinton announced his PIR, huge majorities of blacks reported Clinton had made "substantial progress" in dealing with race relations (71 percent of blacks, only 38 percent of whites), and 71 percent of blacks but only 43 percent of whites thought he would "do so in the future."[145] His job approval rating was exceptionally high among blacks throughout his eight years in office, and highest of all during his darkest moment of political and legal peril: the impeachment crisis (hovering around 86 percent before impeachment in 1997, rising to 92 percent during the impeachment battle, and settling at 89 percent in mid-December 2000).[146]

Other polls show that support for the president was not simply a result of supporting the lesser of two evils. According to a late 1998 poll by the Joint Center for Political and Economic Studies, more blacks felt "favorable" toward Clinton (89 percent) than toward Jesse Jackson (78 percent) and Colin Powell (76 percent). Apparently a large segment of black leaders and masses agreed with Cheryl Miller, the first woman and only black attorney to address the Senate at the trial for removal of the president. Miller proclaimed: "I'm not worried about civil rights, because this president's record on civil rights, on women's rights, on all of our rights is unimpeachable."[147]

There are, however, less sanguine ways to read the evidence on Clinton's commitment to civil rights. His appointment of a record number of blacks to his administration and the federal courts need not necessarily indicate that he was acting fearlessly on behalf of blacks—rather just rewarding them for their heavy support of him in 1992 and 1996, as presidents do any other vigorously supportive group making demands on the administration. Moreover, to give the president so much credit for appointing moderate blacks such as Ron Brown, Mike Espy, Hazel O'Leary, and Franklin Raines is to ignore how quickly he abandoned Lani Guinier, Joycelyn Elders, and ultimately even Mike Espy when the right vigorously attacked them.[148] Arguably, it was blacks' own

145. *Washington Post*/ABC News survey of 1,137 randomly selected adults interviewed by phone June 5–8, 1997.

146. Gallup Polls, Gallup News Service, Princeton.

147. Peter Baker, "Clinton Defense Blasts Evidence as Distorted," *Washington Post,* Jan. 21, 1999. A1.

148. The view that Clinton's appointments in general were good for black America prevailed even in the face of opposition to some of them by other liberal groups. For discussion,

collective action that accounted for the political benefits they received through the appointment process.[149]

Similarly, there is little evidence that white advantage actually declined significantly during the Clinton years. A host of social indicators reveal that the racial gap barely narrowed. Take the white/black ratio of median weekly earnings of adult full-time workers (Table 6.3). In 1979 the earnings of African American full-time, year-round workers were 80 percent of those of compara-

Table 6.3.   Black/white ratios—poverty status, earnings, and unemployment, 1976–2001

Year	Poverty status[1]	Earnings[2]	Unemployment rate
2001	2.91	0.79	2.07
2000	3.04	0.74	2.17
1999	3.06	0.81	2.16
1998	3.18	0.78	2.28
1997	3.08	0.77	2.38
1996	3.30	0.77	2.23
1995	3.45	0.78	2.12
1994	3.26	0.77	2.17
1993	3.34	0.78	2.13
1992	3.48	0.78	2.15
1991	3.48	0.79	2.05
1990	3.63	0.78	2.38
1989	3.70	0.78	2.53
1988	3.73	0.78	2.49
1987	3.72	0.80	2.45
1986	3.31	0.79	2.42
1985	3.23	0.78	2.44
1984	3.38	0.80	2.45
1983	3.31	0.82	2.32
1982	3.36	0.79	2.20
1981	3.60	0.81	2.33
1980	3.57	0.79	2.27
1979	3.83	0.80	2.41

[1]White, not Latino, used in computation of ratios.
[2]Median usual weekly earnings of full-time wage and salary workers 16 years and older, annual averages.

SOURCE: Poverty data from U.S. Department of Commerce, Bureau of the Census, March *Current Population Surveys*, "Historical Poverty Tables—People," http:www.census.gov/hhes/poverty/ hiistpov/hstpov2 .html; earnings data from unpublished tabulations from the *Current Population Surveys*, U.S. Department of Labor, Bureau of Labor Statistics; and data on unemployment from Bureau of Labor Statistics, *Current Population Surveys*, http://www.bls.gov.data.

---

see Thomas B. Edsall, "Liberal Groups Denounce Clinton Nomination to West Coast Appeals Court," *Washington Post*, Feb. 1, 1999, A19.

149. Kennedy, "Is He a Soul Man?" 28.

ble whites; in 2001 they were 79 percent. Indeed, data on the racial earnings gap did not even improve over those of the Reagan-Bush years.[150]

While the poverty gap diminished significantly, the median income of families by race and Hispanic origin of householders shows a pattern similar to that of earnings data. In 1976, black family median income was 58.4 percent that of white family median income; in 2001 the figure was 58.6 percent. Meanwhile, the median income of Latino families relative to white ones showed a more ominous drop. In 1976 Latino family median income was 64.8 percent that of white family median income; in 2001 the figure was only 60.2 percent. (It should be noted, however, that both blacks and Latinos made modest relative improvements in the Clinton years compared to the Reagan and Bush years; in short, they nearly returned to where they had been in the Carter years.)[151]

Finally, despite the fast pace of job growth and the rapidly declining unemployment rate, the pattern (around since World War II) for black unemployment to be at least twice that of whites, no matter how strong a recovery or how deep a recession, remained intact, as Table 6.3 shows. Black unemployment was twice that of whites in 1976; it rose to a high of 2.53 times that of whites during the Bush years (1989) and was 2.28 times that of whites in 1998. Latino unemployment was 1.64 times that of whites in 1976, rising to 1.78 times that of whites in 1989, and continued to rise to 1.85 times that of whites in 1998.

These data for the most part imply that blacks and Latinos were not making substantial progress in closing the racial socioeconomic gap during the Clinton years, in what were presumably good times for all. While improvements in absolute standards of living likely contributed to black support for the president, the question that loomed like a gloomy cloud was what would happen when the good times no longer rolled. In sum, there are little hard data to support the conclusion of many blacks that Clinton improved race relations, altered racial economic inequality, or reduced the privileges of whiteness in any fundamental way. Even socioeconomic indicators that have shown a decline in

150. Since women were gaining in relation to men in this period, however, black women's earnings actually improved in relation to white men's (56.7% in 1979 but 65.7% in 1998) and to black men's (74.4% in 1979, 85.5% in 1998).

151. U.S. Department of Commerce, Bureau of the Census, March Current Population Surveys, "Historical Income Tables—Families."

the racial gap have done so only in comparison with the Reagan-Bush years— improvements just returned racial minorities to their relative positions during the Carter years.

Nor is it clear why so many blacks seemingly accepted the president's assertion that his commitment to racial equality not only needed no defense but was in fact "nonnegotiable." Even if whites (including perhaps the president) bought Clinton's routine on race, African Americans had grounds for questioning it. It is not at all certain that had strong tensions developed between what was politically good for Clinton and what was good for racial minorities, Clinton could be reasonably counted on to support the interests of racial minorities. His failure to support the racial justice act, his shelving of the nominations of controversial black nominees, his ditching of black appointees who faced orchestrated opposition from the right, his signing of the welfare reform and crime bills—all demonstrated an aversion to risking political capital when it came to a fight for policies that would benefit African Americans.

Of course, some may argue that this is just what Clinton did when he supported "mend, not end" affirmative action, but the Supreme Court in *Adarand* had already enunciated just such a policy. Had the president actually been willing to risk considerable political capital in a fight for affirmative action, he would have been more helpful in fighting its opponents in California, Washington, Houston, and beyond. Clinton's rhetorical support for affirmative action, in the context of a record free of any episode of risking considerable political capital on its behalf, should be seen for what it was: recognition of the fact that he had more to lose than gain from outright abandonment of the policy. Such a reversal was likely to bring charges of "playing politics" and alienate black and women Democrats for whom affirmative action was important without garnering the support of people and groups who bitterly opposed the policy. Moreover, Clinton, like the Republicans, understood that the federal courts were the sites of the main action on affirmative action. Hiding behind judicial rulings that were already restricting affirmative action substantially, the president could express his commitment with much less threat of having to pay political costs. It is more than merely plausible that Clinton's limited support for affirmative action was more a consequence of politics than opposition to the privileges of whiteness.[152]

152. Kennedy, "Is He a Soul Man?" 28–29: "There were . . . opportunities for Clinton to show 'special' concern for blacks by taking a real gamble on their behalf. For instance, one of the most outrageous (albeit neglected) stories of judicial policies today is the way in which Jesse Helms and a few other reactionary politicians in the Carolinas have stymied any appointment

In sum, the question that virtually asserts itself is: Where are the instances in which Clinton with a lot at stake rallied to the side of racial minorities and fundamentally attacked white skin privilege—even rhetorically? George Stephanopoulos not only hints that such instances are totally absent from the Clinton record, but infers that much in that record indicates a willingness to make accommodations with gutter supporters of white privilege. He identifies Dick Morris as a case in point. Stephanopoulos points out that Morris had worked in Republican campaigns that had been roundly criticized for their racist overtones, including the infamous "white hands" ad of Jesse Helms, in which Helms's black opponent, Harvey Gantt, was accused of supporting quotas for racial minorities. For another southern Republican candidate Morris had developed a radio ad that defended the symbols of the Confederacy to the tune of "Dixie." In addition, according to Stephanopoulos, Morris claimed to have written the Willie Horton ad that helped George Bush in 1988 (although he said Roger Ailes took credit for it). When Stephanopoulos asked Morris what Clinton knew about the Helms ad, Morris claimed, "Clinton knew all about it. I was talking to him through the whole campaign about how great we were doing with this issue." At the least, Stephanopoulos concludes, Clinton could be accused of "the sin of association" with racists.[153]

The record reveals that Clinton, instead of being a vigilant fighter for civil rights—prepared to foster fundamental change against the status quo even if it took stubbornness to profoundly alter the political landscape (much as Reagan did in the opposite direction)—chose a different course. As William Greider concludes, he "made common cause with selected power blocs— congressional barons of the Democratic Party and major corporate-financial interests normally aligned with Republicans as well as those right-of-center southern Democrats who are traditionally pro-visionists," antilabor, and conservatives on race. "The strategy assumed that once Clinton had satisfied their particular needs, these forces would help him to prevail on crucial reform issues.

---

of distinguished progressive justices to the Fourth Circuit Court of Appeals—a pathetic state of affairs which has meant that no black has ever sat on the federal appeals bench that oversees the federal trial courts in Maryland, Virginia, West Virginia, North Carolina, and South Carolina. It would require a sizeable political investment for the President to attempt seriously to shake Helms's disgraceful stranglehold. The effort might ultimately fail. But even what may seem initially to be a losing effort—and sometimes such efforts surprisingly prevail, as Clinton the student of the civil rights movement should know—at least has the benefit of placing a marker proving beyond a doubt a person's bona fide commitment to the aims he espouses. Clinton can boast no such markers."

153. Stephanopoulos, *All Too Human*, 399–400.

Instead they ate his lunch." Greider further observed that although Clinton made his cabinet "look more like America," he also filled the fiscal areas of his government with Wall Street Democrats, who, "not surprisingly, defined *new Democrat* in their own terms." Consequently, Greider concludes, Clinton's basic economic policy, "despite the partisan bombast from Republicans," was actually not very different from Bush's.[154]

In effect, as Margaret Weir concludes, Clinton ultimately moved to the center of "a political spectrum that had itself been pushed sharply to the right by the congressional Republicans. As the President moved right, he pulled a substantial bloc of congressional Democrats with him on most major issues."[155] In the end, Clinton was a man who had stolen the popular-sounding parts of the Republican agenda, signed them into law, and won. The fact that he sometimes angered part of his base was more a bonus than a problem. The fact that it sometimes contradicted Clinton's past positions and professed beliefs was barely relevant.[156] In sum, without an economic crisis such as occurred in the 1930s, or a political legitimacy crisis spurred by a disruptive mass movement such as occurred in the 1960s, Bill Clinton, a centrist in a long line of centrist Democrats, was pushed to the right, leaving conservative reforms in place.[157]

Yet it is not much of a paradox that blacks so heavily supported Clinton. Few American presidents had sought to demonstrate even sympathy for the plight of the nation's people of color. After the Civil War, Andrew Johnson amply demonstrated his commitment to protecting the privileges of whiteness; FDR, during the New Deal, refused to take on even the semblance of racial justice, whether in his social policies or in the explicit politics of civil rights. After the brief interlude of the civil rights era in the 1950s and 1960s, so too did other presidents. The Reagan and Bush administrations returned to an outright attack on civil rights. That blacks would be so loyal to Bill Clinton is more an expression of the large wounds they suffered historically in presidential administrations, but especially of the fresh wounds left by the Reagan-Bush years. For of all the potential explanations of blacks' commitment to Clinton,

154. William Greider, "Unfinished Business: Clinton at Midterm," *Nation,* Oct. 24, 1994, 8–10.

155. Weir, *Social Divide,* 506.

156. Stephanopoulos, *All too Human,* 336.

157. Gertrude Schaffner Goldberg aid Sheila D. Collins, *Washington's New Poor Law: Welfare Reform and the Roads Not Taken, 1935 to the Present* (New York: Apex, 2001), 90.

the most basic one is that his administration was preceded by those of Reagan and Bush. In the minds of many blacks, they did not have the luxury of turning their backs on a president who at least neither frontally attacked them nor excluded them from the improving economic conditions of his time.

The pronouncements, policies, and actions of Speaker of the House Newt Gingrich and other conservative congressional Republicans kept this understanding alive. Whenever Gingrich said of affirmative action, "Get rid of it," Clinton looked better and better.[158] Whenever the likes of governors such as Mississippi's Kirk Fordice, such congressmen as Tom DeLay and Bob Barr, and such senators as Trent Lott—all white southern Republicans who are the late twentieth-century ideological heirs of the open white supremacists who have always been the nemesis of progress in race relations[159]—took to the floor of Congress or gave interviews to the news media to harangue on and on about the sins of Bill Clinton, African Americans were simply more clear about which side they were on. "The enemy of mine enemy is my friend" was a meaningful proverb for many African Americans in the 1990s.[160]

Yet, despite the clear rationality of such a response in the political climate of the closing years of the twentieth century, it is an indication of the electoral box and outsider status in which blacks remain. Thanks to twelve years of Republican administrations that openly attacked their rights and a Republican-controlled Congress that continued to do so, African Americans have come to expect so little from the political establishment that many were overwhelmed by gratitude for a president who simply treated them as part of the American

158. Ibid.

159. During the Senate removal trial, information surfaced in the news media that Trent Lott had endorsed and asked for the support of the controversial Council of Conservative Citizens (CCC) in 1992. "The CCC, which has strong ties to the old white Citizens Councils, is considered racist by many conservatives and liberals alike. Many of the most prominent figures in the organization are proponents of preserving the white race and culture, which they see as under assault by immigration, intermarriage and growing numbers of Hispanic Americans." According to Alan Dershowitz, Harvard law professor, Rep. Robert L. Barr Jr. (R-Ga.) also spoke to a CCC meeting in Charleston, S.C., in 1992. Jared Taylor, a leader of the CCC in the Washington area, publisher of the magazine *American Renaissance,* and author of a book attacking affirmative action, wrote an essay appearing on the magazine's Web site in which he maintained: "It is certainly true that in some important traits—intelligence, law-abidingness, sexual restraint, academic performance, resistance to disease—whites can be considered 'superior' to blacks." See fuller discussion in Thomas B. Edsall, "Lott Renounces White 'Racialist' Group He Praised in 1992," *Washington Post,* Dec. 16, 1998, A2.

160. Kennedy, "Is He a Soul Man?" 27.

political community. Such gratitude became an expression not only of the lack of electoral choice but the psychological neediness of African Americans at the dawn of a new millennium.[161]

Finally, all people live not only in the sphere of relative progress but perhaps more in the sphere of absolute progress. While people of color made few substantial gains relative to whites, they did make some important progress in absolute terms. When people of color were not excluded from an economy that was "lifting all boats," black and Latino unemployment rates were cut; they shared in the fastest real-wage growth in more than two decades; the EITC and the hike in the minimum wage lifted many out of poverty; and expansion of aid for higher education allowed more to attend college.[162]

In sum, there can be no gainsaying the fact that in absolute terms, the standards of living and other life chances of racial minorities improved during the Clinton years. Poll data confirm that African Americans perceived substantial economic progress. In late 1998, a JCPES poll found that for the first time since they began conducting annual surveys in 1984, African Americans were substantially more likely than whites to report that they were "better off financially" than in the previous year (51 percent of blacks compared with 31.5 percent of whites).[163] For many African Americans, long disabused of the idea that they would ever overcome white privilege, this was as good as it gets.

Conclusion

In 1992 Clinton promised to turn back a dozen years of the politics of racial division.[164] By the time he left office, he had played a little racial politics of his own. By linking a get-tough approach to the racially charged issues of welfare, crime, immigration, and "quotas," the president reduced his vulnerability to the accusations of liberal fundamentalism that had plagued his party for decades. By engaging in the politics of symbolism (particularly appointment poli-

161. Ibid., 28.

162. See CPA and Lifetime Television *Women's Voices* poll, August 2000, Center for Policy Alternatives, Washington, D.C.

163. Nearly two out of five (37%) of respondents in a survey conducted for *Newsweek* in the spring of 1999 gave "a lot" of credit to Clinton administration policies for improving conditions for black Americans but more credited the black church (46%) and black self-help (41%).

164. At the time, Dale Charles, president of the Little Rock chapter of the NAACP, summarized Clinton's record on civil rights as "all style and rhetoric and no substance": Terry Seper, "NAACP Says Clinton Is in Racist Club," *Washington Times*, Mar. 19, 1992, A4.

tics and the PIR), he appeased racial minorities, especially blacks. Both efforts were buttressed by a raging economy that made nearly any actions and behaviors of the president palatable to many blacks in the aftermath of the Bush-Reagan policies and symbolism regarding race.

What was perhaps most striking was that although Clinton's civil right policies continued to be decried by conservatives for political reasons, in actuality there were no important new civil rights policies or laws in the Clinton years. This was a record that even Reagan and Bush did not produce. Albeit forced by Congress to do so, Reagan signed into law the Martin Luther King holiday bill and the reauthorization of the Voting Rights Act. Bush signed into law the Americans with Disabilities Act and the Civil Rights Act of 1991. Bill Clinton's signature graced no new civil rights legislation. Instead symbolism over substance was more than ever the name of the game in the Clinton years.

For Clinton to have performed differently and substantially altered the terrain of social policy and the politics of race would have been difficult in both the circumstances of the 1990s and the historical context of American social policy. The long arm of Andrew Johnson, the racial segmentation of the American social policy regime codified into law during the New Deal, and the development of the Great Society within the New Deal system rather than a transformation of it, when added to the conservative mood of the country that undergirded Reagan-Bush and in which the two administrations sought to expand their appeal—all constrained the Clinton administration.

To be sure, after the harsh conservatism of the Reagan-Bush years, at first it seemed that Clinton just might be willing to act for change, to set both the country and his party on a new course. Yet soon after he took office, the failure of his economic stimulus package, his defeat on health care reform, and his ready acquiescence in conservative demands in crime legislation, NAFTA, GATT, and other economic policies—as well as his withdrawal of support for nominees the right opposed—demonstrated that Clinton either was never really serious or at least could be had.

When Republicans took control of both houses of Congress in 1994, the die was cast. Any reorientation of social policy that took place in the new political context would move rightward, and the partisan politics of race would change only in the sense that not just Republicans but also Democrats now openly embraced a politics that blamed people of color for their own problems and exploited long-term racial/ethnic hostilities and drove up racial fears. Signing a very conservative welfare reform bill, whose preface was laden with racial innuendoes, confirmed this probability.

By the time the Lewinsky scandal turned into an impeachment crisis, the Clinton presidency was virtually finished as a period of policy innovation. As one woman leader put it, Clinton had squandered his all too limited and precious political capital because he "couldn't keep it in his pants."[165] Yet, while presidential missteps are an important part of the narrative of Clinton's failure to reorient the relationship of markets, government, and society and produce a new generation of more equitable social policy and racial justice, legacies from the past combined with economic problems of the present weighed more heavily in explaining the turbulent terrain that doomed the administration's hopes.

The market-based approaches that have structured the American welfare state from its infancy; the pervasive ethos of white skin privilege; the limited American conception of social rights for any group; the tripartite segmentation embodied in the welfare state; a global and technological revolution that generated more bad than good jobs and left many Americans feeling insecure and left behind; budgetary politics in an atmosphere devoted to controlling deficit spending; and the complexities of constructing a coalition in both the electorate and government that could simultaneously differentiate the Democrats from the Republicans, avoid alienating corporate America, and satisfy the president's base among both traditional and New Democrats—all constrained Clinton's opportunities. Given these obstacles, it would perhaps have been unreasonable to expect Clinton either to completely reorient social policy or substantially to improve race relations in eight years. What Clinton could have been expected to accomplish, however, is the development of a clear and consistent message that demystified Republican attempts to scapegoat blacks, the poor, and immigrants and demonstrated to the American people that he understood that white skin privilege still raged in America. But Clinton let pass almost every opportunity to clarify what was really at stake in the reform of social policy—whether welfare reform, civil rights, or improving the living standards of ordinary workers. Instead the president's promise to *balance* responsibilities with rights shifted mightily in ways that ultimately placed considerably more emphasis on responsibility *over* rights for the poor and racially disadvantaged. The 1996 welfare

165. Telephone conversation with Debra Dodson, Center on American Women in Politics, Rutgers University, Jan. 17, 1999.

act exposed women and children in particular to new insecurities by removing the federal guarantee of assistance to families without work. Although Congress appropriated some money for job creation a year after the PRWORA passed, the amounts were enough to provide work opportunities for only a small portion of the million persons ultimately expected to be pushed into the labor market. George W. Bush's tax cuts for the rich, the plunge of the stock market, the return to deficit spending, persistent unemployment, and the crisis of confidence in American corporations threaten to worsen the plight of those who no longer have either a partial guarantee of income support in place or assurance of jobs.

To some it may have seemed ironic that people of color, especially blacks, would give such strong support to a president who restrained the growth of spending on social programs, ended the federal guarantee of a modicum of income security for the nonworking poor, placed new restrictions on both immigration and minority set-aside contracting, supported international trade agreements as unpopular among blacks as they were among organized labor, and engaged in other actions that signaled a shift toward a more conservative, business-oriented philosophy within the Democratic Party. However, to assume that such considerations should have kept African Americans and Latinos at arm's length from Clinton is to presume choices that did not exist in the late 1990s. Legacies of social policy decisions stretching as far back as Reconstruction and segmentation that put people of color and many white women into isolated and unpopular (largely because of the precise constituencies they served) programs during the New Deal not only shaped views of "undeservingness" among privileged whites but also encouraged a reflection of this view among people of color.

Moreover, in the 1990s the Republican Party remained not only patently unwilling to make any fundamental racial commitments that might have changed black voting patterns, but stepped up its campaign against immigrants, vigorously pushing to strip legal immigrants of a host of benefits and making legal entry into the country more difficult. In this setting, it is not surprising that prospects for progressive change were doomed. Thus, with an economy so strong that a plurality of all groups perceived new opportunities and in light of the available options and the social policies and presidential administration that had gone before, the black and Latino embrace of Bill Clinton stood not in contravention of the best interests of their groups, but as a

seven
Whose Welfare System Is It Anyway?
The Three Tracks of Social Citizenship and Racial Inequality

The equation of freedom with citizenship has some very distinctive results in the

republican tradition. Citizenship, like any social status, naturally involves aware-

ness: it means that the citizen, and those with whom she deals, are aware of her

standing, and it means that this awareness is itself a matter of common recognition.

But if citizenship or freedom involves this sort of awareness, then it also means

being able to live without fear or deference; freedom connotes frankness, where

"frankness" is etymologically related to "franchise."

—Philip Pettit

Like a growing number of democratic theorists,[1] Philip Pettit suggests that democratic liberty requires not only simple procedural rights but also what T. H. Marshall called "the social rights of citizenship"—that is, access to public social provision for all of society's members.[2] Thus citizenship is defined not only by law but also by common culturally specific understandings and practices. As Pettit goes on to explain, one common understanding in the republican tradition is that freedom is the opposite of slavery; it involves not being subjected to the will of another, or not being vulnerable. To not be vulnerable, it is necessary not only to eliminate one's subject status but also to be "protected with the best."[3]

1. See also Douglass Rae, "Democratic Liberty and the Tyrannies of Place," in Ian Shapiro and Casiano Hacker-Cordon, eds., *Democracy's Edges* (New York: Cambridge University Press, 1999), and David Johnson, *The Idea of a Liberal Theory* (Princeton: Princeton University Press, 1994).

2. T. H. Marshall, "Citizenship and Social Class," in his *Class, Citizenship, and Social Development: Essays* (Garden City, N.Y.: Doubleday, 1964).

3. Philip Pettit, *The Common Mind: An Essay on Psychology, Society, and Politics* (New York: Oxford University Press, 1993), 415.

African Americans and other people of color have never been "protected with the best." When the Civil War resulted in their putative freedom, most African Americans benefited only from the stingy rations delivered by the short-lived Freedmen's Bureau while benefits from the much more generous and long-lived Civil War veterans' pensions went disproportionately to white males and their widows. Even in the prehistory of the American welfare state proper, preexisting differences in the conceptions of whiteness and blackness meant that two tracks developed for those receiving public assistance.

During the New Deal, when the Social Security Act was passed, a racialized (and gendered) system of stratification resulted. The superior programs disproportionately aided whites and males and they were designed to do so, because that was the dominant image of citizenship in 1935. Old-age insurance, unemployment insurance, and workmen's compensation excluded precisely the kinds of jobs that people of color and women were most likely to have—in small enterprises and agriculture, for low wages, part-time, seasonal, and "casual." Both these exclusions and the defeat of federal standards for "relief" were directed particularly at racial minority workers of both sexes.

In the mid-1940s, when the hidden welfare state was established on a firm footing, women and minority men disproportionately remained excluded. Small and nonunion firms were less likely to offer benefits and people of color and white women were more likely to work for such firms. Firms that offered pensions were not required to offer them to workers with fewer than three years of tenure or to part-time workers, again categories in which people of color and white women were more likely to fall. These same factors (tenure and part-time status) also meant that women and people of color were more likely to fall below the legally mandated minimums for health insurance coverage. Meanwhile, the profoundly disproportionate relegation of people of color to the nonunionized competitive sector (personal services, agriculture, and businesses that pay the lowest wages) in the first place versus the employment of more organized and powerful—and white—workers in the unionized monopoly sector is itself in good part a result of institutionalized racism in the demand for labor. Thus accumulated white skin privilege helps explain why the hidden welfare state, delivered via tax expenditures, loans, and loan guarantees, went proportionally less to the poor and more to the nonpoor, less to blacks and more to whites, and less to women and more to men. Powerful lobbying groups did not simply just win government largesse in the 1940s and 1950s but also succeeded in getting it delivered in ways that camouflaged the state's involvement and disguised the relatively affluent's status as key beneficiaries of public aid. By contrast, direct expenditures on social welfare were both prominent and visible.

Concomitantly, although blacks gained less than whites and women gained less than men from the pre-1960s American welfare state, these groups became stereotyped as chief "recipients" and economic dependents. Those women of subordinated race and class bore the brunt of pejorative stereotypes. They, in particular, were adjudged "undeserving" and parasitic even though at both federal and state levels, most governmental direct and tax expenditures went to relatively privileged whites.

In the midst of prosperity and a vigorous Civil Rights Movement, the Great Society of the 1960s sought to make a substantial dent in the exclusion of people of color from the nation's welfare state. From new manpower training programs directed at people of color to a substantial expansion of relief, the Great Society targeted African Americans in particular for inclusion. More generally, the Great Society sought to reduce inequality by fixing two main problems in the Social Security Act—the creation of public jobs (albeit the commitment here did not go very far) and medical insurance. Certainly, the American welfare state in the 1960s and early 1970s redistributed more resources to the poor, especially poor racial minorities, than ever before in America. Yet the gains "welfare" offered poor minorities were undercut by the reverse redistributive effects of the good, "nonwelfare" programs. Benefits to middle-class and upper-working-class men and their dependents were greater, absolutely and proportionately, than contributions to the poor. Throughout the 1960s and 1970s, the good social insurance programs got steadily better. "OAI benefits were increased, protected against inflation, and extended to more beneficiaries, especially dependents. By contrast, the real value of public assistance programs fell, and in the 1970s eligibility criteria began to exclude proportionately more of the poor."[4] By 1980, 80 percent of the nation's social welfare budget (counting direct spending alone) went to the nonpoor.[5]

---

4. Michael R. Sosin, "Legal Rights and Welfare Change," in Sheldon Danziger, Robert Haveman, and Robert Plotnick, eds., *Fighting Poverty: What Works and What Doesn't* (Cambridge: Harvard University Press, 1986), 276.

5. Sheldon Danziger, Robert Haveman, and Robert Plotnick, "Antipoverty Policy: Effects on the Poor and the Nonpoor," in Danziger et al, *Fighting Poverty*, 66–67; and Marcus D.

To be sure, there were many reasons that direct spending on welfare came under attack, but central among these was the stereotype of the "typical" beneficiary. In the 1980s, while all Americans paid taxes (even those without income pay sales taxes and higher prices to compensate business for its taxes), believing they were overtaxed to pay benefits for a colored other, affluent white Americans became especially hostile toward rising taxes. In this context, the conservative attack on the welfare state convinced many whites that the conflict was between those who want to increase and those who want to reduce government aid. Actually, a better debating point would have been how government aid was distributed—for even as the real value of public assistance fell, the call to eliminate "welfare" grew louder.

It was no coincidence that support for eliminating welfare was linked to white attitudes toward blacks. As empirical studies demonstrate, white views of blacks as lazy or dependent figured prominently in their hostility toward "welfare." Despite passage of a weak welfare reform bill (the Family Support Act of 1988), however, welfare rolls continued to climb throughout the Reagan and Bush administrations.

Ironically, it was a candidate heavily supported by blacks, Latinos, and lower-income and poor Americans who dealt the most prominent public assistance program, AFDC, a fatal blow. As the sixty-year entitlement program was terminated, legislation put in place a new system, TANF, with severe sanctions. After literally millions of families exited welfare rolls, those left behind were disproportionately brown and black. Social citizenship for these groups by the end of the 1990s was weaker than at any time since the mid-1930s.

In sum, race has been a powerful determinant of the nation's welfare state from its very beginnings. American social policy did not create inequality in social citizenship but solidified it. American social policy actively contributed to civil, political, and social inequities, exclusions from "the edifice of citizenship."[6] Today social insurance and hidden welfare appear as rights and deserved benefits that increase a citizen's awareness, self-esteem, and feeling of entitlement. Public assistance beneficiaries are daily told they are freeloaders. Symbolically and practically, the insurance programs and hidden welfare tax

Pohlman, "Profits, Welfare, and Class Position: 1965–1984," *Journal of Sociology and Social Welfare* 15, no. 3 (September 1988): 3–28.

6. Michael Walzer, "Exclusion, Injustice, and the Democratic State," *Dissent,* Winter 1993, 55–64.

expenditures extend the meaning of first-class American citizenship to include an economic shield against impoverishment, creating social citizenship alongside civil and political citizenship.[7] By contrast, the third track of American welfare, public assistance programs, embodies a lack of national social citizenship, underlined by sending the poor to the states to get help and forcing the near-poor to become impoverished and humiliated before help is forthcoming. Public assistance constructs despair through lack of opportunity—the determining condition of the alleged underclass.

As a result, most people of color, especially blacks, have never found freedom as Pettit defines it. Instead white skin privilege characterized two tracks of the American welfare state (social insurance and hidden welfare), providing whites a powerful feeling of entitlement—even while people of color remained disproportionately trapped in the inferior third track and were stigmatized as undeserving. This result was not an accidental artifact of an expanding and therefore complex welfare state, but the product of political and ideological conflict in which the "facts" are always constructed by contestation. This is why one cannot understand the attack on programs dubbed "welfare" without considering the larger context of a welfare state and all its recipients.

Who Gets What in the American Welfare State Today?

Are there still different tracks of social citizenship? And if so, what are the political and economic implications?

Table 7.1, based on data from the Census Bureau, demonstrates that as late as 2001 (the most recent year for which statistics are available at this writing), the good tracks still disproportionately benefited whites. As the table shows, blacks were heavily overrepresented in every category of social welfare, rising from being 2.4 times more likely to be beneficiaries of the Women, Infants, and Children's (WIC) program than the black proportion of the population would predict to 3.2 times more likely to be represented among beneficiaries of poor housing, for instance. In short, even descriptive statistics show that there is a strong association between race and the likelihood of receiving means-tested assistance such as TANF, Supplemental Security Income, and food stamps.

---

7. Linda Gordon, *Pitied but Not Entitled: Single Mothers and the History of Welfare* (New York: Free Press, 1994), 303.

Table 7.1.   Average annual participation in social programs and dollar value of annual benefits received, non-Latino whites and blacks 15 years and over, 2001

General statistic/ program	Number with benefit			Average annual benefit/income		Racial difference[1]
	Total number	Percent white	Percent black	White	Black	
Population	200,814	73.6%	11.1%	$33,049	$24,092	− $8,957
Social Welfare						
Public assistance (TANF, other, both)	2,225	43.3	31.2	3,016	2,888	− 128
SSI	5,002	54.0	26.9	5,013	5,256	243
Food stamps	25,383	61.3	33.3	2,928	3,300	372
Medicaid	29,332	62.9	31.0	NA	NA	NA
Poor housing assistance	12,206	58.7	35.7	1,656	1,668	12
Received free or reduced-price school lunch and/ or breakfast	46,743	64.9	29.4	NA	NA	NA
Received energy assistance	19,071	66.5	28.6	168	156	− 12
Women, Infants & Children coverage	3,846	68.6	26.8	1,560	1,716	156
Social Insurance						
Veterans' payments	2,523	79.3	12.7	9,365	8,446	− 919
Medicare	33,964	89.0	9.0	NA	NA	NA
Unemployment compensation	7,374	71.3	12.7	3,323	3,152	− 171
Worker's compensation	2,135	73.9	12.2	5,475	5,005	− 470
Social Security payments	39,699	82.3	9.4	9,621	8,205	− 1,416
Survivor payments	2,737	87.2	7.7	10,627	6,608	− 4,019
Disability payments	1,583	70.3	16.7	9,675	7,936	− 1,739
Hidden Welfare						
Private health insurance	199,860	76.5	10.2	NA	NA	NA
Private pension plan	11,210	91.8	6.9	13,792	11,874	− 1,918
Mortgages held	2,188	95.5	2.6	4,080	924	− 3,156
Govt. educational assistance	7,798	79.7	14.8	3,703	2,427	− 1,276

[1]Racial difference = black − white income or benefit.

SOURCE: U.S. Bureau of the Census, *Current Population Survey, March 2002* and *Survey of Income and Program Participation, 1996.*

By contrast, blacks are underrepresented in several key social insurance programs. In the most popular social insurance programs (Social Security and Medicare), blacks were only 88 percent and 81 percent respectively as likely to be represented as their share of the relevant population would predict, while whites were overrepresented.

Even as the new century began, Social Security, perhaps the most popular universal policy of all, remained rife with distributional inequalities. In 2001 (according to data on source of income from the Census Bureau's Current Population Survey) 86.9 percent of Latinos sixty-five years old and older and 87.6 percent of African Americans were receiving income from Social Security (compared to 93.6 percent of non-Hispanic whites); and the average Social Security benefit, reflecting the lifetime experience of racial pay differentials, was substantially lower for racial minorities than for non-Latino whites. The mean annual income from Social Security for whites not of Latino origin was $9,621; for blacks, $7,691; and for Latinos, $8.205, or roughly 18 percent less for people of color than for whites.

Moreover, people of color tend to subsidize whites on Social Security, in part because racial minorities have a lower life expectancy than whites. In 1996, the average life expectancy of blacks at age sixty was significantly lower than that of whites. Sixty-year-old white women could expect to live another 23.0 years and white men 19.4 years. By contrast, sixty-year-old black women had a life expectancy of another 20.7 years and black men only 16.7 years.

Furthermore, as Jill Quadagno concludes, African Americans remain disadvantaged also in the share of earnings they pay in Social Security taxes because of "black/white differences in the proportion of wages subject to Social Security taxes."[8] In sum, although people of color on average pay a disproportionate share of taxes on earnings, their low lifetime earnings mean they receive lower benefits.

In part, this distribution of benefits reflects market inequities. Yet there are aspects of the current nature of Social Security that penalize some blacks even when the program bypasses the market in the distribution of benefits. One such aspect is the way women who marry, stay married, and do not work are rewarded. Women who remain married for at least ten years, whether or

---

8. Jill Quadagno, *The Color of Welfare: How Racism Undermined the War on Poverty* (New York: Oxford University Press, 1994), 160–62.

not they have ever worked for wages or salaries, are eligible for a spouse benefit. Although working women pay full payroll taxes, most find that when they retire, the spouse benefit pays more than their own earned benefit, because women earn lower wages than men and have more sporadic work histories. Thus Social Security transfers income from those in the labor force to home-makers.

The subsidy to wives doubly disadvantages black women. Not surpris-ingly, black women receive a relatively small benefit from Social Security. In 1994 the average monthly Social Security benefit of white men was $703; for white women, $536; for black men, $526; but only $454 for black women (that is, 35 percent lower than that of white men and 15 percent or more less than white women and black men). One reason is that black women are far less likely than white women to qualify for a spouse benefit, because fewer have been legally married for ten years. In the 1990s, many more white women aged 45–64 were married compared to black women. In addition, black married women with a spouse in the labor force remained more likely than white women to have paid employment. Hence their Social Security taxes tend to subsidize the spouse benefits of white housewives.[9]

Racial and gender inequalities in social insurance programs, however, are dwarfed by those in hidden welfare. As Table 7.1 indicates, with the exception of government educational assistance (and perhaps the earned income tax credit[10]—data here are unavailable), blacks are dramatically underrepresented in the hidden welfare sector. Regarding private pensions, blacks are only half as likely (54 percent) as their share of the population would predict while whites are overrepresented among private pensioners by 10 percentage points. Indeed, nearly all of the tax expenditures devoted to private pensions and the mortgage interest deduction flowed to whites in 1994. There were also signifi-cant differences in private health insurance coverage, with whites much more likely than blacks to be covered. More than 61 percent of whites were covered by private health insurance, compared to 42 percent of blacks and 39 percent of Latinos.[11]

9. Ibid.

10. The EITC is the only key tax expenditure for the poor—and then only for the working poor. Tax credits and tax deductions for child care and tax incentives to lure employers into inner cities represent more modest tax expenditures targeted toward the working poor.

11. U.S. Bureau of the Census, *Poverty in the United States, 1992,* Current Population Reports, P60–185 (Washington, D.C., 1993), 148ff.

In sum, hidden welfare benefits remain dramatically unequal by race, class, and gender—benefiting whites over blacks, affluent over poor, and men over women. This is partially a result of the nature of the most prominent type of hidden welfare, tax expenditures. Tax expenditures tend to be regressive because high-income households are generally able to spend more on the activities that are subsidized, and the value of the deduction is greatly affected by one's tax bracket. For instance, nearly 90 percent of the mortgage interest deduction went to households earning more than $50,000 in 1995, but while roughly half of white families were in this cohort, only a quarter of black families were.[12]

In addition, some data suggest that even when people of color and women receive hidden welfare benefits, inequality remains virtually constant. Take the impact of employer-provided pensions and health insurance. Differences in benefit status for these two programs increase the gap in total compensation by gender and race.[13] Table 7.2, comparing hourly wages with total compensation, reveals that black men and women are less likely than white men to be covered by employer-sponsored benefits. Although these data must be interpreted in light of the insights provided above for differential coverage (size of firm, tenure, and so forth), they indicate that total hourly compensation (including employers' dollar expenditures on benefits) exceeds wage compensation by $2.54, $0.94, $1.05, and $0.90 for white male, white female, black male, and black female workers, respectively. In effect, racial and gender inequality tends to grow when total compensation is considered.

Further analysis of these data suggests that more than market forces are at work. Observable worker characteristics explain only part of the differences by race and gender in either hourly wages or total compensation; rather a substantial amount of the difference reflects discrimination on the basis of race and gender. The results of probit analysis of these data, which appear in Table 7.3 (see appendix for regression equations), demonstrate that both hourly wage and

12. Joint Committee on Taxation, *Estimates of Federal Tax Expenditures for Fiscal Years 1995–1999*, prepared for the Committee on Ways and Means and the Committee on Finance, Nov. 9, 1994; and U.S. Bureau of the Census, *Money Income in the United States, 1999*, Current Population Reports, P60–209 (Washington, D.C., 2000), text table C.

13. Joni Hersch and Shelley White-Means, "Employer-Sponsored Health and Pension Benefits and the Gender/Race Wage Gap," *Social Science Quarterly* 74, no. 4 (December 1993): 851. I thank Hersch and White-Means for providing a model for analyzing the differential impact of fringe benefits on racial and gender groups.

Table 7.2.   Hourly wage and total compensation[1] by selected average worker characteristics, 1999

	White males	White females	Black males	Black females
Median hourly wage	$15.38	$11.70	$11.70	$10.00
	(6.14)	(4.88)	(4.88)	(4.11)
Median hourly wage + benefits	$17.92	$12.64	$12.75	$10.90
	(6.47)	(5.19)	(5.27)	(4.54)
Tenure with employer (years)	3.9	3.4	3.6	3.4
	(7.73)	(6.34)	(7.01)	(6.74)
Full-time worker	0.87	0.70	0.86	0.77
	(0.21)	(0.40)	(0.29)	(0.39)
Union member	0.16	0.11	0.21	0.15
	(0.39)	(0.22)	(0.40)	(0.36)
Firm size				
Under 25 persons	0.32	0.29	0.22	0.17
	(0.34)	(0.27)	(0.41)	(0.37)
25–99 persons	0.14	0.12	0.13	0.11
	(0.36)	(0.35)	(0.32)	(0.33)
100–499 persons	0.14	0.14	0.15	0.14
	(0.36)	(0.38)	(0.41)	(0.37)
500–999 persons	0.05	0.06	0.06	0.07
	(0.17)	(0.20)	(0.20)	(0.21)
1,000 persons or more	0.36	0.39	0.45	0.51
	(0.49)	(0.50)	(0.54)	(0.48)
Covered by pension	0.47	0.42	0.42	0.40
	(0.50)	(0.46)	(0.46)	(0.47)
Covered by health benefits	0.59	0.48	0.53	0.51
	(0.42)	(0.47)	(0.44)	(0.48)
Sample size	7,286	6,167	481	566

[1]Hourly wages plus employer-sponsored pensions and health insurance. The estimate is derived by adding to each worker's hourly wage the approximate value of benefits available to the worker, based on the worker's industry.

SOURCE: Data on full-time worker status from U.S. Bureau of the Census, *Current Population Survey,* P-60 Series, 2000; data on tenure with employer, firm size, benefits, and union membership from U.S. Chamber of Commerce, Labor and Employee Benefits Division, 2000; data on hourly wages from U.S. Bureau of Labor Statistics, "Real Earnings," 2000; and data on health and pension benefits from U.S. Bureau of Labor Statistics, National Compensation Survey, 2000.

total compensation regression equations are virtually the same. These equations indicate that slightly less than half of the log-earning gap between white and black men is explained by differences in qualifications. Following the trend among economists when faced with inequality not explained by observable dif-

Table 7.3. Percentage of earnings gap attributable to differences in average qualifications, 1999

Earnings measure	White women–white men	Black men–white men	Black women–white men
All workers			
Hourly wage	32.8%	46.8%	20.8%
Hourly wage + benefits	34.3	46.1	20.6
Benefit-sector workers			
Hourly wage	31.5	45.8	20.7
Hourly wage + benefits	33.6	46.1	21.7
Nonbenefit-sector workers			
Hourly wage	44.4	15.0	18.7

SOURCE: Analysis based on data on full-time worker status from U.S. Bureau of the Census, *Current Population Survey*, P-60 Series, 2000; data on tenure with employer, firm size, benefits, and union membership from U.S. Chamber of Commerce Labor and Employee Benefits Division, 2000; data on hourly wages from U.S. Bureau of Labor Statistics, "Real Earnings," 2000; and data on health and pension benefits from the U.S. Bureau of Labor Statistics, National Compensation Survey, 2000.

ferences in qualifications, tenure on the job, geography, and so forth,[14] we may attribute the remaining 54 percent to discrimination. For women, especially black women, the log-wage and log-compensation gaps are explained even less by differences in qualifications, suggesting that discrimination may be a far more important component of the gender-race wage gap. Over 65 percent of the log-earnings gap between white women and white men and about 80 percent of that between black women and white men are unexplained by observable worker characteristics and may be attributable to discrimination. This analysis demonstrates that instead of hidden welfare diminishing inequality, at best the measured gender and racial gaps in earnings of private employees are only slightly affected by basing earnings ratios on total compensation (wages plus pension and health benefits) rather than on wages alone. While fringe benefits in the form of health insurance and pensions have been heralded as equalizers in the employment setting, they have only a small impact at best on gender and race differences in earnings gaps and/or the return on qualifications. Black women, white women, and black men still face a large disadvantage in comparison with white men when fringe benefits are taken into consideration.

Moreover, the effects of fringe benefits are very likely underestimated in

14. Ibid., and William E. Ewen and David A. Macpherson, "The Gender Gap in Pensions and Wages," *Review of Economics and Statistics* 72 (1990): 259–65.

the data presented here, since only a few such benefits are included. A full listing would include paid time off (holidays, vacations, personal leave, funeral leave, jury duty leave, military leave, sick leave, family leave), unpaid family leave, disability benefits (short-term and long-term), insurance (health, dental, vision, life), retirement (defined benefit, defined contribution), savings and theft, deferred profit sharing, employee stock ownership, money purchase pension, tax-deferred savings , income continuation plans (severance pay, supplemental unemployment benefits), family benefits (child care, adoption assistance, long-term care insurance, flexible workplace), health promotion programs (wellness programs, employee assistance programs, fitness centers), and a host of miscellaneous benefits such as job-related travel accident insurance, nonproduction bonuses, substantial commuting, and job- and non-job-related educational assistance.[15]

These benefits—privileging whites more than people of color and the middle class more than the poor—are expensive to the public treasury. According to Christopher Howard, in 1995 the federal government spent $160–200 billion on income security via tax expenditures, making it roughly half the hidden welfare state. Subsidies for homeownership alone cost roughly $90 billion per year—a fact that undercuts the prevailing image of a nation doing too much to subsidize the rental housing of the poor. In the same year that $19 billion in taxes were returned as a result of the EITC, more than $50 billion in taxes were refunded as a result of the mortgage interest deduction. Allowing employers to write off the costs of providing pensions and health insurance for workers constituted a huge subsidy of billions more. One study found that in the mid-1990s, high-income families were subsidized 33 cents for every dollar spent, while working-class families received a subsidy of only 15 cents. The unemployed poor, who paid no income taxes, received no benefits from hidden welfare.[16]

In sum, to a substantial extent, blacks and whites tend to be covered by different tracks of the American welfare state, and concomitantly have a different experience with social citizenship. Several observations summarize the current situation. First, despite differential treatment by track, within each track whites remain privileged in some key programs. For example, in 2001 whites

15. For a more complete listing, see Christopher Howard, *The Hidden Welfare State: Tax Expenditures and Social Policy* (Princeton: Princeton University Press, 1997), 20–23.
16. Ibid., 177.

received on average $128 more a year than blacks in TANF, $1,416 more in Social Security, and $1,918 more in private pensions (Table 7.1).

Second, and more important in the reproduction of racial inequality, whites and people of color remain disproportionately covered by different tracks of the American welfare state. To be sure, many—and indeed a growing number—of each racial group receive benefits from each track, but even as the twentieth century drew to an end, whites had higher participation rates in the good (more generous) tracks (social insurance and hidden welfare programs) and people of color and women had higher participation rates in the bad (more stingy) programs (direct social welfare). Third, far more from the public treasury is devoted to the programs in which whites benefit more heavily. For example, in 1995 social insurance programs (exclusive of Medicare) accounted for 65.3 percent of social spending (or $2,632 per capita) while AFDC and other public assistance accounted for 19.1 percent of social spending (or $714 per capita).[17]

Furthermore, the data presented here in all likelihood paint the picture for people of color rosier than it is. For example, in 1994 African Americans made up 11.4 percent of all those receiving unemployment compensation, but only 22.6 percent of the black unemployed received any unemployment compensation; 77.4 percent of the black unemployed received nothing. By contrast, 38.0 percent of the white unemployed received unemployment compensation.[18] Given factors such as higher poverty rates, deeper poverty, secular decline in the labor force participation rate for young black men, and so forth, these data probably underestimate the true magnitude of exclusion of blacks from income security programs.

Thus, people of color (and many white women) either remain underrepresented or receive lower benefits than white middle- and working-class male wage and salary earners in the social insurance and hidden welfare tracks. Together these two tracks account for most of the welfare state beneficiaries and the bulk of federal expenditures for social policy.

In short, whites have been and continue to be the beneficiaries of the most generous programs of the American welfare state. Preferential treatment

17. *Social Security Bulletin* 60, no. 3 (1997).
18. Calculated from data provided in Martina Shea, *Dynamics of Economic Well-Being: Program Participation, 1990 to 1996*, Current Population Reports, P70–41 (Washington, D.C., 1999), and unemployment statistics from *Historical Data Series*, <http://www.bls.gov>.

for whites is so successfully institutionalized in American social policy that most people of all races are unaware of it.[19] The programs that disproportionately serve people of color have a shorter history and provide lower benefits than the "universal" programs that disproportionately serve middle-class whites. Thus, in contrast to the stereotype, blacks as a group have received the least benefits for the shortest time. Even today blacks are underrepresented in the programs that pay higher benefits; and within programs, they tend to receive lower benefits.

Thus, an examination of all three tracks of the American welfare state in the 1990s demonstrates that it is a misconception that American social programs primarily benefit the poor and a downright falsehood that they advantage people of color. The visible programs of social insurance and social welfare benefit more whites than people of color and the hidden welfare tax expenditures significantly escalate the benefits going to the white middle class. Tax expenditures, loans, and loan guarantees flow overwhelmingly to those with above-average incomes,[20] who in the 1990s remained disproportionately white.

In the light of these data, the use of race to undercut the American welfare state has been based on one of the greatest hoaxes of the twentieth century. Only if the true history and current reality of who actually benefits most from American social policy is faced up to will it be possible to build sustained support for a more generous American social policy regime.

Political Ramifications of a Racially Stratified Three-Track Welfare State

Extrapolating from this conclusion, one sees not only that the politics of race has played a key role in producing a racially stratified welfare state but that that fragmented state has had a variety of deleterious political consequences, and not just for the poor and people of color. Policy, interest group politics, and party politics have been reshaped constantly as a result of the three-track welfare state.

One outcome is registered in the ease with which some tracks of welfare are maintained and expanded and the difficulty for others. Hidden welfare, carried on by tax expenditures in particular, is a prime example. Tax expenditures

19. Andrew Hacker, *Two Nations: Black and White, Separate, Hostile, Unequal* (New York: Ballantine, 1995), 32.

20. Howard, *Hidden Welfare State*, 25–39.

have political advantages because they can be (and almost always are) presented as tax reductions, not new social spending. Because they are tied closely to tax policy, and tax policy is a common site of party competition, parties matter directly to the hidden welfare state.[21] The fact that Republicans have, more often than not, been out front on tax expenditures has strengthened their appeal to tax-weary voters, who, ignorant of the heavy government subsidies making so-called private benefits possible, strengthened their loyalties to the private sector, weakened their support for the state, and consequently heightened their support for the party supposedly committed to the free market and limited government. These considerations, along with the complexity of the tax code, the difficulty of explaining the concept of tax expenditures, and the salience of the word "tax" in contemporary American politics, have made it impossible to persuade many advantaged Americans to support the policy reforms that might have allowed a more activist agenda.

A second outcome is registered in interest group politics. Inequities of benefits, respect, and rights institutionalized in social policy reproduced and expanded political inequities. To provide just a few examples: The fact that Social Security and private pensions were not considered to be "welfare" strengthened the lobbying power of organizations representing the elderly (e.g., the American Association of Retired Persons). This strength has helped these organizations to maintain benefit levels and further reinforced their identity as citizens with social rights. By contrast, AFDC/TANF beneficiaries, always stigmatized as poor single mothers and since the 1960s further stereotyped as black mothers living in big cities, economically dependent and spawning a criminal class, grew politically weaker because of their continuing poverty and increasing discouragement. Their indigence and stigmatization in turn undercut their ability to organize to create political pressure, and their lack of organizational strength further weakened the respect they could evoke. Perhaps better than any other demonstration of this result, the experience of the National Welfare Rights Organization (NWRO) is central. When "welfare" clients organized during the late 1960s and the NWRO was strong, they made substantial gains; these gains eroded as the organization weakened in the 1970s.

A third outcome is registered in the experience of racial politics more

21. Ibid., 10.

generally. As argued above, it was the unraveling of the New Deal coalition beginning in the late 1940s—long before the Great Society—that inspired the Democrats to seek new voters among blacks. They did so by not only support- ing voting rights but also by creating new programs targeting blacks for inclu- sion. The more the politics of the 1960s produced programs targeted to people of color, especially blacks, the more the American welfare system exacerbated resentments. There is little evidence that Joe Sixpack or Suzy Yuppie was ever committed to a new racially just Garden of Eden, so that when the costs of targeted programs rose and when whites feared losing their advantages, mem- bers of the privileged white middle class called for their abandonment. As a result, blacks became more, not less, politically marginalized even as the vast majority were just attaining political and legal rights.

The deleterious consequences of fragmentation has had important conse- quences for the Democratic Party. Over time the resulting politics of resent- ment weakened the Democratic Party. While many, if not most, analyses of the demise of the New Deal coalition have implicated an overexpansion of the welfare state, particularly during the Great Society, the fragmentation of wel- fare into three tracks was at least equally culpable. By providing differential benefits according to track, the Social Security Act of 1935 deepened fissures among the Democrats' own motley electoral coalition and undermined the legitimacy of its own welfare compromises. In view of southerners' control of key committees in Congress, the disenfranchisement of blacks in the South, the related weakness of organized labor in that region, and the general acceptance of the ethos of white privilege nationwide, these may have been politically unavoidable decisions in the 1930s. It is nevertheless important to understand what happened; and what happened was that the actual operations of the New Deal welfare state nourished divisions among the Democratic electorate. Most destructive were those between the beneficiaries of social insurance and hidden welfare—privileged- upper-working-class and middle-class white men—and those who got "welfare." As taxes increased, recipients of "welfare" became scapegoats. In particular, the rise of private health insurance and pensions les- sened middle-class and upper-working-class white voters' support for a shared social citizenship and further distanced them from those who could not get or could not afford hidden welfare benefits.

John Petrocik's analysis of the decline of the New Deal coalition indicates that defections from the Democratic Party among union members, Polish and

Irish Catholics, and lower-status white southerners in the 1970s were connected to attitudes on racial and welfare issues and the perceived position of the Democratic Party on these issues. While blacks became overwhelmingly liberal on such issues, and thus more strongly Democratic over the 1970s, white unionists and ethnics in the North and white southerners in general became less liberal and less Democratic.[22] In sum, it is readily apparent that since 1964 there has been a sharpening bifurcation within the Democratic Party between the social insurance and hidden welfare constituencies on one side and the "welfare" constituencies on the other that paralleled their structural relation to the American welfare state.[23]

In the electoral arena, this meant that national Democratic politicians, as the 1976 presidential election first demonstrated, had to target the swing voters who (erroneously) did not feel dependent on the welfare state. The neglected and maligned poor who did support the welfare state increasingly became nonvoters, political noncitizens. The more the poor did not vote, the more the Democrats focused their appeals on conservative swing voters. Polls found such voters concentrated among white middle-income families served by hidden welfare and the white elderly served by social insurance. Throughout the 1980s such voters gravitated in huge numbers to the Republican Party. In 1992 and 1996, however, Bill Clinton was able to break the Republican juggernaut temporarily by largely ignoring the party's base.

Cumulative White Skin Privilege at the Close of the Twentieth Century

The role of the three-tier American welfare state in both reproducing racial inequality and impeding a politics of change helps explain why whites remained substantially advantaged compared to blacks and Latinos as the twentieth century came to an end. To be sure, whites were less privileged than they had been a half-century earlier. In fact, a crowning achievement of the twentieth century was its demonstration that through vigilant struggle, racism can be reduced and white supremacy challenged.

The benefits of the mid-century challenge to white skin privilege and the

---

22. John Petrocik, *Party Coalitions: Realignments and the Decline of the New Deal Party System* (Chicago: University of Chicago Press, 1981), 77–97.

23. Michael K. Brown, *Remaking the Welfare State: Retrenchment and Social Policy in America and Europe* (Philadelphia: Temple University Press, 1988), 202.

new laws and social policies it encouraged dramatically improved the lots of some people of color. Certainly, overall data on the economic well-being of people of color mask the fact that a substantial minority of each racial/ethnic group (the best educated and most highly skilled) made significant progress since the 1960s. The middle class among people of color grew in a relatively short time and had a firmer footing than it had ever had before.

Yet blacks remain at the bottom of whichever class they are in, even as the public image of an affluent and growing black middle class tends to deflect attention not only from the worsening plight of a large new unemployed class of blacks that has become the first casualty of globalization, automation, and the new displacement technologies, but also from the overall dramatic inequality among racial and ethnic groups that persists.

As Figure 7.1 demonstrates, even a cursory look at indicators of well-being validates the conclusion that whites, as a group, remain substantially advantaged over people of color in achieving positions of affluence and influence. For instance, the indicators demonstrate that Latino and black per capita income is only slightly more than half of non-Latino.

Data on attainment of college degrees help explain why Asian-Pacific Americans are slightly advantaged over whites in national per capita income data. Indeed, Asian Americans' exceptionally high rate of college graduation raises the question of why they do not also have exceptionally superior per capita income compared to whites. The data show that the 37 percent of Asian-Pacific Americans fifteen years old and older who hold bachelor's or higher degrees is one and a half times the proportion of comparable non-Latino whites (24.6 percent) who hold such degrees. Apparently there must be a very low glass ceiling operating against Asian Americans. By contrast, Latinos and African Americans represent exceptionally disadvantaged groups when it comes to attaining college degrees. The racial/ethnic equality index shows that Latinos are a third as likely as non-Latino whites and blacks slightly more than half as likely to obtain college degrees. Although none of the indicators in and of themselves explain why inequalities persist and instead are devoted to simply demonstrating the reality of ongoing white advantage (contrary to many whites' claims that racial parity has been achieved),[24] it seems nearly obvious

24. See, e.g., Richard Morin, "A Distorted Image of Minorities," *Washington Post,* Oct. 8, 1995, A1, A26, A27.

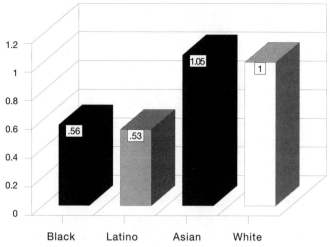

Figure 7.1. Racial/ethnic cumulative equality index

Averages of the eight following indices for black and Latinos and of seven indices for Asian and Pacific Islanders when compared to non-Latino whites.

Race/ethnic equality indices use ratios of minority group to whites. A ratio of 1.0 is the point where the minority group and whites are equal in relation to that index. The proportion below 1.0 indicates the minority group's average deficit when compared to whites; above 1.0, the minority group is advantaged over whites.

Race/Ethnic Equality Index by Category:

	Black	Latino	Asian
Per capita income, 2001	0.57	0.50	0.93
College degree or more, 2001	0.55	0.34	1.50
Managerial/prof. employment of coll. graduates, 2001	0.66	0.44	1.18
Md earnings of year-round, full-time coll. graduates, 2001	0.87	0.84	0.98
Mortgage acceptance rate, 2001	0.76	0.92	1.06
Home ownership rates, 2001	0.64	0.64	0.73
Business ownership rate, 1997	0.25	0.43	0.94
Net worth/wealth, 1995	0.14	0.15	NA

SOURCES: U.S. Bureau of the Census, *Current Population Survey,* March 2001; *Housing Vacancies and Home Ownership* (Washington, D.C., 2001), and *Survey of Businesses* (1997); *Asset Ownership* (1995); and Federal Reserve System, *Home Mortgage Disclosure Act Study* (2001).

that there is a dialectical relationship between the low incomes and low attainment of college degrees of African Americans and Latinos. While there is considerable complexity involved in attaining a college degree, including personal choice, preparation for college work, and expectations of what the job market will offer graduating students, college graduation is undoubtedly influenced by the ability to finance higher education, to secure student loans and repay them, and to secure financial and other support from parents, spouses, and other family members. Those with higher incomes are advantaged in attaining higher educations, and as a result are likely to have better occupations with higher incomes.

Comparing people of color to non-Latino whites in employment in two traditionally defined high-status occupational categories that provide high monetary rewards, managerial and professional specialty occupations, one finds that again whites and Asian Americans remain substantially advantaged over Latinos and African Americans. African Americans are two-thirds as likely as their non-Latino white counterparts to be employed in managerial and professional occupations, and Latinos are less than half as likely. Meanwhile, Asian Americans are more likely than whites to be employed in these two high-status occupational categories.

Nor are returns to investment in higher education equal. Even when employed year-round, full-time, people of color with college degrees remain substantially disadvantaged and whites substantially advantaged in total earnings. Blacks' earnings are 87 percent those of whites, Latinos' 84 percent, and even the highly educated Asian-Pacific Americans' earnings are slightly less (98 percent) than those of whites. Higher educational achievement apparently lessens the racial/ethnic divide, but white advantage remains palpable even among the college-educated population.

Beyond income, education, work, and earnings, a host of other social indicators demonstrate continuing white advantage in arenas most valued in American society. The remaining data are simply illustrative of the big picture. Homeownership (a value at the core of the American dream) provides additional evidence of continuing white advantage. Data on mortgage availability support this conclusion, since in the United States most homes are bought on credit. Thus attaining credit is tremendously important to attaining homeownership. Recent federal data, however, reveal that while Asian Americans do not differ from whites (or even are slightly advantaged) in their mortgage application acceptance rates, blacks and Latinos are substantially different from whites, with blacks having the lowest acceptance rate of all. Federal Reserve data demonstrate that wealthy blacks with spotless credit records are turned down more often than whites with below-average income and poor credit records. In addition, the rejection rates for federal government-backed mortgages are similar to those for conventional loans: blacks, 26.3 percent; whites, 12.1 percent; Latinos, 18.4 percent; and Asian Americans, 12.8 percent.

Given the difficulty of securing home mortgages, it is not surprising that there are dramatic differences by race and ethnicity when it comes to actual homeownership. In 2001 both African Americans and Latinos were less than two-thirds as likely as whites to own homes and Asian Americans less than three-fourth as likely. That pinnacle of the American dream was still disproportionately likely to be the province of whites. Almost three out of every four whites own houses compared to only approximately one out of every two members of a racial minority group.

At least partially as a result of discriminatory practices in lending and investment, business ownership as a route to wealth demonstrates especially large gaps between people of color and whites. In 1997, blacks were only one-fourth as likely as non-Latino whites to own businesses and Latinos only two-fifths as likely. However, Asian Americans were statistically indistinguishable from whites in regard to business ownership. The percentages of businesses owned, however, reveal a more favorable picture than the percentages of business sales and receipts of each major racial/ethnic group. In 1997, to achieve parity with non-Latino whites in sales receipts, blacks would have had to receive 90 percentage points more, Latinos nearly 80 more, and Asians–Pacific Islanders nearly 15 more.

The most stunning evidence of continuing white advantage, however, is seen in regard to wealth. As Melvin Oliver and Thomas Shapiro argue, asset holding or wealth perhaps better captures the actual financial status of families and individuals than income.[25] Wealth determines how long a family or individual can withstand setbacks in income (for example, when one loses a job);

25. Melvin L. Oliver and Thomas M. Shapiro, *Black Wealth, White Wealth: A New Perspective on Racial Inequality* (New York: Routledge, 1995), 5.

and wealth can be used as collateral to acquire more assets. The data in Figure 7.1 reveal that whites own a whopping seven times more assets than do African Americans or Latinos. In 1995, white households had a median measured net worth of $49,030, while the figure for Latino households was $7,255 and for black households $7,073. Wealth, of course, is both acquired and inherited. The disparities in homeownership undoubtedly play an important role in the huge gaps in wealth, since equity in one's own home accounts for a large proportion of total net worth. In 1995, home equity accounted for 62.4 percent of African American households' total net worth and 70.6 percent of white households' total net worth. The historical dimension of wealth is perhaps even more important since it is a significant factor in solidifying white skin privilege, no matter how egalitarian laws or even income structures become. In short, the wealth indicator describes the extent to which people of color have assets, such as a home, business, or other investments, that enhance their economic power and provide a cushion against income fluctuations. It reveals a more complete picture of people's economic well-being, demonstrating stark white advantage.

For illustration purposes only, Figure 7.1 provides a composite index of the eight racial/ethnic equality indexes shown below it. The composite figure suggests that while Asian Americans have reached parity with non-Latino whites, both Latinos and African Americans are only slightly more than half as likely as non-Latino whites to have achieved society's desired goals, such as a higher income, education, occupation, and wealth. It would take a change of 44 percentage points for blacks and 47 percentage points for Latinos to reach parity with whites.

It is clear, however, that the composite index leaves out many important indicators and probably severely underestimates the extent of continuing white advantage in the United States. From life expectancy to access to health care to securing the computer skills needed to prosper in the new economy, and on and on, blacks and Latinos fare worse than whites and Asians. In more subtle but politically hot areas, white drivers are less likely to be pulled over by the police; whites are more likely to be free to live in neighborhoods and send their children to schools of their choice, and quite simply to live lives free of suspicion, mistrust, hostility, and disrespect in the perceptions of dominant elites. This does not minimize the real struggles and difficulties that many white men and women face, but the evidence is clear: whites remain privileged in America. As David Johnston points out in his discussion of liberty, the cumulative advantages of white skin privilege mean that even if, "counter-factually . . . black Americans did enjoy fair equality of opportunity with whites," they would still be at a disadvantage, given the centuries of accumulated white skin privilege.[26]

Among people of color, only Asians–Pacific Islanders appear to be outliers from the trend in white skin privilege. They tend to live in what some economists call the "bicoastal economy," areas of above-average income concentrated in California and northeastern megalopolises. Several studies have cogently shown that when the statistics are analyzed against the numerical realities of dependents and of persons working per family, educational attainment, residence in high-cost cities, and other factors, the conclusion is that Asian Americans have not actually reached equality with whites. Indeed, in cities where several communities of color account for large proportions of the population, they are in much more competitive positions. In San Francisco, for instance, Asian Americans composed 30.8 percent of the population in 2000, Latinos 14.1 percent, and blacks 7.8 percent. There the per capita incomes of the groups were close: $19,534 for Latinos, $21,560 for blacks, and $22,181 for Asians–Pacific Islanders. The per capita income of whites, who accounted for 49.7 percent of San Francisco's population, was $51,006. Thus per capita income of Latinos in San Francisco was only 38 percent that of whites; per capita income of blacks was only 42 percent; and per capita income of Asian Americans was only 44 percent that of non-Latino whites. Similar patterns emerge in other cities with large numbers of diverse minorities, for example, Los Angeles, New York, and Chicago.[27] In short, Asian Americans too face continuing barriers of racism and exclusion that not even their superior educational achievement has been able to overcome in a supposedly meritocratic society. For African Americans and Latinos, even the national data are straightforward and unambiguous: both groups would nearly have to double their representation in desirable categories representing socioeconomic well-being to be equal to whites. Non-Latino whites remain dramatically advantaged in American society—a situation mainly reproduced or, most disturbing of all, heightened by the nation's welfare state.

26. David Johnston, *The Idea of a Liberal Theory: A Critique and Reconstruction* (Princeton: Princeton University Press, 1994), 156–57.
27. U.S. Bureau of the Census, Internet—1990 Census Lookup (1,4), 1990 U.S. Census Data, Database: C90STF3A.

Conclusion

As the new millennium began, despite significant progress[28] and the kudos blacks gave the Clinton administration, racial inequality remained stark. The racially segmented welfare state that had roots as far back as Reconstruction and was codified in law beginning in the 1930s remains intact in the twenty-first century.

Segmentation had material impacts not only up through the 1980s but throughout the 1990s. Today the three tracks of welfare disproportionately serving different racial clienteles mean in effect that the American welfare state is itself an embodiment of institutionalized racism. Although first created in full consciousness of its function in reproducing the nation's racial hierarchy, as debates in Congress in the 1930s showed, it now performs this service on much more neutral grounds. The greater poverty of blacks and Latinos guarantees their disproportionate share in the poorly funded means-tested programs. The greater affluence of whites guarantees they reap the lion's share of benefits in the hidden welfare state. Standing in between in regard to the generosity of benefits, social insurance programs also tend to benefit whites disproportionately as a result of accumulated differential experiences in the workplace and the hardships that lower the life expectancies of people of color.

In both originally producing and sequentially reproducing these results, racial politics historically and currently set the stage for debates over social policy from era to era. In effect, race has always figured in the calculations of policy makers and by the twenty-first century a racial mythology of the welfare state not only remained fully incorporated in party politics but continued to constrain policy options. To paraphrase Antonio Gramsci, debates over social policy, like those over party politics, inculcate in the general public a folk "common sense" or hegemonic conception.[29] Today virtually no well-organized constituency questions whether hidden welfare actually plays a justifiable role

28. Just a few examples: More students of color attend majority-white colleges and universities than ever before. More people of color work in the higher echelons of the occupational world—in the professions and in management, especially in the public sector—than ever before. There are more black-, Latino-, Asian-, and Native American–owned businesses and elected officials than ever before. The civil rights agenda is still best characterized as unfinished, but America is simply not what it was in the 1950s.

29. Quoted in Michael Omi and Howard Winant, "The Los Angeles 'Race Riot' and Contemporary U.S. Politics," in Robert Gooding-Williams, ed., *Reading Rodney King/Reading Urban Uprising* (New York: Routledge, 1993), 101.

in producing the common good; and the distributional inequalities in social insurance programs also tend to be ignored. Meanwhile, those programs that disproportionately serve people of color are everywhere questioned and sharply eroded. The cumulative advantages of whiteness have in time become so institutionalized as to become normalized.

eight
"The Problem of Race"
American Social Policy at the Dawn of a New Century

White skin privilege is the flip side of discrimination. While discrimination is
negative and overt, white skin privilege is negative but passive. It's a great blind
spot more than a painful boil, but in a subtle way it is far more destructive. . . .
For me, the quest for racial unity remains the defining moral issue of our time.
I say to you who are young, take this issue and find a way of making it yours.
—Bill Bradley

Near the start of his short-lived campaign for the Democratic presidential nomination, Bill Bradley did what no contender for a major party's nomination had
done before. In a speech on April 18, 1999, at New York City's Cooper Union,
where Abraham Lincoln signaled his intention to run for president on an anti-
slavery platform in 1860, Bradley not only promised to make racial unity the
centerpiece of his candidacy in 2000 and, if elected, the most important attribute of his administration, but also spoke of the "blind spot" in which white
skin privilege acts as an organizing principle of life in the United States. This
book has sought to make a contribution toward bringing white skin privilege,
particularly in regard to its impact on the politics of social policy making, into
clear view.

I have argued that there is no race problem per se; instead, "race problem" is a euphemism for "white skin privilege."[1] The real problem is the social

1. Bradley's challenge to white Americans to look at both their own indifference and the
privileges that accrue to them simply by virtue of their color was followed almost immediately
by a dare to African Americans to overcome their own suspicions, fears, and frustrations with
the racial barriers and discrimination that still exist—making it seem that abandoning white
supremacy and black patience and understanding were parallel and equal challenges, goals,
and duties.

and political construction of race in a way that advantages whites over people of color in economic markets, political institutions, and social policies. There can be little genuine progress in solving the so-called race problem or in creating the kind of social citizenship all Americans deserve unless and until continuing white skin privilege is openly acknowledged and addressed. In effect the problem of the twenty-first century is not the color line but finding a way to successfully challenge whiteness as ideology and reality.

Assessing Progress Made in the Twentieth Century

As Oliver Cox stressed in 1948, to understand racism, it must be set in class and economic contexts,[2] and those contexts have changed. Indeed, important progress was made in moderating white skin privilege over the past century, especially in its latter half.[3] There are significantly more people of color in the middle and upper classes than there were at mid-century. There has been a dramatic decline in the overt daily horrors posed by both white terrorist groups such as the Ku Klux Klan and institutional forces such as the police. At least some racial minorities are visible in positions of leadership, affluence, and influence in almost every sector of American life. The number of people of color who are public officials—elected and appointed—has grown impressively. Not only has the number of racial minorities in colleges grown significantly but their enrollment in predominantly white universities would have been unthinkable midway through the twentieth century. Similarly, at mid-century there were virtually no people of color on *Fortune* 500 corporate boards, few on entertainment television, and none anchoring television news. Nor were there hardly any people of color among daily newspaper editors or among presidents and administrators of colleges, universities, and hospitals that were not historically black. That is no longer the case.

In short, there is little doubt that both economic and political structures have changed since the pre–civil rights era. The United States of America is, simply, not what it was in the 1950s. In 1991 one could even see Malcolm X's

2. Oliver Cromwell Cox, *Caste, Class, and Race: A Study in Social Dynamics* (Garden City, N.Y.: Doubleday, 1948).

3. For an exceptionally optimistic argument in regard to racial progress, see William Julius Wilson, *The Declining Significance of Race: Blacks and Changing American Institutions,* 2d ed. (Chicago: University of Chicago Press, 1990).

radical visage peering out at America from the improbable perch of a 33-cent U.S. postage stamp.

Alterations in the nation's social policy regime—from civil rights to social rights—have played a key role in producing positive changes in race relations and racial progress. To be sure, people of color were included only on a discriminatory basis at the inception of the American welfare state, but even the crumbs of the New Deal were more than they had gotten before. On the cusp of the force of the Civil Rights Movement in the 1950s and 1960s, new civil rights laws were enacted and the Great Society was born. Programs of this era, more than any other, began the slow improvements in conditions for people of color and made some incursions into white skin privilege.

Looking at this fifty-year history, some have declared victory. For example, as this book went to press, a Washington, D.C., newspaper published a series, "Black Money," dedicated to showing that blacks were truly "making it."[4] According to Steve Miller, the author of the series, the median household income of blacks grew substantially faster than that of whites during the 1990s; the number of black-owned firms increased faster than U.S. firms overall between 1992 and 1997. Miller concluded: "The figures undermine the steadfast proclamations of the civil rights industry, that times are hard and racism is thriving and striving to keep black America in poverty." In toto, the series suggested not only that African Americans are alive and well in America but also that the quest for racial equality is complete.

But Miller's recitation of only two sets of figures regarding the rate of progress left unnoted the radical differences between black and white socioeconomic statuses that Chapter 7 demonstrates. Rather than tackle the data on the persistent set of racial disparities and particularly the fact that in regard to many of them, particularly wealth, there has been little or no progress at all, Miller concentrates on anecdotes about the experiences of a few black families who have achieved success. Undoubtedly such anecdotes about outliers find a warm acceptance among most white Americans. National polls show a majority saying that when it comes to jobs, income, health care, and education, black Americans are doing just as well as whites. Not surprisingly, the vast majority

---

4. Steve Miller, "Black and Rich," *Washington Times,* Feb. 18, 2002; "Graduating to Success," ibid., Feb. 19, 2002; "Striking Gold in California," ibid., Feb. 20, 2002; and "Blacks Thriving Economically," ibid., Feb. 21, 2002.

of whites oppose even symbolic gestures (such as an apology for slavery) to redress the most blatant exercises of white skin privilege in the past.[5]

Such anecdotes and opinions add up to what Franklin D. Raines, director of the Office of Management and Budget in the Clinton administration, has labeled "a peril of self-delusion."[6] In essence, writers such as Miller use a new form of an old tactic. As so often in American history, stories of individual mobility are used both to create and to recreate Horatio Alger–style myths and at the same time undercut group solidarity. Anecdotes about impressive individual families (just like anecdotes full of ugly stereotypes of criminality among very poor families)—chosen precisely because they are exceptions to the rule—are paraded about as if they were the rule. Newsworthy because they are so "new," different, atypical, and unusual, they encourage consumers of the news to treat them as if they were routine.

To be sure, the meaning of race and the nature of racial identity have become far more problematic and far more ambiguous than they were at the peak of the Civil Rights Movement. It is abundantly clear that race now involves significant antagonisms among ethno-racial groups and class conflicts within each ethno-racial group. Nonetheless, as we have seen, the growing significance of one set of variables (for example, class) in no way need indicate the declining significance of another set of variables (for example, race). Massive differences between people of color and whites persist. If racial parity had been achieved, African Americans would have 2 million more high school degrees, 2 million more college degrees, nearly 2 million more professional and managerial jobs, and roughly $200 billion more in income. If there were no racial gaps,

5. For example, in a 1997 Gallup poll, whites opposed the idea of apologizing to Americans whose ancestors were enslaved by whites by a 67–26% margin (while blacks favored the idea by almost the same margin, 65–28%). White southerners were solidly opposed to an official apology, by a 51-point margin: 22% in favor of an apology, 73% opposed. That these differences were related to any policy that attempts to make up for the accumulated privileges of whites is suggested by the fact that the racial gap is similar to those recorded in other polls asking Americans about such issues as affirmative action and the need for increases in civil rights legislation. As Hugh Heclo concludes, even if "justice is seen to demand reparation . . . there seems no realistic political prospect for building antipoverty policy on white guilt for racism": Heclo, "The Nature, Causes, and Cures of Poverty: Accomplishments from Three Decades of Poverty Research and Policy," in Sheldon H. Danziger, Gary D. Sandefur, and Daniel H. Weinberg, *Confronting Poverty: Prescriptions for Change* (Cambridge: Harvard University Press, 1994), 471.

6. Franklin D. Raines, "Charter Day Address," Charter Day 2002 Convocation, Howard University, Mar. 8, 2002.

3 million more African Americans would own their own homes; African Americans would have $760 billion more in home equity value, $200 billion more invested in the stock market, $120 billion more in private pension funds, and $80 billion more in savings accounts. "That alone," Raines points out, "would total over $1 trillion more in wealth."[7] Despite racial progress over the course of the last century, there remains a long journey indeed to racial parity.

Add to this the dirty little secret of continued racial discrimination (all too often breaking wide open in the 1990s at places like Texaco, Bell Atlantic, Denny's, Fleet Finance, the Bureau of Alcohol and Firearms, Eddie Bauer's, the Agriculture Department, and so forth),[8] segregated neighborhoods and schools, growth of memberships in white supremacy groups, racial bias, hate crimes, and racial hostility of all sorts, and one must conclude that overcoming whiteness as reality and ideology remains unfinished business. One is not surprised, then, by conclusions of the "civil rights industry."

In fact, in the context of the full picture of today's racial disparities, denying that race still matters is perhaps the most effective tactic of what has been called the "new racism." By 2000, a veritable bevy of polls showed that the vast majority of Americans did not think of themselves as racist, nor did they want to. Although many whites negatively stereotyped blacks and to a lesser extent Latinos and Asian Americans, most whites had accepted racial equality in principle. Fewer and fewer whites were willing to openly make claims of biological superiority to people of color. Moreover, since racial discrimination had been outlawed formally, in some places and at some times its practice had serious legal repercussions. How, then, does one hang on to white skin privilege not only materially but ideologically in this new context?

Ironically, the very gains from the civil rights "revolution" of the 1960s have been transformed in nearly Orwellian fashion into a weapon to be used against people of color in the new reconstruction of race and poverty. The new racism virtually hinges on the insistence that "discrimination is illegal; everyone has equal rights, so what's the problem?" The answer, of course, is that it must be "them." To make this answer believable and acceptable, a second tactic (per-

7. Ibid.
8. In all these companies and government agencies, evidence of old-style bigotry as well as institutionalized discriminatory practices against blacks were on display and widely covered by the news media in 1995, 1996, and 1997, forcing lawsuits and out-of-court settlements or consent decrees.

haps the most important) is to completely ignore history as having valid implications and material legacies for the present. Only a completely ahistorical analysis can fail to discover that the problem is that political and social citizenship are very recent phenomena for most people of color and that this result was hardly accidental.

What Barrington Moore has called "suppressed historical alternatives" that could have produced the world's first multicultural democracy[9] virtually litter the American experience since the nation's beginning. What if "while white pioneers were claiming and settling the frontier which created a strong tradition of and quest for individual property rights, blacks had not been property but instead had property rights?"[10] What might have happened if, as the United States was establishing the world's strongest system of property rights and protections,[11] the formerly enslaved had been allowed to own property they could turn into assets that generated capital, not eliminated from competition by black codes and Jim Crow laws—making a mockery of the Fourteenth Amendment's protection of property rights for the formerly enslaved? What would have happened if Reconstruction-era blacks had been allowed to get and keep the lands in General Sherman's Special Field Order 15—the land below Charleston, South Carolina, which includes what are now the resort islands of Hilton Head and Kiawah, some of the most beautiful beachfront properties on the Eastern Seaboard, where today a four-bedroom beach house on one acre of land is listed for $3 million? What would have happened if the homestead law in such states as Texas had not explicitly prohibited the distribution of public lands to blacks?

How early might effective civil rights laws have been enacted if Senator Sumner's proposal to establish the Freedmen's Bureau as a permanent agency with a secretary of Cabinet rank had not been rebuffed? What might have been if white terrorists dressed in white robes had not been allowed to systematically drive black families from their land and businesses when a few were allowed to purchase them? What would the plight of the black elderly be if a federal system of insurance for all categories of all races of workers suffering involuntary

9. Barrington Moore, *The Social Basis of Obedience and Revolt* (Armonk, N.Y.: M. E. Sharpe, 1978).

10. Raines, "Charter Day Address."

11. Hernando de Soto, *The Mystery of Capital: Why Capitalism Triumphs in the West and Fails Everywhere Else* (New York: Basic Books, 2000).

unemployment, including domestics, agricultural workers, laborers, and people who worked part-time as well as professionals and the self-employed, as Lundeen proposed in 1935, had become the law of the land? What would have happened if the GI Bill had barred housing loans to veterans of World War II if they purchased from real estate companies such as the Levittowns (the first major planned suburban developments in the United States) that discriminated against "persons other than members of the Caucasian race"? What might have happened if the countless calls of civil rights leaders from the 1930s through the late 1990s for an entitlement to work (the assurance of jobs at living wages for all men and women as the primary strategy for ending poverty), not just an entitlement to welfare, had been heeded?[12] What if black leaders, organized labor, women leaders, and other civil rights activists were strong constituencies heavily engaged in social policy issues today?

Once history is brought into focus, few can doubt that the authentic problem is twofold: first, that the denial of equality of opportunity for people of color and the privileging of whites has been anything but unintentional; rather that it has been far more often than not conscious, systematic, de jure, and de facto; and second, that only four generations have passed since there was even a halfhearted attempt to alter this pattern. For example, it has been less than a century and a half since African Americans were even permitted to learn to read, work for income, and own assets. Less than half a century has passed since most African American could vote. The majority of today's African Americans have great-grandparents who were enslaved by whites; grandparents who were propertyless sharecroppers working "from sunup to sundown" for whites; parents who could not vote and lived under Jim Crow, and often experience de facto denial of equal education, equal employment, and fair lending today. African Americans today are heirs of more than 400 years and thirteen generations of superexploitation, subjugation, humiliation, segregation, and discrimination—de facto and de jure. By contrast, many whites have grandparents who lived in the epoch of slavery and the vast majority have great-grandparents who did. Slave master or not, these whites all benefited from the ability to become property owners, vote for their leaders, and be constructed as socially and psychologically superior to people of color. The problem

12. Martin Luther King Jr., *Where Do We Go from Here? Chaos or Community* (Boston: Beacon, 1968), 163.

is that one generation cannot reverse the impact of that past.[13] That is why the reconstruction of race and the securing of white skin privilege in the early twenty-first century, in a manner reminiscent of the pseudo science of Social Darwinism in the nineteenth century, depends on ignoring history and in its place giving credence to individualistic interpretations of the exceptional who have beaten the odds versus the ordinary who remain trapped behind race and class barriers. In so doing, a rationale for rampant inequality and hands-off government is provided.

To break the pattern of denial and self-delusion that lies at the heart of the new racism and complete the long journey of making people of color full participants in American society, one must, however, realize that the nation's single step is not and will not be enough. One must openly confront white skin privilege as reality and ideology and to do so in a capitalist system requires finding means to a significant redistribution of income and wealth, more consumption, and less capitalization. This is the task of social policy.

But this book has demonstrated that historically American social policy has been anything but up to this task. Instead, it has been documented here that American social policy has been culpable of both constraining redistribution and reproducing white advantage. To be sure, there has never been a time in which the American welfare state in its entirety or its fractions exclusively served one race only. Recall that in its prehistory, so many whites benefited from the Freedmen's Bureau's work that one *New York Times* journalist asked: Whose bureau is it anyway? Simultaneously, some black veterans garnered enough benefits from the Civil War veterans' pension system to become members of the middle class and leaders in their communities. During the New Deal, a small but important portion of blacks in covered occupations benefited from old-age insurance as well as private pensions, mostly in the North. At the same time, more whites than blacks benefited from relief. When the Great Society finally included people of color on a mass basis, hundreds of thousands of previously excluded white women and their children also swelled welfare rolls. As eligibility requirements were tightened and ultimately the federal guarantee was eliminated in 1996, both the poorest sector of whites and poor people of color found themselves losing social protection. Thus from its very beginning understanding the relationship between race and the tracks of the

13. Raines, "Charter Day Address."

American welfare state has meant understanding proportional and differential inclusion, not total exclusion of any racial group.

Some analysts might see the conflicting trends in the role of the welfare state vis-à-vis racial inequality as a paradox. They are not. The essence of the dual role of American social policy—improving the conditions of people of color on one hand and reproducing white skin privilege on the other—can be summarized by two observations. First, just as there has been a dual labor market, with primary sector jobs reserved for whites and blacks relegated to a secondary sector of low-paying, low-status jobs, reinforcing the subordinate position of the black worker,[14] so too has a three-tiered social policy regime disproportionately reserved the superior tracks for whites and the inferior tracks for people of color. In effect the privilege generated for whites is directly implicated in the penalization generated for people of color. Second, people live in both the absolute and the relative. While expanding social protections, like economic prosperity, lifts all boats, those boats already floating are buoyed while those stuck at the bottom rise a little but remain mired underwater. In short, as long as the "good" welfare programs (hidden welfare and social insurance) disproportionately benefit whites and the "bad" welfare programs (social welfare) disproportionately benefit blacks and most other people of color, American social policy acts as a reproducer of stratification, not a reducer of inequality. Depending on the precise nature of the social policies produced, all racial groups may or may not find their conditions improving in absolute terms. For example, blacks and whites both gain when Social Security paychecks go up as a result of cost-of-living increases (COLAs). But there may be no relative gains among the races. Since fewer blacks are covered by Social Security, proportionately fewer will benefit from the new COLAs; since blacks begin with lower payments, a 3 percent gain, for example, will mean less in actual money for them than for whites; and since blacks have a much shorter life expectancy, they subsidize the benefits of whites. In short, unredressed historical wrongs aggravate current market-based inequalities and inbuilt biases in contemporary American social policies to reproduce racial inequality. A system in which everyone has basic economic security and shares equally in social protections has failed to materialize. What might such a system look like?

14. Wilfrid David, "Black America in Development Perspective," pt. 2, *Review of Black Political Economy* 3, no. 4 (Summer 1973): 82.

Where Should America Go from Here?

It is not only typical, but popular, to act as if there were a huge mystery about what is to be done. This posture is good for economic elites who want to do nothing because change would threaten their power and profits, for many whites who want to hold on to privileges they believe they got "the old-fashioned way—they earned them"; for politicians who benefit from pandering to stereotypes of people of color in general and welfare recipients in particular while ignoring premier beneficiaries of the nation's most generous social policies; and for policy researchers who want to secure grants to rediscover the obvious. But social policy options that would both provide economic security for all and eliminate white skin privilege are not really a big puzzle. They do not require a presidential commission to study race relations and economic injustice. In most instances, relevant facts and knowledge have already been established and confirmed both by the American past and by researchers and practices of the welfare states of other nations. A minimal set of first principles flows from this body of amassed knowledge.[15] Each requires a sharp break with some of the United States' most important social policy legacies.

One first principle is that social policy should no longer be made in a vacuum as if it were not linked to labor market or other macroeconomic policies. This should be axiomatic: for example, welfare mothers need programs that help them to be wage earners *and* to meet domestic labor obligations; a social policy that encourages men to meet domestic labor obligations also remains vital. Thus welfare and labor market policies are tangled, and macroeconomic policy making must deal with both an entitlement to welfare *and* an entitlement to work. While the United States has had a partial entitlement to welfare, it has never had an entitlement to work. Both are needed, but particularly the latter. The assurance of jobs at good wages and in safe working conditions for all men and women who are neither disabled, elderly, nor performing essential work in the home is the best strategy for ending poverty. For all people to develop a feeling of ownership in liberal individualism, all must have their needs for sufficient income, adequate material resources, and opportunities to be productive, contributing members of their communities and society met.

15. For a sampling of policy recommendations and strategies, see William Julius Wilson, *When Work Disappears: The World of the New Urban Poor* (New York: Vintage Books, 1997); and Gertrude Schaffner Goldberg and Sheila D. Collins, *Washington's New Poor Law: Welfare Reform and the Roads Not Taken, 1935 to the Present* (New York: Apex, 2001).

Another sharp break with the nation's social policy legacy is to comprehend the welfare state as a whole. The treatment of direct spending on social welfare, social insurance, and indirect spending on hidden welfare must be conjoined so that they are understood as a single stream of American social policy, with an eye to equalizing benefits. Traversing the three tracks of the American welfare state and understanding them as part of a whole would lead to development of more rational budgetary decisions. For example, treating tax expenditures that disproportionately benefit the white middle and upper classes as an open part of the welfare system would expose the dirty little secret of hidden welfare (how expensive and how class- and race-biased it is). Imagine what might happen if politicians and journalists started regularly referring to private pensions, student loans, and home mortgage deductions as "welfare." Only if issues of accountability and control over public monies are extended to hidden welfare will it be possible to break the vicious cycle in which the stigma of direct-spending welfare programs and the stigmatized color, gender, and class of their recipients stop reinforcing each other. Only then will there be the possibility for the fragmentation that has weakened political support for the American welfare state to subside and the potential for equal social citizenship alongside civil and political citizenship grow.

A third principle for new social policy making is to break out of the box of incrementalism with its focus on the immediate conjuncture. Focusing on investments whose biggest payoffs will be realized only in the future rather than on the balance sheets of today is in the interest of the nation as a whole if it is to remain globally competitive. First and foremost, this means targeting children (who all—regardless of ideology—should be able to agree are deprived through no fault of their own) for assistance rather than continuing the constant American preoccupation with altering parental behaviors in regard to a presumed lack of adherence to the American ethos. After all, few if any empirical studies demonstrate that poor parents differ significantly from more affluent parents in regard to attitudes toward work, marriage, and education. What differentiates the poor from others are opportunities and expectations, not ideals. Prioritizing social protections for children, regardless of the ills of their parents and indeed to compensate for such ills, needs to be brought to center stage in a new social policy regime in America.

Creating an entitlement to work as well as welfare, treating tax expenditures like direct social spending, and focusing social policy on children are all universal policies that stand to create greater economic security for Americans of all races. But even if such universal policies were enacted, history has shown that like Social Security, the GI Bill, and other universal policies, they would in all likelihood reproduce racial inequality. If the booming economy of the late 1990s revealed nothing else, it is that inequality of class or race will not fix itself. Despite the longest peacetime recovery, improved international competitiveness, the lowest unemployment rate in more than forty years, modest inflation, declining welfare rates, and so forth, these good socioeconomic trends failed to reverse three disturbing long-run trends: stagnant or falling real earnings for the majority of workers; increasing income inequality among workers, families, and households; and relative inequality among ethno-racial groups. For those living in hard-hit Appalachia, economically starved black and Latino communities, or poverty-soaked Indian reservations, it is clear that the soaring economy of the 1990s had its gaping holes. These holes revealed that neither the Democrats' favored solution (economic growth) nor the Republicans' favorite policy tool (tampering with tax rates) will fix class and racial inequality. In short, white skin privilege must be attacked directly. Thus a fourth principle for a new social policy regime is to provide racism-sensitive safeguards, such as strong and enforceable preventive antidiscrimination provisions in current policies and provide more, not fewer, compensatory policies to overcome the legacies of past discrimination. As this book has shown, the right's argument for a color-blind society far exceeds what the nation's most basic institutions, policies, and practices have made possible. Color still matters; as Martha Minow put it: "If the goal is to avoid identifying people by a trait of difference, but the institutions and practices make that trait matter, there seems to be no way to remedy the effects of difference without making difference matter yet again."[16] Those who seriously support racial equality, not just in principle but also in implementation, must also support compensatory programs based on race at this historical conjuncture if the nation is ever to get beyond the accumulated privileges of whiteness. Challenges to whiteness cannot be race-blind.

Finally, in the world's premier capitalist system, there is no escaping the need to democratize capital through an asset-building strategy. As Chapter 7 showed, of all the challenges for achieving ethno-racial parity, wealth is the

---

16. Quoted in Michael B. Katz, *The Undeserving Poor: From the War on Poverty to the War on Welfare* (New York: Pantheon, 1989), 167.

stiffest. With wealth, individuals can buy other assets, insure them against loss, borrow against them, and pass them on to their descendants. In effect, assets have a second life because they generate capital.[17] The lack of wealth among people of color helps to explain why racial disparities persist in education, jobs, income, and property ownership. "Without wealth, it's hard to send your kids to college. Without college, it's hard to get a good job. Without a good job, it's hard to earn a good income. Without a good income, it's hard to obtain property, And without property and the capital to leverage it, it's hard to create wealth to send your kids to college."[18] And so the cycle of inequality continues. Thus beyond the focus on work, income adequacy, education, and all the rest, there must also be an asset-building strategy. Then all people, regardless of education or income, could harness their human capital, their ability and willingness to work, into appreciable assets and thereby harness the ability of compound interest to build wealth.

Each of these five general principles suggests a readily identifiable set of programs with strong potential to generate equal social protections. For example, linking policies such as welfare to labor market policy as part of a single policy stream would, in all probability, lead to development of a full-employment policy. A full-employment policy in turn would depend on programs for improving education, job training, and retraining, and would probably result in a shorter workday or workweek; more paid leave in the form of vacations, sick leave, and family leave; job-creating public investment in the nation's crumbling infrastructure; controls on capital flight; replacement of a corporate-driven trade agenda with one concerned to enhance the lives of workers; revitalization of the public sector; and strategies for a just transition for workers and communities away from corporate degradation of the environment. Meaningful full employment would mean a living wage through expansion of the EITC and increasing the minimum wage but also through what economists such as James Meade (winner of the Nobel Prize in 1977) and John Kenneth Galbraith refer to as a "citizen's income"—a guarantee for every citizen to have a minimum acceptable level of income, equaling perhaps the prevailing local wage, indexed to the cost of living, and funded by individual and corporate income taxes and inheritance and gift taxes.[19] Such a program could effectively

17. De Soto, *Mystery of Capital.*
18. Raines, "Charter Address."
19. J. E. Meade, *Full Employment Regained? An Agathotopian Dream* (New York: Cambridge University Press, 1995). The citizen's income, also known as a basic income or universal bene-

contain increasing income inequality. It could also have a salutary effect on race relations. While it is simplistic to think that if you guarantee all people a job with decent wages, their hearts and minds will follow, it is nonetheless likely that full employment at decent wages in safe working conditions would encourage interracial cooperation as well as racial justice. Competition for scarce jobs and widening disparities of wealth and income deepen racial competition and hostility.

Similarly, a social policy agenda focused first and foremost on children, as in Europe and Canada, leads to a set of easily identifiable programs. For example, stronger enforcement of child support, while a step in the right direction, must be accompanied by child assurance. Some noncustodial parents—especially men of color—are so hampered by unemployment, underemployment, and low wages that even when they pay their maximum in child support, children are left poor and hopeless. Child assurance, through creating a child's allowance and a caregiver's allowance, available in most countries in the West, would protect children whether the child support from absentee parents was adequate or not. Other programs that must be coupled with child assurance include the increasingly well known agenda: access to comprehensive and universal health care, quality child care, quality schools, affordable housing; allowing parents who are beneficiaries of social welfare to count education and training as work; and adequate provision of ancillary/support services such as transportation and drug counseling. Among these programs, the most important of all to the future of children is improving the education prospects, especially for poor children, through equalizing resources, from school finances to class size to prepared teachers to technology. If "it takes a village to raise a child," providing resources and encouragement for schools to facilitate and coordinate service provision by other institutions of civil society, families, and government would also constitute a good programmatic tool. Creating a family

---

fit, would not destroy work incentives if it were not withdrawn as the citizen earned other income. In an increasingly insecure labor market, Meade argued, where many if not most workers must come to see themselves as "permanent trainees," moving from one job to another, a citizen's income takes on a new urgency, enabling all workers to have a secure financial base on which they can build. The citizen's income concept has attracted not only European economists such as Meade but many other distinguished economists. John Kenneth Galbraith has argued that everyone in the good society "should have a basic source of income. If this is not available from the market system, as it is now called, it must come from the state. Nothing, let us not forget, sets a stronger limit on the liberty of the citizen than a total absence of money": Galbraith, *The Affluent Society*, 4th ed. (Boston: Houghton Mifflin, 1984), 251–52.

policy that first and foremost focuses on poor children's educational prospects would help people of color especially, since they compose a large share of the poor. Moreover, given a demographic picture in which children are already experiencing diversity first (for example, there are already more Latino children than African American ones, and children of color will exceed white children before adults of color exceed white adults in number), a family policy focused on improving schooling for poor minority children is in the interests of the economic future of white children, who will depend increasingly on the talents of children of Americans of color.

Advancing the antidiscrimination principle suggests programs that strengthen enforcement of current civil rights laws, not only maintaining but expanding compensatory programs such as affirmative action; enacting new laws against racial bias and hate crimes, subjecting all policy proposals and changes to equity impact statements, conducting racial audits to identify and assess levels of current discrimination in the implementation of policies, and periodic reviews of departments and agencies of federal, state, and local governments regarding whether they are furthering racial equality. Ultimately, given the dramatic reach of 400-plus years of ethno-racial oppression and current institutional racism, there may be little short of reparations that can complete the long journey of people of color from enslaved or colonized and oppressed and discriminated peoples to full and equal participants in American society.

Finally, asset-building strategies suggest programs not only such as minority business set-asides, but perhaps more important for the masses of people of color and the poor in general, expanding opportunities for homeownership. Studies show that "homeownership leads to stronger families and safer, more close-knit communities with better schools and services." Thus there are society-wide benefits to homeownership, but homeownership is critical to closing the wealth gap. More Americans generate wealth through owning a home—the most important and only leveraged investment available to most—than they do investing in the stock market. For most American families, it is the only way to transmit wealth from generation to generation. In effect, "owning a home is the working man and woman's capital engine," a step toward the democratization of capital.[20] A program building a public-private partnership to rescue people of color from costly subprime and predatory lend-

20. Raines, "Charter Address."

ing institutions could be an important first step to expanding wealth that can be transmitted from generation to generation in communities of color. The subprime consumer is charged a higher rate of interest than the prime consumer. The interest for subprime borrowers is usually far higher than their credit histories would indicate is justified. There are also (usually) exorbitant prepayment penalties on subprime loans (subprime lenders claim the greater risk they take by making loans to people with faulty credit histories requires a commensurate return—that is, higher profits). Subprime loans are five times more likely in black than white neighborhoods. Homeowners in high-income black areas are twice as likely as homeowners in low-income white areas to have subprime loans.[21]

In sum, the broad outline of a social policy agenda that works is not the fundamental puzzle. It is not nearly so much a question of what is to be done as finding a politics to do it.

Political Will at the Start of the Twenty-first Century

Only a Pollyanna thinks that the nation is on the precipice of endorsing the kinds of first principles for a new social policy regime outlined above. As discussed in earlier chapters, political will has been racing in the opposite direction since at least 1980. The main new social initiatives that were enacted in the 1980s and 1990s involved cutbacks, devolution, and elimination of the entitlement to welfare—all actions threatening the very heart of a social policy regime around since the New Deal and making any advances beyond it all the more unlikely.

The presidential campaign of 2000, its results, and the actions of the Bush administration indicate more of the same. To be sure, there were some important differences between the two major-party nominees, Vice President Al Gore (Democrat) and Texas Governor George W. Bush (Republican). The candidates differed on the extent to which they would protect reproductive choice and affirmative action, cut taxes, and reform Social Security and health care for the elderly, for example. Like Clinton, Gore would likely have pursued trade and domestic agendas that continued the steady undermining of social gains; but he would not have engaged in a frontal assault upon them. In no way should these differences be trivialized.

21. "Unequal Burden," Huduser, April 2000, <http://www.huduser.org/publications>.

Nevertheless, it is also true that neither party nominated a bona fide friend of the working-class, poor, and racial constituencies. Both candidates generally ignored these groups and indicated they would continue the right-ward drift. For all his promises to "fight for you," Gore, like Clinton, was the candidate of Wall Street, welfare reform with heavy sanctions, and unfettered global trade for corporations. Like Clinton, he sought to perform a balancing act. For example, running against Bill Bradley, the more progressive candidate in the Democratic primaries, at the Apollo Theater in Harlem Gore seized the opportunity to declare that he was a firm supporter of affirmative action, a declaration he repeated throughout the primaries. Yet he was always careful to emphasize that he was against "quotas," or numeric standards for measuring affirmative action's success. This stance was in keeping with Gore's reinventing a government task force proposal to abolish affirmative action guidelines in government procurement, a proposal that "eventually died a bureaucratic death."[22] Gore repeatedly pledged to help "those left behind" by the booming economy; yet he praised welfare reform efforts that denied education and train-ing (not to mention health insurance and a job guarantee) to workfare partici-pants. His choice of Senator Joseph Lieberman of Connecticut as his running mate helped him deliver on his promise to be a centrist, and regarding some policy arenas, a conservative. Lieberman, one of the most visible and militant leaders of the party's conservative wing, had campaigned for California's anti–affirmative action proposition and supported school vouchers, punitive welfare reform, and many other conservative measures. In sum, the Democrats in 2000 could not be depended on to propose, much less fight for, the kind of progres-sive first principles in social policy discussed above. Nor was there an organized force in the party that sought to spur the party's nominees in that direction. Even African American leadership, often considered to be the left flank of the Democratic Party, was essentially silent. Left-of-center Democrats had virtually no leverage within the Democratic Party in the 2000 campaign.

Shut out in their party, a small segment of the left turned to the Green Party candidate, Ralph Nader. As Nader put it, his goal was to "end the right-wing domination of the Democratic Party." But in a real sense Nader never reached out to communities of color. His whole strategy of addressing the

---

22. George Stephanopoulos, *All Too Human: A Political Education* (Boston: Little, Brown, 1999), 208–9.

needs of the poor and downtrodden and white advantage was a simple claim that he would make the nation better for *all* so that he need not discuss issues like poverty and civil rights. In effect, although Nader addressed some of the big issues affecting people of color—corporate globalization, environmental abuse, child poverty, opposition to the death penalty, legal services for the poor—he almost never pointed to the racial dimensions of these issues. Of the nineteen issues listed on the official Nader 2000 Web site, including such entries as "Clinton-Bush-Gore," "Fair Trade," and "Industrial Hemp," concern for racial justice was not obvious. When criticized by some black progressives for demonstrating a kind of "color-blindness," Nader defended himself by saying, "I've come to believe that in a political campaign, if you don't focus on basic, fundamental, democracy issues and corporate power, the media will scatter you in terms of other issues." This seemed to indicate that to Nader, anathema to racial exclusiveness and promotion of inclusiveness are apparently addenda to the "real" issues of democracy.

But if Gore and Nader showed how weak the prospects for a new and progressive social policy agenda were in 2000 in Democratic and Independent politics, George W. Bush was anything but an alternative. Although Bush sought to present himself as a "compassionate conservative," near the start of his campaign he stirred up controversy when he visited the segregationist Bob Jones University and when he stood behind states' rights in a controversy over whether the Confederate flag should still fly over South Carolina's statehouse.[23] Even as he modestly stepped up the Republicans outreach to black voters (for instance, he visited inner-city schools and churches, spoke at the NAACP 2000 convention, and prominently featured General Colin Powell and Condoleezza Rice at the Republican National Convention in July 2000), Bush simultaneously promised the kind of justices he would nominate to the Supreme Court would be like Antonin Scalia and Clarence Thomas—the two most conservative justices—and promised as the centerpiece of his administration a $1.3 trillion income tax cut that would go overwhelmingly to the rich, partial privatization of Social Security to allow younger workers to use a portion of their payroll taxes to set up personal retirement accounts, support for school vouchers, weakening of affirmative action, and deregulation of industries from

23. Tamar Jacoby, "Voters and Victims: How Blacks Lost—No Matter What," *National Review,* Dec. 4, 2000.

oil to health care. These were anything but policies that would either generate spending on new social programs or infringe on white skin privilege. For instance, few blacks stood to gain from the heavy overall tax cut going to the rich or the elimination of estate taxes; and even eliminating the marriage penalty would help whites more than blacks. In addition, the more Bush pointed to Texas—with its 1.4 million children without health insurance (a huge proportion of whom were Latinos), squandered surplus, appalling pollution record, exaggerated assessment of school standards, housing crisis, and death factory—as the poster child and validation for his presidential race, the clearer it was how much people of color stood to lose.

In sum, in the first presidential election of the twenty-first century, neither Bush, Gore, nor Nader seriously addressed the poor, city dwellers, or racial minorities. Instead, with the race for the presidency one of the tightest ever, the campaign zeroed in on the undecided or swing voters—mainly said to be affluent suburban and elderly whites. The surgically tailored themes, emerging from focus groups and polls of "likely voters"—a practice that already eliminated nonvoters and infrequent voters (mainly low-income and poor people and racial minorities) even before the candidates hit the campaign trail—patently ignored the concerns of those whose boats had not been lifted by the nation's longest economic boom. Preempted from the general election campaign were the most immediate and critical issues concerning many Americans who favored a more inclusive social policy agenda and racial justice. There was no space for debate about real national health care in a publicly funded health care system; access to decent, secure jobs at a living wage, not to mention a guarantee of a citizen's income; protections and extension of workers' right to organize and bargain collectively and to exercise in the workplace their constitutional rights of free speech and assembly and curtailment of employers' prerogatives that often amount to imposing involuntary servitude; elimination of the war on poor people being conducted via the 1996 welfare reform, the war on drugs, and a draconian criminal justice policy that has incarcerated more than two million people (disproportionately black and Latino), the double whammy of federal support for urban redevelopment initiatives that displace minority, poor, and working people and eliminate affordable housing combined with the federal retreat from direct provision of low-income housing, and on and on.

Indeed, the view that it fundamentally mattered whether Gore or Bush was elected was more a result of the language and techniques of marketing and press desires for a horse race than the candidates' own stances. The candidates actually muted their differences and co-opted each other's issues. Gore's problem as a candidate was not just that he kept reinventing his personality but that he sent mixed messages on his program. When Bush charged that Gore wanted to increase public spending, Gore might have said: "You bet I do. How else are we going to finance drug coverage for seniors, or health insurance for all kids, or better schools, or secure those leaving welfare for work when recession hits?" Instead Gore took the charge as an insult and insisted that he was a champion cutter of big government. Both nominees claimed their party deserved credit for firmly altering welfare, producing falling crime rates, narrowing immigration quotas, and cutting back affirmative action and other racially charged policies. Each was so successful in these claims that polls showed that Republicans enjoyed only a small advantage on matters such as crime, drugs, welfare, and affirmative action—issues on which they had long fared far better than Democrats. No wonder voters were confused. In sum, in 2000 the nation was drawn into a debate on terms set by the bipartisan consensus reduced to a handful of issues that, although meaningful enough on their own, were treated as symbolically encasing the concerns of identifiable groups that easily could be marginalized as "special interests."

Ironically, it was these marginalized interests that produced the most unusual American election in the twentieth century and kept Gore's election chances alive for thirty-five days. For instance, the black vote played a prominent role in enabling Gore to take the lead in the national popular vote (by 539,897 votes). Bush won the white vote (54 percent with Gore winning only 42 percent), but Gore outpolled Bush among blacks by 90 percent to 9 percent. Nationally, Gore also won the votes of Latinos, Asian Americans, Jews, members of labor unions, the poor, and women. Black women and Latinas in particular supported Gore nationally. Indeed, much of the 12-point gender gap is explained by women of color, since white women narrowly split their votes (49 percent for Bush; 48 percent for Gore).[24] Nationally, the vote was so close that the thousands of black ex-felons (mostly males locked up wholesale over the previous eight years for nonviolent offenses as a result of the Clinton administration's own crime bill, and who had now served their time in prison and

24. Marjorie Connelly, "Who Voted: A Portrait of American Politics," *New York Times,* Nov. 12, 2000, Week in Review.

gone on to lead productive and reformed lives) would have been enough to alter election results—*if* they could have voted.[25]

Nonetheless, it is noteworthy that it was the black vote (15 percent of the Florida electorate) that propelled Gore to a strong enough position to contest the vote in Florida. There Gore won 93 percent of the black vote compared with 7 percent for Bush. Meanwhile Bush won the white women's vote, the Latino vote, and almost all other demographic categories in Florida. Thus black marginalized interests were key in producing an election so close that a decision over who won would come only after the five most conservative justices on the Supreme Court set a new precedent by weighing in and in effect awarding election to George W. Bush, although controversy continued for months over whether a manual recount of the votes would show that Gore was the actual victor.

That two men seemingly so close to the center line of politics, what Adolph Reed calls "Republicrat convergence," could stir such different emotions said more about the nation than it did about the candidates. Electoral division on November 7, 2000, was a visceral expression of a country divided over the interpretation of its past, the understanding of its present, and the hopes for its future, regardless of whether either of the two candidates actually represented these fault lines. What mattered more than the candidates' actual differences were the disparate constituencies, donors, and patrons that supported them.

In a visceral sense, the Bush entourage was disproportionately made up of constituencies that had previously supported Reagan-Bush and their firm commitment to conservative moral values, unfettered opportunities for the corporate elite, cutting back the welfare state, and white skin privilege. These were groups who had never accepted Bill Clinton and had waited eight years for him to leave office. Despite the fact that Clinton certainly had not produced a liberal, much less progressive, policy record, these groups had regarded him as an illegitimate president because he was stereotyped as giving certain quarters of American power a hard time—characterized by a new term in the Wall Street lexicon during the immediate aftermath of the 2000 election: "Bush stocks"—and giving comfort to certain other quarters—"the blacks." Now the

25. According to Reuters News Service, nationally 13% of all black men cannot vote because of incarceration and past felony convictions; in Florida, one in three.

groups supporting George W. Bush were dedicated to turning back. So much was his victory a restoration of the past that a substantial proportion of his Cabinet and aides came from his father's prior administration (including his two most important symbols of commitment to diversity, Powell and Rice). Clearly the Democrats, despite their desertion of the substantive policy concerns of racial minorities and liberals in general and despite their emphasis on being "new" Democrats, were not left better off than before Clinton came into office. When he was elected in 1992 the Democrats had 57 senators; they came out of the 2000 election with 50.[26] They controlled the House with a majority of 266 in 1993; in the immediate aftermath of the 2000 election, they had become a minority of 211. The Democrats held 28 governorships and a majority of state legislatures in 1992; they had only 17 governorships and a minority of state assemblies after the 2000 elections. Still there was little to indicate that these dismal election outcomes would encourage the party to rethink its strategies and policy priorities.

Meanwhile, the selection of Bush as the first American president "elected" in the twenty-first century confirmed that social policy would continue to move rightward, at least in the short term. As Bush entered office, it appeared that the narrowness of his official victory, the pall of illegitimacy that surrounded his presidency, and the very close partisan balance in both houses of Congress would force the new president to cut back his ambitiously conservative agenda in some distinctive ways.

Nonetheless, from the start the kind of racial politics and its implications for social policy were clear. Bush's first two nominees were two blacks—Powell as secretary of state and Rice as national security adviser. He used the occasion of their nomination not only to reify once again the links between the American ethos and the ideology of whiteness but to engage in the new racism that substituted individual for group mobility. As Bush put it, the nominations of Powell, Rice, and Albert Gonzales showed that "people who work hard and make the right decisions in America can achieve anything they want." The implication, of course, is that the nation needs no longer to be concerned with the ideology and practice of whiteness. There would be no new emphasis on achieving racial equality.

26. Only when James Jeffords of Vermont left the Republican Party and became an Independent did the Democrats acquire a one-vote working majority in the Senate.

Even the social program touted to be "the most significant revision of schools policy since the Elementary and Secondary Education Act of 1965"[27] pointedly took no notice of racial disparities. While it increased standards and testing for schools, provided a system of punishment and rewards, and sought to deliver more federal aid to the neediest schools,[28] it failed to address the dramatic disparities in pupil funding across the country, as a result of antiquated practices of financing schools primarily through state and local taxes—a process that translates the vast socioeconomic differences between neighborhoods, counties, and states into vast differences in school funds. That these disparities exist disproportionately in minority communities remained unaddressed. With less than one-tenth of school funding actually coming from the federal government, Congress and the White House engaged in what was little more than substituting symbolism for substance. While the bill provided marginal increases in funds to the poorest school districts, it was not nearly enough to begin to level the playing field nationwide or between minority and white schools. In general, the welfare state continued to shrink, not grow, in the first year of the George W. Bush administration.

The events of September 11, 2001, when a terrorist attack killed more than 2,000 at the World Trade Center in New York City and hundreds more at the Pentagon and in the Pennsylvania countryside, had ominous portents for the trend of stagnation and deterioration in the commitment to social rights in the United States and the patent lack of concern for the continuing racial divide. To be sure, in the immediate aftermath of September 11 it appeared as if there would be an opportunity to promote greater unity across the races. Newspaper stories were flush with anecdotal accounts indicating that the "old racial division" among blacks, Latinos, and whites was abating.[29] Blacks and whites were said to be united in an understanding of September 11 as an attack on all Americans, regardless to race. Here, at least, there was no white skin privilege. Typical in such stories were comments from blacks such as: "I just thought of myself as black. But now I feel like I'm an American, more than ever."[30] Poll data backed up journalistic accounts: the data reported enhanced

27. Dana Milbank, "With Fanfare, Bush Signs Education Bill," *Washington Post,* Jan. 9, 2002, A3.

28. Ibid.

29. Somini Sengupta, "Sept. 11 Attack Narrows the Racial Divide," *New York Times,* Oct. 10, 2001.

30. Quoted ibid.

trust across ethno-racial divisions and even greater open-mindedness toward intermarriage.[31]

Ironically, however, the newfound Americanness across race and ethnicity perhaps told more about the tendency in the United States to view developments through a racial prism than not. As the traditional racial divisions were tweaked momentarily, many turned to a new ethno-racial enemy. Racial profiling previously centered on "driving while black" turned into racial profiling centered on "flying while brown"—a new phrase coined to refer to harassment at airports of anyone who stereotypically looked like an Arab or Muslim American. Not only was trust in Arab Americans 10 percent below the level expressed toward other ethno-racial groups in a post–September 11 poll,[32] but seemingly, at least, blacks and Latinos joined whites in supporting this new target of racial profiling. For example, a month after the September 11 attacks, of the 120 alleged bias incidents reported to the New York police, 80 were against Arabs and South Asians and the suspects were whites, blacks, and Latinos. Moreover, nearly as many blacks as whites supported regarding Middle Eastern travelers with "more suspicion" than others in one early October poll.[33] Apparently some blacks experienced a newfound Americanness by supporting racist attitudes and views. But obviously a single event, even one so tragic as the September 11 terrorist attacks, could hardly be expected to displace the "old racial division" for long. Only a few months later, conflict erupted over a memorial to the firefighters who had behaved heroically in the wake of the disaster: should the memorial show whites only lifting the American flag, as a popular photograph had portrayed, or one white, one black, and one Latino? In addition, the willingness of a majority of respondents to polls to give up some civil liberties in exchange for "security" hardly demonstrated fertile new ground for a battle against white skin privilege. Even George W. Bush's job approval rating received a mighty boost among blacks. As late as November 27, 2001, 46 percent strongly approved and 35 percent approved somewhat of the way Bush was "handling his job as president." Of course, this remained far below Clinton's consistently high job approval among blacks and substantial racial gaps persisted between the levels of approval, but 81 percent of blacks

31. Robert D. Putnam, "Bowling Together," <http://www.prospect.org/print/V13/3/putnam-r.html>.

32. Ibid.

33. Sengupta, "Sept. 11 Attack."

approving a Republican president was a monumental change. Meanwhile, nothing had changed in the president's approach to racial politics or the social policy agenda. Nor was Congress responding favorably to the civil rights and social policy agenda of blacks. The NAACP's "report card"—its rating system—found that more than half the members had voted against every piece of legislation on their agenda in the first session of the 107th Congress.[34] These developments seem to indicate that the pressures for altering the course of social policy in a leftward direction were declining, not growing.

Perhaps the most devastating setback of all for prospects of social policy was the way developments flowing from the September 11 tragedy deepened economic precariousness and depleted funding for the domestic agenda. With the budget surplus already eliminated by the economic slowdown and Bush's huge tax cut passed in the spring of 2001, faced with the decision to increase spending on military and national security initiatives and the spiraling costs of bailouts for the airline and other travel industries, a consensus emerged in the White House and Congress to allow budget deficits in 2002 and support an economic stimulus package. The sheer economics of the moment virtually ensured that few new social programs requiring substantial spending had a ghost of a chance of passage, and true to expectations, the politics of the moment produced a stimulus package that, while costing $41 billion over the next ten years, provided less than $3 billion to help the jobless and 90 percent or more of the total new spending in assistance for business. The new tax write-offs for business in the stimulus package promised to deepen the damage done to state budgets by the recession by reducing corporate tax obligations by an estimated $14.6 billion over the next three years, rendering the states less capable of helping the indigent.[35]

As perhaps the most potent symbol of the failure of the earlier stimulus package and the large tax cuts already enacted, by January 2003 unemployment had crept back up to 6.0 and the Bush administration proposed yet another stimulus package. Like the administration's previous one, the January proposal included little that would immediately stimulate the economy and much that would provide tax cuts for the rich. Of the $674 billion proposed

34. "Legislative Report Card for the 107th Congress, First Session, Final Edition" (Washington, D.C.: Washington Bureau of the NAACP, July 2002)
35. David S. Broder, "No Stomach for the 'Stimulus,'" *Washington Post,* Mar. 13, 2002, A29.

package, more than half the benefits would go to those making more than $200,000 annually and a whopping quarter to people making more than $1 million a year. It was class warfare unvarnished—the wealthy class who needed help least was getting most of the help. With lower revenues to follow and the proposal to fight at least two costly wars (a war in Iraq and the War on Terrorism, as well as perhaps a war against North Korea), expected budget deficits would be again the pretext to do nothing in the social policy arena.[36] The conclusion is nearly inescapable: these were the worst of times for the kind of social policy agenda proposed above.

36. Paul Krugman, "An Irrelevant Proposal," New York Times, Jan. 7, 2003.

Conclusion

I refuse to accept the idea that an individual is mere flotsam and jetsam in the river of life, unable to influence the unfolding events which surround him.
—Martin Luther King Jr.

Despite the dismal current scenario for social citizenship, there is, of course, always the possibility for change. Those committed to change must not throw up their hands in despair; rather they must begin to build a new politics for bringing about a new social policy regime when the next window of opportunity opens. They must prepare for the long haul, for it is unlikely that American public opinion, the dominance of conservative politics, the role race plays in it, and the nation's constrictive social policy agenda can be transformed swiftly. After all, it took conservatives roughly thirty years in the wilderness of American national politics, from Goldwater's humiliating defeat in 1964 to Republicans' recapture of control of Congress in 1994, to consolidate their dominance over both public opinion and the nation's agenda. With equally dedicated commitment, organization, and hard work, in time a countermovement can develop and restore opportunities for a new public philosophy centered on equal social rights.

How might one mount the long, hard struggle for the public mind and the mobilization of massive public support for a new social policy regime? How might a multiracial coalition be forged to attack white skin privilege, its structures and institutions, organizational forms, policies, and cultural practices, and create in its stead a transformative, oppositional alternative—what Antonio Gramsci called a "war of position"?

In regard to this last question, the importance of white skin privilege poses a fundamental conundrum: given the material and sociopsychological interests in white privilege that have been driving much of the history of social policy, what would it take for the white majority to become willing to support equal social rights for all?

The main argument that has been advanced to answer this question can be called the "universalist" solution. Universalists maintain that if advocates of social citizenship focus on issues that serve the white middle class as well as the nonwhite poor, a multiracial coalition will emerge. In William Julius Wilson's view, for example, it makes little political sense to pursue race-based social policies that make African Americans a special class of recipients. He implies that today such specialism, not racism, generates hostility against assistance for poor and low-income African Americans. Wilson thus calls for universal programs rather than compensatory group-targeted ones to halt the deterioration of inner-city communities. His "hidden agenda" is to improve the life chances of groups such as the "ghetto underclass" by emphasizing programs in which the more advantaged groups of all races can positively relate.[1] The political logic, according to Wilson, is that the needs of middle-class whites—for more and better jobs, access to higher education and health care, and reductions in drug trafficking and crime—can be linked to those of the African American poor if the wedge issue of race can be blunted.

Theda Skocpol takes Wilson's argument a step further by suggesting that universal programs will generate "collective solidarity" that eventually will benefit poor people of color. Affluent whites will not think of assistance for the poor in "us" versus "them" terms if universal policies are the goal. According to Skocpol, since the 1930s the southern racial caste system of political and economic inequalities has crumbled. The groups the 1960s social welfare programs were designed to appease—people of color (especially blacks), Appalachian and other poor whites, and the white middle class—are now competing with each other over pieces of a rapidly shrinking economic pie. Today's policy battles, Skocpol continues, are framed as a contest between advocates of racial minorities who fight for targeted benefits and conservative politicians who exploit white opposition to "special" benefits for people of color.[2]

Thus Skocpol concludes that if advocates for poor people of color "were

---

1. William J. Wilson, *The Truly Disadvantaged: The Inner City, the Underclass, and Public Policy* (Chicago: University of Chicago Press, 1987), 120.

2. Theda Skocpol, "The Limits of the New Deal System and the Roots of Contemporary Welfare Dilemmas," in Margaret Weir, Ann Orloff, and Theda Skocpol, eds., *The Politics of Social Policy in the United States* (Princeton: Princeton University Press, 1988), 308.

more supportive of universal programs oriented toward the white middle class, then the white middle class would reciprocate out of a newfound solidarity."[3] Universal programs would "create new opportunities" because such programs would have a "consistent moral voice," and would "reinforce fundamental American values such as rewards for work, opportunities for individual betterment, and family and community responsibility for the care of children and other vulnerable people." In Skocpol's view, like Wilson's, when civil rights advocates are not "preoccupied with defending affirmative action or pushing for measures targeted on the nonwhite poor," conservatives will lose a political rallying point and universalist social policies will lead to collective solidarity across race, class, and region.[4]

Skocpol admits that in her version of universalism, benefits would initially accrue to the white middle class, whose political support is needed to implement it. Thus hers is a trickle-down universalism, dictated by political goals. She argues that poor African Americans would benefit later, after group identities have been reshaped through government programs." Hence Skocpol concludes that African Americans and other people of color are probably best served by quietly mobilizing support for those leaders of the white middle class who support universalism.

To be sure, the universalist argument has a seductive logic that can be buttressed by the large number of issues that threaten people across the races and even across nations (depletion of the industrial workforce, growth of the poorly paid ranks of the service sector, suffering parts of the agricultural sector, destruction of the environment, the declining clout of trade unionism, and lack of access to decent health care, affordable housing, and quality education, to name just a few) as well as evidence revealing that poor people of color are politically weak or even irrelevant and cannot produce change on their own. However, a number of problems surface in regard to the universalists' claim that if blacks and other people of color would give up their demands for group-specific policies, a wide swath of people in all racial groups (including middle-class whites) would realize that the American dream does not work for them; recognize that their own interests are at stake, be more likely to see their commonalities with people of color, and move in cross-race solidarity.

3. Ibid.
4. Theda Skocpol, "Targeting within Universalism: Politically Viable Policies to Combat Poverty in the United States," in Christopher Jencks and Paul Peterson, eds., *The Urban Underclass* (Washington, D.C:. Brookings, 1991), 429.

First, there is the problem of rationally and accurately determining one's self-interest. American history is replete with miscalculations in which people's *subjective* interests (their conscious preferences) are diametrically opposed to their *objective* interests (those interests that affect their life chances whether they know it or not).[5] Put succinctly, it should not be taken for granted that conscious orientations or actions approximate objective class interests. Indeed, people of all races are often mistaken about what their objective economic interests are—especially when such interests are in the long rather than short run. Take, for example, an issue such as health care, which is not nearly as deeply infused with racial politics as many other social issues. Although trend data collected by the Census Bureau show that more and more Americans are uninsured and public opinion polls find that large majorities prefer universal health insurance,[6] the coalition for health care reform splinters when voters are told even small tax increases might be sought to put it in place—this despite the fact that studies show most middle-class and low-income Americans would gain far more from universal health insurance than they would lose from higher taxes.[7] In short, one should not underestimate how difficult the project of building solidarity for universalism is, even when racial issues are not at the fore.

Another error stems from neglecting nonmaterial motives for racism. To be certain, material interests matter significantly and perhaps most dramatically, but the politics of race goes deeper than mere economic self-interest. Only an economic determinist refuses to understand that social status competition often plays a more important role in generating racism than narrow economic interest. As scholars from W. E. B. Du Bois to Howard Winant conclude, there are cultural and moral dimensions of white skin privilege.[8]

A third problem of universalist thinking derives from the role attributed to blacks in collective action. More to the point, if it is in no way certain that

5. For discussion, see Isaac D. Balbus, "The Concept of Interests in Pluralist and Marxian Analysis," *Politics and Society* 1 (1971): 14–41; and Ralf Dahrendorf, *Class and Class Conflict in Industrial Society* (Stanford: Stanford University Press, 1959), 174–76.

6. U.S. Bureau of the Census, *Health Insurance Coverage: 2001,* Current Population Reports, P60–220, Table 14101; "Gallup Poll Analyses—Health Care an Important Issue This Year" (Sept. 28, 2000), <http://www.gallup.com/health>.

7. Kaiser Foundation Survey, Nov. 8, 1994.

8. W. E. B. Du Bois, *Dusk of Dawn: Autobiography of a Race Concept* (New York: Schocken, 1968), 205; Howard Winant, "Behind Blue Eyes: Whiteness and Contemporary U.S. Racial Politics," in Michelle Fine, Lois Weis, Linda C. Powell, and L. Mun Wong, eds., *Off White: Readings on Race, Power, and Society* (New York: Routledge, 1997), 45–47.

poor and middle-class whites can be encouraged to participate in solidary actions with people of color, it is equally doubtful that poor and middle-class African Americans—the only group universalists such as Wilson and Skocpol ask to stop advocating for themselves—will relinquish their historically grounded demands for justice in exchange for guidance by the political interests of the white middle class. In fact, universalism requires African Americans to invest a high degree of trust in whites, particularly in white political leadership. Yet no one ever explains exactly why African Americans should believe that white Americans will ultimately make a connection between their own interests and the interests of poor people of color. Instead, if history is a guide, shared oppression need no more generate solidarity than it necessarily breeds contempt. Much depends on the type of leadership that emerges, and, unfortunately, so far American history indicates that far fewer white leaders have sought to encourage whites to believe that eliminating the suffering of poor people of color is in their own interest than conversely have sought to divide the working class by race and conquer. Indeed, past eras of widespread common suffering have all too often resulted in scapegoating African Americans, religious minorities, and immigrants, not joining them.[9] Moreover, this has happened despite the fact, as Dona and Charles Hamilton show in copious detail, that national civil rights groups in every decade beginning with the inception of the American welfare state have *never* focused solely on policies directed toward helping people of color alone, but rather have consistently emphasized "(1) a preference for a *universal* social welfare system and (2) jobs for *all* in the regular labor market."[10] Thus, if there are good reasons to doubt that white Americans would automatically support the implementation of universalist policies, there are just as few reasons to expect African Americans to abandon their particularistic demands and place their trust in suspect political strategies that offer vague promises that whites will embrace African Americans at some undefined point in the future.[11]

The very notion of a "hidden agenda" contradicts the claim that racism is of "declining significance" and need not be specifically addressed in social

9. Jill Quadagno, *The Color of Poverty: How Racism Undermined the War on Poverty* (New York: Oxford University Press, 1994), 74–114.

10. Dona Cooper Hamilton and Charles V. Hamilton, *The Dual Agenda: Race and Social Welfare Policies of Civil Rights Organizations* (New York: Columbia University Press, 1997), 3–4.

11. Thompson, "Universalism and Deconcentration."

policy and coalition formation. Indeed, it is because of racism that universalists such as Wilson and Skocpol feel compelled to hide their agenda in the first place. Apparently "the underlying premise is that the United States is so racist—so utterly indifferent to the plight of people of color, so implacably opposed to any indemnification for centuries of racial oppression—that it becomes necessary to camouflage policies intended for people of color behind policies that offer benefits to the white majority."[12] Not only have past experiences with universal policies from Social Security to the GI Bill not lifted all boats equally but the universalists' silence on, ambivalence about, or suppression of black claims for racial justice reinforce black fears that they will never see the promised fruit of collective solidarity.

What counts is what people see as the causes of their oppression. As long as white skin privilege is ignored as a cause of the oppression of people of color, there will be an organizational impasse, for such lack of consideration cements distrust between people of color and whites and weakens grounds for cooperation. Without openly tackling the racial divide, one should not expect those many multiracial Americans who have not benefited from the most recent wave of prosperity to comprehend their common interests in new social policies.

In short, as difficult as it may be to build a multiracial coalition that owns up to racial injustice, there is little probability that ignoring the politics and policy of white skin privilege will produce a strong and sustainable coalition for change. Only a successful project that clarifies the real statuses of people of color and the effects on them of not just past but current discrimination could invert the logic of the bill of goods sold by conservative Republicans and Democrats.

Thus, rather than blunting the wedge issue of race, as universalists such as Wilson and Skocpol advocate, both the commonalities that bind *and* the race-specific experiences that objectively separate whites from most people of color must be components of the new political logic. Both targeted compensatory and universal benefits are needed. Collective solidarity across race, class, and region can happen only, if at all, when both racial minorities and middle-class whites feel their interests are being addressed in the short run. If conservatives triumph by diverting white Americans from legitimate class concerns to

---

12. Stephen Steinberg, *Turning Back: The Retreat from Racial Justice in American Thought and Politics* (Boston: Beacon, 1995), 124.

focus on racial ones, a progressive alternative must begin by focusing on legitimate race concerns and move to class concerns. Only through facing up to ongoing racial discrimination and the continuing unequal plight of people of color within each class and as ethno-racial groups can one begin to demonstrate how advancing the struggle for racial equality fosters not just the struggle for democracy in some abstract sense but socioeconomic well-being for all groups in a very material sense. Only when this happens will group identities be reshaped through government programs in a way that leads to cross-racial solidarity and justice.

In effect, this means that leaders must help people realize that racial advancement has nearly always meant class and gender advancement. As noted in the introduction to this study, in the nineteenth century, white women, struggling for abolition of slavery, found voice for their own claims for suffrage and equal rights. Providing education for "freedmen" after the Civil War boosted public school provision for whites, too, throughout the South. Eliminating the poll tax brought far more poor whites to the voting booths than it brought blacks in the early 1960s. Expanding welfare in the mid-1960s gave millions of poor white mothers and children access to improved government aid. Even a policy stigmatized as "race-specific," affirmative action, helped hundreds of thousands of the sisters, mothers, daughters, and wives of white men enter colleges, secure employment, and gain promotions. Conversely, when poor people of color lose benefits, so do far more whites. Thus, when poor people of color were subjected to racist stereotypes depicting them as undeserving and public assistance programs were stereotyped as "programs for them," poor whites also suffered negative consequences, most recently in respect to the 1996 welfare reform act.[13]

In short, there must be an open, frontal exposure of right-wing politicians who interpret civil rights, equal opportunity, and affirmative action as distinct from and unfair to the interests of poor whites. It must be disclosed that the host of analytic thumb-twisting over the impact of race versus the impact of class, as if there were a contest about which was the most pressing as a source of disadvantage and which deserved attention, is little more than a diversionary tactic. Such analyses undermine the potential to advance the understanding of

---

13. Kenneth J. Neubeck and Noel A. Cazenave, *Welfare Racism: Playing the Race Card against America's Poor* (New York: Routledge, 2001), 223.

the universal side of the demand for civil and social rights. Thus, moving from race to class means the explicit effort to link the interests of people of color with those of the white working and middle classes. But this cannot be done by pretending that class issues have supplanted racial ones any more than it can be done by pretending that racial discrimination is the only factor impeding the progress of blacks. Race and class inequality are inextricably linked and collective solidarity across the races can be achieved only by fleshing out the connections. What is needed is risk-taking. Those of any color leading comfortable lives in the current ethno-racial status quo must accept the risks involved in going against the prevailing wind if a democracy that is substantive, not just procedural, and a citizenship that is social, not just political, are ever to emerge.

The historical experience presented in this book demonstrates that this is precisely what has happened at the few critical historical conjunctures in which whites—a substantial number of leaders and mass—were persuaded to join the challenge to white skin privilege. In sum, history shows that at critical turning points in the politics of race and social policy, an impressive number of whites were persuaded to join the struggle for equal rights. They took risks— sometimes in regard to political fortunes and sometimes in regard to socioeconomic ones and sometimes in regard to life itself—to expand the very definitions of American citizenship and democracy to include people of color.

In short, alongside the more dispiriting history chronicled here, at important historical moments key white leaders have been willing to grant and the white majority has been willing to accept important expansions of minority rights. Such historical moments include but are not limited to the work of Radical Republicans in the Reconstruction era, the presidential administrations of Harry Truman and Lyndon Johnson in the post–World War II/Cold War era, and the white champions of civil rights in what is often called the Second Reconstruction during the Vietnam War era. In each of these instances, an impressive contingent of whites joined people of color and supported advances for minority rights at great risk to their own political ambitions and individual welfare. Far more than a few whites were threatened, ostracized, beaten, jailed, and killed for their commitment to civil rights and the abolition of white skin privilege.[14]

14. See, e.g., G. McLeod Bryan, ed., *These Few Also Paid a Price: Southern Whites Who Fought for Civil Rights* (Macon, Ga.: Mercer University Press, 2001).

What is common about these instances that can be instructive for creating a new window of opportunity for building a multiracial coalition in support of social citizenship for all? What conditions appear to prefigure struggles when people of color are joined by whites in relatively successful efforts to expand and equalize the reach of American social policy?

First, as Antonio Gramsci explained, it is difficult for a new regime, a new public philosophy, or even a new policy agenda to break through and become the public will. Here his concept of hegemony is useful. According to Gramsci, in ordinary times power in advanced capitalist societies is expressed through the construction of a folk common sense that explains, rationalizes, and reinforces the rule of dominant groups. That is, a hegemonic bloc of capitalists, state officials, media personnel, and intellectuals exercise moral and cultural leadership by winning the consent of subordinate social forces to its rule, and this consent is the result of acceptance of the hegemonic bloc's particular interests as the general interest. Gramsci further explains, however, that because hegemony is a negotiated process, it is never complete or absolute. Economic and political crises create contradictions between people's lived experiences and the dominant ideology and thereby provide opportunities for subordinate social forces to question the taken-for-grantedness of the folk common sense.[15]

This implies, then, that ordinarily neither whites nor people of color question the hegemonic construction of race. Only under exceptional conditions has white skin privilege been opposed and assaulted. Such an assault has typically occurred during times of national crisis. The most important challenges to white skin privilege and alterations in the nation's social policy regime all occurred in *extraordinary* times—when the nation was in the midst of political and usually military crises. In these instances, the state faced a crisis of legitimacy—a development that seemingly weighed heavier than crises that were principally economic. For example, while an economic crisis such as the Great Depression led to dramatic alteration of the social policy regime, the challenge to whiteness was virtually nil. The three key periods that generated racial progress supported by multiracial coalitions (the Civil War and its aftermath, World War II and its aftermath, and the Cold War and the war in Vietnam) were all

---

15. Antonio Gramsci, *Selections from the Prison Notebooks* (New York: International Publishers, 1971).

times of state legitimacy crises. Indeed, in the 1960s, the period of the greatest policy change and advance for people of color, the nation was experiencing unprecedented economic prosperity. State legitimacy crises, more than economic ones (although the two are obviously related), call into question hegemonic claims about the nature of America. They put into sharp focus the contradictions between the nation's two open ideologies (liberal individualism and republicanism) and its just as real but secret one (ascriptive inegalitarianism). As people of color were called upon to help America fight enemies of democracy and stepped up their own challenge for the nation to live up to its open democratic ideals, they were joined by whites jarred by the disclosure of ugly revelations regarding that secret ideal.

Second, the instances in which people of color gained white allies in attacking white skin privilege occurred in moments when significant fault lines and contradictions developed within the hegemonic bloc itself due to conflicting interests, capacities, and perceptions. Upheaval and crisis affect dominant groups differently, undermining the power of some segments and enlarging the power of others, so that dominant groups split among themselves. This dissonance tends to erode their authority and the authority of the institutional norms they uphold; in the ensuing competition within the hegemonic bloc, some factions seek to enlist the support of the subordinated by naming their grievances as just. This stirs the hope of the subordinated groups for change and further weakens the legitimacy of current arrangements.[16] For example, the economic interests of northern industrialists and the southern plantocracy differed in the Reconstruction period and led them to differing perceptions of a "free labor" system in the South. Altruistic pressures in civil society combined with the political ambitions of the Radical Republicans and the economic ambitions of cotton mill operators and manufacturers, interested in driving down the costs of raw cotton by breaking the southern plantocracy's semimonopoly in its production, to create fissures in that day's hegemonic bloc.

During World War II, black militancy grew as blacks, especially northern ones, found racism in the military particularly galling. Their disclosures in the context of the growth of fascism and America's coming new global role forced some whites to begin to challenge the racial inequalities in their midst. Some

---

16. Frances Piven and Richard Cloward, *Poor People's Movements: Why They Succeed, How They Fail* (New York: Pantheon, 1977), 13.

dominant elites, such as the government officials whose job it was to win the war, began to complain that racial outrages at home provided grist for German and Japanese propaganda mills while dominant elites in the South remained adamant in their defense of Jim Crow. Manpower shortages combined with pressure from blacks also encouraged a fraction of the industrial elite to challenge the dominant construction of race in that period.[17] Political elites in northern cities with fast-growing black populations also posed new challenges to that day's racial attitudes. In general, electoral considerations motivated a fraction of Democratic Party elites to modestly challenge whiteness.[18]

Similarly, during the Cold War, while southern elites by and large resisted any moderation of white skin privilege, northern elites fretted increasingly about how incidents of racial discrimination adversely affected the nation's international efforts to reach out to the uncommitted people of the Middle East, Africa, and Southeast Asia. The international activities of corporate leaders encouraged some, such as members of the Business Council, to become concerned about the foreign implications of white skin privilege even as Cold War concerns made many ordinary white Americans more attuned to the nation's global vulnerability on civil rights. As the Civil Rights Movement became increasingly disruptive, a growing number of whites began to see moderation of white skin privilege as one means by which Americans could keep together a society that seemed to be coming apart. In sum, hegemonic crises with implications for state legitimacy, the protest movements of people of color, and renegotiations within the hegemonic bloc itself have typically been preconditions for emergence of a multiracial coalition committed to advancing social citizenship for all. To be sure, to date renegotiation within the hegemonic bloc has resulted in only modest material concessions, co-opting the disclosure of challengers, and bringing moderate groups into the hegemonic bloc while marginalizing more radical ones. While these actions produced important social change, it was social change that fell far short of a war of position critically challenging white skin privilege. Still the historical conjunctures in which a significant number of whites (some elites and some masses) joined people of color to challenge white skin privilege provide a glimpse into what it takes for a window of opportunity to materialize.

17. Note, however, that some of the same developments reinforced the nation's "Yellow Peril" racist traditions.

18. Philip A. Klinkner with Rogers K. Smith, *The Unsteady March: The Rise and Decline of Racial Equality in America* (Chicago: University of Chicago Press, 1999), chap. 7.

These conditions (a crisis of state legitimacy brought on by political or military crisis, as opposed to mere partisan positioning and bickering, a vigorous protest movement among people of color challenging hegemonic conceptions of race and social policy, and significant fault lines within the hegemonic bloc regarding the politics of race) were certainly not present in the 1990s. Perhaps, then, it is not surprising that Bill Clinton, the putative heir to the New Deal, co-opted the conservative agenda and declared that "the era of big government is over."[19]

Whether conditions associated in the past with advancing the possibilities of a multiracial coalition for equal social rights will appear again in the near future is a question impossible to answer. Only time will tell whether the complex subtext regarding race in the "War on Terrorism," the global interests of corporate America, and a large-scale mobilization of people of color will produce conflict within the hegemonic bloc, call into question the legitimacy of the state, bring into sharp relief the contradictions in the nation's multiple ideologies, and encourage a significant fraction of whites to join the now multifarious array of people of color in challenging white skin privilege as ideology and reality. All that is certain is that if leaders have not already prepared the way to walk through the narrow and rapidly closing window of opportunity that the emergence of such conditions could reopen, even the pace of progress achieved in similar previous eras will not materialize.

Much, then, depends on what leaders are doing today. What is needed is leaders who will not seek to divide the working class by race and conquer, but instead encourage the white masses to understand that eliminating the suffering of the "least of these" is in their own interest. Such leaders seem to be in critically short supply. Not only the Republican but the Democratic leadership has virtually abandoned overturning centuries of white skin privilege as an important goal. When it comes to racial politics, there are few risk-takers on the political stage today.

Thus the new millennium begins as a political era full of peril—not just of partisan blockage or international threats, but of a deeper social and economic malaise. The question is not just whether the nation can withstand the menace of outside enemy forces but whether its own civic and social fabric will

---

19. Bill Clinton, *Between Hope and History: Meeting America's Challenges for the 21st Century* (New York: Random House, 1996), 90.

hold. A state legitimacy crisis, especially accompanied by a deep and sustained recession, could show that the current veneer of "One America," free, just, and equal, is like the emperor with no clothes, and throw into bold relief the divisiveness and polarization that still undermine the nation. The growing transnational movement challenging global capitalism not only provides a new stage for battle but could escalate a focus on the local roots and causes of opposition politics. If this happens, the politics of race, the struggle over privilege, the debate over social policy could become hostile.

The press often compared the presidential election of 2000 with the election of 1876. The focus was on what happened when a candidate who lost the popular vote was declared the victor by extraordinary actions on the part of political elites. What was striking was how few commentators sought to focus on the role racial politics played in settling that election controversy. In the election of 1876, when Rutherford B. Hayes (Republican) was awarded the electoral college vote although Samuel J. Tilden (Democrat) won the popular vote, one means of overcoming the crisis was to sell out the rights of blacks and firmly bolster the privileges of whites. The facts are quite clear: to win the support of Democrats in the House of Representatives, Hayes's allies met for weeks with key southerners, promising that if elected, Hayes would withdraw occupying troops from the last three southern states (South Carolina, Florida, and Louisiana), invest in the South's economic development, and do all he could to promote a return to normalcy. In secret and not so secret deals, southern Democrats agreed to support Hayes. On March 2, 1877, Hayes was named the victor, and he took the oath of office the next day. Within five weeks, Hayes had ordered the withdrawal of the last federal troops from the South. The officials in the southern states who had given him the margin of victory ended up, with almost no exception, in federal jobs, after losing their state jobs to new, mostly Democratic local governments. In the months and years that followed, Hayes helped create the coalition of conservative southern Democrats and northern Republicans that dominated American politics for much of the next eight decades and set the stage for both constraining the development of the welfare state and shaping it in a way to privilege whites. The impact of the compromise on black citizens was remarkably negative.

In 2000, black voters in Florida reported a string of vigorous efforts to keep them from voting or ratchet up the probability that their votes would not be counted as a result of confusing ballots and outmoded voting machines in their voting precincts while new, more high-tech machines were in middle-class white areas. Yet selling out the black vote seemed hardly more important to Democrats or Republicans than it had been in 1876. Bush, of course, did not want to risk a full recount, and Gore sued on grounds that did not include black complaints about either violations of voting rights or "overvotes." Nor did Clinton's Justice Department weigh in by investigating the complaints of black voters. As Bob Herbert put it, "The tactics have changed, but the goal remains depressingly the same: Keep the colored, the blacks, the African Americans—whatever they're called in the particular instance—keep them out of the voting booths. Do not let them vote! If you can find a way to stop them, stop them."[20]

In sum, once again in 2000 the American ethos, the ideology of white skin privilege, and the politics of race played a central role in shaping electoral outcomes and concomitantly the fundamental nature of the system and its weak welfare state. If even only a bare majority of white working-class people voted consistently for the same candidates supported by people of color, one could have some kind of social democracy that would provide much more social justice than the conservative regimes since 1968 have produced. But exploitation of ethno-racial loyalties and white skin privilege interfere with the development of class loyalties and collective solidarity.

Many whites, perhaps especially poor and working-class ones, still think that cutting social spending means cutting programs for "the blacks." At the same time, after both long-run historical precedents and more recent years of conservative leadership, people of color seemingly have come to expect so little from American presidents that even just an administration that does not daily insult their sensibilities wins not only support but celebration and gratitude. Virtually the same situation (the mere absence of an open attack on blacks) encourages whites to believe their interests are actually being challenged.

If the left does not come up with a new convincing public philosophy that provides a better explanation to whites and people of color alike about what is really at stake and gives people hope that a new social policy regime can be built through a coordinated strategy of law, protest, and politics, the right will continue to succeed in selling their interpretation. A rightist explana-

---

20. Bob Herbert, "Keep Them Out!" *New York Times,* Dec. 7, 2000, Op-Ed.

tion can continue to be successful only if it constantly sharpens the class divide, heightens factionalism not only between people of color and whites but among people of color, and encourages global bigotry.

Today it is popular to bemoan the disappearance of civic life in the United States. Pointing to the declining rates of participation in everything from membership in voluntary organizations and other forms of civic participation to voting and other forms of political participation, scholars and popular writers fret over the challenges presented to American democracy when citizens refuse to act. Rarely, however, is it recognized that true citizenship has economic preconditions. In a capitalist system, economic independence is a precondition for self-esteem and self-development. Without some minimum level of security, well-being, and dignity, people cannot function as citizens: thus the necessary connection between political and social citizenship; thus the need for the democratization of capital—the fundamental responsibility of effective social policy.

Yet a new generation of social policy depends on millions of individuals combining and connecting across the races to demand it. This could happen, for as Dr. King concluded, people are far from flotsam and jetsam in the river of life. We all have the power to influence the unfolding events that surround us. Much, then, depends on whether the true friends of racial equality and social justice take seriously their responsibility to act. The answer to the historic inextricably linked problem of the politics of race and social policy is in their hands.

Appendix

A. Earnings equations for all workers

	White males		White females		Black males		Black females	
	In wage	In wage + benefits	In wage	In wage + benefits	In wage	In wage + benefits	In wage	In wage + benefits
Experience	.024	.029	.041	.044	.039	.039	.031	.033
	(.002)	(.002)	(.004)	(.004)	(.007)	(.007)	(.011)	(.011)
Tenure	.021	.021	.031	.033	.028	.030	.028	.031
	(.002)	(.002)	(.002)	(.002)	(.007)	(.007)	(.007)	(.007)
Education	.050	.050	.064	.063	.040	.041	.042	.044
	(.002)	(.002)	(.003)	(.003)	(.010)	(.009)	(.009)	(.009)
Full-time	.414	.441	.224	.267	.107	.157	.237	.261
	(.024)	(.021)	(.014)	(.014)	(.071)	(.067)	(.047)	(.046)
White-collar	.128	.127	.188	.194	.264	.254	.241	.247
	(.014)	(.013)	(.014)	(.014)	(.051)	(.051)	(.041)	(.040)
Metropolitan location	.157	.147	.154	.154	.097	.089	.147	.140
	(.012)	(.011)	(.014)	(.014)	(.054)	(.052)	(.050)	(.049)
South	−.049	−.048	−.048	−.041	−.067	−.057	−.131	−.124
	(.011)	(.011)	(.013)	(.012)	(.046)	(.044)	(.039)	(.037)
Union	.113	.134	.142	.169	.188	.207	.185	.220
	(.015)	(.014)	(.025)	(.024)	(.057)	(.055)	(.052)	(.051)
Firm size								
25–99	.067	.101	−.007	.019	.051	.094	.021	.057
	(.017)	(.017)	(.018)	(.017)	(.077)	(.074)	(.067)	(.064)
100–499	.080	.121	.115	.154	−.074	−.027	.174	.219
	(.017)	(.016)	(.018)	(.017)	(.064)	(.061)	(.062)	(.060)
500–999	.111	.157	.060	.011	−.057	−.017	.111	.181
	(.028)	(.027)	(.032)	(.032)	(.114)	(.109)	(.097)	(.094)
1,000 or more	.138	.136	.097	.141	−.044	0.14	.161	.221
	(.014)	(.014)	(.015)	(.015)	(.059)	(.057)	(.055)	(.054)
Inverse Mill's ratio		.104		.104		.097		.127
		(.010)		(.010)		(.034)		(.031)
Intercept	.664	.687	.327	.317	.991	.964	.604	.557
	(.037)	(.035)	(.042)	(.041)	(.150)	(.144)	(.137)	(.131)
Adjusted R^2	.37	.41	.31	.37	.31	.34	.39	.47
Sample size	7,286	7,286	6,167	6,167	481	481	566	566

NOTE: Latinos (called Hispanics by the Census Bureau) may be of any race. Including Latinos in other racial populations, in the estimated 1998 population: blacks composed 12.7 percent of the population, Asian Americans composed 3.8 percent; Native Americans composed 0.9 percent; and whites composed 82.6 percent.

SOURCE: U.S. Census Bureau

B. Profile of ethno-racial population of the United States, 2000

Percent of total population

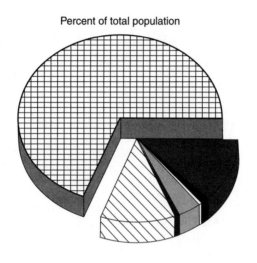

⊞ White, not Hispanic
⊠ Black, not Hispanic
■ American Indian and Alaska native, not Hispanic
▨ Asian, not Hispanic
☐ Native Hawaiian and Other pacific Islander, not Hispanic
■ Some other race, not Hispanic
■ Hispanic or Latino

One race	
White, not Hispanic	69.1%
Black, not Hispanic	12.1
American Indian and Alaska Native, not Hispanic	0.7
Asian, not Hispanic	3.6
Native Hawaiian and Other Pacific Islander, not Hispanic	0.1
Some other race, not Hispanic	0.2
Two or more races, not Hispanic	1.6
Hispanic or Latino	12.5

In 2000, the U.S. Bureau of the Census created a new social construction of race. Unlike in previous censuses, respondents were given the option of selecting one or more race categories to indicate their identities. Hispanic origin and race continued to be considered to be two separate and distinct concepts, but unlike in the 1990 census, the question on Hispanic origin was asked directly before the question on race—that is, the question order was reversed in the 1990 census. For these reasons, the census data on race are not directly comparable with data from earlier censuses. As the census constructs race:

"White" refers to people having origins in any of the original peoples of Europe, the Middle East, or North Africa. "Black or African American" refers to people having origins in any of the black racial groups of Africa. "American Indian and Alaska Native" refers to people having origins in any of the original peoples of North and South America (including Central America) and who maintain tribal affiliation or community attachment. "Asian" refers to people having origins in any of the original peoples of the Far East, Southeast Asia, or the Indian subcontinent. "Native Hawaiian and Other Pacific Islander" refers to people having origins in any of the original peoples of Hawaii, Guam, Samoa, or other Pacific Islands. "Some other race" refers to people who were unable to identify with the five Office of Management and Budget race categories.

Index